Absolutely Every*

BED &
BREAKFAST
*Almost

NORTHERN CALIFORNIA

Edited by Carl Hanson

SASQUATCH BOOKS
SEATTLE

Copyright ©1999 by Sasquatch Books
All rights reserved. No portion of this book may be reproduced or utilized in any form, or by any electronic, mechanical, or other means without the prior written permission of the publisher.

Printed in the United States of America.
Distributed in Canada by Raincoast Books Ltd.
03 02 01 00 99   5 4 3 2 1

Cover design: Jane Jeszeck
Cover illustration: Christopher Irion/The Image Bank
Interior design and composition: Alan Bernhard
Editor: Carl Hanson
Copy editors: Diane Sepanski, Christine Clifton-Thornton

ISSN 1522-5488
ISBN 1-57061-188-2

Sasquatch Books
615 Second Avenue
Seattle, Washington 98104
(206) 467-4300
books@SasquatchBooks.com
http://www.SasquatchBooks.com

Contents

ABSOLUTELY EVERY BED & BREAKFAST SERIES xviii
HOW TO USE THIS BOOK xix

AHWAHNEE	Apple Blossom Inn Bed & Breakfast 1
	Homestead, The 1
	Silver Spur Bed & Breakfast 2
ALAMEDA	Garratt Mansion 3
	Krusi Mansion Bed & Breakfast 4
	Morning Rose Boat & Breakfast 5
	Webster House 5
ALBION	Albion River Inn 6
	Fensalden Inn 7
	Wool Loft, The 8
ALTA	Crystal Springs Inn 8
ALTURAS	Dorris House B&B 9
AMADOR CITY	Imperial Hotel 10
	Mine House Inn 11
ANGELS CAMP	Cooper House Bed & Breakfast 11
ANGWIN	Forest Manor 12
APTOS	Apple Lane Inn 13
	Bayview Hotel Bed & Breakfast Inn, The 13
	Inn at Manresa Beach 14
	Mangels House 14
ARCATA	Cats' Cradle Bed & Breakfast .15
	Lady Anne Victorian Inn 15
ARNOLD	Lodge at Manuel Mill 16
AUBURN	Power's Mansion Inn 16
BASS LAKE	Bass Lake Bed & Breakfast 17
	Lakehouse Bed & Breakfast 17
BEN LOMOND	Chateau des Fleurs 17
	Fairview Manor 18
BENICIA	Captain Walsh House 19
	Painted Lady Bed & Breakfast, The 20
	Union Hotel 20
BERKELEY	Bancroft Club Hotel 21
	Beau Sky Hotel 21
	Bonita Studio Bed & Breakfast 22
	Clarinett Cafe Bed & Breakfast 22
	Elmwood House 22

	Gramma's 23
	Hillegass House 23
BISHOP	Chalfant House, The 24
	Matlick House, The 25
BODEGA	Bodega Estero Bed & Breakfast 26
	Bodega Harbor Inn 26
BOLINAS	Blue Heron Inn Restaurant Bed & Breakfast 27
	One Fifty-Five Pine 27
	Thomas' White House Inn 27
BOONVILLE	Anderson Creek Inn 28
	Boonville Hotel, The 28
	Toll House Restaurant & Inn 29
BRENTWOOD	Brentwood Oaks.............................29
BRIDGEPORT	Cain House, The 29
BROWNSVILLE	Mountain Seasons Inn 30
CALISTOGA	Brannan Cottage Inn 30
	Calistoga Bear Flag Inn 31
	Calistoga Country Lodge 32
	Calistoga Wayside Inn 32
	Christopher's Inn 32
	Elms Bed & Breakfast, The 32
	Eurospa & Inn 33
	Falcon's Nest 33
	Fanny's 33
	Foothill House Bed & Breakfast 34
	Hillcrest Bed & Breakfast 35
	La Chaumiere, a Country Inn 36
	Larkmead Country Inn 36
	Meadowlark Country House 37
	Mountain Home Ranch 37
	Pink Mansion, The 38
	Quail Mountain 39
	Scarlett's Country Inn 39
	Scott Courtyard 41
	Silver Rose Inn..............................42
	Trailside Inn Bed & Breakfast 43
	Washington Street Lodging 43
	Wine Way Inn 43
	Wisteria Garden Bed & Breakfast 44
	Zinfandel House 44

Capitola-by-the-Sea	Inn at Depot Hill	45
	Monarch Cove Inn	46
Cassel	Clearwater House	46
Catheys Valley	Chibchas	47
Cazadero	Cazanoma Lodge	47
	House of a Thousand Flowers	48
Chester	Bidwell House, The	48
	Cinnamon Teal Bed & Breakfast	49
Chico	Esplanade Bed & Breakfast, The	49
	Johnson's Country Inn	50
	L'Abri Bed & Breakfast	51
	Music Express Inn	52
Clio	White Sulphur Springs Ranch Bed & Breakfast	53
Cloverdale	Abrams House Inn	54
	Vintage Towers Bed & Breakfast	55
	Ye Olde Shelford House	55
Coloma	Coloma Country Inn, The	56
Columbia	Blue Nile Inn	57
	Columbia City Hotel	58
	Fallon Hotel	58
	Harlan House	59
Corning	Doc's Country Inn	60
Coulterville	Hotel Jeffery	60
	Sherlock Homes Bed & Breakfast	61
Crescent City	Fernbrook Inn	61
	Pebble Beach Bed & Breakfast	61
Cromberg	Twenty Mile House	61
Crowley Lake	Rainbow Tarns Bed & Breakfast at Crowley Lake	62
Davenport	New Davenport Bed & Breakfast Inn	64
Davis	Aggie Inn	65
	Davis Bed & Breakfast Inn	65
	University Inn Bed & Breakfast	65
Dillon Beach	Windmist Cottage	66
Dorrington	Dorrington Hotel & Restaurant, The	66
	Dorrington Inn	67
Dorris	Hospitality Inn	68
Downieville	Sierra Shangri-La	69
Duncans Mills	Inn at Duncans Mills, The	69
	Superintendent's House, The	70
Dunsmuir	Dunsmuir Inn	71
	Riverwalk Inn B&B	72

ELK	Elk Cove Inn	72
	Greenwood Pier Inn	73
	Griffin House at Greenwood Cove	74
	Harbor House	75
	Sandpiper House Inn	75
EMIGRANT GAP	Emigrant Gap Inn	76
ETNA	Bradleys Alderbrook Manor	76
EUREKA	Abigail's Elegant Victorian Mansion Bed & Breakfast	77
	Café Waterfront Bed & Breakfast	79
	Carter House, Carter Cottage, Bell Cottage, and Little Hotel Carter, The	79
	Cornelius Daly Inn	80
	Dreamwalkers Old Town Bed & Breakfast Inn	81
	Weaver's Inn, A	82
FELTON	Felton Crest Hanna's Guest House	83
FERNDALE	Gingerbread Mansion Inn	84
	Grandmother's House Bed & Breakfast	85
	Shaw House Bed & Breakfast Inn	85
FISH CAMP	Karen's Yosemite Bed & Breakfast	86
	Scotty's Bed & Breakfast	87
	Yosemite's Carriage House	87
FOLSOM	Bradley House	88
FORESTVILLE	Farmhouse Inn & Restaurant, The	88
FORT BRAGG	Avalon House	89
	Claudia's Garden	90
	Country Inn Bed & Breakfast	91
	Glass Beach Bed & Breakfast Inn	92
	Grey Whale Inn	92
	Jughandle Beach Country Bed & Breakfast	93
	Lodge at Noyo River, The	94
	Old Stewart House Inn	94
	Pudding Creek Inn	95
	Rendezvous Inn & Restaurant	96
	Riverview House	96
	Todd Farmhouse Country Bed & Breakfast	96
FORT JONES	Wild Goose Victorian Bed & Breakfast, The	97
FREESTONE	Green Apple Inn	98
FREMONT	Lord Bradley's Inn	98
FRENCH GULCH	French Gulch Hotel	99
GARDEN VALLEY	Mountainside Bed & Breakfast	100
GAZELLE	Hollyhock Farm Bed & Breakfast	101

GEORGETOWN	American River Inn	101
GEYSERVILLE	Campbell Ranch Inn	102
	Hope-Merrill House & Hope-Bosworth House	103
	Isis Oasis	104
GLEN ELLEN	Above the Clouds Inn	104
	Glenelly Inn	105
	Jack London Lodge	106
	Tanglewood House	107
GLENHAVEN	Kristalberg Bed & Breakfast	108
GOODYEARS BAR	Helm's St. Charles Inn	109
GRASS VALLEY	Elam Biggs Bed & Breakfast	109
	Golden Ore Bed & Breakfast Inn	110
	Holbrooke, The	110
	Murphy's Inn	110
	Peacock Inn	111
	Swan-Levine House	111
GROVELAND	Berkshire Inn	112
	Groveland Hotel, an Historic Country Inn, The	112
	Hotel Charlotte	113
	Inn at Sugar Pine Ranch	113
GUALALA	Inn at Getchell Cove	114
	North Coast Country Inn	114
	Old Milano Hotel, The	115
	Saint Orres	116
	Whale Watch Inn	117
GUERNEVILLE	Applewood	118
	Creekside Inn & Resort	119
	Ridenhour Ranch House Inn	119
	Santa Nella House	120
HALF MOON BAY	Cypress Inn on Miramar Beach	121
	Harbor House	122
	Mill Rose Inn	123
	Old Thyme Inn	123
	Pacific Victorian Bed & Breakfast	124
	San Benito House	124
	Zaballa House Bed & Breakfast, The	124
HEALDSBURG	Belle de Jour Inn	125
	Calderwood Inn	126
	Camellia Inn	127
	Frampton House	128
	George Alexander House, The	128

	Grape Leaf Inn 129
	Haydon Street Inn 130
	Healdsburg Inn on the Plaza 130
	Honor Mansion 131
	Madrona Manor 131
	Raford House, The 132
	Villa Messina 133
Hope Valley	Sorensen's Resort 133
Hopland	Thatcher Inn and Restaurant, an 1890 Bed & Breakfast 134
Inverness	Ark, The 135
	Bayshore Cottage 136
	Blackthorne Inn 136
	Dancing Coyote Beach 137
	Fairwinds Farm Cottage 137
	Hotel Inverness 138
	Laurel Ridge Cottage Inn 139
	Marsh Cottage Bed & Breakfast 139
	Patterson House 140
	Rosemary Cottage 140
	Sandy Cove Inn 141
	Ten Inverness Way 142
	Tree House, The 143
Ione	Heirloom, The 144
Jackson	Court Street Inn 145
	Gate House Inn 146
	Wedgewood Inn, The 147
Jamestown	National Hotel, The 148
	Palm Hotel Bed & Breakfast, The 149
	Royal Hotel 150
Jenner	Jenner Inn 150
Klamath	Klamath Inn 151
	Rhode's End Bed & Breakfast 152
Kneeland	Abe's Ocean View Redwoods Wilderness Chalet 152
La Porte	Gold Country 153
Lake Arrowhead	Carriage House Bed & Breakfast 153
Lake Tahoe	Chaney House 154
	Cottage Inn at Lake Tahoe 155
	Mayfield House 155
	Norfolk Woods Inn 155
	River Ranch Lodge 156

	Rockwood Lodge 157
	Shore House at Lake Tahoe, The 157
	Stanford Alpine Chalet, The 158
	Tahoma Meadows Bed & Breakfast 159
LAKEHEAD	Lake Shasta's True Bed & Breakfast 159
LAKEPORT	Arbor House Inn 160
	Forbestown Bed & Breakfast Inn, The 161
	Thompson House, The 161
	Wooden Bridge Bed & Breakfast, The 162
LEWISTON	Old Lewiston Inn 163
LITTLE RIVER	Blanchard House, The 164
	Glendeven 164
	Heritage House 164
	Rachel's Inn 166
	Seafoam Lodge, The 166
	Victorian Farmhouse Bed & Breakfast 166
LIVERMORE	Purple Orchid Inn Resort & Spa 166
LODI	Wine & Roses Country Inn 167
LOLETA	Southport Landing 167
LOOMIS	Emma's Bed & Breakfast 167
	Old Flower Farm Bed & Breakfast 167
LOTUS	Golden Lotus 167
LOWER LAKE	Big Canyon Inn 168
MAMMOTH LAKES	Snow Goose Inn 169
	White Horse Inn, The 170
MANCHESTER	Victorian Gardens 170
MARIPOSA	5th Street Inn 171
	Boulder Creek Bed & Breakfast 171
	Dubord's Restful Nest 172
	Finch Haven 172
	Granny's Garden 172
	Highland House.............................173
	Mariposa Hotel & Inn 173
	Mariposa Meadows Ranch 174
	Meadow Creek Ranch Bed & Breakfast Inn 174
	Pelennor Bed & Breakfast, The 175
	Poppy Hill 175
	Rockwood Gardens 176
	Shangri La Bed & Breakfast 176
	Shiloh Bed & Breakfast 176

	Sierra House Bed & Breakfast ...176
	Villa Monti Bed & Breakfast ...177
McCloud	McCloud River Inn ...177
	Stoney Brook Inn ...178
Meadow Valley	Haskins Valley Inn ...178
Mendocino	Agate Cove Inn ...178
	Blair House Inn ...179
	Brewery Gulch Inn ...180
	Captain's Cove Inn ...180
	Headlands Inn, The ...181
	John Dougherty House ...181
	Joshua Grindle Inn ...182
	MacCallum House Inn ...183
	Mendocino Farmhouse ...184
	Mendocino Village Inn ...185
	Reed Manor ...186
	Sea Gull Inn ...186
	Sea Rock Bed & Breakfast Inn ...186
	Stanford Inn by the Sea—Big River Lodge ...187
	Whitegate Inn Bed & Breakfast ...188
Merced	Rambling Rose Bed & Breakfast ...189
Mi Wuk Village	Christmas Tree Inn ...189
Mill Valley	Mill Valley Bed & Breakfast ...189
	Mill Valley Inn ...190
	Mountain Home Inn ...190
Modesto	Vineyard View ...191
Mokelumne Hill	Mokelumne River Lodge ...191
Montara	Goose & Turrets Bed & Breakfast ...191
Monte Rio	Highland Dell Inn ...192
	House of a Thousand Flowers ...193
	Huckleberry Springs Country Inn and Spa ...194
Monterey	Old Monterey Inn ...195
Moraga	Hallman Bed & Breakfast ...195
Moss Beach	Seal Cove Inn ...196
Mount Shasta	Dream Inn Bed & Breakfast ...198
	Mount Shasta Ranch Bed & Breakfast ...199
	Wagon Creek Inn ...199
	Ward's Big Foot Ranch ...200
Muir Beach	Pelican Inn, The ...201
Murphys	Dunbar House, 1880 ...201
	Redbud Inn, The ...202

MYERS FLAT	Myers Country Inn	203
NAPA	Arbor Guest House	203
	Beazley House	204
	Blue Violet Mansion	205
	Candlelight Inn, The	206
	Cedar Gables Inn	207
	Churchill Manor Bed & Breakfast	208
	Country Garden Inn	209
	Crossroads Inn	210
	Elm House, The	210
	Hennessey House	210
	Hillview Country Inn	211
	Inn on Randolph	212
	La Belle Epoque	213
	La Residence Country Inn	214
	McClelland-Priest Bed & Breakfast	215
	Napa Inn, The	215
	Oak Knoll Inn	216
	Old World Inn	217
	On Mayacamas	218
	Stahlecker House Bed & Breakfast, Country Inn, and Gardens	218
	Tall Timbers Chalets	219
	Trubody Ranch Bed & Breakfast	219
NEVADA CITY	Deer Creek Inn	220
	Downey House Bed & Breakfast	221
	Emma Nevada House	221
	Flume's End	222
	Grandmere's Inn	223
	Kendall House, The	224
	Marsh House	225
	Parsonage Bed & Breakfast, The	225
	Piety Hill Inn	225
	Red Castle Inn, Historic Lodgings	226
	U. S. Hotel Bed & Breakfast	227
NICE	Gingerbread Cottages Bed & Breakfast	227
O'BRIEN	O'Brien Mountain Inn	229
OAKHURST	Chateau du Sureau	229
	China Creek	230
	Hound's Tooth Inn	230
	Pine Rose Inn	231

OAKLAND	Bedside Manor	231
	Dockside Boat & Bed	232
	Tudor Rose Bed & Breakfast	232
	Washington Inn, The	232
OLEMA	Bear Valley Inn	232
	Olema Inn	233
	Point Reyes Seashore Lodge	233
	Ridgetop Inn & Cottages	234
	Roundstone Farm Bed & Breakfast	234
ORLAND	Inn at Shallow Creek Farm	234
OROVILLE	Jean's Riverside Bed & Breakfast	235
	Lake Oroville Bed & Breakfast	236
PALO ALTO	Hotel California	237
	Victorian on Lytton, The	237
PESCADERO	Old Saw Mill Lodge	238
	Pescadero Creek Inn Bed & Breakfast	239
PETALUMA	Cavanagh Inn	239
PETROLIA	Lost Inn, The	241
PHILO	Philo Pottery Inn	242
	Pinoli Ranch Country Inn	242
PINE GROVE	Druid House Bed & Breakfast	242
PLACERVILLE	Chichester-McKee House	242
	Combellack Blair House	243
	Fitzpatrick Winery & Lodge	244
	River Rock	245
	Seasons Bed & Breakfast, The	245
	Shadowridge Ranch & Lodge	246
	Shafsky House Bed & Breakfast Inn, The	246
PLEASANTON	Evergreen	247
	Plum Tree Inn	248
PLYMOUTH	Amador Harvest Inn	248
	Indian Creek Bed & Breakfast	249
	Plymouth House Inn	250
POINT ARENA	Coast Guard House	251
	Point Arena Bed & Breakfast	251
POINT REYES STATION	Carriage House Bed & Breakfast	251
	Crickett Cottage	252
	Ferrando's Hideaway and Cottages	252
	Holly Tree Inn	253
	Jasmine Cottage	254
	Knob Hill	254

	Terri's Homestay 255
	Thirty-Nine Cypress and Redwing Cottage 255
	Windsong Cottage 256
PORTOLA	Pullman House Bed & Breakfast 257
	Silver Lady Bed & Breakfast 257
PRINCETON-BY-THE-SEA	Pillar Point Inn Bed & Breakfast 257
QUINCY	Feather Bed, The 258
RED BLUFF	Faulkner House, The 260
	Jarvis Mansion Bed & Breakfast 261
	Jefferson House 261
	Jeter Victorian Inn 262
REDDING	Palisades Paradise Bed & Breakfast 262
	Redding's Bed & Breakfast 263
	Tiffany House Bed & Breakfast Inn 264
RICHMOND	East Brother Light Station 265
	Hotel Mac 266
RUTHEFORD	Rancho Caymus 266
SACRAMENTO	Abigail's Bed & Breakfast 267
	Amber House Bed & Breakfast Inn 268
	Hartley House Bed & Breakfast Inn 269
	Inn at Parkside 270
	Moon River Inn 271
	On the Bluffs 271
	Savoyard Bed & Breakfast 271
	Vizcaya 272
SAN ANDREAS	Courtyard Bed & Breakfast 272
	Robin's Nest, The 273
	Thorn Mansion Inn 274
SAN FRANCISCO	Abigail Hotel 274
	Adelaide Inn 274
	Alamo Square Inn 275
	Albion House Bed & Breakfast 275
	Alexander Inn 275
	Amsterdam Hotel, The 275
	Andora Inn 275
	Andrews Hotel, The 276
	Archbishop's Mansion 276
	Art Center Bed & Breakfast 277
	Bed & Breakfast Inn, The 277
	Black Stallion Inn 277
	Bock's Bed & Breakfast 278

Carol's Cow Hollow Inn 279
Casa Arguello Bed & Breakfast 280
Casita Blanca 280
Chateau Tivoli 281
Chez Duchene 281
Church Street Bed & Breakfast 281
Cornell Hotel 282
Dockside Boat & Bed 282
Dolores Park Inn 282
Edward II Bed & Breakfast 283
Golden Gate Hotel 283
Herb'n Inn, The 284
Hill Point Bed & Breakfast 284
Hotel David 285
Inn 1890 285
Inn on Castro 285
Inn San Francisco 286
Jackson Court 286
Mansions Hotel, The 287
Marina Inn 287
Monte Cristo Bed & Breakfast 288
No Name Victorian Bed & Breakfast 288
Nob Hill Lambourne, The 289
Noe's Nest 289
Obrero Hotel 290
Parker House 290
Pensione International 291
Petite Auberge 292
Queen Anne Hotel 292
Red Victorian Bed, Breakfast, and Peace Center 293
Shannon-Kavanaugh House 294
Sheehan Hotel 294
Spencer House 295
Stanyan Park Hotel Bed & Breakfast 296
Sunset Edwardian 297
Twenty-Four Henry 297
Union Street Inn, The 297
Victorian Inn on the Park 298
Washington Square Inn 299
White Swan Inn 300
Willows Bed & Breakfast Inn 300

SAN GREGORIO	Rancho San Gregorio	.300
SAN JOSE	Briar Rose Bed & Breakfast Inn	.302
	Hensley House, The	.303
SAN MARTIN	Country Rose Inn Bed & Breakfast	.304
SAN MATEO	Coxhead House Bed & Breakfast	.305
	Palm House, The	.306
SAN RAFAEL	Gerstle Park Inn	.306
	Panama Hotel	.307
SANTA CLARA	Madison Street Inn	.307
SANTA CRUZ	Babbling Brook Bed & Breakfast	.309
	Chateau Victorian, a Bed & Breakfast Inn	.309
	Cliff Crest Bed & Breakfast Inn	.310
	Darling House, a Bed & Breakfast Inn by the Sea, The	.311
	Hummingbird Hill Bed & Breakfast	.312
	Inn at Pasatiempo	.312
	Pleasure Point Inn	.312
SANTA ROSA	Gables Inn, The	.313
	Melitta Station Inn	.314
	Pygmalion House	.315
	Vintners Inn	.315
SAUSALITO	Casa Madrona Hotel	.316
	Gables Inn Sausalito	.317
SEBASTOPOL	Gravenstein Inn	.317
	Vine Hill Inn Bed & Breakfast	.317
SHINGLETOWN	Weston House	.318
SIERRA CITY	High Country Inn Bed & Breakfast	.319
SMITH RIVER	Casa Rubio Oceanfront Lodging	.320
SODA SPRINGS	Royal Gorge's Rainbow Lodge	.321
	Traverse Inn, The	.322
SONOMA	Adriana's Bed & Breakfast	.322
	Eller House Bed & Breakfast	.322
	Magliulo's Bed & Breakfast	.322
	Sonoma Chalet	.323
	Starwae Inn	.323
	Thistle Dew Inn	.324
	Victorian Garden Inn	.325
SONORA	Barretta Gardens Bed & Breakfast Inn	.326
	Hammons House Inn Bed & Breakfast	.327
	Lavender Hill	.327
	Mountain View Bed & Breakfast	.329

	Ryan House Bed & Breakfast	329
	Serenity, a Bed & Breakfast Inn	330
	Wy's Acres	330
SOQUEL	Blue Spruce Inn	331
SOUTH LAKE TAHOE	Christiania Inn, The	332
	Tamarack Creek Bed & Breakfast	334
ST. HELENA	Ambrose Bierce House	334
	Asplund Country Inn	335
	Barro Station Bed & Breakfast	335
	Bartels Ranch & Country Inn	336
	Bylund House Bed & Breakfast	337
	Chestelson House	337
	Cinnamon Bear Bed & Breakfast	337
	Deer Run Inn	338
	Elsie's Conn Valley Inn	339
	Erika's Hillside Bed & Breakfast	339
	Glass Mountain Inn	339
	Harvest Inn	339
	Hilltop House Bed & Breakfast	340
	Hotel St. Helena	340
	Ink House Bed & Breakfast	341
	La Fleur Bed & Breakfast Inn	342
	Milat Bed & Breakfast	343
	Oliver House Bed & Breakfast	343
	Prager Winery Bed & Breakfast	343
	Rose Garden Inn	343
	RustRidge Ranch Bed & Breakfast	343
	Shady Oaks Country Inn	345
	Spanish Villa Inn	345
	Sunny Acres Bed & Breakfast	346
	Taylor's Creekside Inn	347
	Vineyard Country Inn	347
	White Ranch Bed & Breakfast	347
	Wine Country Inn	347
	Zinfandel Inn	348
STINSON BEACH	Casa del Mar	348
	Redwoods Haus	349
STIRLING CITY	Stirling City Hotel	349
STOCKTON	Old Victorian Inn	350
SUTTER CREEK	Clementines Bed & Breakfast	350

	Foxes in Sutter Creek, The 350
	Grey Gables Bed & Breakfast 351
	Hanford House Bed & Breakfast Inn, The 352
	Picturerock Inn 353
	Sutter Creek Inn 353
TRINIDAD	Lost Whale Bed & Breakfast Inn, The 354
	Trinidad Bay Bed & Breakfast 355
	Turtle Rocks Oceanfront Inn 356
TRUCKEE	Bocks 10064 House 357
	Donner Country Inn Bed & Breakfast 357
	Richardson House Bed & Breakfast Inn 357
	Truckee Hotel 358
TUOLUMNE	Oak Hill Ranch Bed & Breakfast 358
TWAIN HARTE	Country Inn at Sugar Pine 359
	McCaffrey House Bed & Breakfast 360
UKIAH	Sanford House Bed & Breakfast 362
	Vichy Hot Springs Resort Bed & Breakfast 363
VOLCANO	St. George Hotel, The 364
WALNUT CREEK	Diablo Mountain Inn 365
	Secret Garden Mansion, The 365
WESTPORT	Blue Victorian Inn 366
	DeHaven Valley Farm Country Inn 367
	Howard Creek Ranch 368
	Pelican Lodge & Inn 369
WHITEHORN	Shelter Cove Bed & Breakfast 369
WINDSOR	Country Meadow Inn 369
YOSEMITE	Yosemite Peregrine Bed & Breakfast 370
NATIONAL PARK	Yosemite West High Sierra Bed & Breakfast 370
YOUNTVILLE	Bordeaux House 371
	Burgundy House 372
	Maison Fleurie 372
	Oleander House 373
	Vintage Inn—Napa Valley 373
YUBA CITY	Harkey House Bed & Breakfast 373

INDEX 375

Absolutely Every Bed & Breakfast Series

Welcome to *Absolutely Every° Bed & Breakfast: Northern California (°Almost)*, a comprehensive guide to virtually every bed and breakfast establishment in Northern California. We've done the work for you: Everything you need to know in choosing a bed and breakfast is included on these pages, from architectural style to atmosphere, from price range to breakfast variety. Listings are in alphabetical order by town, so locating the perfect stay at your destination is a snap, and the simple format makes comparing accommodations as easy as turning the page. So whether you're looking for an elegant Victorian inn, a stunning chateau in the heart of wine country, or a cozy seaside cottage, *Absolutely Every° Bed & Breakfast: Northern California (°Almost)* will help you find it.

In addition to Northern California, the *Absolutely Every* series covers Arizona, Colorado, New Mexico, Southern California, Oregon, Washington, and Texas; look for the latest edition of each in your local bookstore. The guides list small- and medium-sized inns, hotels, and host homes that include breakfast in the price of the room. The lists of B&B establishments are compiled from a variety of sources, including directories, chambers of commerce, tourism bureaus, and the World Wide Web. After gathering a complete list, the editors send each innkeeper a survey, asking for basic lodging information and for those special details that set them apart. The completed surveys are then examined and fact-checked for accuracy before inclusion in the book. The °*Almost* in the series title reflects the fact that a small number of innkeepers may choose not to be listed, may neglect to respond to the survey and follow-up phone calls, or are not listed because of negative reports received by the editors.

The editors rely on the honesty of the innkeepers in completing the surveys and on feedback from readers to keep the *Absolutely Every Bed & Breakfast* series accurate and up-to-date. (*Note:* While innkeepers are responsible for providing survey information, none are financially connected to the series, nor do they pay any fees to be included in the book.) Please write to us about your experience at any of the bed and breakfasts listed in the series; we'd love to hear from you.

Enjoy your bed and breakfast experience!

—The editors, *Absolutely Every Bed & Breakfast*

How to Use This Book

Absolutely Every Bed & Breakfast: Northern California is organized alphabetically by town and by establishment name, and includes a comprehensive index. The concise, at-a-glance format of the complete bed and breakfast listings covers fifteen categories of information to help you select just the right bed and breakfast accommodation for your needs. This edition offers you a choice of establishments in cities, towns, and outlying areas.

THE BED & BREAKFAST LISTINGS

Note that although specifics of each establishment have been confirmed by the editors, details such as amenities, decor, and breakfast menus have been provided by the innkeepers. Listings in this guide are subject to change; call to confirm all aspects of your stay, including price, availability, and restrictions, before you go. Some bed and breakfast listings offer only selected information due to lack of response or by request of the innkeeper; complete listings include the following information.

Establishment name

Address: Note that street addresses often vary from actual mailing addresses; confirm the mailing address before sending a reservation payment.

Telephone numbers: Includes any toll-free or fax numbers.

Innkeeper's languages: Languages spoken other than English.

Location: Directions from the nearest town, highway, or landmark.

Open: Notice of any seasonal or other closures.

Description: Overview of architecture, furnishings, landscaping, etc.

Rooms: Number of rooms with private bathrooms vs. shared baths; availability of suites and/or additional guesthouses; and the innkeeper's favorite room.

Rates: Range of room prices, which vary based on private or shared bathroom, season, and individual room amenities. Also noted here are any minimum stay requirements and cancellation policies (usually two weeks' notice is required for a full refund).

Breakfast: Description of breakfast served (full, continental, continental plus, or stocked kitchen).

Credit cards: Indicates which, if any, credit cards are accepted. Note that credit cards may be listed for reservation confirmation purposes only; be prepared to pay by check or cash.

Amenities: Details any special amenities that are included.

Restrictions: Lists any restrictions regarding smoking, children, and pets. Also listed here are any resident pets or livestock.

Awards: Any significant hospitality or historic preservation awards received.

Reviewed: Publications in which the B&B has been reviewed.

Rated: Indicates whether the B&B has been rated by institutions such as the American Automobile Association (AAA), American Bed & Breakfast Association (ABBA), or the Mobil Travel Association.

Member: Indicates membership in any professional hospitality associations or organizations.

Kudos/Comments: Comments from guests who have stayed in the establishment.

AHWAHNEE

Located on historic Highway 49 in California's gold country, Ahwahnee is in a prime position for excursions to Yosemite, 20 miles to the north. Check out the Yosemite Mountain Sugar Pine Railroad or ski Badger Pass ski area.

APPLE BLOSSOM INN BED & BREAKFAST

44606 Silver Spur Court, Ahwahnee, CA 93601 559-642-2001
WEBSITE *www.sierranet.net/web/apple/* 888-687-4281

THE HOMESTEAD

41110 Road 600, Ahwahnee, CA 93601 209-683-0495
Cindy Brooks & Larry Ends, Innkeepers FAX 209-683-8165
Spanish spoken
EMAIL *homesteadcottages@sierratel.com*
WEBSITE *www.homesteadcottages.com*

LOCATION	Four-and-a-half miles north of the junction of Highways 41 and 49; 2.5 miles southwest of Highway 49 on Road 600.
OPEN	All year
DESCRIPTION	Four 1992 one-story country bungalows of adobe and stone construction nestled under the oaks on 160 acres. Each cottage has a theme: Country, Santa Fe Ranch, Native American, and Garden. Natural gardens and meandering rock walls surround the cottages.
NO. OF ROOMS	Five rooms with private bathrooms.
RATES	Year-round rates are $115-125 for a single or double and $149-225 for a suite. There is a minimum stay during weekends and cancellation requires seven days' notice for a full refund.
CREDIT CARDS	American Express, Discover, MasterCard, Visa
BREAKFAST	Continental breakfast is served in the guestrooms. In each cottage is a fully equipped kitchen stocked with coffee, teas, hot chocolate, cider, fresh juice, muffins, and fruit.
AMENITIES	Air conditioning, fireplaces, one cottage handicapped accessible, private sitting areas, no shared walls, flowers, robes, full kitchens, outdoor barbecue, gold panning, 160 acres of hiking.
RESTRICTIONS	No smoking, no pets. Charlotte is the resident cat and Gracie is the dog. There are also Arabian horses. The cat and dog are not allowed in the guest cottages.

REVIEWED	The Best Places to Kiss in Northern California
MEMBER	Professional Association of Innkeepers International, California Association of Bed & Breakfast Inns
RATED	AAA 3 Diamonds, Mobil 2 Stars

SILVER SPUR BED & BREAKFAST

44625 Silver Spur Trail, Ahwahnee, CA 93601   559-683-2896
Bryan & Patty Hays, Innkeepers   888-359-9178
WEBSITE *www.sierranet.net/web/silver*

LOCATION	From the intersection of Highways 41 and 49 in Oakhurst, travel north on Highway 49 for eight miles to Silver Spur Trail. Turn right on Silver Spur Trail; the inn is the second driveway on the left.
OPEN	All year
DESCRIPTION	A 1986 two-story log lodge with American lodge decor, located in the California Sierras.
NO. OF ROOMS	Two rooms with private bathrooms.
RATES	Year-round rates are $50-60 for a single or double. There is a two-night minimum stay on holidays and cancellation requires 48 hours' notice.
CREDIT CARDS	Discover, MasterCard, Visa
BREAKFAST	Continental breakfast is served in the dining room and includes bread or pastry (cinnamon rolls, muffins, or specialty bread), assorted fresh fruit, juice, coffee, and tea.
AMENITIES	Private entrances, outdoor picnic area, air conditioning, close to many outdoor activities, hosts are knowledgeable about the area and will help you plan your trip to Yosemite.
RESTRICTIONS	No smoking in rooms. The inn is home to three cats, Pharoah, Whiskers, and Tabby; a dog, Rocky; and 12 chickens. "Pharoah is available for companionship to those who are cat lovers."
REVIEWED	Bed & Breakfast U.S.A.

ALAMEDA
(OAKLAND)

If you love islands and airplanes, you'll love it here. West of Oakland on San Francisco Bay, this once-thriving resort community is now home to Alameda Naval Air Station. During fall and winter, watch for loons, grebes, and other birds at Robert C. Crown Memorial Beach. The Crab Cove shoreline is a designated estuarine marine reserve with great exhibits of undersea creatures. The town is handy to all the goodies in Oakland.

GARRATT MANSION

900 Union, Alameda, CA 94501   510-521-4779
Royce & Betty Gladden, Resident Owners   FAX 510-521-6796
EMAIL garrattm@pacbell.net   WEBSITE www.garrattmansion.com

LOCATION	From Highway 880 take the High Street/Alameda exit. Go west for five blocks on High Street, then turn right onto Central Avenue. Go 1.5 miles, turn left onto Union Street, and go four blocks to the inn on the corner of Clinton and Union.
OPEN	All year
DESCRIPTION	A 1893 three-story colonial revival mansion with antique furnishings.
NO. OF ROOMS	Five rooms with private bathrooms and two rooms share two bathrooms.
RATES	Year-round rates are $95 for a single or double with a private bathroom and $80 for a single or double with a shared bathroom. The suite is $130. There is no minimum stay and cancellation requires three days' notice.

Garratt Mansion, Alameda

CREDIT CARDS	American Express, MasterCard, Visa
BREAKFAST	Full breakfast, served in the dining room, changes daily and may include cheese blintz soufflé with fresh strawberries, chicken and apple sausage, fresh-squeezed orange juice, and other beverages.
AMENITIES	Robes, telephones, fresh flowers in every room, TV room with popcorn and old movies, chocolate chip cookies, California-grown pistachios, hot and cold drinks, and area maps and menus.
RESTRICTIONS	No smoking in the house, no pets
REVIEWED	*Bed & Breakfast California, Northern California Best Places, Frommer's*
MEMBER	California Association of Bed & Breakfast Inns, Professional Association of Innkeepers International, American Bed & Breakfast Association
RATED	ABBA 3 Crowns
AWARDS	1996, Jones Dairy Farm national contest winner; 1997, Alameda Newspaper Group best lodging
KUDOS/COMMENTS	"Betty Gladden thinks of every little detail; I stole a bunch of ideas from her. Beautiful house."

KRUSI MANSION BED & BREAKFAST

2033 Central Avenue, Alameda, CA 94501   *510-864-2300*
Ty & Sonja Taylor, Innkeepers   *FAX 510-864-2336*
EMAIL *kmansion@dnai.com*   WEBSITE *www.krusimansion.com*

LOCATION	From San Francisco, cross the Bay Bridge and take Highway 880 to Alameda. Go five miles to the 23rd Avenue exit. Go 0.5 mile to the bridge and another seven blocks to Central Avenue; turn right and go four long blocks.
OPEN	All year
DESCRIPTION	A restored 1888 two-story blend of Victorian and colonial revival architecture with authentic period antiques throughout.
NO. OF ROOMS	Four rooms with private bathrooms. Try the Rose Room.
RATES	Year-round rates are $100-130 for a single or double. Cancellation requires 48 hours' notice.
CREDIT CARDS	American Express, Diners Club, MasterCard, Visa
BREAKFAST	Continental plus is served in the dining room and includes fresh orange juice, fresh fruit salad, homemade muffins and breads, custard, fruit pies and cobblers, cheese pie, and vegetarian quiche.
AMENITIES	Flowers, candy, wine or beer, champagne for special occasions.

Krusi Mansion Bed & Breakfast, Alameda

RESTRICTIONS   No smoking, no pets, children over 14 are welcome. Children must have their own room—there are no extra beds in rooms.

MEMBER   California Association of Bed & Breakfast Inns

MORNING ROSE BOAT & BREAKFAST

1070 Marina Village Parkway, Alameda, CA 94501   510-523-9600
WEBSITE *www.compassrosecharters.com*

WEBSTER HOUSE

1238 Versailles Avenue, Alameda, CA 94501   510-523-9697
Susan McCormack, Resident Owner

ALBION

Nestled on the Mendocino Coast and Albion River and famous for its salmon and crab fishing, this is the perfect place for divine eating. Not to be missed is Van Damme State Park—it's a gem. Albion is between Fort Bragg and Point Arena on Highway 1.

ALBION RIVER INN

3790 North Highway 1, Albion, CA 95410 707-937-1919
Peter Wells & Flurry Healy, Resident Owners 800-479-7944
Some Spanish spoken FAX 707-937-2604
EMAIL *ari@mcm.org* WEBSITE *www.albionriverinn.com*

LOCATION	Three miles north of the intersection of Highway 128 and Highway 1, just 0.1 mile north of the Albion Bridge.
OPEN	All year
DESCRIPTION	A 1983 two-story New England clapboard inn and cottages with comfortable country furnishings, situated on 10 cliff-top acres overlooking the Pacific Ocean and Albion River Cove.
NO. OF ROOMS	Twenty rooms with private bathrooms. Try room 20.
RATES	Year-round rates are $170-260 for a single or a double. There is a two-night minimum stay when Saturday is involved, and cancellation requires seven days' notice.
CREDIT CARDS	American Express, MasterCard, Visa
BREAKFAST	Full all-you-can-eat breakfast is served in the dining room. Dinner is available in the gourmet restaurant.
AMENITIES	Robes, complimentary local wines, fireplaces, binoculars, telescopes, all rooms have private garden entrances, 18 rooms have decks, no TVs in rooms, piano in restaurant, handicapped accessible, weddings and receptions catered.
RESTRICTIONS	No smoking, no pets. Albion is the resident cat.
REVIEWED	*Weekends for Two in Northern California: 50 Romantic Getaways; The Best Places to Kiss in Northern California; Karen Brown's California Country Inns & Itineraries*
MEMBER	California Lodging Industry Association
RATED	AAA 3 Diamonds, Mobil 3 Stars
KUDOS/COMMENTS	"Comfortable rooms with beautiful views of the Pacific Ocean. Great restaurant!"

FENSALDEN INN

38810 Navarro Ridge Road, Albion, CA 95410　　　707-937-4042
Evelyn Hamby, Innkeeper　　　　　　　　　　　　800-959-3850
WEBSITE www.fensalden.com　　　　　　　　　FAX 707-937-2416

LOCATION	Seven miles south of Mendocino, two miles north of Highway 128.
OPEN	All year
DESCRIPTION	An 1860 two-story Victorian farmhouse with period antiques.
NO. OF ROOMS	Nine rooms with private bathrooms. The Hawthorne Suite is the best room.
RATES	April through December, rates are $120-175 for a single or double, $155-165 for a suite, and $175 for the guesthouse. January through March, rates are $10 less. There is a minimum stay on weekends and holidays, and cancellation requires one weeks' notice (two weeks for holidays and six weeks for the entire inn).
CREDIT CARDS	MasterCard, Visa
BREAKFAST	Full breakfast is served in the dining room and includes assorted juices, baked or cold fruit, a hot entrée, fresh-baked muffins or coffeecake, assorted hot beverages, and champagne on Sunday. Special dietary needs can be accommodated, and catered lunches and dinners are available for groups.
AMENITIES	Fresh flowers and fireplaces in all rooms; refrigerators with complimentary wine on arrival; radio, CD and tape players in all rooms; books, games, telescope, TV/VCR in main room; telephone, fax, copier, data port in library; wine and hors d'oeuvres in evening; meeting facilities; handicapped accessible; grand piano; croquet; volleyball.
RESTRICTIONS	No smoking, no pets, no children. The resident dogs are Suki, a golden retriever, and Roxanne, a mixed breed.
REVIEWED	*Country Inns of the Far West; Historic Country Inns of California; The Official Guide to American Historic Bed & Breakfast Inns and Guesthouses; More Weekends for Two in Northern California*
MEMBER	California Association of Bed & Breakfast Inns, Professional Association of Innkeepers International
KUDOS/COMMENTS	"Peaceful, genteel, with a view; decompression comes easily here."

THE WOOL LOFT

32751 Navarro Ridge Road, Albion, CA 95410   707-937-0377
Richard & Roberta Ollenberger, Innkeepers
EMAIL *woolloft@mcn.org*   WEBSITE *www.designjk.com/woolloft*

LOCATION	Six miles south of the historic town of Mendocino. From Highway 1, take Navarrow Ridge Road East for 1.2 miles. The inn is on the right side of road.
OPEN	All year
DESCRIPTION	A two-story contemporary inn with contemporary decor, located high on Navarro Ridge.
NO. OF ROOMS	Four rooms with private bathrooms. Try the Ewe View Room.
RATES	May through October, rates are $85-120 for a single or double and $145 for a suite. There is a minimum stay during holidays and cancellation requires seven days' notice with a $25 charge.
CREDIT CARDS	American Express, MasterCard, Visa
BREAKFAST	Full breakfast includes juice, seasonal fruit, a main entrée, and fresh-baked bread or muffins. Vegetarian diets are accommodated by request. Resident chickens provide fresh eggs and the garden supplies herbs and veggies in season.
AMENITIES	Evening wine and hors d'oeuvres; large hot tub off back deck garden area; queen beds with down comforters and bed warmers; flowers and champagne available for special occasions with advance notice.
RESTRICTIONS	Children OK in the Loft Studio only. Claudia, Charity, Arial, and Fannie Mae are the resident sheep, and there are a number of Rhode Island Red chickens.
KUDOS/COMMENTS	"Great river view, fun hosts, nice accommodations."

ALTA

CRYSTAL SPRINGS INN

34818 E Towle Road, Alta, CA 95701   530-389-2355

ALTURAS

Set in a semi-arid landscape between Modoc National Forest and the South Warner Wilderness, the Modoc county seat is the marketing center for local livestock, potatoes, and prime alfalfa. The geology of this area is fascinating: Rock hounds should keep an eye out for quartz crystals, jasper, obsidian, and perlite. There's good bird-watching in Modoc National Wildlife Refuge on the shores of Dorris Reservoir, abundant fish and few people at Goose Lake. In town, do the historic tour and the County Museum, and remember that on Saturday nights the cowboys come into town! Alturas is in the northeast corner of the state, a short zip into Oregon. The Pitt River runs through it.

DORRIS HOUSE B&B

County Road 57, Alturas, CA 96101 530-233-3786
Karol & Mary Woodward, Resident Owners

LOCATION	Four miles east of Alturas on Country Roads 56 and 57.
OPEN	All year
DESCRIPTION	A 1912 two-story ranch furnished with family heirlooms and antiques, on Dorris Lake.
NO. OF ROOMS	Four rooms share two bathrooms. Mary recommends Kathy's room.
RATES	Year-round rates are $40-45 for a single or double. There is no minimum stay and cancellation requires ten days' notice with a $5 cancellation fee.
CREDIT CARDS	No
BREAKFAST	Continental plus is served in the dining room or on the deck and includes homemade muffins, banana bread, all available fruit, homemade jams, and homegrown strawberries and raspberries in season.
AMENITIES	Wine available at cocktail hour, located on a lake with bass and catfish fishing, bird-watching, horse pasture, parlor with piano, large deck.
RESTRICTIONS	No pets, children over 12 are welcome. Lucky the cat and Hershey the horse are the resident critters.
REVIEWED	*Northern California Best Places*

AMADOR CITY

Once the "saddle on the Mother Lode," the state's smallest incorporated city is only one block long. Lined with false-fronted antique and specialty shops, browsing the block is the main event in town. North of Sutter Creek on Highway 49.

IMPERIAL HOTEL

14202 Highway 49, Amador City, CA 95601 209-267-9172
Bruce Sherrill & Dale Martin, Resident Owners 800-242-5594
WEBSITE www.imperialamador.com FAX 209-267-9249

LOCATION	Northwest corner of Highway 49 and Water Street.
OPEN	All year except Christmas Eve
DESCRIPTION	A two-story gothic brick hotel with Victorian furnishings, a veranda, fountains, and a waterfall.
NO. OF ROOMS	Six rooms with private bathrooms.
RATES	Year-round rates are $75-105 for a single or double. There is a two-night minimum stay when a Saturday is involved and cancellation requires seven days' notice and a $10 fee.
CREDIT CARDS	American Express, Diners Club, Discover, MasterCard, Visa
BREAKFAST	Continental plus is served in the dining room or guestrooms, or on the patio or balcony and includes eggs, fresh fruit, homemade breads, and beverages. Dinner and Sunday brunch is also available and features mostly California ingredients.
AMENITIES	Flowers, morning paper, hair dryers, room service, bar, air conditioning, meeting space, and AV equipment available.
RESTRICTIONS	No smoking, no pets. There are four "adopted" resident cats: Carla, Perl, Jose, and Hose-B.
REVIEWED	*The Best Places to Kiss in Northern California, Best Places to Stay in California, Northern California Best Places, America's Wonderful Little Hotels & Inns*
MEMBER	California Association of Bed & Breakfast Inns, Amador Bed & Breakfast Association
KUDOS/COMMENTS	"An excellent opportunity to spend a night in an 1800s vintage hotel."

Mine House Inn

14125 Highway 49, Amador City CA 95601   209-267-5900
Allen & Rose Mendy, Resident Owners   800-646-3473
Fluent Spanish, some German and French spoken
WEBSITE *www.minehouseinn.com*

LOCATION	Five miles north of Jackson on Highway 49
OPEN	All year except December 24 and 25
DESCRIPTION	An 1879 Federal-style Victorian inn and a 1930s home that formerly housed the superintendent of the mine. Listed on the California State Historic Register. Victorian antiques from the 1800s furnish all the rooms.
NO. OF ROOMS	Nine rooms with private bathrooms.
RATES	Year-round rates are $85-185 for a single or a double. There is a two-night minimum stay on weekends and cancellation requires seven days' notice and a $10 fee.
CREDIT CARDS	American Express, Discover, MasterCard, Visa
BREAKFAST	Full breakfast is served in guestrooms and includes juices, fresh fruit, baskets of bread and pastries, yogurt, a hot entrée, coffee, and tea.
AMENITIES	Outdoor swimming pool and patio overlooking hillside and Amador City, enclosed outdoor spa.
RESTRICTIONS	No smoking, no pets
MEMBER	Professional Association of Innkeepers International, Amador County Bed & Breakfast Association

Angels Camp

Cooper House Bed & Breakfast

1184 Church Street, Angels Camp, CA 95222   209-736-2145

ANGWIN

It's in wine country, but wine is not welcome here (no coffee, tea, meat, or cigarettes are sold in the local store either). The Seventh-day Adventist Pacific Union College is here, and most of the populace belongs to the church. But it is in Napa Valley and away from the madness of Highway 29's wine spine. Check out the Newton Observatory nearby and Los Posadas State Forest. Angwin is in the hills just east of St. Helena, via Deer Park and Howell Mountain roads.

FOREST MANOR

415 Cold Springs Road, Angwin, CA 94508 707-965-3538
Randi & Richard Theobald, Innkeepers 800-788-0364
EMAIL ricktheobald@fcs.net FAX 707-965-1962
WEBSITE www.forestmanor.com

LOCATION	Located in the Napa Valley wine country, five miles east of St. Helena. Go north through St. Helena on Highway 29 for one mile. Turn right (east) on Deer Park Road and proceed six miles. Turn right on Cold Springs Road.
OPEN	All year
DESCRIPTION	A 1981 three-story English Tudor manor house with eclectic, elegant interior decor, surrounded by 20 landscaped acres. The building features hand-hewn beams, vaulted ceilings, and verandas.
NO. OF ROOMS	Seven rooms with private bathrooms. The William Shakespeare Suite is the best in the house.

Forest Manor, Angwin

RATES	Year-round rates are $210-350 for a single or double. There is a two-night minimum stay and cancellation requires 14 days' notice.
CREDIT CARDS	American Express, Discover, MasterCard, Visa
BREAKFAST	Full breakfast is served in the dining room, guest rooms, or library, or on the veranda, and includes pastries, egg dishes, waffles, or soufflés, all made from scratch.
AMENITIES	Complimentary wine tastings, cordials/cognac for nightcap, robes, pool, large spa, air conditioning, hiking trails, mountain bikes, coffee-maker and refrigerator in every room, fireplace and private Jacuzzi in most rooms.
RESTRICTIONS	No smoking, no pets, no children. "The three resident Airedales, three macaws, and the Maine coon cat, Mozart, run the place!"
REVIEWED	*The Best Places to Kiss in Northern California*
MEMBER	California Association of Bed & Breakfast Inns

Aptos

Aptos is a southern suburb of Santa Cruz at the upper reaches of Monterey Bay, on the east side of Highway 1. This is the entrance into the Nature Conservancy's Forest of Nisene Marks State Park, an oasis of pristine solitude and a hiker's dream (also epicenter of the devastating 1989 earthquake). There are art galleries and craft shops galore. The world's shortest parade can be seen (briefly) on July 4th weekend. Aptos offers handy access to Seacliff State Beach and coastal redwoods.

Apple Lane Inn

6265 Soquel Drive, Aptos, CA 95003   408-475-6868

The Bayview Hotel Bed & Breakfast Inn

8041 Soquel Drive, Aptos, CA 95003   408-688-8654
Dan Floyd & Suzie Lankes, Innkeepers   800-422-9843
WEBSITE www.bayviewhotel.com   FAX 831-688-5128

LOCATION	Approximately eight miles south of Santa Cruz. Take the Seacliff Beach/Aptos exit off Highway 1 and turn right on Soquel Drive. The hotel is 1.25 miles up the drive.
OPEN	All year

DESCRIPTION	A 1978 three-story Italianate Victorian inn listed on the California Historic Register.
NO. OF ROOMS	Eleven rooms with private bathrooms. Try the Arano Room.
RATES	Year-round rates are are $90-160 for a double and $145 for a suite. A two-night minimum stay is required over Saturday night and cancellation requires ten days' notice.
CREDIT CARDS	American Express, MasterCard, Visa
BREAKFAST	Continental plus is served in the dining room and includes assorted pastries and breads, juices, fresh fruit, dried fruit, cereals, yogurt, coffee, tea, and cocoa.
AMENITIES	Flowers, feather beds, small conference facilities for up to 12 people, handicapped accessible, massage available, restaurant on premises.
RESTRICTIONS	No smoking
MEMBER	California Association of Bed & Breakfast Inns, Professional Association of Innkeepers International
RATED	AAA 3 Diamonds

INN AT MANRESA BEACH

6901 Freedom Boulevard, Aptos, CA 95003   408-728-1000

MANGELS HOUSE

570 Aptos Creek Road, Aptos, CA 95003   408-688-7982
Jacqueline Fisher, Resident Owner
Spanish and French spoken

LOCATION	From Highway 1, take the Seacliff Beach exit. Take Soquel Drive south to Aptos Creek Road east. The inn is one mile from the exit.
OPEN	All year except December 24 through 27
DESCRIPTION	An 1886 Italianate Victorian with eclectic interior furnishings, on 4 acres.
NO. OF ROOMS	Six rooms with private bathrooms.
RATES	Please ask about current rates and cancellation information.
CREDIT CARDS	American Express, MasterCard, Visa

BREAKFAST	Full breakfast is served in the dining room and includes beverages, an egg dish, homemade scones, muffins or coffeecake, French bread, butter, and jams.
AMENITIES	Large formal gardens, fresh flowers, robes in some rooms, sherry and shortbread in the afternoon, table tennis, darts and croquet on the porch and lawn.
RESTRICTIONS	No smoking in the bedrooms, no pets, children over 12 are welcome.
REVIEWED	*The National Trust Guide to Historic Bed & Breakfasts, Inns, and Small Hotels; Karen Brown's California Country Inns & Itineraries; The Best Places to Kiss in Northern California*
MEMBER	California Association of Bed & Breakfast Inns, Bed & Breakfast Innkeepers of Santa Cruz, American Bed & Breakfast Association
KUDOS/COMMENTS	"Mansion on the edge of a 10,000-acre forest park. Six lovely rooms and a lovely hostess."

ARCATA

Home to the California State University at Humboldt, a liberal arts school, Arcata is like most college towns in that everyone tends to lean toward the left. Environmentalism, artistry, good beads, and good bagels are indispensable elements of the Arcatian philosophy, as is a cordial disposition toward tourists. A two-minute drive east of downtown on 11th Street will take you to Arcata's beloved Redwood Park. Surrounding the park is the Arcata Community Forest, 600 acres of lush second-growth redwoods favored by hikers, mountain bikers, and equestrians.

CATS' CRADLE BED & BREAKFAST

815 Park Place, Arcata, CA 95521   707-822-2287

LADY ANNE VICTORIAN INN

902 14th Street, Arcata, CA 95521   707-822-2797
Sam Pennisi, Resident Owner

ARNOLD

LODGE AT MANUEL MILL

PO Box 998, Arnold, CA 95223   209-795-2622

AUBURN

This was one of the first towns built in Gold Country, and Auburn still has an old-fashioned downtown area and many Victorian homes, though it's fast giving way to encroaching suburban sprawl. Check out the many fine museums, or head out to the Auburn State Recreation Area. Interesting doings include April's Pro-Rodeo, the Western States Gold Fair and Panning Championships in July, and the hilarious Funk Soap Box Derby Nationals in August. Auburn is northeast of Sacramento via I-80 and Highway 49.

POWER'S MANSION INN

164 Cleveland Avenue, Auburn, CA 95603   530-885-1166
Jean & Arno Lejnieks, Innkeepers   FAX 530-885-1386
German and Latvian spoken
EMAIL powerinn@westsierra.net
WEBSITE www.vfr.net/~powerinn

LOCATION	Take the Elm exit in Auburn and turn left. At the first traffic light turn right, then left at the next traffic light.
OPEN	All year
DESCRIPTION	An 1898 two-story Victorian inn with Victorian furnishings. Listed on the California Historic Register.
NO. OF ROOMS	Thirteen rooms with private bathrooms. The best room in the house is the Honeymoon Suite.
RATES	Year-round rates are $79-149 for a single or a double; the suite is $149; and the entire B&B rents for $1285. There is no minimum stay and cancellation requires 72 hours' notice.
CREDIT CARDS	American Express, MasterCard, Visa
BREAKFAST	Full breakfast is served in the dining room.
AMENITIES	Robes, telephones, TV, heart-shaped Jacuzzi in Honeymoon Suite, air conditioning, skylights, two rooms have fireplaces, wedding and meeting facilities.

RESTRICTIONS	No smoking, no pets
REVIEWED	The Complete Guide to Bed & Breakfasts, Inns, and Guesthouses; Fodor's California; Frommer's; Northern California Best Places; The Official Guide to American Historic Inns; The National Trust Guide to Historic Bed & Breakfasts, Inns and Small Hotels

BASS LAKE

BASS LAKE BED & BREAKFAST

53489 N Shore Drive, Bass Lake, CA 93604   209-642-3618
EMAIL *basslake@sierranet.net*

LAKEHOUSE BED & BREAKFAST

PO Box 309, Bass Lake, CA 93604   209-683-8220

BEN LOMOND

Ben Lomond is about 16 miles north of Santa Cruz along the San Lorenzo River. From here it's a short drive to Big Basin Redwoods State Park. For sandy beaches and good swimming, try Highlands County Park or Ben Lomond County Park.

CHATEAU DES FLEURS

7995 Highway 9, Ben Lomond, CA 95005   831-336-8943
Lee & Laura Jonas, Resident Owners   800-291-9966
German spoken
WEBSITE *www.chateaudesfluers.com*

LOCATION	From Highway 17, take the Mount Vernon Road turnoff through Scott's Valley to Felton. Turn right at Graham Hill Road. After one block, turn right onto Highway 9 and go two miles.
OPEN	All year
DESCRIPTION	An 1879 French country Victorian inn decorated with antiques.

NO. OF ROOMS	Three rooms with private bathrooms.
RATES	Year-round rates for a single or double are $100-130. There is a two-night minimum stay on all holiday weekends and during UCSC graduation. Five days' notice is required for cancellation.
CREDIT CARDS	American Express, Discover, MasterCard, Visa
BREAKFAST	Full breakfast, served in the dining room, includes fresh fruit, pastry, a hot entrée such as quiche, blintzes, French custard toast, or cheese soufflé, and beverages.
AMENITIES	Wine and hors d'oeuvres, phone available, meeting rooms for up to 30, fireplaces in some rooms.
RESTRICTIONS	No smoking, no pets
REVIEWED	*Bed & Breakfast California, Bed & Breakfast in California*
MEMBER	California Association of Bed & Breakfast Inns, Bed & Breakfast Association of Santa Cruz County

FAIRVIEW MANOR

245 Fairview Avenue, Ben Lomond, CA 95005   408-336-3355
Nancy Glasson, Resident Owner
EMAIL nancy@fairviewmanor.com
WEBSITE www.fairviewmanor.com

LOCATION	From Highway 17, take the Mt. Herman/Glen Canyon exit. Stay on Mt. Herman for exactly four miles to Felton. Go right (north) on Highway 9 for three miles to Ben Lomond. Turn left on Fillmore then left on Fairview Avenue. The inn is 100 yards down on the left.
OPEN	All year
DESCRIPTION	A mid-1920s country redwood inn with country English furnishings, situated on the banks of the San Lorenzo River.
NO. OF ROOMS	Five rooms with private bathrooms.
RATES	Year-round rate is $119 for a single or double. There is no minimum stay.
CREDIT CARDS	MasterCard, Visa
BREAKFAST	Full breakfast, served in the dining room, includes fruit, juice, muffins, an egg dish, meat, and potatoes.
AMENITIES	Soft drinks, coffee, and tea available at all times; wine and hors d'oeuvres; gazebo, walking paths, deck overlooking the river; Great Room with stone fireplace; meeting facilities.
RESTRICTIONS	No smoking, no pets, children over 12 are welcome.

REVIEWED	*Recommended Country Inns—West Coast; Bed, Breakfast & Bike Northern California; Cooking and Traveling Inn Style; Bed & Breakfast California*
MEMBER	California Association of Bed & Breakfast Inns, Bed & Breakfast Innkeepers of Santa Cruz County

BENICIA

This splendid little town had a short reign as the state capital from 1853–1854. Set along the northern edge of Suisun Bay, it is now experiencing overall revitalization and an art-community boom. The town features lots of historic architecture, notably St. Paul's Episcopal Church, and Benicia Capital State Historic Park. Along the strait, Benicia State Recreation Area is fine for some outdoor fun, and it's a short drive to Marine World/Africa U.S.A. Pick your route northeast of Oakland.

CAPTAIN WALSH HOUSE

235 East L Street, Benicia, CA 94510 707-747-5653
Reed & Steve Robbins, Resident Owners FAX 707-747-6265
EMAIL cwhinn.com WEBSITE www.cwhinn.com

LOCATION	From San Francisco, go north on Highway 80 to East 780 and take the Central Benicia/East Second Street exit. Turn left onto East Second Street, go to L Street, and turn left. The inn is the third building on the left.
OPEN	All year
DESCRIPTION	An 1849 two-story Gothic Revival inn with Gothic Victorian decor, listed on the National and California Historic Registers.
NO. OF ROOMS	Five rooms with private bathrooms. Try the Epiphania Room.
RATES	Year-round rates for a double are $125-150. There is a two-night minimum stay and cancellation requires seven days' notice.
CREDIT CARDS	American Express, MasterCard, Visa
BREAKFAST	Three-course gourmet breakfast is served in the dining room and includes fruit "art" plate; fresh-baked goods; puff-pastry pillow with smoked quail, herbs, gouda, egg, and chutney. Lunches, dinners, and special meals are available upon request.
AMENITIES	Hors d'oeuvres and wine, silver coffee service to rooms before breakfast, robes, flowers, individually controlled heating and air conditioning, fireplaces, full wedding facility.
RESTRICTIONS	No smoking, no pets. Bill, the clumber spaniel, has graced the cover of *Dog World* magazine.

REVIEWED	*Frommer's California Bed & Breakfast Inns, Northern California Best Places, Fodor's San Francisco Focus*
AWARDS	Finalist for the 1998 Entrepreneur of the Year, selected by the Small Business Administration

THE PAINTED LADY BED & BREAKFAST

141 East F Street, Benicia, CA 94510 707-746-1646
Sally Watson, Resident Owner
WEBSITE *www.placestostay.com/Benicia-PaintedLady*

LOCATION	Located in historic downtown Benicia.
OPEN	All year
DESCRIPTION	An 1896 Victorian cottage with Victorian and country furnishings, surrounded by an old-fashioned garden.
NO. OF ROOMS	Two rooms with private bathrooms.
RATES	Year-round rates are $75-90 for a single or double. There is no minimum stay and cancellation requires four days' notice.
CREDIT CARDS	MasterCard, Visa
BREAKFAST	Full breakfast is served in the dining room or on the patio and might include breakfast breads, waffles, pancakes, omelets, fruits, and beverages "depending on the cook's whim and what's in season." Will cater luncheons and small parties.
AMENITIES	Robes, wine in room, books, tape player, games.
RESTRICTIONS	No smoking in the house, children welcome if guests rent both rooms. Outdoor cats, Miss Kitty and Beau, are affectionate hosts.
MEMBER	California Lodging Industry Association, California Association of Bed & Breakfast Inns

UNION HOTEL

401 First Street, Benicia, CA 94510 707-746-0100
Bruce Inderato, Resident Manager 800-544-2278
  FAX 707-746-6458

LOCATION	From San Francisco, take Highway 101 to I-80 across the Carquinez Bridge to I-780. Take the 2nd Street exit left to the first light. Turn right on Military and go to First Street.
OPEN	All year

DESCRIPTION	A historic 1882 three-story bordello and restaurant, renovated in 1982, with individually decorated rooms.
NO. OF ROOMS	Twenty rooms with private bathrooms.
RATES	Year-round rates are $105-140 for a single or double. Rates are cheaper during midweek. There is no minimum stay and cancellation requires 48 hours' notice.
CREDIT CARDS	American Express, Diners Club, Discover, MasterCard, Visa
BREAKFAST	Continental breakfast is served in the dining room. Lunch and dinner are also available.
AMENITIES	Queen- and king-size beds, TV, Jacuzzi tubs, atrium and gazebo for weddings and parties, meeting room, live music five nights a week, parking on premises.
RESTRICTIONS	No pets

BERKELEY

The wild days of this now middle-aged, upper–middle-class burg are gone. Although hot-button issues can still spark a march or two at the University of California at Berkeley, these days most UC Berkeley students seem more interested in cramming for exams than in mounting protests in People's Park. In some respects, the action has moved from the campus to City Hall, where the town's residents rage on against everything from Columbus Day (Berkeley celebrates Indigenous People's Day instead) to the opening of a large video store downtown (too lowbrow and tacky). The San Francisco Chronicle recently called Berkeley the "most contentious of cities," and it's a mantle most of its inhabitants wear with pride.

BANCROFT CLUB HOTEL

2680 Bancroft Way, Berkeley, CA 94704

EMAIL reservations@bancroft.com
WEBSITE www.brancrofthotel.com

510-549-1000
800-549-1002
FAX 510-549-1070

BEAU SKY HOTEL

2520 Durant Avenue, Berkeley, CA 94704

510-540-7688

Bonita Studio Bed & Breakfast

On Bonita between Rose & Vine Street 510-525-6416
Berkeley, CA 94709
Marie Minghini, Innkeeper
EMAIL bonitasstudio@yahoo.com
WEBSITE www.bbonline

LOCATION	In Northern Berkeley, two blocks from Chez Panisse.
OPEN	All year
DESCRIPTION	A two-story turn-of-the-century Victorian.
NO. OF ROOMS	Two rooms with private bathrooms.
RATES	Year-round rates are $85-150 for a double.
CREDIT CARDS	No
BREAKFAST	Expanded continental breakfast includes a selection of teas, gourmet coffee, breads and cheese, fruit salad, homemade jams and jellies. Dietary restrictions and preferences are accommodated.
AMENITIES	Private entrances, radiant heat, marble floors, double showers, telephone, queen-size beds, reading area, newspaper delivered to guestrooms in the morning, refrigerator, microwave, electric tea kettle in one room.
RESTRICTIONS	No smoking, no pets, no children

Clarinett Cafe Bed & Breakfast

1908 Shattuck Avenue, Berkeley, CA 94704 510-644-1070

Elmwood House

2609 College Avenue, Berkeley, CA 94704 510-540-5123
John Ekdahl & Steve Hyske, Resident Owners
French and German spoken

LOCATION	From Highway 24 west, exit onto Clairmont Avenue and go left to College Avenue. From Highway 24 east, exit onto College Avenue and go right.
OPEN	All year

DESCRIPTION	A two-story turn-of-the-century Berkeley Bay host home with redwood-trimmed interior.
NO. OF ROOMS	Two rooms have private bathrooms and two rooms share two bathrooms. John recommends the Maybeck Room.
RATES	Please call for current rates and cancellation information.
CREDIT CARDS	American Express, MasterCard, Visa
BREAKFAST	Continental breakfast is served.
AMENITIES	Private phone in each room.
RESTRICTIONS	No smoking, no pets. The resident cats are called Ruby and Bebe.
MEMBER	American Bed & Breakfast Association, California Association of Bed & Breakfast Innkeepers

GRAMMA'S

2740 Telegraph Avenue, Berkeley, CA 94705   510-549-2145

HILLEGASS HOUSE

2834 Hillegass Avenue, Berkeley, CA 94705   510-548-5517
Richard Warren, Resident Manager   800-400-5517
EMAIL rpwarren@slipnet.com   FAX 510-548-9302
WEBSITE www.travelassist.com/reg/ca/1285

LOCATION	Two blocks west of College Avenue and one block north of Ashby Avenue. Eight blocks south of the University campus.
OPEN	All year
DESCRIPTION	A restored 1904 three-story Craftsman inn decorated with eclectic decor and many antiques, located on an oversized wooded lot in a quiet residential neighborhood.
NO. OF ROOMS	Four rooms with private bathrooms.
RATES	Year-round rates are $70-110 for a single or double. There generally is a two-night minimum stay during weekends and cancellation requires 10 days' notice less a $10 charge.
CREDIT CARDS	American Express, MasterCard, Visa
BREAKFAST	Full breakfast is served in the dining room and includes fresh-squeezed orange juice, fresh fruit salad, yogurt (Russian style), muesli, granola, cheese, a variety of baked goods (breads and pastries), coffee, and tea.

Hillegass House, Berkeley

AMENITIES	Large multilevel deck overlooking the garden; sauna; two large parlors; off-street parking; very convenient location; easy walk to university, shops, and restaurants; convenient public transportation to San Francisco.
RESTRICTIONS	No smoking, no pets, well-behaved children are welcome.
REVIEWED	Northern California Best Places, Frommer's San Francisco

BISHOP

At the southeastern edge of the Sierras, this is the gateway to the Inyo National Forest. From here it's a straight shot to the Mammoth Lakes area for serious trout fishing. Local happenings include the Early Sierra Trout Derby in March, Mule Days Celebration over Memorial Day, Wild West Rodeo over Labor Day, and Millpond Blue Grass Festival in September.

THE CHALFANT HOUSE

213 Academy Street, Bishop, CA 93514   760-872-1790
Fred & Sally Manecke, Resident Owners

LOCATION	One block off Highway 395 in the center of Bishop, on the corner of Academy and Warren.
OPEN	All year
DESCRIPTION	An 1898 country inn with Victorian furnishings.
NO. OF ROOMS	Seven rooms with private bathrooms. Try the Blanche Room.

RATES	Please call for current rates and cancellation information.
CREDIT CARDS	American Express, MasterCard, Visa
BREAKFAST	Full breakfast is served on china and silver in the dining room.
AMENITIES	Handmade quilt and flowers in the rooms, old-time ice-cream sundaes every night from 8–9 p.m., orange frosty drink in the afternoon, iced tea and hot apple cider in the winter.
RESTRICTIONS	No smoking, children over eight are welcome.
REVIEWED	*The Definitive California Bed & Breakfast Touring Guide, Non-Smokers Guide to Bed & Breakfasts*
RATED	AAA 3 Diamonds, Mobil 3 Stars

THE MATLICK HOUSE

1313 Rowan Lane, Bishop, CA 93515   760-873-3133
Ray & Barbara Showalter, Innkeepers   800-898-3133

LOCATION	Two miles north of Bishop on Highway 395. The inn is located behind Kragen's Auto Parts.
OPEN	All year
DESCRIPTION	A 1906 two-story ranch house with wraparound verandas and antique furnishings.
NO. OF ROOMS	Five rooms with private bathrooms. Barbara's favorite room is Lena's Room.
RATES	Year-round rates are $75-85 for a single or double. Cancellation requires seven days' notice and a $15 fee.
CREDIT CARDS	American Express, Discover, MasterCard, Visa
BREAKFAST	Full country breakfast is served in the dining room and includes juice, fresh fruit, eggs, homemade biscuits, coffee, and tea. Sack lunches and dinner are also available.
AMENITIES	Common area with fireplace and TV, wine and hors d'oeuvres served in the evening.
RESTRICTIONS	No smoking, no pets, children over 15 are welcome.
REVIEWED	*Fodor's*
MEMBER	Professional Association of Innkeepers International, California Association of Bed & Breakfast Inns

BODEGA

A little jewel to be savored, especially in the fall when the crowds go home. But anytime is fine to explore the headlands and tide pools, comb the beach, and whale-watch. This is a working fishing village, and the seafood is to dream about. Do a walking tour of settings from *The Birds*, and plan to be here for the Fishermans' Festival and Blessing of the Fleet in April. Bodega is on the Sonoma Coast, north of San Francisco on Highway 1.

BODEGA ESTERO BED & BREAKFAST

17699 Highway 1, Bodega, CA 94922　　　　　　　　707-876-3300
Edgar A. Furlong & C. Michael O'Brien, Resident Owners　800-422-6321

LOCATION	Located on Highway 1, 1,000 feet from the turnoff into Bodega.
OPEN	All year
DESCRIPTION	A 1984 contemporary geodesic dome with 50-foot ceilings and country antique furnishings.
NO. OF ROOMS	Four rooms with private bathrooms.
RATES	Year-round rates are $75-135 for a double. There is a two-night minimum stay on Saturdays and a seven-day cancellation policy.
CREDIT CARDS	MasterCard, Visa
BREAKFAST	Continental plus is served in the dining room and includes fresh fruit salad, homemade scones, muffins, quiche, a hot dessert such as apple Betty, and beverages.
AMENITIES	Down comforters, fireplace, wine and desserts in the evening, handicapped accessible.
RESTRICTIONS	No smoking, no pets. Resident pets and farm animals include goats; sheep; llamas; exotic birds; a potbellied pig, Piggy Lee; Baby the Siamese cat; and a dog named Phoebe.

BODEGA HARBOR INN

1345 Bodega Avenue, Bodega CA 94923　　　　　　　707-875-3594
Bill & Elda Stevens, Resident Owners
WEBSITE www.bodegaharborinn.com

LOCATION	On the bluffs off the east side of Highway 1 at the north end of Bodega Bay. Turn east on Bodega Avenue.
OPEN	All year
DESCRIPTION	A 1950 bungalow-style cottage furnished with antiques.

NO. OF ROOMS	Sixteen rooms with private bathrooms.
RATES	Year-round rates are $53-100. There is a minimum stay of two nights on weekends during the high season and holiday weekends all year round. Cancellation requires 48 hours' notice, three weeks during holidays.
CREDIT CARDS	MasterCard, Visa
BREAKFAST	Continental breakfast is served on holidays and weekends year-round and on weekdays from June through October.
AMENITIES	TV in rooms, courtesy phone for guests, views of Bodega Harbor and the surrounding fishing village.
RESTRICTIONS	No pets

BOLINAS

Down at the far south end of the Point Reyes Peninsula, this is a prime ocean spot. From San Francisco, it's a short drive north on Highway 1. Once in town, the Bolinas Lagoon, surrounded by a crescent-shaped sand spit, is serene.

BLUE HERON INN RESTAURANT BED & BREAKFAST

11 Wharf Road, Bolinas, CA 94924   415-868-1102

ONE FIFTY-FIVE PINE

PO Box 62, Bolinas, CA 94924   415-868-0263

THOMAS' WHITE HOUSE INN

118 Kale Road, Bolinas, CA 94924   415-868-0279
Jacqueline Thomas, Innkeeper
www.coastallodging.com/thomas/thomas.html

LOCATION	Twenty-seven miles north of San Francisco off Highway 1, 4.5 miles north of Stinson Beach.
OPEN	All year

DESCRIPTION	A 1979 two-story New England-style inn with an observation tower, located on a bluff overlooking San Francisco.
NO. OF ROOMS	Two rooms with a shared bathroom.
RATES	Year-round rates for a double are $100-110. A minimum stay is required on weekends and holidays and cancellation requires 10 days' notice.
CREDIT CARDS	No
BREAKFAST	Continental plus is served in the dining room and includes fresh fruit, pastries, and beverages.
AMENITIES	TV/VCR, phone, fireplace in common room, gardens, window seats with great views.
RESTRICTIONS	No smoking, children are welcome. Resident pets include cats Misha and Nicholas and several zebra finches.
REVIEWED	*Northern California Best Places, Offbeat Overnights*
MEMBER	Coastal Lodging Association

BOONVILLE

This speck of a town in the heart of the Anderson Valley is best known for a regional dialect called Boontling, developed by townsfolk at the beginning of the century. No one really speaks Boontling anymore, though a few old-timers remember the lingo. While you're in town, grab a copy of the *Anderson Valley Advertiser*, a rollicking, crusading (some might say muckraking) small-town paper with avid readers from as far away as San Francisco and the Oregon border.

ANDERSON CREEK INN

12050 Anderson Valley Way, Boonville, CA 95415   707-895-3091
Rod & Nancy Graham, Resident Owners

KUDOS/COMMENTS   "Delightful, peaceful retreat on Anderson Creek, beautifully decorated and impeccably clean; charming innkeepers."

THE BOONVILLE HOTEL

Highway 128 and Lambert Lane, Boonville, CA 95415   707-895-2210
WEBSITE *www.boonvillehotel.com*

TOLL HOUSE RESTAURANT & INN

15301 Highway 253, Boonville, CA 95415   707-895-3630

BRENTWOOD

BRENTWOOD OAKS

1850 Arabian Lane, Brentwood, CA 94513   925-634-0378
EMAIL WSgibs@aol.com   925-634-0197

BRIDGEPORT

Surrounded by Toiyabe National Forest in the eastern Sierras, this is an exceedingly good place to stop before heading farther into the wilderness. While here, check out Big Hot Warm Springs and sample the good trout fishing in Twin Lakes southwest of town (with trailhead access into the Hoover Wilderness). Bridgeport is on scenic Highway 395 between Lake Tahoe and Bishop, just outside the Nevada border.

THE CAIN HOUSE

340 Main Street, Bridgeport, CA 93517   760-932-7040
Chris & Marachal Gohlich, Resident Owners   800-433-2246
Some Spanish and German spoken   FAX 760-932-7419
EMAIL thecainhouse@msn.com

LOCATION	On Highway 395, 0.1 mile from the center of town, 55 miles north of Mammoth Lakes, and 113 miles south of Reno.
OPEN	April 25 through October 25
DESCRIPTION	A 1920s two-story western ranch-style inn with English country furnishings.
NO. OF ROOMS	Seven rooms with private bathrooms Try the J. S. Cain Room.
RATES	Rates are $85-135 for a single or double and $700 for the entire B&B. There is no minimum stay and cancellation requires 48 hours' notice.
CREDIT CARDS	American Express, Discover, MasterCard, Visa

BREAKFAST	Full or continental breakfast is served in the dining room, in the guestrooms, or outside on the deck. There are four menus to choose from daily.
AMENITIES	Wine and cheese, fruits and breads in the evenings; rooms all have private phones, TVs, robes, coffee-makers, hot pots, air conditioning, movies.
RESTRICTIONS	No smoking, no pets, only two people per room. The resident cat is called Amadeus ("Amy").
REVIEWED	Best Places in Northern California; America's Favorite Inns, B&Bs, & Small Hotels
MEMBER	Professional Association of Innkeepers International, California Association of Bed & Breakfast Inns
RATED	AAA 3 Diamonds, ABBA 3 Crowns, Mobil 3 Stars

BROWNSVILLE

MOUNTAIN SEASONS INN

9067 La Porte Road, Brownsville, CA 95919   530-675-2180

CALISTOGA

Mud baths, mineral pools, and massages are still the main attractions of this charming little spa town, founded in the mid-19th century by California's first millionaire, Sam Brannan. In 1859 he purchased 2,000 acres of the Wappo Indians' hot springs land and built a first-class hotel and spa. He then watched his fortunes grow as affluent San Franciscans paraded into town for a relaxing respite from city life. These days, more than a dozen enterprises touting the magical restorative powers of mineral baths line the town's Old West-style streets. From Calistoga, a 10-mile drive up Mount St. Helena gets you to Robert Louis Stevenson State Park, where he honeymooned and wrote.

BRANNAN COTTAGE INN

109 Wapoo Avenue, Calistoga, CA 94515   707-942-4200
Dieter Back, Resident Owner
German spoken

LOCATION	From Highway 29, go east on Lincoln Avenue into town. Wapoo Avenue angles off to the left.
OPEN	All year
DESCRIPTION	An 1863 Victorian cottage with 11-foot ceilings, oak floors, stencils, and antiques. Listed on the National Historic Register.
NO. OF ROOMS	Six rooms with private bathrooms.
RATES	April through October, rates are $125-165 for a single or double. November through March, rates are $90-140 for a single or double. There is a two-night minimum stay on weekends and cancellation requires seven days' notice with a $20 fee.
CREDIT CARDS	MasterCard, Visa
BREAKFAST	Full breakfast is served buffet style in the parlor or garden.
AMENITIES	Down quilts, flowers, off-street parking.
RESTRICTIONS	No smoking, no pets, children over 12 are welcome.
MEMBER	Napa Valley Bed & Breakfast Association

CALISTOGA BEAR FLAG INN

2653 Foothill Boulevard, Calistoga, CA 94515   707-942-5534
Marge & Dennis McNay, Resident Owners   FAX 707-942-8761
EMAIL *bearflaginn@bestlodgings.com*

LOCATION	One mile northwest from the center of town on Highway 128.
OPEN	All year
DESCRIPTION	A 1930s two-story farmhouse and cottage furnished with period antiques.
NO. OF ROOMS	Four rooms with private bathrooms.
RATES	Year-round rates are $150-175 for a single or double. There is a two-night minimum stay over Saturday and cancellation requires seven days' notice.
CREDIT CARDS	Discover, MasterCard, Visa
BREAKFAST	Full breakfast, served in the dining room, includes fruit, an entrée, meat, potatoes, pastry, and beverages.
AMENITIES	Swimming pool and spa, flowers, robes, hot tub, wine and hors d'oeuvres, vineyard, parlor with fireplace and piano, TVs in guest rooms.
RESTRICTIONS	No smoking inside, no pets

Calistoga Country Lodge

2883 Foothill Boulevard, Calistoga, CA 94515   707-942-5555

Calistoga Wayside Inn

1523 Foothill Boulevard, Calistoga, CA 94515   707-942-0645
KUDOS/COMMENTS   "Small but very helpful and nice."

Christopher's Inn

1010 Foothill Boulevard, Calistoga, CA 94515   707-942-5755
WEBSITE www.christophersinn.com

The Elms Bed & Breakfast

1300 Cedar Street, Calistoga, CA 94515   707-942-9476
Stephen & Karla Wyle, Resident Owners   800-235-4316
Spanish, Italian, German, French, and Flemish spoken   FAX 707-942-9479
EMAIL 103702.1043@compuserve.com   WEBSITE www.theelms.com

LOCATION	Go north on Highway 29 to the flashing light at Lincoln Avenue. Turn right on Lincoln, go two blocks to Cedar Street, and turn left.
OPEN	All year
DESCRIPTION	An 1871 French Victorian inn with Victorian and French furnishings and enormous elm trees in front. Listed on the National Historic Register.
NO. OF ROOMS	All rooms have private bathrooms. Try La Chambre.
RATES	Year-round weekend rates are $125-185; weekday rates are $100-155. There is a two-night minimum stay on weekends, three nights on some holidays. Cancellation requires seven days' notice with a $20 charge.
CREDIT CARDS	MasterCard, Visa
BREAKFAST	Full three-course gourmet breakfast is served in the dining room.

AMENITIES	Robes, coffee-makers, chocolates, TV, fireplaces, and port in rooms; telephone; air conditioning; wine and cheese served in the afternoon; full concierge service.
RESTRICTIONS	No smoking, no pets. The inn is not suitable for young children. The resident golden retriever is called Ivory.
MEMBER	California Association of Bed & Breakfast Inns

EUROSPA & INN

1202 Pine Street, Calistoga, CA 94515 707-942-6829
WEBSITE www.eurospa.com

FALCON'S NEST

471 Kortum Canyon Road, Calistoga, CA 94515 707-942-0758
Michael & Yvonne Rich, Resident Owners
WEBSITE www.falconsnestbb.com

FANNY'S

1206 Spring Street, Calistoga, CA 94515 707-942-9491
Deanna Higgins, Resident Owner FAX 707-942-4810

LOCATION	Follow Highway 29 north into Calistoga. Continue past the blinking light for two blocks and turn right at Spring Street. Go one block to the big red house on the right.
OPEN	All year
DESCRIPTION	A 1915 two-story Craftsman cottage with a big front porch, rockers, and a porch swing.
NO. OF ROOMS	All rooms have private bathrooms.
RATES	Year-round rate for a double is $95. There is a two-night minimum stay on weekends.
CREDIT CARDS	No

Fanny's, Calistoga

BREAKFAST	Continental plus is served in the dining room and features fresh seasonal dishes such as frittatas, breakfast wraps, and quiches.
AMENITIES	Fireplace in the living room, large common area upstairs.
RESTRICTIONS	No smoking, no pets, children over 12 are welcome. The resident pets include Muttley the Dandy Dinmont, and two cats, Krusty and Zoe.
REVIEWED	*Fodor's Wine Country*

FOOTHILL HOUSE BED & BREAKFAST

3037 Foothill Boulevard, Calistoga, CA 94515　　707-942-6933
Gus & Doris Beckert, Resident Owners　　800-942-6933
　　FAX 707-942-5692

LOCATION	From the point where Highway 29 becomes Highway 128 (Foothill Boulevard at the intersection of Lincoln Boulevard), continue north 1.5 miles. The B&B is on the left.
OPEN	All year except Thanksgiving and Christmas Day
DESCRIPTION	An 1893 farmhouse and cottage with country antique furnishings and landscaped gardens with waterfalls and freshwater ponds.
NO. OF ROOMS	Three rooms with private bathrooms. Gus and Doris recommend the Quail's Roost.
RATES	Year-round rates are $165-295. There is a two-night minimum stay over Saturday night and cancellation requires seven days' notice and a $10 fee.
CREDIT CARDS	American Express, Discover, MasterCard, Visa

BREAKFAST	Full breakfast is served in the dining room, guestrooms, or gazebo, or on the patio, and includes fresh fruit, croissants, muffins, baked soufflés, and coffee. Guests with food allergies can be accommodated.
AMENITIES	Evening wine and hors d'oeuvres, fresh flowers, robes, wood-burning stoves or fireplaces in all rooms, TV, phones, in-room tape players, air conditioning/ceiling fans, turndown service with sherry and cookies.
RESTRICTIONS	No smoking, no pets, children over 12 are welcome in selected rooms. There are koi fish in the pond, and Grizzie is "a 'fraidy cat that came with the inn."
REVIEWED	The Best Places to Kiss in Northern California, Best Places to Stay in Northern California, America's Wonderful Little Hotels & Inns, Northern California Best Places
MEMBER	Professional Association of Innkeepers International, California Association of Bed & Breakfast Inns
RATED	ABBA 4 Crowns, Mobil 3 Stars, Best Places to Kiss 4 Lips
KUDOS/COMMENTS	"Great innkeepers. Wonderful place to stay." "Beautifully decorated; caring innkeepers." "Nice rooms." (1999)

HILLCREST BED & BREAKFAST

3225 Lake County Highway, Calistoga, CA 94515   707-944-6334
Debbie O'Gorman, Innkeeper

LOCATION	Two miles north of Calistoga on Highway 29 as you begin to climb Mount St. Helena. The B&B is the first driveway on the left.
OPEN	All year
DESCRIPTION	A 1961 rambling ranch house filled with antiques and rare art, located on a hilltop that overlooks lush vineyards and the wooded hillsides of Napa Valley on land that has been in the same family since 1870.
NO. OF ROOMS	Four rooms with private bathrooms and two rooms share one bathroom.
RATES	Year-round rates are $60-165 for a single or double with a private bathroom and $60-135 for a single or double with a shared bathroom. There is a two-night minimum stay during weekends and holidays and cancellation requires one weeks' notice.
CREDIT CARDS	American Express, MasterCard, Visa

BREAKFAST	Large continental breakfast is served in the dining room on a 12-foot antique table and includes fruit juice, coffee, tea, cereal, turnovers, ham and cheese croissants, peach cobbler, or large muffins.
AMENITIES	Conference room, 12-foot antique table by fireplace overlooking the valley, 40,000-gallon pool, Jacuzzi under the stars, fishing pond, 40 acres for hiking, minimuseum of antique silver china, rare artwork, oriental rugs, family photos showing what valley life was like in the 1800s, rooms with balconies and valley views, TV with HBO, trampoline, fireplace in guest parlor, air conditioning, old books, boating on pond.
RESTRICTIONS	No smoking inside. Taz and Bamboo are the resident Labs.

La Chaumiere, a Country Inn

1301 Cedar Street, Calistoga, CA 94515
Gary Venturi, Resident Manager
WEBSITE www.lachaumiere.com

707-942-5139
800-474-6800
FAX 707-942-5199

LOCATION	Greater downtown Calistoga.
OPEN	All year
DESCRIPTION	A 1910 English Cotswald country inn with French interior.
NO. OF ROOMS	All rooms have private bathrooms. Gary recommends the Cottage.
RATES	Year-round rates are $150-175 for a double and $185-225 for the cottage. There is a two-night minimum stay on weekends, three nights during holidays. Cancellation requires seven days' notice plus a $20 fee.
CREDIT CARDS	American Express, MasterCard, Visa
BREAKFAST	Full breakfast, served in the dining room, includes a fruit platter, sausage frittata, home fries, croissant, coffee, and orange juice.
AMENITIES	Wine and cheese in the afternoon, in-house massage in tree house under huge redwood tree, hot tub, port, fresh flowers in the room.
RESTRICTIONS	No smoking, no pets, the inn is not suitable for children.

Larkmead Country Inn

1103 Larkmead Lane, Calistoga, CA 94515   707-942-5360

MEADOWLARK COUNTRY HOUSE

601 Petrified Forest Road, Calistoga, CA 94515   707-942-5651
Kurt Stevens, Resident Owner
German and Italian spoken
WEBSITE www.meadowlarkinn.com

LOCATION	From Calistoga, follow Highway 128 for one mile to Petrified Forest Road.
OPEN	All year
DESCRIPTION	An 1886 two-story California country inn decorated with simple elegance, situated on a 20-acre estate.
NO. OF ROOMS	Seven rooms with private bathrooms.
RATES	April through November, rates are $185 for a double. December through March, rates are $125-150 for a double. There is a two-night minimum stay on weekends and holidays, and cancellation requires seven days' notice.
CREDIT CARDS	MasterCard, Visa
BREAKFAST	Full gourmet breakfast is served in the dining room or guestrooms and includes fruit, baked goods, eggs, granola, and beverages.
AMENITIES	Complimentary soft drinks, hot tub, swimming pool (clothes optional at pool!), sun deck, all rooms with TV/VCR, fax, phones, secluded sunning area past the pool, terraces, decks.
RESTRICTIONS	No smoking, pets are allowed with prior arrangement. The resident cat is called Miss Kitty; guinea hens. Sport horses are bred and trained here.
REVIEWED	Karen Brown's California Country Inns & Itineraries
MEMBER	California Association of Bed & Breakfast Inns, Bed & Breakfasts of Napa Valley, Bed & Breakfasts of Calistoga
KUDOS/COMMENTS	"We booked this place by mistake—the best mistake we ever made."

MOUNTAIN HOME RANCH

3400 Mountain Home Ranch Road, Calistoga, CA 94515   707-942-6616
                                                   FAX 707-942-9091

LOCATION	Five miles southeast of Calistoga. Mountain Home Ranch Road is off of Petrified Forest Road. The lodge is at the end of the road.
OPEN	All year

DESCRIPTION	A 1953 lodge and cabins with modern furnishings.
NO. OF ROOMS	Thirteen rooms with private bathrooms and six rooms share one bathroom.
RATES	Please call for rates and cancellation information.
CREDIT CARDS	MasterCard, Visa
BREAKFAST	Either continental or full breakfast is served in the dining room. Dinner and special meals are available.
AMENITIES	Tennis; fishing; five miles of hiking trails; sulphur springs; facilities for meetings, retreats, weddings, and large barbecues.
RESTRICTIONS	Ask about restrictions.

THE PINK MANSION

1415 Foothill Boulevard, Calistoga, CA 94515   707-942-0558
Toppa Epps, Resident Owner   800-238-7465
Spanish spoken   FAX 707-942-0558
WEBSITE www.pinkmansion.com

LOCATION	From Highway 29, at the stoplight in Calistoga, go one block; the inn is on the right.
OPEN	All year
DESCRIPTION	A 1875 two-story Victorian inn with antique furnishings.
NO. OF ROOMS	Six rooms with private bathrooms.
RATES	Year-round rates are $135-225 for a single or double. There is a two-night minimum stay on weekends and holidays, and cancellation requires seven days' notice.
CREDIT CARDS	Discover, MasterCard, Visa
BREAKFAST	Full gourmet breakfast served in the dining room or guestrooms.
AMENITIES	Flowers in the rooms, hot tub and indoor pool, air conditioning, handicapped access, wine and cheese in the afternoon, some rooms have TVs and fireplaces.
RESTRICTIONS	No smoking
MEMBER	California Association of Bed & Breakfast Inns

QUAIL MOUNTAIN

4455 North St. Helena Highway, Calistoga, CA 94515   707-942-0316
Eric & Kathy Amadei, Innkeepers   FAX 707-942-0315

LOCATION	Two miles south of Calistoga off Highway 29 (St. Helena Highway) on Quail Mountain Lane across from Stonegate Vineyard.
OPEN	All year
DESCRIPTION	A 1984 two-story contemporary estate with classic contemporary decor, situated on 26 acres with a Cabernet vineyard.
NO. OF ROOMS	Three bedrooms with private bathrooms. Try the Fern Room.
RATES	Year-round rates are $130-150 for a single or double. There is a minimum stay during weekends and holidays, and cancellation requires seven days' notice with a 10 percent charge.
CREDIT CARDS	American Express, Diners Club, Discover, MasterCard, Visa
BREAKFAST	Full breakfast is served in the dining room and includes juice, fruit, a hot entrée with meat, fresh-baked goods, coffee, and tea.
AMENITIES	Pool and hot tub, robes, fresh flowers, air-conditioned rooms, wine and hors d'oeuvres before dinner.
RESTRICTIONS	No smoking, no pets, no children
REVIEWED	Karen Brown's California Country Inns & Itineraries; America's Wonderful Little Hotels & Inns; Northern California Best Places; Fodor's Bed & Breakfast Country Inns and Other Weekend Pleasures; Bed & Breakfast Homes: Best of the West Coast
MEMBER	Professional Association of Innkeepers International, California Association of Bed & Breakfast Inns
KUDOS/COMMENTS	"Excellent!"

SCARLETT'S COUNTRY INN

3918 Silverado Trail, Calistoga, CA 94515   707-942-6669
Scarlett Dwyer, Innkeeper   FAX 707-942-6669
EMAIL scarletts@aol.com   WEBSITE members.aol.com/scarletts

LOCATION	On Highway 29, travel four miles north of St. Helena and turn right on Bole Lane. Turn left on Silverado Trail and go exactly 0.5 mile.
OPEN	All year
DESCRIPTION	A 1900 two-story French country farmhouse furnished with antiques, located in a canyon overlooking vineyards.

Scarlett's Country Inn, Calistoga

NO. OF ROOMS	Three rooms with private bathrooms. Scarlett recommends the Camellia Suite.
RATES	Year-round rates are $115 for a single or double and $135-175 for a suite. The guesthouse is $310 and the entire B&B rents for $425. There is no minimum stay.
CREDIT CARDS	No
BREAKFAST	Full breakfast is served in the dining room or guestrooms and includes fresh fruit, fresh-squeezed orange juice, coffee, tea, and a hot dish such as French toast, pancakes, or eggs.
AMENITIES	Fresh flowers in rooms, robes, down pillows, microwaves, refrigerators, TVs, afternoon refreshments, turndown service, swimming pool, patios with tables and chairs, air conditioning, cribs, special children's plates, lawns, flowers, fireplaces, wet bar, aviary with finches, suites have private entrances.
RESTRICTIONS	No smoking, no pets. The resident pets include two dogs, Chili and Frond; four cats, Huckle, Pesto, Matt, and Miss Kitty; and three chickens, Tony, Woppo, and India. "All co-exist and take care of each other."
REVIEWED	*Karen Brown's California Charming Inns & Itineraries; B&Bs, Inns, and Guesthouses; America's Favorite Inns, B&Bs, & Small Hotels; The Official Guide to American Historic Inns; Bed and Breakfast U.S.A.*
MEMBER	California Association of Bed & Breakfast Inns, Professional Association of Innkeepers International
KUDOS/COMMENTS	"Peaceful, quiet; attention to detail; comfy; cozy; wonderful hostess."

SCOTT COURTYARD

1443 Second Street, Calistoga, CA 94515
Joe & Lauren Scott, Innkeepers

707-942-0948
800-942-1515
FAX 707-942-5102

LOCATION	Two blocks from downtown Calistoga. From Highway 29 north, turn left on Fairway and drive two blocks to Second Street.
OPEN	All year
DESCRIPTION	A 1920s Mediterranean villa and bungalows with tropical art deco interior and courtyard gardens and pool.
NO. OF ROOMS	Six rooms with private bathrooms. Lauren recommends the Tropical Room and Joe prefers the Palisades Room.
RATES	April through November, rates are $125-135 for a single or double and $175 for a suite or the guesthouse. December through March, the suites and guesthouse rent for $175 per night. Weekends require a two-night minimum stay, three nights during holidays; and cancellation requires seven days' notice with a 10 percent charge.
CREDIT CARDS	American Express, Discover, MasterCard, Visa
BREAKFAST	Full breakfast is served buffet style in the dining room and includes coffee, cereal, juice, fresh fruit, tea, and cocoa. Breakfast may include French toast, chicken apple sausage, quiche burritos, bread pudding, pancakes, and bacon.
AMENITIES	Wine and appetizers in the afternoon; fresh flowers in rooms; robes; iron and ironing boards; coffee machines in rooms; large bird aviary; pool; art workshop; television room; air conditioning; winery and spa information.
RESTRICTIONS	No smoking. Children welcome in some rooms.
REVIEWED	*Northern California Wine Country Access; The Best Places to Kiss in Northern California; Country Inns and Back Roads: California; Northern California Best Places; The Napa & Sonoma Book*
MEMBER	Professional Association of Innkeepers International, California Association of Bed & Breakfast Inns, California Lodging Industry Association
RATED	Mobil 3 Stars

SILVER ROSE INN

351 Rosedale Road, Calistoga, CA 94515
J. Paul & Sally Dumont, Innkeepers
EMAIL silvrose@napa.net
WEBSITE www.silverrose.com

707-942-9581
800-995-9381
FAX 707-942-0841

LOCATION	Twenty-five miles north of San Francisco in the Napa Valley. One mile east of Calistoga off the Silverado Trail.
OPEN	All year
DESCRIPTION	A 1986 three-story inn decorated with elegant western furnishings and surrounded by mountains and vineyards.
NO. OF ROOMS	Twenty rooms with private bathrooms. J. Paul's favorite is the Vineyard Suite.
RATES	Year-round rates are $150-270 for a single or double. There is a minimum stay on weekends and holidays, and cancellation requires seven days' notice.
CREDIT CARDS	American Express, Discover, MasterCard, Visa
BREAKFAST	Continental plus is served in the dining room or guestrooms and includes a fresh seasonal fruit plate, homemade breads, juices, coffee, and tea.
AMENITIES	Robes, swimming pools, outdoor Jacuzzi, wine and cheese, air conditioning, handicapped accessible, tennis courts, chipping and putting green, meeting facilities.
RESTRICTIONS	No smoking, no pets, children over 14 are welcome. The two cats, Patches and Pumpkin, are "gentle and loving."
REVIEWED	Karen Brown's California Country Inns & Itineraries, Northern California Wine Country Access, The Best Places to Kiss in Northern California, Best Places to Stay in California, Country Inns & Back Roads: California, America's Wonderful Little Hotels & Inns, The Napa and Sonoma Book, Bed and Breakfast California, Recommended Country Inns—West Coast
MEMBER	California Hotel and Motel Association, United States Hotel and Motel Association
RATED	Mobil 3 Stars
KUDOS/COMMENTS	"Beautifully maintained, excellent location, spacious rooms."

TRAILSIDE INN BED & BREAKFAST

4201 Silverado Trail, Calistoga, CA 94515   707-942-4106
WEBSITE www.trailsideinn.com

WASHINGTON STREET LODGING

1605 Washington Street, Calistoga, CA 94515   707-942-6968
Joan Ranieri, Resident Owner

LOCATION	Head north on Main Street, turn left at Washington Street. The inn is between 4th and Lake Streets.
OPEN	All year
DESCRIPTION	An 1873 country farmhouse with five cottages decorated with country furnishings.
NO. OF ROOMS	Five rooms with private bathrooms.
RATES	Please call for current rates and cancellation information.
CREDIT CARDS	No
BREAKFAST	Continental breakfast is served in the cottages.
AMENITIES	Down comforters, fresh flowers, three cottages on the Napa River, two with decks, all cottages have kitchens.
RESTRICTIONS	None

WINE WAY INN

1019 Foothill Boulevard, Calistoga, CA 94515   707-942-0680
Moye & Cecil Stephens, Resident Owners   800-572-0679

LOCATION	On Highway 29, one block south of Lincoln Avenue.
OPEN	All year except December 21 through 25
DESCRIPTION	A 1915 two-story Craftsman with antique furnishings.
NO. OF ROOMS	Six rooms with private bathrooms. Cecil suggests the Calistoga Room.
RATES	Please call for current rates and cancellation information.
CREDIT CARDS	American Express, MasterCard, Visa
BREAKFAST	Full breakfast is served in the dining room.

CALISTOGA

AMENITIES	Wine and hors d'oeuvres, robes, sherry in parlor, full-service spa, three-level deck.
RESTRICTIONS	No smoking, no pets
REVIEWED	*Northern California Wine Country Access, America's Wonderful Little Hotels & Inns*
RATED	Mobil 1 Star

WISTERIA GARDEN BED & BREAKFAST

1508 Fair Way, Calistoga, CA 94515   707-942-5358
Carmen Marb, Resident Owner

LOCATION	From Main Street in Calistoga, take Lincoln Avenue one block to Fair Way.
OPEN	All year
DESCRIPTION	A 1916 Victorian shaded by a 150-year-old oak tree.
NO. OF ROOMS	Two rooms with private bathrooms.
RATES	Please call for current rates and cancellation information.
CREDIT CARDS	MasterCard, Visa
BREAKFAST	Continental breakfast is served in the guestrooms.
AMENITIES	Cable TV, fresh flowers, microwave, refrigerator, and coffee-makers.
RESTRICTIONS	Smoking outside the rooms only.

ZINFANDEL HOUSE

1253 Summit Drive, Calistoga, CA 94515   707-942-0733
Bette & George Starke, Innkeepers   FAX 707-942-4618
EMAIL zinhouse@pon.net   WEBSITE www.geocities.com/napavalley/1510

LOCATION	Halfway between St. Helena and Calistoga. Call for directions.
OPEN	All year
DESCRIPTION	A 1980 redwood host home with a mixture of traditional and antique furnishings, situated on a hillside.
NO. OF ROOMS	Two rooms with private bathrooms and two rooms share one bathroom. Ask for the room with the king-size bed and balcony.

RATES	Year-round rates are $95-120 for a single or double with a private bathroom and $80-85 for a single or double with a shared bathroom. There is a two-night minimum stay on weekends and cancellation requires five days' notice and a 10 percent fee.
CREDIT CARDS	Discover, MasterCard, Visa
BREAKFAST	Full breakfast is served in the solarium or on the deck.
AMENITIES	Views of mountains and vineyards, fresh flowers, telephones available for all rooms, complimentary wine and snacks, food and wine library, air conditioning.
RESTRICTIONS	No smoking, no pets. Due to steep steps, not convenient for children or the handicapped.
REVIEWED	Karen Brown's California: Charming Inns & Itineraries; The Complete Guide to Bed & Breakfasts, Inns, and Guesthouses
MEMBER	California Association of Bed & Breakfast Inns

CAPITOLA-BY-THE-SEA

Just east of Santa Cruz sits Capitola-by-the-Sea, a tiny, very popular resort town nestled around a small bay. The intimate downtown is only a few blocks long; it's a quaint, jumbled mix of restaurants, gift shops, and beachwear boutiques reminiscent of resort towns of yesteryear. Capitola's broad, sandy beach attracts lots of sun worshippers, primarily because it's sheltered from the wind; it's also bordered by a charming promenade. At the west end of town is the bustling 867-foot-long Capitola Pier—a great place to hang out, admire the view of the town, and, on weekends, listen to live music.

INN AT DEPOT HILL

PO Box 1950, Capitola-by-the-Sea, CA 95010 831-462-3376
Suzie Lankes & Dan Floyd, Innkeepers 800-572-2632
German and Spanish spoken FAX 831-462-3697
EMAIL lodging@innatdepothill.com WEBSITE www.innatdepothill.com

LOCATION	One-and-a-half hours south of San Francisco and four miles south of Santa Cruz, the inn is on a hill overlooking the village of Capitola-by-the-Sea, just one mile west of Highway 1.
OPEN	All year
DESCRIPTION	A 1901 restored two-story railroad depot with rooms named and decorated to resemble grand destinations of the world, such as Paris, Portofino, Côte d'Azur.
NO. OF ROOMS	Twelve rooms with private bathrooms. Suzie recommends Valencia.

RATES	Year-round rates are $190-250 for a double, and $210-275 for a suite. There is a two-night minimum stay on weekends.
CREDIT CARDS	American Express, Diners Club, MasterCard, Visa
BREAKFAST	Full breakfast is served in the dining room or guestrooms, or on the patio, and includes a variety of entrées, fruit, croissants, cinnamon rolls, raspberry granola, and beverages.
AMENITIES	Fireplaces, private garden patios with hot tubs, TV/VCR, stereos, phones with fax and data ports, robes, flowers, in-room coffee, afternoon wine and hors d'oeuvres, evening dessert, port and sherry, conference room, one room is handicapped accessible.
RESTRICTIONS	No smoking inside, no pets
REVIEWED	*The Best Places to Kiss in Northern California; Karen Brown's California Country Inns & Itineraries; American Historic Inns; America's Favorite Inns, B&Bs, & Small Hotels; Bed and Breakfast in California; Best Places to Stay in California; Complete Guide to American Bed & Breakfast; Country Inns and Backroads; Frommer's; Elegant Small Hotels; Northern California Guide for Fun, Excitement, and Romance; The Complete Guide to Bed & Breakfasts, Inns, and Guesthouses; Northern California Best Places; Recommended Country Inns—West Coast; Weekends for Two in Northern California: 50 Romantic Getaways*
MEMBER	Professional Association of Innkeepers International, International Innkeepers Association, California Association of Bed & Breakfast Inns, California Historic Country Inns, California Lodging Industry Association, California Hotel and Motel Association
RATED	Mobil 4 Stars
KUDOS/COMMENTS	"A wonderful getaway, close to beach and dining; the rooms are done to perfection." "My second favorite inn in California."

Monarch Cove Inn

620 El Salto Drive, Capitola-by-the-Sea, CA 95010   408-464-1295
WEBSITE *www.pointinfopoint.com/monarch*

Cassel

Clearwater House

21568 Cassel Road, Cassel, CA 96016   530-335-5500

Catheys Valley

Chibchas

2747 State Highway 140, Catheys Valley, CA 95306   209-966-2940

Cazadero

Bring an umbrella. It rains a lot here, about 80–100 inches a year, but it's greener than anywhere else, too. The Kruse Rhododendron State Reserve is a beauty, about nine miles west of this tiny town. Get gas and directions before going, and do the reserve before the vineyards and wine tasting. Cazadero is about 23 miles north of Bodega Bay via Highway 1.

Cazanoma Lodge

1000 Kidd Creek Road, Cazadero, CA 95421   707-632-5255
Randall Neuman, Innkeeper   888-699-8499
    FAX 707-632-5256

LOCATION	Three miles off Highway 116, turn left on Kidd Creek Road, and drive one mile to the lodge.
OPEN	March 1 through December 1
DESCRIPTION	A 1926 three-story lodge in a 147-acre redwood and fir forest.
NO. OF ROOMS	Four rooms with private bathrooms and two cabins. Randall suggests the Canyon View Room.
RATES	Year-round rates are $70-110 for a single or double, $95-110 for a suite, and $125-135 for a cabin. There is two-night minimum stay during weekends and cancellation requires four days' notice.
CREDIT CARDS	American Express, MasterCard, Visa
BREAKFAST	Continental plus is served in the guestrooms and includes fresh-baked breads, fruit platter, juice, cereal, milk, coffee, and hot chocolate. Dinner and Sunday brunch are also available.
AMENITIES	Brie, crackers, fruit, and choice of white wine or champagne; fruit basket; firewood for fireplaces; fine food and wine list in restaurant; large deck overlooking waterfall, trout pond, creeks, and redwoods; full-service cocktail lounge.
RESTRICTIONS	No pets in rooms, pets OK in cabins. The resident critters are dogs, cats, and raccoons.

House of a Thousand Flowers

PO Box 369, Monte Rio, CA 95462   707-632-5571

Chester

In the shadow of Lassen Peak, this little logging town has limited southern access to Lassen Volcanic National Park (a geologic wonderland) via the Chester–Warner Valley Road. It's also on the north shore of Lake Almanor, a good reason in itself to be here. About 32 miles west of Susanville via Highway 35.

The Bidwell House

1 Main Street, Chester, CA 96020   530-258-3338
Kim & Ian James, Resident Managers   FAX 530-258-3338

LOCATION	Located on Highway 36 at the east end of Chester, 0.5 mile from the city center.
OPEN	All year
DESCRIPTION	A 1902 two-story farmhouse furnished with antiques, located on the southeast slope of Mount Lassen.
NO. OF ROOMS	Twelve rooms with private bathrooms and two rooms share one bathroom. Try Robin's Roost or Meadow View.
RATES	May through October, rates are $109-163.50 for a single or double with a private bathroom and $81.75 for a single or double with a shared bathroom. November through April, rates are $93-127 for a single or double with a private bathroom and $65.40 for a single or double with a shared bathroom. All rates include tax. There is a two-night minimum stay on weekends and cancellation requires four days' notice.
CREDIT CARDS	MasterCard, Visa
BREAKFAST	Full breakfast is served in the dining room and includes gourmet omelets, fresh seasonal fruits, ham, bacon, or chicken cherry sausages, muffins or breads. Dinner is available on Thursday, Friday, and Saturday, and special meals are available for weddings, dinner parties, or retreats.
AMENITIES	Wheelchair accessible, flower gardens, herb and vegetable gardens, organic produce grown on site used in dishes, meeting room with a view of Lake Almanor, Jacuzzi tubs in seven rooms, wood-burning stoves in three rooms, great food, cookies, cooking and gardening tips, games, coffee, and tea.

The Bidwell House, Chester

RESTRICTIONS	No smoking, no pets. Scout, the inn's Rhodesian Ridgeback, lives in a converted barn with the managers.
REVIEWED	*Northern California Best Places*
MEMBER	Professional Association of Innkeepers International
RATED	AAA 2 Diamonds

CINNAMON TEAL BED & BREAKFAST

227 Feather River Drive, Chester, CA 96020   530-258-3993

CHICO

The town's founders, John and Annie Bidwell, left a legacy of well-laid-out, tree-shaded streets, parks, and a college that is now a California State University campus. When the warm weather rolls in, plan a picnic or a stroll among the trees in the 2,400 acres of pretty Bidwell Park. To find out what's currently going on around town, settle in at Caffe Paulo with a pastry and espresso and thumb through the *Chico News and Review*, the city's fine alternative-press newspaper.

THE ESPLANADE BED & BREAKFAST

620 The Esplanade, Chico, CA 95926   530-345-8084
Lois I. Kloss, Innkeeper
WEBSITE now2000.com/esplanade

LOCATION	One block from downtown Chico, across the street from the Bidwell Mansion and three blocks from CSU–Chico.

OPEN	All year
DESCRIPTION	A 1915 two-story Craftsman home with comfortable turn-of-the-century furnishings.
NO. OF ROOMS	Five rooms with private bathrooms.
RATES	Year-round rates for a single or double are $65-85. There is no minimum stay; ask about a cancellation policy.
CREDIT CARDS	MasterCard, Visa
BREAKFAST	Full breakfast is served buffet style in the dining room or guestrooms, or on the patio or porch, and includes fresh orange juice, fresh fruit, eggs, meat, fresh-baked muffins, and beverages.
AMENITIES	Wine and hors d'oeuvres, robes, Jacuzzi, bubble bath, great location, friendly atmosphere.
RESTRICTIONS	No smoking indoors, pets welcome with a refundable $20 deposit.
MEMBER	California Association of Bed & Breakfast Inns

JOHNSON'S COUNTRY INN

3935 Morehead Avenue, Chico, CA 95928   530-345-7829
Joan & David Johnson, Resident Owners   FAX 530-345-7829 (call first)
EMAIL j.c.inn@pobox.com   WEBSITE www.pobox.com/~j.c.inn

LOCATION	Turn west at the intersection of Highway 32 and West 5th Street (becomes Chico River Road) and travel one mile to Morehead Avenue. From the intersection of Chico River Road and Morehead Avenue, proceed 0.5 mile to the inn.
OPEN	All year
DESCRIPTION	A 1992 two-story Victorian farmhouse with a veranda, reading and conversation nooks, and antique furnishings.
NO. OF ROOMS	Four rooms with private bathrooms. Joan likes the Harrison Room.
RATES	Year-round weekend rates are $80-125 for a single or double; weekday rates are $72-105. There is no minimum stay and cancellation requires seven days' notice.
CREDIT CARDS	American Express, MasterCard, Visa
BREAKFAST	Full breakfast is served in the dining room and includes fresh-squeezed orange juice, vegetable-cheese frittata, zucchini waffles, apple-almond coffeecake, locally made apple sausage, inn-grown fruits, and beverages.

Johnson's Country Inn, Chico

AMENITIES	Fresh flowers; robes; telephones; wine; hors d'oeuvres; one room with a fireplace and Jacuzzi; coffee, juice, or tea delivered to the room before breakfast; one room is handicapped accessible; meeting facilities; parlor with fireplace; game room; horseshoes; croquet; badminton; fully air-conditioned.
RESTRICTIONS	No smoking, no pets, children over 10 are welcome. Zackary Taylor is the resident dog and Puss, the resident cat.
REVIEWED	*Northern California Best Places, Fodor's California Best Bed & Breakfasts*
MEMBER	California Association of Bed & Breakfast Inns
RATED	AAA 3 Diamonds, Northern California Best Places 4 Stars

L'ABRI BED & BREAKFAST

14350 Highway 99, Chico, CA 95973　　　530-893-0824
Jeff & Sharon Bisaga, Innkeepers　　　800-489-3319
Spanish spoken　　　FAX 530-895-0735
WEBSITE now2000.com/l'abri

LOCATION	Located seven minutes north of the downtown Chico exit on Highway 99. The driveway is exactly 0.5 mile north of Kegfer Road on the east side of Highway 99.
OPEN	All year
DESCRIPTION	A 1972/1995 one-story ranch-style country inn with country furnishings.
NO. OF ROOMS	Three rooms with private bathrooms. Teddi's Room has the best view.

RATES	Year-round midweek rates are $65-75 for a single or double; weekend rates are $15 more. There is no minimum stay and cancellation requires five days' notice for a full refund.
CREDIT CARDS	MasterCard, Visa
BREAKFAST	Full breakfast is served in the dining room or guestrooms and includes an egg dish, muffins or scones, fresh fruit, and juice. Weekday breakfast does not include an egg dish.
AMENITIES	Fresh flowers in rooms, afternoon goodies and cider, robes, double-seated showers, morning paper and coffee brought to room, great views, friendly pets (in common areas only).
RESTRICTIONS	No smoking indoors, no pets. Several pets call the inn home: Bonita the dog, cats Daisy and Halloween, and sheep Split Pea, Sweet Pea, and Isaiah. The sheep can be hand-fed, and there is also an aviary with doves, finches, chickens, and a rooster.

MUSIC EXPRESS INN

1091 El Monte Avenue, Chico, CA 95928   530-891-9833
Irene Cobeen, Innkeeper   FAX 530-893-8521
EMAIL icobeen@aol.com   WEBSITE www.now2000.com/musicexpress

LOCATION	Three blocks east of the Highway 99 and Highway 32 interchange, on the northwest corner of Highway 32 and El Monte Avenue.
OPEN	All year
DESCRIPTION	A 1977 one- and two-story country inn decorated with elegant country furnishings and family antiques, located on three acres.
NO. OF ROOMS	Nine rooms with private bathrooms. Irene recommends Scott's Room or, for handicapped guests, the Fall Room.
RATES	Year-round rates are $55-85 for a single or double. There is a minimum stay on Race Weekend in September and graduation weekend in May, and cancellation requires 48 hours' notice.
CREDIT CARDS	American Express, Discover, MasterCard, Visa
BREAKFAST	Full breakfast, served in the dining room, includes fresh fruit, juice, a hot entrée, bread or rolls, coffee, and tea.
AMENITIES	Handicapped accessible, refrigerators, microwaves, private phone lines, TV, Jacuzzi tubs, meeting rooms, wedding gardens, fax, copier, air conditioning, king-size beds, rooms with two beds.
RESTRICTIONS	Smoking in designated areas only. The resident tail-free manx is Purrfect and the cocker spaniel is Tascha.
REVIEWED	America's Favorite Inns, B&Bs, and Small Hotels; B&B Encyclopedia; The Complete Guide to Bed & Breakfasts, Inns, and Guesthouses

Music Express Inn, Chico

MEMBER   Professional Association of Innkeepers International
RATED   AAA 3 Diamonds

CLIO

Clio is a tiny hamlet in the eastern Sierra on Highway 89, just south of the intersection with I-70, halfway between Quincy and Truckee. Continuing northwest will get you into Lassen Volcanic National Park, or head south to Lake Tahoe.

WHITE SULPHUR SPRINGS RANCH BED & BREAKFAST

2200 Highway 89, Clio, CA 96106   530-836-2387
Karen & Don Miller, Owners   800-854-1797
WEBSITE www.whtssbb@psln.com   FAX 530-836-4457

LOCATION	Five miles south of Graeagle on Highway 89.
OPEN	All year
DESCRIPTION	Originally a stage coach stop, this 1852 two-story modified Greek revival inn is furnished with antiques and country furnishings, located on 42 acres.
NO. OF ROOMS	Two cottages with private bathrooms and five rooms share two bathrooms. Try the Fern Room.

RATES	Year-round rates are $100-140 for a single or double or a cottage with a private bathroom and $80-90 for a single or double with a shared bathroom. A minimum stay is required during weekends in July and August and over holidays. A 14-day cancellation notice is required.
CREDIT CARDS	Discover, MasterCard, Visa
BREAKFAST	Full breakfast, served in the dining room or delivered to cottages, includes a hot entrée such as sausage and spinach frittata or stuffed French toast, homemade breads, home-style spuds, fruit, and beverages.
AMENITIES	Robes, Olympic-size natural warm-springs pool, piano, pump organ, evening treats in rooms.
RESTRICTIONS	No smoking, no pets. Prefer younger children in the cottages.
MEMBER	Professional Association of Innkeepers International

CLOVERDALE

The clover around here has long since been replaced by grapes. This is a charming town with lots going on: the Fiddle Contest in January, the Citrus Fair in February, the Russian River Wine Fest in May, and the Annual Grape Festival in September. In winter, whitewater rafting on the Russian River is spectacular. Cloverdale is about 87 miles north of San Francisco and 17 miles north of Healdsburg.

ABRAMS HOUSE INN

314 North Main Street, Cloverdale, CA 95425   707-894-2412
Betsy Fitz-Gerald, Patti & Ray Roberts, Resident Owners   800-764-4466
FAX 707-894-2412

LOCATION	Exit Highway 101 at Citrus Fair Drive. Turn right on Cloverdale Boulevard, and go five blocks to Third Street; turn right, then left on Main Street. The inn is three houses down on the right.
OPEN	All year
DESCRIPTION	An 1872 two-story Victorian inn furnished with antiques.
NO. OF ROOMS	Two rooms have private bathrooms, and two rooms share a bathroom.
RATES	Call for current rates and the cancellation policy.
CREDIT CARDS	American Express, MasterCard, Visa
BREAKFAST	Full breakfast is served in the dining room.

AMENITIES	Afternoon tea and lemonade, evening dessert, flowers, robes, hair dryers in rooms, wine available. Prearranged wine tasting and food sampling for small groups.
RESTRICTIONS	Smoking in designated areas, no pets
REVIEWED	*Best Places in Northern California*
MEMBER	Professional Association of Innkeepers International, California Association of Bed & Breakfast Inns, California Lodging Industry Association, California Hotel & Motel Association

VINTAGE TOWERS BED & BREAKFAST

302 North Main Street, Cloverdale, CA 95425   707-894-4535
www.vintagetowers.com

YE OLDE SHELFORD HOUSE

29955 River Road, Cloverdale, CA 95425   707-894-5956
Ina & Al Sauder, Resident Owners   800-833-6479
WEBSITE *www.shelford.com*

LOCATION	From Highway 101 north to Cloverdale, take the Citrus Fair Drive exit. Go right to Asti Road, left to First Street, right on First Street, and go one mile to the inn.
OPEN	All year
DESCRIPTION	An 1885 two-story country Victorian and carriage house furnished with family antiques.
NO. OF ROOMS	Six rooms with private bathrooms.
RATES	Please call or visit the website for current rates and cancellation information.
CREDIT CARDS	American Express, MasterCard, Visa
BREAKFAST	Full breakfast is served in the dining room.
AMENITIES	Flowers, homemade quilts, wraparound Victorian porch with swing, cookies, beverages, hot tub on sun deck, gazebo, pool, bikes, recreation room, piano, Ping-Pong, exercise equipment, antique car wine tour with picnic lunch available.
RESTRICTIONS	No smoking indoors, children OK with prior arrangement.
REVIEWED	*Karen Brown's California Country Inns & Itineraries; Country Inns and Back Roads: California*
MEMBER	Wine Country Inns of Sonoma County

Coloma

As every California schoolchild knows, the Gold Rush began here when carpenter James Marshall found traces of the precious metal at John Sutter's sawmill on January 24, 1848. A full-scale working replica of the famous sawmill and other gold-related exhibits are displayed at Marshall Gold Discovery State Historic Park, a 280-acre expanse of shaded lawns and picnic tables that extends through three-quarters of the town; on Highway 49. Stop at the park's small Gold Discovery Museum for a look at Native American artifacts and James Marshall memorabilia, and pick up the self-guided tour pamphlet outlining the park's highlights.

The Coloma Country Inn

345 High Street, Coloma, CA 95613   530-622-6919
Alan & Cindi Ehrgott, Innkeepers   FAX 530-622-1795
Spanish spoken
WEBSITE *www.colomacountryinn.com*

LOCATION	Sixty miles east of Sacramento.
OPEN	All year
DESCRIPTION	An 1852 two-story New England farmhouse furnished with American country decor, on five acres with a large pond, rose gardens, and an orchard.
NO. OF ROOMS	Four rooms with private bathrooms, three rooms share two bathrooms. The Lavender Room is Cindi's favorite.
RATES	Year-round rates are $100-140 for a single or double with a private bathroom, $90 for a shared bathroom, and $130-180 for a suite. There is a minimum stay on holidays and cancellation requires two weeks' notice.
CREDIT CARDS	No
BREAKFAST	Full breakfast is served in the dining room or guest rooms, or outside by the pond, and includes fresh-baked goods, fruit dish, egg entrée, orange juice, and fresh-ground coffee. Catered meals are available.
AMENITIES	Fresh flowers, canoeing on the pond, heritage rose garden, gazebo, tree swing, gold panning, hiking, air conditioning, afternoon cookies and tea, hot air ballooning, whitewater rafting one block from river, inn is inside an historic 300-acre state park.
RESTRICTIONS	No smoking, no pets. Children are welcome (but please call ahead).
REVIEWED	*Karen Brown's California Country Inns & Itineraries, Best Places to Stay in California, The Best Places to Kiss in Northern California, The Official Guide to American Historic Inns*

The Coloma Country Inn, Coloma

MEMBER California Association of Bed & Breakfast Inns, Historic Country Inns of El Dorado

KUDOS/COMMENTS "Excellent in all respects." (1999)

COLUMBIA

Some mighty fortunate 49ers unearthed a staggering $87 million in gold in this former boisterous mining town, once the state's second largest city. But when the gold no longer panned out in the late 1850s, Columbia's population of 15,000 nearly vanished. In 1945, the entire town was turned into Columbia State Historic Park. This is the Mother Lode's best-preserved park, filled with historic facades and mining artifacts. Follow the free, short, self-guided park tour, and don't miss the Wells Fargo Express Office, a former stagecoach center, and the restored Columbia Schoolhouse. Big-time Gold Rush buffs who want more area history should pick up the inexpensive walking-tour booklet at the visitors center or sign up for a guided mine tour. For a more leisurely view of the park, hop aboard one of the horse-drawn stagecoaches.

BLUE NILE INN

11250 Pacific Street, Columbia, CA 95310   209-532-8041
EMAIL *Innkeeper@Blue-Nile-Inn.com*   WEBSITE *www.Blue-Nile-Inn.com*

COLUMBIA CITY HOTEL

22768 Main Street, Columbia, CA 95310 209-532-1479
Tom Bender, Innkeeper 800-532-1479
EMAIL info@cityhotel.com FAX 209-532-7027

LOCATION	Three miles north of Sonora off Highway 49.
OPEN	All year
DESCRIPTION	An 1856 two-story Victorian inn with period Victorian decor. Listed on the National and State Historic Registers.
NO. OF ROOMS	Ten rooms with two shared bathrooms. Try the Balcony Rooms.
RATES	Year-round rates are $80-105 for a single or double. There is no minimum stay and cancellation requires 72 hours' notice.
CREDIT CARDS	American Express, Discover, MasterCard, Visa
BREAKFAST	Continental plus is served in the dining room and includes freshly baked breads, muffins, granola, yogurt, quiche, orange juice, and house-blend coffee. Dinner is also available.
AMENITIES	Each room has a basket to take to the shower with a robe, slippers, towels, soap, and shampoo; sherry is served in the parlor each evening; cuisine that combines the fundamentals of French cooking with contemporary flavors; an exceptional wine list.
RESTRICTIONS	No smoking, no pets, children are welcome.
RATED	AAA 3 Diamonds, Mobil 2 Stars

FALLON HOTEL

11175 Washington Street, Columbia, CA 95310 209-532-1470
Tom Bender, Innkeeper 800-532-1479
EMAIL info@cityhotel.com FAX 209-532-7027
WEBSITE www.cityhotel.com

LOCATION	Three miles north of Sonora off Highway 49.
OPEN	All year
DESCRIPTION	An authentically restored 1857 two-story Victorian inn listed on the National and State Historic Registers. Many of the antiques and furnishings are original to the hotel.
NO. OF ROOMS	One room with a private bathroom and 13 rooms share three bathrooms.

RATES	Year-round rates are $70-75 for a single or double with a private bathroom, $55-105 for a single or double with a shared bathroom, and $50-155 for a suite. There is no minimum stay and cancellation requires 72 hours' notice.
CREDIT CARDS	American Express, Discover, MasterCard, Visa
BREAKFAST	Continental plus is served in the ice-cream parlor and includes fresh coffee, tea, orange juice, homemade granola, quiche, freshly baked muffins, coffeecake, and rolls. Dinner is also available.
AMENITIES	All rooms have air conditioning; meeting facilities available; located in Columbia State Historic Park—guests can take advantage of all the park's concessions; a getaway weekend package offers lodging, dining, and theater for a reduced price. Room 114 is completely handicapped accessible.
RESTRICTIONS	No smoking, no pets, children are welcome.
RATED	AAA 2 Diamonds, Mobil 3 Stars

HARLAN HOUSE

22890 School House, Columbia, CA 95310   209-533-4862
Samantha O'Brien, Resident Owner
WEBSITE www.go-native.com/inns/0049.html

LOCATION	From Sonora, take Highway 49 to Parrot's Ferry Road. Turn right at Columbia Street, right at Pacific Street, and follow signs to Historic School. The B&B is across the street from the school.
OPEN	All year
DESCRIPTION	A 1900 two-story Victorian furnished with period antiques.
NO. OF ROOMS	Four rooms with private bathrooms. Samantha suggests the Wine Cellar Suite, which includes a spa.
RATES	Year-round rates are $85-90 for a double and $130 for a suite. There is no minimum stay and cancellation requires five days' notice.
CREDIT CARDS	American Express, MasterCard, Visa
BREAKFAST	Full country breakfast, served in the dining room or outside, includes hashbrowns, special eggs, fresh fruit, ham, fresh muffins, and beverages.
AMENITIES	Flowers, phones, TV/VCRs, sherry, all rooms with fireplaces.
RESTRICTIONS	No smoking, no pets, children over eight are welcome. There are five resident cats.
AWARDS	1993, Tuolumne Historical Society

CORNING

In the Sacramento Valley off I-5, between Redding and Sacramento, Corning features the Jr. Rodeo, an Olive Festival, and a Civil War re-enactment. Car and boat races and livestock shows abound.

Doc's Country Inn

256 Solano Street, Corning, CA 96021   530-824-1800

LOCATION	One mile east of I-5 on Corning's main street.
OPEN	All year
DESCRIPTION	An elegant 1915 three-story Victorian mansion with hardwood floors and light, airy theme rooms.
NO. OF ROOMS	Two rooms with private bathrooms and three rooms with two shared bathrooms. Try the Cowboy Room.
RATES	Year-round rates are $129 for a single or double with a private bathroom, $89 for a single or double with a shared bathroom, and $500 for the entire B&B. There is no minimum stay and cancellation requires seven days' notice.
CREDIT CARDS	Discover, MasterCard, Visa
BREAKFAST	Continental plus is served in the dining room. "We try to cater to our guests." Full brunch is served when a Saturday night stay is involved. Lunch and dinner are also available.
AMENITIES	Robes are available for use with shared baths; complimentary kitchenette stocked with soda, juice, fruit, and snacks.
RESTRICTIONS	No pets
KUDOS/COMMENTS	"Newly opened; six great rooms plus a full restaurant on the first floor with excellent food; pub in basement."

COULTERVILLE

The entire town is a State Historic Landmark, with original, unrestored buildings and a must-see museum. Check it out at the Mariposa County Historic Center. Coulterville is located along Highway 49 east of Merced, with direct access to Yosemite National Park.

Hotel Jeffery

PO Box 440, Coulterville, CA 95311   209-878-3471
WEBSITE www.hoteljeffrey.com

SHERLOCK HOMES BED & BREAKFAST

5006 Main Street, Coulterville, CA 95311   209-878-3915
WEBSITE www.yosemitegold.com/sherlocks/index.html

CRESCENT CITY

The northern gateway to the popular Redwood National and State Parks along Highway 101, but not a major tourist mecca. Take a side trip to the North Coast Marine Mammal Center. This nonprofit organization was established in 1989 to rescue and rehabilitate stranded or injured marine mammals. Other interesting local sites include the operational Battery Point Lighthouse, built in 1856 on a small island off the foot of A Street. Do some fishing and crabbing off the city's 800-foot-long pier. If you're not one to get your hands dirty, take a shoreline tour along Pebble Beach Drive from the west end of Sixth Street to Point St. George. You're bound to see a few seals and sea lions at the numerous pullouts.

FERNBROOK INN

4650 N Bank Road, Crescent City, CA 95531   707-458-3202

PEBBLE BEACH BED & BREAKFAST

1650 Macken Avenue, Crescent City, CA 95531   707-464-9086

CROMBERG

In the Plumas National Forest on scenic Highway 70. From here, you can explore Plumas–Eureka State Park and the Lakes Basin Recreation Area.

TWENTY MILE HOUSE

Old Cromberg Road, Cromberg CA 96103   530-836-0375
Barbara Gage, Innkeeper   FAX 530-836-2128
French and German spoken
EMAIL TwentyMH@aol.com

LOCATION	In Cromberg, one mile south of Highway 70 down Old Cromberg Road (or Cemetary Road) to the river. Cromberg is between Quincy and Portola, one hour from Reno and Truckee.
OPEN	All year
DESCRIPTION	An 1854 two-story western-style Victorian brick country inn.
NO. OF ROOMS	Three rooms with private bathrooms. Barbara recommends the Parlor Room.
RATES	Year-round rates are $125 for a single or double and $135 for the guesthouse. There is no minimum stay and cancellation requires one weeks' notice.
CREDIT CARDS	No
BREAKFAST	Full gourmet breakfast is served in the dining room and includes French roast coffee, fresh juice, breakfast meat, and an egg or pancake dish.
AMENITIES	Flowers in all rooms; afternoon tea or wine; fly fishing on a private, two-mile section of the middle fork of the Feather River; wedding location.
RESTRICTIONS	No smoking. Pets and children are welcome with previous arrangements. Dylan is the resident golden retriever; Riff, Balou, and Pumba are the resident cats.
REVIEWED	Karen Brown's California Charming Inns & Itineraries; Northern California Best Places
RATED	Northern California Best Places 3 Stars

CROWLEY LAKE

Positioned halfway between Mammoth and Bishop off a very scenic stretch of Highway 395. In the summer, don't forget your fly pole, as this is prime trout-fishing country. Winter is for snow skiing in the Sierras.

RAINBOW TARNS BED & BREAKFAST AT CROWLEY LAKE

505 Rainbow Tarns Road, Crowley Lake, CA 93546   760-935-4556
Brock & Diane Thoman, Innkeepers   888-588-6269

LOCATION	Take Highway 395 to the Rock Creek/Crowley Lake Drive exit (between Bishop and Mammoth Lakes) and go west past Tom's Place on Crowley Lake Drive for 0.75 mile to Rainbow Tarns Road. Turn right and go to the end of the road.

Rainbow Tarns Bed & Breakfast at Crowley Lake, Crowley Lake

OPEN	April through February
DESCRIPTION	A 1920s log cabin lodge with major additions in the 1970s and 1990, perched at 7,000 feet in the Sierra Mountains.
NO. OF ROOMS	Three rooms with private bathrooms. Try the Rainbow Room.
RATES	May through October, rates are $115-140 for a single or double (midweek rates for stays of two or more nights are $95-125). April and November through February, rates are $90-120 for a single or double (midweek rates for stays of two or more nights are $75-100). There is a minimum stay during weekends and cancellation requires seven days' notice with a $20 charge.
CREDIT CARDS	No
BREAKFAST	Full breakfast is served in the dining room and includes fresh fruit, sweet rolls, juice, eggs, pancakes, meats, potatoes, etc. Fresh coffee is served early. Picnic lunches are also available.
AMENITIES	Wine and hors d'oeuvres in the afternoon, champagne and snack platter upon arrival, whirlpool tubs in private baths, robes in rooms, games and puzzles in main sitting room, fishing ponds.
RESTRICTIONS	No smoking, no pets, children over 12 are welcome. Crowley is the Austrian shepherd mix. Larry, Mo, and Curly Joe are the mallard ducks.
REVIEWED	*Hot Showers, Soft Beds, and Dayhikes in the Sierra; Best Places to Stay in Northern California; Official Guide to American Historic Inns; Complete Guide to Bed & Breakfast Inns & Guesthouses*
MEMBER	Professional Association of Innkeepers International

DAVENPORT

This quiet, uncrowded seaside town is the perfect stopping place on the way to Ano Nuevo State Preserve, a breeding ground and rookery for sea lions and seals. This is also a great spot for sailing. Twelve miles north of Santa Cruz on Highway 1.

NEW DAVENPORT BED & BREAKFAST INN

1 Davenport Avenue, Davenport, CA 95017   831-425-1818
Marcia & Bruce McDougal, Resident Owners   800-870-1817
WEBSITE www.swanton.com   FAX 831-423-1160

LOCATION	Nine miles north of Santa Cruz on Highway 1.
OPEN	All year
DESCRIPTION	A 1906 cottage and 1978 Old West-style building furnished with crafts and antiques.
NO. OF ROOMS	Twelve rooms with private bathrooms.
RATES	Year-round rates are $78-140 for a double. There is two-night minimum stay during three-day holiday weekends and cancellation requires four days' notice.
CREDIT CARDS	American Express, Discover, MasterCard, Visa
BREAKFAST	Full breakfast is served in the restaurant, except on Sundays. Lunch and dinner are available at the restaurant.
AMENITIES	Phones, gift shop, bar on premises, limited handicapped access.
RESTRICTIONS	No smoking, no pets
REVIEWED	Best Places to Stay in California; America's Wonderful Little Hotels & Inns; California B&B Guide; Hidden Coast of California; The Official Guide to American Historic Bed & Breakfasts, Inns, and Guesthouses
MEMBER	Bed & Breakfast Innkeepers of Santa Cruz, California Association of Bed & Breakfast Innkeepers
AWARDS	ABBA 2 Crowns

DAVIS

The University of California at Davis is this little city's claim to fame, particularly the college's respected veterinary science and enology schools. The urban-village atmosphere of downtown Davis draws shoppers, diners, and browsers to its charming streets, and on the southeastern outskirts of town is The Palms Playhouse, an intimate, down-home spot that features nationally known blues, country, jazz, and folk acts that will save you a trip to Austin.

AGGIE INN

245 1st Street, Davis, CA 95616   530-756-0352

DAVIS BED & BREAKFAST INN

422 A Street, Davis, CA 95616   530-753-9611

UNIVERSITY INN BED & BREAKFAST

340 A Street, Davis, CA 95616   530-756-8648
Lynda & Ross Yancher, Resident Owners   800-756-8648
Spanish, French, German, and Japanese spoken   FAX 530-753-6920
EMAIL Yancher@aol.com

LOCATION	Directly adjacent to the University of California at the southeast corner of Fourth and A Streets.
OPEN	All year
DESCRIPTION	A 1925 Spanish inn with country and southwest furnishings.
NO. OF ROOMS	Four rooms with private bathrooms.
RATES	Year-round rates are $48-65 for a double and $48-75 for a suite. There is a two-night minimum stay during special events (rates are also slightly higher then). Nonrefundable prepayment is required to confirm reservations.
CREDIT CARDS	American Express, Diners Club, Discover, MasterCard, Visa
BREAKFAST	Continental plus is served and catered picnic lunches and celebratory hors d'oeuvres are available with advance notice.
AMENITIES	Phones, cable TV, refrigerator, off-street parking, microwave, complimentary tea and chocolates, flowers.
RESTRICTIONS	No smoking inside. Ask about pets.

DILLON BEACH

A wonderful spot at the mouth of lovely Tomales Bay, Dillon Beach features boating, clamming, and dunes galore. Across from Tomales Bay State Park via Highway 1.

WINDMIST COTTAGE

524 Oceana Drive, Dillon Beach, CA 94929   707-878-2465

DORRINGTON

It's probably not on the map, but it's worth a visit. Here in Calaveras County in Sierra Nevada Gold Country, the offerings are splendid: Calaveras Big Trees State Park, the first giant redwood grove ever discovered by white explorers; Mercer and Moaning Caverns; and winter sports at Cottage Springs and Bear Valley. Check the ongoing festivals and events at Bear Valley and neighboring Arnold. Dorrington is directly northeast of Stockton and Angel's Camp via very scenic Highway 4.

THE DORRINGTON HOTEL & RESTAURANT

3431 Highway 4, Dorrington, CA 95223   209-795-5800
Bonnie & Arden Saville, Resident Owners

LOCATION	Center of town on the north side of Highway 4.
OPEN	All year
DESCRIPTION	An 1852 two-story Mother Lode clapboard inn and restored stagecoach stop decorated with country furnishings. The inn is listed on the California Historic Register.
NO. OF ROOMS	One room has a private bathroom and five rooms share two bathrooms. Pick room 2.
RATES	Year-round rates are $80-85 for a single or double and the cabin is $125 per night. There is no minimum stay and cancellation requires five days' notice with a $10 cancellation fee.
CREDIT CARDS	MasterCard, Visa
BREAKFAST	Continental breakfast is served in the guestrooms and includes freshly ground coffee, homemade baked goods, and fresh fruit.
AMENITIES	Morning coffee and newspaper at guests' doors, robes, fruit and sherry in the rooms, brass beds, armoires, quilts, and the ghost of Rebecca Dorrington Gardner (the original owner).

The Dorrington Hotel & Restaurant, Dorrington

RESTRICTIONS	No smoking, no pets; the inn is not suitable for children.
REVIEWED	Northern California Best Places; The National Trust Guide to Historic Bed & Breakfast, Inns and Small Hotels; The National Directory of Haunted Places; Historic Inns of California's Gold Country Cookbook and Guide
MEMBER	California Association of Bed & Breakfast Inns

DORRINGTON INN

3450 Highway 4, Dorrington, CA 95223 209-795-2164
Bob & Dennis, Innkeepers 888-874-2164
Some Spanish spoken FAX 209-795-1543
EMAIL innkeeper@dorringtoninn.com WEBSITE www.dorringtoninn.com

LOCATION	Calaveras County, seven miles east of Arnold, two miles east of Calaveras Big Trees State Park on Highway 4.
OPEN	All year
DESCRIPTION	Three A-frame cottages and a main building with a mix of modern decor and antiques, set in the High Sierra Gold Country of Calaveras County.
NO. OF ROOMS	Eight rooms with private bathrooms. Try a cottage.
RATES	Year-round rates are $100-140 for a single or double. There is a minimum stay during ski season weekends and cancellation requires 10 days' notice, 21 days during holidays.

CREDIT CARDS	American Express, Discover, MasterCard, Visa
BREAKFAST	Continental plus is served in the dining room and includes homemade baked goods, fresh fruit, hard-boiled eggs, cheese, gourmet coffee from a local roaster, tea, and juice.
AMENITIES	Fresh flowers; Caswell Massey soaps and shampoo; down comforters; fireplace; TV/VCR and a large film library; microwave; small refrigerator; evening apéritifs.
RESTRICTIONS	No smoking, no pets. Winston is the resident golden retriever. The inn is located in the middle of the Stanislaus National Forest, so there are a wide variety of critters nearby.
MEMBER	California Association of Bed & Breakfast Inns

DORRIS

At the far north-central edge of Siskiyou County, just short of the Oregon line, Dorris lies in Mount Shasta country. From Weed, Highway 97 cuts along Klamath National Forest and continues past Dorris to Klamath Falls and Upper Klamath Lake. From town, it's easy access to Lower Klamath National Wildlife Refuge, internationally known for its diverse wildlife and habitats. Or there's Lower Klamath and Meiss Lakes. Drive northeast from Redding via I-5 and Highway 97.

HOSPITALITY INN

200 South California Street, Dorris, CA 96023   530-397-2097
Donna & Jeff Burcher, Resident Owners
A little Spanish spoken
EMAIL *dburcher@yahoo.com*

LOCATION	Fifty miles north of Weed, 22 miles south of Klamath Falls, Oregon; one block off Highway 97, at the corner of Second and California Streets.
OPEN	All year
DESCRIPTION	A two-story turn-of-the-century hospital that has been converted into an inn with French country and Victorian furnishings.
NO. OF ROOMS	Four rooms share two bathrooms.
RATES	Year-round rates are $52 for a single or double. There is no minimum stay and cancellation requires 24 hours' notice.
CREDIT CARDS	No
BREAKFAST	A wholesome country breakfast is served in the dining room.

AMENITIES	Private sitting room, full basement with antique pool table, boat parking, tandem bike, liquid refreshments, hors d'oeuvres, and dog kennel. Near Lava Beds National Monument and the gateway to Crater Lake National Park. "Duck hunters' paradise!"
RESTRICTIONS	None. The resident pets include Duke, a Lab, Molly, a minischnauzer, and Grey Kitty, who "may sleep with you."
AWARDS	Best Christmas Decorations (two years in a row), Butte Valley Chamber of Commerce

DOWNIEVILLE

SIERRA SHANGRI-LA

12 Jim Crow Canyon, Downieville, CA 95936   530-289-3455
WEBSITE *www.sierrashangrila.com*

DUNCANS MILLS

This stretch of the Russian River, once called Slavianka (Little Beauty) by Russian fur traders, is good for steelhead in winter and floating all summer. The tiny hamlet is surrounded by redwoods and wine country. Explore Armstrong Redwoods State Reserve or head down to the Sonoma State Beach. From San Francisco, go north on Highway 1 and east on Highway 116.

THE INN AT DUNCANS MILLS

25233 Steelhead Boulevard, Duncans Mills, CA 95430   707-865-1855
Christina Harrison, Resident Owner

LOCATION	Just off Highway 116 in central Duncans Mills, which is really only a wide spot in the road. Four miles east of Highway 1 on Highway 116, turn south on Moscow Road.
OPEN	All year
DESCRIPTION	A 1989 redwood country guesthouse furnished with eclectic antiques and nestled along the Russian River in a redwood forest.
NO. OF ROOMS	Four rooms with private bathrooms. A three-bedroom apartment

	or guesthouse is also available.
RATES	Please call for current rates and cancellation information.
CREDIT CARDS	American Express, MasterCard, Visa
BREAKFAST	Full breakfast is served in the community room, kitchen, or guestrooms. Other meals are available with prior arrangement.
AMENITIES	Flowers, telephones, wine, appetizers and fruit upon arrival, meeting facilities, catering, croquet, horseshoes, putting green, river access, game room, VCR and videos, handicapped accessible.
RESTRICTIONS	No smoking, no pets

THE SUPERINTENDENT'S HOUSE

24951 Highway 116, Duncans Mills, CA 95430   707-865-1572
Phil Dattola, Resident Owner

LOCATION	From the east on Highway 116, go 100 yards past the "Duncans Mills, pop. 20" sign and turn right at the windmill. Wind your way up to the red and white Victorian home. From the west on Highway 116, go 300 yards past town and turn left at the old metal windmill.
OPEN	All year
DESCRIPTION	An 1880 two-story redwood Victorian roadhouse listed on the State Historic Register. It features 12-foot ceilings, large windows, hardwood floors, and an old fashioned porch.
NO. OF ROOMS	Five rooms share two bathrooms.
RATES	Please call for current rates and cancellation information.
CREDIT CARDS	No
BREAKFAST	Full breakfast is served in the dining room or on the porch.
AMENITIES	Parlor with TV/VCR and video library.
RESTRICTIONS	No pets, no smoking

Dunsmuir

The Sacramento River runs through this unspoiled old railroad town on the National Historic Register. The scenery around here is sublime. Railroad buffs: check out Railroad Park, Archives, and Library. Railroad Days picks up steam in June. This is also the gateway into Castle Crags State Park, a haven for trekkers and serious rock climbers. The Pacific Crest Trail swings through here. Dunsmuir is just south of Mount Shasta.

Dunsmuir Inn

5423 Dunsmuir Avenue, Dunsmuir, CA 96025 530-235-4543
Jerry & Julie Iskra, Resident Owners 888-386-7684
FAX 530-235-4154

LOCATION	From I-5, take the Central Dunsmuir exit. At the stop sign, turn left onto Dunsmuir Avenue and follow for 0.5 mile to the inn.
OPEN	All year
DESCRIPTION	A 1925 two-story inn with country furnishings.
NO. OF ROOMS	Five rooms with private bathrooms. The suite is the best room.
RATES	Year-round rates are $60-70 for a single or double, the suite is $70, and the entire inn rents for $250. There is a minimum stay during holiday weekends and cancellation requires 72 hours' notice and a $10 fee.
CREDIT CARDS	American Express, Diners Club, Discover, MasterCard, Visa
BREAKFAST	Full breakfast is served in the kitchen and includes baked French toast, bacon, quiche, fresh fruit cup, coffee, tea, and juice. Lunch is also available.
AMENITIES	Air conditioning, complimentary pick-up and delivery to the local Amtrak station and airport, meeting area for small groups.
RESTRICTIONS	No smoking, no pets, all children are welcome. Misty is the resident basset, Sadie is the Queensland, and the Lab is called Penny. The potbellied pig is called Rosie.
MEMBER	California Association of Bed & Breakfast Inns, California Lodging Industry Association
KUDOS/COMMENTS	"Roomy, friendly atmosphere; nice sandwich shop and ice cream parlor."

Riverwalk Inn B&B

4300 Stagecoach Road, Dunsmuir, CA 96025 530-235-4300
WEBSITE *www.dunsmuir.com*

Elk

This tiny hamlet perched on the coastal bluffs was once a lumber port. Central to the town is Greenwood Creek State Beach and Park, a great spot for picnics and ocean fishing. Visit the historic exhibits at the park's visitor center. Elk is halfway between Point Arena and Mendocino, with handy access to both.

Elk Cove Inn

6300 South Highway One, Elk, CA 95432 707-877-3321
Elaine Bryant, Innkeeper 800-275-2967
Spanish and German spoken FAX 707-877-1808
EMAIL *elkcove@mcn.org* WEBSITE *www.elkcoveinn.com*

LOCATION	From Cloverdale, turn west on Highway 128. Elk is located on Highway 1, six miles south of the intersection of Highway 128 and Highway 1.
OPEN	All year
DESCRIPTION	An 1873 French Victorian oceanfront inn, a former lumber baron's guest house, is nestled in peaceful seclusion atop a bluff with access to the beach. Listed on the National Historic Register.
NO. OF ROOMS	Fourteen rooms with private bathrooms.
RATES	High season and weekend rates are $108-278 for a single or double and $248-278 for the suites. Regular season and weekday rates are $98-248 for a single or double and $218-278 for a suite. There is a two-night minimum stay, three nights during Saturdays; cancellation requires 14 days' notice, 30 days during holidays, with a $10 per night fee.
CREDIT CARDS	American Express, MasterCard, Visa
BREAKFAST	Full gourmet buffet is served in the oceanfront dining room and includes juice, coffee, and hot dishes such as Belgian waffles with fresh fruit, pasta frittata, corn pudding, a meat of the day, baked fruits, hot croissants, biscuits, scones, and cinnamon rolls. "We always offer hot oatmeal and cold cereals plus a huge assortment of fruits, yogurt, and our famous morning pie. On winter weekday mornings we offer a full breakfast served in the room." Dinners are served on Tuesday and Wednesday nights only.

AMENITIES	All rooms have coffeemakers with fresh-ground regular and decaf coffee, teas, and hot chocolate; fresh flowers from the organic gardens; port and chocolates; robes; fluffy down pillows and comforters; comfortable rocking chairs; gift basket with a bottle of wine, fresh fruit, and our very own giant chocolate chip cookies on arrival; full bar with a special martini menu plus local wines and beer; common sitting room with a rooftop sun deck, microwave, refrigerator, VCR, movies, and lots of games and books; hammock and glider rockers; gazebo; private steps to a driftwood-strewn beach.
RESTRICTIONS	No smoking, no pets, children over 12 are welcome. Asta is the wire-haired fox terrier, Boomer is the black German shepherd, and Tommy is the large, white and orange cat. "Asta runs a complimentary beach tour guide service. She is somewhat famous, having been a model in Martha Stewart's magazine a few times."
REVIEWED	*The Best Places to Kiss in Northern California, Recommended Country Inns—West Coast*
MEMBER	California Association of Bed & Breakfast Inns, Professional Association of Innkeepers International, Mendocino Coast Inn Association, California Lodging Industry Association, California Hotel & Motel Association
RATED	AAA 3 Diamonds, Mobil 3 Stars

GREENWOOD PIER INN

5928 South Highway 1, Elk, CA 95432 707-877-9997
Kendrick Petty, Resident Owner FAX 707-877-3439
EMAIL gwpier@mcn.org WEBSITE www.elkcoast.com/greenwoodpier

LOCATION	Three-and-a-half miles north of San Francisco between Point Arena and Mendocino.
OPEN	All year
DESCRIPTION	Six two-story Craftsman and Victorian buildings with eclectic decor, located on a bluff above the Pacific Ocean with magnificent views of ocean rock formations.
NO. OF ROOMS	Twelve rooms with private bathrooms.
RATES	Year-round weekend rates and weekday rates during the summer and fall are $120-235 for a single or double and $165-235 for a suite. Weekday rates from November through May are $120-235 for a single or double and $150-220 for a suite. There is a two-night minimum stay during weekends, three nights during holidays in the suites. Cancellation requires one week's notice.
CREDIT CARDS	American Express, MasterCard, Visa

BREAKFAST	Continental breakfast is served in the guestrooms and includes scones, rolls, and sticky buns, plus fresh fruit salad and coffee. Lunch, dinner, and meals for special events are also available.
AMENITIES	Lavish gardens, flowers, robes, hot tub on ocean bluff, fireplaces or stoves, coffee-makers, refrigerator, CD players or tape decks.
RESTRICTIONS	No smoking, pets allowed in some rooms. There are two resident cats.
REVIEWED	*Weekends for Two in Northern California: 50 Romantic Getaways; The Best Places to Kiss in Northern California; Country Inns of America: California*
MEMBER	California Lodging Industry Association
KUDOS/COMMENTS	"Interesting and eclectic rooms with great gardens; on bluffs overlooking the Pacific Ocean." (1999)

GRIFFIN HOUSE AT GREENWOOD COVE

5910 South Highway 1, Elk, CA 95432   707-877-3422
Leslie Griffin Lawson, Resident Owner
Spanish spoken
WEBSITE www.griffinn.com

LOCATION	Center of "downtown" Elk (pop. 250) on the ocean side of Highway 1; watch for signs.
OPEN	All year
DESCRIPTION	A carriage house, rural Victorian cottages, and a restaurant.
NO. OF ROOMS	Seven rooms with private bathrooms. There is also a carriage house.
RATES	November through April, weekend rates are $90-100 for the garden cottages and $165 for the oceanfront cottages. Weekday prices are reduced 25 percent. May through October, the garden cottages are $95-115 and the oceanfront cottages are $165. The carriage house is $225 year-round. A minimum stay is required on weekends and cancellations require 72 hours' notice (no fee if room is rebooked).
CREDIT CARDS	MasterCard, Visa
BREAKFAST	Full hot breakfast is served in the guestrooms and includes cheese and egg soufflés, waffles, pancakes; turkey, ham, and sausages; fruits; and juices. Dinner is available seven nights a week in Bridget Dolan's Irish Pub.
AMENITIES	All cottages have wood-burning stoves, split of local wine on arrival, and fresh flowers. Several cottages include clawfoot tubs, separate parlors, and oceanfront private decks.

RESTRICTIONS	No smoking inside, no pets. Assorted cats adorn the grounds: Lucky, Rosie, and "G Pat the Cat."
REVIEWED	Karen Brown's California Country Inns & Itineraries, Northern California Best Places, Bed & Breakfast Northern California
MEMBER	Professional Association of Innkeepers International, California Lodging Industry Association

HARBOR HOUSE

5600 South Highway 1, Elk, CA 95432   707-877-3203
WEBSITE www.theharborhouseinn.com

SANDPIPER HOUSE INN

5520 South Highway 1, Elk, CA 95432   707-877-3587

LOCATION	From Highway 101, go north to Cloverdale. Take the Highway 128 exit west to Highway 1. The Sandpiper is six miles south of the junction of Highways 128 and 1.
OPEN	All year
DESCRIPTION	A 1916 two-story California Craftsman with traditional furnishings and European antiques, perennial gardens, and a private beach.
NO. OF ROOMS	Five rooms with private bathrooms.
RATES	Please call for current rates and cancellation information.
CREDIT CARDS	American Express, MasterCard, Visa
BREAKFAST	Full breakfast is served in the dining room and includes fresh fruit, a main course, meats, baked goods, and beverages.
AMENITIES	Afternoon tea and fresh-baked pastries, sherry, fresh flowers, massage available, private beach access from the garden.
RESTRICTIONS	Children over 10 are welcome.
REVIEWED	America's Wonderful Little Hotels & Inns, Karen Brown's California Country Inns & Itineraries
MEMBER	Professional Association of Innkeepers International, California Association of Bed & Breakfast Inns

EMIGRANT GAP

EMIGRANT GAP INN

42380 Emigrant Gap Road, Emigrant Gap, CA 95715   530-389-7021

ETNA

This small, remote community lies on the doorstep of Marble Mountain Wilderness, about 25 miles southwest of Yreka. In September, help the locals celebrate Balloon Faire. In May, the rodeo kicks in.

BRADLEYS ALDERBROOK MANOR

836 Sawyers Bar Road, Etna, CA 96027   530-467-3917
Joyce C. Bradley, Resident Owner   FAX 530-467-3936
German, Russian, and some French spoken
EMAIL joybrad@sisqtel.net
WEBSITE www.sisqtel.net/~joybrad

LOCATION	Take I-5 north to the first Yreka exit (Ft. Jones/Etna). Go under I-5 to the light, turn left on Highway 3, and go 23 miles. When Highway 3 turns left at the town entrance, keep going straight to Etna (Collier Way). Once in Etna, go three blocks to the dead end on Main Street. Turn right and go three blocks.
OPEN	All year
DESCRIPTION	An 1877 two-story Victorian country home with international ambiance, mountain views, and gardens.
NO. OF ROOMS	One room with a private bathroom and four rooms share two bathrooms.
RATES	Year-round rates are $60 for a single or double with a private bathroom and $45 for a single or double with a shared bathroom. There is no minimum stay.
CREDIT CARDS	No
BREAKFAST	Continental plus is served in the dining room and includes juice, fruit, beverage, yogurt, cereal, ham, cheese, hard-boiled eggs, homemade breads and jams, and various toaster treats.
AMENITIES	Handicapped accessible, horse corral, dog kennel, robes, cocktails on arrival, mountain views from all rooms, game room, two landscaped acres with a pond and treehouse, folk art collection.

Bradleys Alderbrook Manor, Etna

RESTRICTIONS   No smoking or food in rooms. Lady Velvet is the resident cat and official greeter; she is constantly amazed that the Arucana chickens lay green eggs.

REVIEWED   *Northern California Best Places*

EUREKA

Named after the popular gold-mining expression "Eureka!" (Greek for "I have found it"), this town is the largest city on the North Coast (population 30,000). The heart of Eureka is Old Town, a 13-block stretch of shops, restaurants, and hotels, most of which are housed in painstakingly preserved Victorian structures. Stroll through the Clarke Memorial Museum, which has one of the top Native American displays in the state, showcasing more than 1,200 examples of Hupa, Yurok, and Karok basketry, dance regalia, and stonework. Take a bay cruise on skipper Leroy Zerlang's *Madaket*, the oldest passenger vessel on the Pacific Coast. The 75-minute narrated tour is a surprisingly interesting and amusing perspective on the history of Humboldt Bay.

ABIGAIL'S ELEGANT VICTORIAN MANSION BED & BREAKFAST

1406 C Street, Eureka, CA 95501   707-444-3144
Doug & Lily Vieyra, Resident Owners   FAX 707-442-5594
French, Dutch, and German spoken
WEBSITE *www.eureka-california.com*

Abigail's Elegant Victorian Mansion Bed & Breakfast, Eureka

LOCATION	At the corner of 14th and C Streets in Eureka. From Highway 101 north, turn right at the Denny's restaurant. From Highway 101 south, turn left at C Street and continue south 10 blocks to 14th Street.
OPEN	All year
DESCRIPTION	An 1888 two-story Victorian inn constructed entirely of 1,000-year-old California redwood with gingerbread architecture and furnished with opulent Victorian pieces. Listed on the State and National Historic Registers.
NO. OF ROOMS	Two rooms have private bathrooms, and two rooms have shared bathrooms. Doug recommends the Governor's Suite.
RATES	Year-round rates are $135-185 for a single or double with a private bathroom and $85-155 for a single or double with a shared bathroom. There is no minimum stay and cancellation requires 10 days' notice and a $25 charge.
CREDIT CARDS	MasterCard, Visa
BREAKFAST	Elaborate multicourse gourmet breakfast, served in the dining room, includes French and Belgian specialties. Special dietary needs are accommodated upon request.
AMENITIES	Complimentary bay cruise and horseless carriage ride, sauna, croquet, Victorian flower gardens, movies, ice-cream sodas, bicycles, tennis courts, valet parking.
RESTRICTIONS	No smoking, no pets, children over 13 are welcome. Talented resident birds include Victoria the Ostrich, Victoria the Peacock, and Albert the Parrot. The parrot talks and the peacock dances.
REVIEWED	*Frommer's California, Fodor's America's Best Bed & Breakfasts, America's Wonderful Little Hotels & Inns, Northern California Best Places, Best Places to Stay in California*

MEMBER	Professional Association of Innkeepers International, Bed & Breakfast Innkeepers International, California Association of Bed & Breakfast Inns, Historic Inns of America, National Bed & Breakfast Association
RATED	AAA 3 Diamonds, ABBA 3 Crowns, Mobil 3 Stars, Chambres D'Hotes 4 Stars
KUDOS/COMMENTS	"Small but elegant Victorian inn; outstanding breakfasts; and warm, welcoming innkeepers." "Charming Victorian building, decor, and furnishings; hosts are delightful; lovely gardens."

CAFÉ WATERFRONT BED & BREAKFAST

102 F Street, Eureka, CA 95501   707-476-1818
Diane Smith, Resident Owner

LOCATION	Overlooks Humboldt Bay and Eureka's historic Old Town District.
OPEN	All year
DESCRIPTION	An 1892 Queen Anne Victorian restored to period with high ceilings and wallpaper frieze work. Listed on the National and State Historic Registers.
NO. OF ROOMS	Two rooms with private bathrooms.
RATES	Please call for current rates and cancellation information.
CREDIT CARDS	MasterCard, Visa
BREAKFAST	Choose from a breakfast menu at the Café Waterfront downstairs.
AMENITIES	Fresh flowers, phones, TVs, stereo, CD player, washer, dryer, kitchen, horse and carriage pick up.
RESTRICTIONS	No smoking, no pets, children are not encouraged.
AWARDS	1994, Governer's Award for Excellence in Bed & Breakfast Design

CARTER HOUSE, CARTER COTTAGE, BELL COTTAGE, AND THE LITTLE HOTEL CARTER

301 L Street, Eureka, CA 95501   707-444-8062
Mark & Christi Carter, Resident Owners   800-404-1390
French spoken   FAX 707-444-8062

LOCATION	From Highway 101, turn left onto L Street and go two blocks to 3rd and L Street (Highway 101 is 5th Street).

OPEN	All year
DESCRIPTION	This three-building complex includes a three-story reconstruction of a Eureka Victorian hotel.
NO. OF ROOMS	All rooms have private bathrooms.
RATES	Year-round rates are $125-295. A honeymoon house is $495. There is a minimum stay on selected holidays and cancellation requires 72 hours' notice.
CREDIT CARDS	American Express, Carte Blanche, Diners Club, Discover, MasterCard, Visa
BREAKFAST	Full breakfast is served in the dining room and includes hot entrée, variety of muffins and pastry, and beverages. Dinner and special meals are available in the restaurant.
AMENITIES	Robes, phones, TV/VCR, fireplaces, spa and soaking tubs, feather beds, CD players, minibars, wine and hors d'oeuvres, turn-down service, on-site restaurant, gardens, dining room with classical guitarist on weekends. There is a 1,000-square-foot honeymoon house with private kitchen (chefs will prepare up to an eight-course dinner for up to six), private deck with fountain, two fireplaces, two-person shower, and Jacuzzi.
RESTRICTIONS	No smoking, no pets
REVIEWED	*The Best Places to Kiss in Northern California; Weekends for Two in Northern California: 50 Romantic Getaways; Fodor's*
MEMBER	California Association of Bed & Breakfast Inns
RATED	AAA 3 Diamonds, Mobil 3 Stars, Northwest Best Places 4 Stars
AWARDS	Recipient of Wine Spectator's Grand Award for the restaurant's wine list; Pamela Lanier's Best Inns of America; Uncle Ben's award for Best Inns; Grand Hotel and Inn Award by Focus magazine.

CORNELIUS DALY INN

1125 H Street, Eureka, CA 95501   707-445-3638
Sue & Gene Clinesmith, Innkeepers   800-321-9656
EMAIL *dalyinn@humboldt1.com*   FAX 707-444-3636
WEBSITE *www.humboldt1.com/~dalyinn*

LOCATION	Turn east off Highway 101 onto H Street and continue to the corner of 12th Street.
OPEN	All year except Christmas holiday
DESCRIPTION	A 1905 three-story colonial revival mansion completely furnished with antiques and surrounded by gardens.

NO. OF ROOMS	Three rooms with private bathrooms, two rooms with a shared bathroom. For the best view, try the Garden View Suite.
RATES	May through October, rates are $125 for a single or double with a private bathroom, $85-100 for a single or double with a shared bathroom, and $150 for a suite. November through April, rates are $105 for a single or double with a private bathroom, $75-90 for a single or double with a shared bathroom, and $125 for suites. There is a minimum stay on three-day weekends, and cancellation requires seven days' notice for a full refund.
CREDIT CARDS	American Express, Discover, MasterCard, Visa
BREAKFAST	Full breakfast is served in the dining room, guestrooms, or breakfast room and includes homemade coffeecake or muffins, an egg entrée, meat, fruit, and beverages. "My grandmother's sticky buns are my speciality."
AMENITIES	Robes, guest telephone, flowers, wine and hors d'oeuvres each evening, chocolate truffles with turndown service, Victorian garden with fish pond and waterfall.
RESTRICTIONS	No smoking, no pets, children are welcome.
REVIEWED	Karen Brown's California Country Inns & Itineraries
MEMBER	California Association of Bed & Breakfast Inns, Eureka Bed & Breakfast Association, Professional Association of Innkeepers International, Northern Redwoods B&B Association
RATED	AAA 3 Diamonds, Mobil 3 Stars
KUDOS/COMMENTS	"Beautiful, large, well-appointed room. Lovely baths." "One of the most outstanding cooks I've met."

DREAMWALKERS OLD TOWN BED & BREAKFAST INN

1521 Third Street, Eureka, CA 95501 707-445-3951
Leigh & Diane Benson, Resident Owners 800-331-5098
Spanish and Italian spoken FAX 707-268 0231
EMAIL otb-b@dreamwalkerusa.com
WEBSITE www.dreamwalker-usa.com/otb-b

LOCATION	At 3rd and P Streets, just east of the Old Town National Historic District.
OPEN	All year except most of January
DESCRIPTION	An 1871 two-story Greek revival/Italianate inn furnished with antiques and plush, semi-Victorian decor. The inn is on the State Historic Register.

NO. OF ROOMS	Four rooms with private bathrooms and two rooms share one bathroom. Carlottas is the best room.
RATES	Year-round rates are $80-140 for a double with a private bathroom and $70-80 for a double with a shared bathroom. The entire inn rents for $650. There is no minimum stay and cancellation requires three days' notice.
CREDIT CARDS	American Express, Carte Blanche, Diners Club, Discover, MasterCard, Visa. There is a 5 percent discount for cash or check payments.
BREAKFAST	Country gourmet breakfast from Diane's Country Kitchen is served family style in the dining room. "We publish and sell our own cookbook."
AMENITIES	Fresh flowers from the gardens; soaps, shampoo, conditioner, razors, and shaving cream, floss, earplugs; afternoon cookies, teas, cocoa; restaurant menus, maps, and brochures; teakwood hot tub; gardens; handmade robes, slippers, bath sheets; fireplaces.
RESTRICTIONS	No smoking, no pets, children over 10 are welcome. "We will consider children under 10 by prior arrangement." The cats go by Sa'a-Ha (Say-ha) and Chotahla.
REVIEWED	*The Official Guide to American Historic Inns; Recommended Country Inns—West Coast; Hidden San Francisco and Northern California; Northern California Handbook; Bed & Breakfast Guide: California; Non-Smokers Guide to Bed & Breakfasts; Best of the Pacific Coast; Bed & Breakfast California*
MEMBER	Professional Association of Innkeepers International, Eureka Bed & Breakfast Association, Northern Redwoods Bed & Breakfast Association
RATED	ABBA 3 Crowns, Mobil 2 Stars
KUDOS/COMMENTS	"Fun decor and entertaining innkeepers."

A WEAVER'S INN

1440 B Street, Eureka, CA 95501 707-443-8119
Lea L. Montgomery, Innkeeper 800-992-8119
EMAIL *weavrinn@humboldt1.com* FAX 707-443-7923
WEBSITE *www.humboldt1.com/~weaverinn*

LOCATION	If coming from the south, Highway 101 becomes Broadway. Make a right onto 14th Street, go seven blocks to B Street, and make another right. The inn is the fourth house on the right. If coming from the north, Highway 101 becomes 4th Street. Turn left onto E Street, go 10 blocks, turn right onto 14th Street, go three blocks, and take a left onto B Street. The inn is the fourth house on the right.

OPEN	All year
DESCRIPTION	A meticulously restored 1883 two-story Queen Anne inn with textured wallpaper, picture-frame moldings, wood floors, and Victorian furnishings.
NO. OF ROOMS	Three rooms with private bathrooms and two rooms with one shared bathroom. Try the Pamela Suite.
RATES	May through October, rates are $85-110 for a single or double with a private bathroom, $65-90 for a single or double with a shared bathroom, and $115-125 for a suite. November through April, rates are $75-100 for a single or double with a private bathroom, $55-80 for a single or double with a shared bathroom, and $105-115 for a suite. There is no minimum stay and cancellation requires four days' notice.
CREDIT CARDS	American Express, Diners Club, Discover, MasterCard, Visa
BREAKFAST	Four-course gourmet breakfast is served in the dining room and includes juice frappé, coffee, tea, hot chocolate; homemade coffeecakes, muffins, breads, or scones; fresh fruits; peach upside-down French toast, mushroom crepes, eggs Florentine, or egg strata; apple crisp or broiled berries and cream.
AMENITIES	Fresh flowers from the garden, robes, complimentary wine, locally made chocolate truffles at bedtime, down comforters, custom-made soaps and lotions, fireplaces, cozy parlor and elegant dining room, large yard with spacious lawn, croquet, beautiful cottage-style gardens.
RESTRICTIONS	Outdoor smoking areas. Tigra and Gracie are the resident cats. They are not allowed inside the inn.
MEMBER	California Association of Bed & Breakfast Inns, Professional Association of Innkeepers International, California Hotel & Motel Association, Northern Redwoods Bed & Breakfast Association

FELTON

FELTON CREST HANNA'S GUEST HOUSE

780 El Solyo Heights Drive, Felton, CA 95018   408-335-4011
WEBSITE www.feltoncrest.com
KUDOS/COMMENTS "Unique excellence."

FERNDALE

Even if Ferndale isn't on your itinerary, it's worth a detour off Highway 101 to stroll its colorful Main Street, browsing through the art galleries, gift shops, and cafes that are strangely reminiscent of Disneyland's "old town." Ferndale, however, is for real, and hasn't changed much since it was the agricultural center of Northern California in the late 1800s. In fact, the entire town is a National Historic Landmark because of its abundance of well-preserved Victorian storefronts, farmhouses, and homes. What really distinguishes Ferndale from the likes of Eureka and Crescent City, however, is the fact that Highway 101 doesn't pass through it—which means no cheesy motels, liquor stores, and fast-food chains. For a trip back in time, view the village's interesting memorabilia—working crank phones, logging equipment, and a blacksmith shop—at the Ferndale Museum.

GINGERBREAD MANSION INN

400 Berding Street, Ferndale, CA 95536 707-786-4000
Ken Torbert, Innkeeper 800-952-4136
EMAIL kenn@Humboldt1.com FAX 707-786-4381
WEBSITE www.gingerbread-mansion.com

LOCATION	Take the Ferndale exit off Highway 101. From the north, go to the second stop sign and turn right. From the south, go to the first stop sign and turn left. Continue over the bridge into Ferndale, approximately five miles, and turn left at the bank.
OPEN	All year
DESCRIPTION	An 1899 three-story Queen Anne Victorian inn with Victorian decor, nestled between the rugged Pacific Coast and the giant redwoods. Listed on the National and California Historic Registers.
NO. OF ROOMS	Eleven rooms with private bathrooms. Try the Empire Suite.
RATES	Year-round rates are $120-185 for a single or double, $230-265 for a suite, and $350 for the guesthouse. There is no minimum stay and cancellation requires seven days' notice with a 10 percent charge.
CREDIT CARDS	American Express, MasterCard, Visa
BREAKFAST	Full gourmet breakfast is served in the dining room or guestrooms and includes baked egg dishes, hot side dishes, and several accompanying items.
AMENITIES	English tea, English gardens, four lovely parlors, bathrobes, turndown service with chocolates, fireplaces, clawfoot tubs, grand suites.
RESTRICTIONS	No smoking, no pets, children over nine are welcome.
MEMBER	California Historic Country Inns, California Association of Bed & Breakfast Inns

RATED	AAA 4 Diamonds, ABBA 4 Crowns, Mobil 3 Stars
KUDOS/COMMENTS	"Great hosts, outstanding guest rooms." "Like stepping into another era." "Wonderful. Couldn't say enough about it."

GRANDMOTHER'S HOUSE BED & BREAKFAST

861 Howard Street, Ferndale, CA 95536   707-786-9704
Richard & Jacqueline Ramirez, Resident Owners

LOCATION	Four blocks north of downtown Ferndale. One block past the high school as you come into town on Highway 101.
OPEN	All year
DESCRIPTION	A 1901 Queen Anne Eastlake Victorian with "light" Victorian decor.
NO. OF ROOMS	One room with a private bathroom and two rooms share one bathroom.
RATES	Year-round rates are $65-75 for a single or double. Call about a cancellation policy.
CREDIT CARDS	Discover, MasterCard, Visa
BREAKFAST	Continental plus is served in the dining room.
AMENITIES	Robes, porches overlooking grazing cattle and buffalo, fireplace, self-service snacks available.
RESTRICTIONS	No smoking, no pets, children of any age are welcome. Outdoor pets include three dogs (Chewy, Huey, and Sadie) and two cats.

SHAW HOUSE BED & BREAKFAST INN

703 Main Street, Ferndale, CA 95536   707-786-9958
    FAX 707-786-9958

LOCATION	Approximately four miles off Highway 101 in greater historic downtown Ferndale.
OPEN	All year
DESCRIPTION	An 1854 two-story carpenter Gothic with French windows, six gables, and French doors and balconies, listed on the National Historic Register.
NO. OF ROOMS	Six rooms with private bathrooms.
RATES	Please call for current rates and cancellation information.
CREDIT CARDS	American Express, MasterCard, Visa

BREAKFAST	Full breakfast is served in the dining room and changes daily.
AMENITIES	Flowers, robes, slippers, cookies and coffee in the afternoon, bicycles, 1-acre of grounds with benches and gazebo.
RESTRICTIONS	No pets, children over five are welcome.
REVIEWED	Northern California Best Places
MEMBER	American Bed and Breakfast Association, California Lodging Industry Association
RATED	ABBA 3 Crowns
KUDOS/COMMENTS	"She offers first-class hospitality; warm and homey." (1999)

FISH CAMP
(YOSEMITE NATIONAL PARK)

What a spot! Fish Camp is located at the south entrance to Yosemite National Park and the Mariposa Grove of Giant Sequoias. See them all summer via the open-air tram. From Fresno, it's 54 miles north on scenic Highway 41. Bass Lake is a nice stop on the way for water recreation.

KAREN'S YOSEMITE BED & BREAKFAST

1144 Railroad Avenue, Fish Camp, CA 93623　　　209-683-4550
Karen Bergh, Resident Owner　　　　　　　　　　800-346-1443
EMAIL karenbnb@sierratel.com　　　　　　　　FAX 209-683-8127
WEBSITE www.karensyosemitebnb.com

LOCATION	One mile south of Yosemite and 0.25 mile south of the Chevron station on Highway 41.
OPEN	All year
DESCRIPTION	A 1989 two-story contemporary country inn with country furnishings.
NO. OF ROOMS	Three rooms with private bathrooms.
RATES	Year-round rates are $85-90 for a single or double. There is a two-day minimum stay on holiday weekends. Cancellation requires seven days' notice (21 days for holidays) and a $10 cancellation fee.
CREDIT CARDS	No
BREAKFAST	Full breakfast is served in the dining room and includes hot drinks; fruit juice; fresh fruit; waffles, pancakes, or muffins; breakfast meats; eggs; and potatoes.

AMENITIES	Afternoon refreshments; video and reading library; seasonal drinks; cookies, cakes, breads, fruit, cheese, and nuts; tour information for Yosemite.
RESTRICTIONS	No smoking (inside), no pets. Buster the cat weighs 20 pounds.
REVIEWED	America's Wonderful Little Hotels & Inns, Bed & Breakfast California, Bed & Breakfast in California

SCOTTY'S BED & BREAKFAST

1223 Highway 41, Fish Camp, CA 93623   209-683-6936

YOSEMITE'S CARRIAGE HOUSE

7731 Forest Drive, Fish Camp, CA 93632   209-683-8139
Mike & Judy Durr, Innkeepers   FAX 209-683-8139 (call first)
EMAIL durr@sierratel.com   WEBSITE www.fresnomall.com/carriagehouse

LOCATION	In Fish Camp, turn off Highway 41 onto Summit Road. Go right on Forest Drive to the first place on the right past the fire station.
OPEN	All year
DESCRIPTION	A 1994 two-story mountain cabin with western and romantic decor.
NO. OF ROOMS	One room with a private bathroom.
RATES	Year-round rates are $110 for a single or double. There is no minimum stay and cancellation requires seven days' notice.
CREDIT CARDS	Discover, MasterCard, Visa
BREAKFAST	Continental breakfast is served in the guestroom and includes juice, fruit, roll, bread, and coffee.
AMENITIES	Spa tub, CD player, TV/VCR, microwave, refrigerator, balcony with porch swing. Hosts have lived and worked in Yosemite for over 20 years and can offer advice on visiting the park.
RESTRICTIONS	No smoking, no pets, no children

FOLSOM

BRADLEY HOUSE

606 Figueroa Street, Folsom, CA 95630   916-355-1962

FORESTVILLE

Forestville is north of San Francisco at the center of Sonoma's wine country—in the shadow of the redwoods and just south of the Russian River. It is located on Highway 116 between Highways 1 and 101.

THE FARMHOUSE INN & RESTAURANT

7871 River Road, Forestville, CA 95436   707-887-3300
Rebecca Smith, Resident Owner   800-464-6642
EMAIL innkeep@sonic.net   FAX 707-887-3311
WEBSITE www.farmhouse.com

LOCATION	From Highway 101, take the River Road exit (Santa Rosa), and head west on River Road. The inn is 7.5 miles on the left, across the street from Wohler Road.
OPEN	All year
DESCRIPTION	A restored 1878 two-story traditional farmhouse and cottages with white picket fences and gardens.
NO. OF ROOMS	Eight rooms with private bathrooms. Try room 1.
RATES	Year-round rates for a double are $105-195. There is a two-night minimum stay on weekends and cancellation requires ten days' notice.
CREDIT CARDS	American Express, MasterCard, Visa
BREAKFAST	Full breakfast, served in the dining room or outside on the deck, includes cereal, muffins, fruit, a hot entrée, and beverages. Lunch and dinner are available at the restaurant in the main house.
AMENITIES	Swimming pool, English gardens, phone, clock-radios, fireplace, sauna, Jacuzzi tubs, wedding facilities for up to 250, wheelchair accessible.
RESTRICTIONS	No smoking, no pets. Arthur, a feral cat, is still adjusting to domestic life.

REVIEWED   Northern California Wine Country Access
MEMBER   Country Inns of the Russian River

FORT BRAGG

Fort Bragg's two largest festivals are Paul Bunyan Days on Labor Day weekend, which features a big parade, log-cutting races, and a demolition derby (of all things); and the annual Whale Festival, held the third Saturday of March, which includes ranger-led talks about the cetaceans, a Whale Run, and a beer- and chowder-tasting contest. Check out the city's popular Skunk Train (named for the odoriferous mix of diesel fuel and gasoline that once powered the train) for a scenic eight-hour round-trip journey through the magnificent redwoods to the city of Willits and back again (or you can take the three-and-a-half-hour round-trip excursion to Northspur). One of the prettiest public beaches on the Mendocino Coast is at MacKerricher State Park, located three miles north of Fort Bragg off Highway 1.

AVALON HOUSE

561 Stewart Street, Fort Bragg, CA 95437   707-964-5555
Anne Sorrells, Innkeeper   800-964-5556
EMAIL anne@theavalonhouse.com   FAX 707-964-5555
WEBSITE www.theavalonhouse.com

LOCATION	Ten miles north of the town of Mendocino, one block west of Main Street (Highway 1). Turn left on Fir Street and left again onto Stewart.
OPEN	All year
DESCRIPTION	A 1905 three-story Craftsman-style inn with period furnishings, listed on the Fort Bragg Historic Register.
NO. OF ROOMS	Six rooms with private bathrooms. Anne's favorite is the Yellow Room.
RATES	Year-round rates are $70-140 for a single or double. Take 20 percent off these rates Monday through Thursday (excluding holidays). There is a minimum stay on weekends and no cancellation policy.
CREDIT CARDS	American Express, Discover, MasterCard, Visa
BREAKFAST	Full breakfast is served in the dining room and includes fruit, juice, homemade scones, and an entrée such as omelets or pancakes.
AMENITIES	Flowers; sherry and port; down comforters; feather pillows; some rooms have whirlpool tubs, fireplaces, decks, and ocean views.

Avalon House, Fort Bragg

RESTRICTIONS	No smoking, no pets. Toby is the resident Maine coon cat.
REVIEWED	*More Weekends for Two in Northern California: 50 All-New Romatic Getaways*
MEMBER	California Association of Bed & Breakfast Inns, California Lodging Industry Association

CLAUDIA'S GARDEN

32450 Simpson Lane, Fort Bragg, CA 95437   707-964-5574
Claudia Ellis, Resident Owner   FAX 707-964-5574
WEBSITE *www.infinityguest.com/bnblist/california/claudia's gardens*

LOCATION	At the intersection of Highway 1 and Highway 20, turn left and go 0.5 mile to Simpson Lane. Take another left and go 0.5 mile. The inn is on the left.
OPEN	All year
DESCRIPTION	A 1974 one-and-a-half-story redwood guesthouse, surrounded by a redwood forest.
NO. OF ROOMS	One room with a private bathroom.
RATES	Call for year-round rates and cancellation information.
CREDIT CARDS	No
BREAKFAST	Continental breakfast is served in the guestroom and includes coffee, tea, juice, fruit, rolls, cream cheese, eggs.

Claudia's Garden, Fort Bragg

AMENITIES   Fresh flowers in rooms, robes, hot tub, fresh herb garden, lots of privacy.

RESTRICTIONS   Sandy is the Lab and Spot is the Australian shepherd. These two are kept company by Pretty Pretty, the calico, while the ducks patrol the garden for snails and slugs and the rabbit makes his home over the compost bin.

COUNTRY INN BED & BREAKFAST

632 North Main Street, Fort Bragg, CA 95437   707-964-3737
Bruce & Cynthia Knauss, Resident Owners   800-831-5327
WEBSITE www.beourguests.com

LOCATION   In downtown Fort Bragg.

OPEN   All year

DESCRIPTION   An 1892 two-story Victorian townhouse with hanging flower baskets and contemporary and old-fashioned furnishings, listed on the Fort Bragg Historic Register.

NO. OF ROOMS   Eight rooms with private bathrooms.

RATES   Year-round rates are $89-139 for a single or double. There is a two-night minimum stay on summer weekends, three nights during holiday weekends. Ask about a cancellation policy.

CREDIT CARDS   American Express, MasterCard, Visa

BREAKFAST   Full breakfast is served in the parlor.

AMENITIES	Wine in evenings, fresh-cut flowers, brass and white enameled beds, hurricane lamps, maps, history books, off-street parking.
RESTRICTIONS	No smoking, no pets, children over 15 are welcome.
REVIEWED	Bed & Breakfast California; Country Inns, Lodges and Historic Hotels; Bed & Breakfast USA

Glass Beach Bed & Breakfast Inn

726 North Main Street, Fort Bragg, CA 95437   707-964-6774

Grey Whale Inn

615 North Main Street, Fort Bragg, CA 95437   707-964-0640
John & Colette Bailey, Resident Owners   800-382-7244
Spanish spoken   FAX 707-964-4408
EMAIL stay@greywhaleinn.com   WEBSITE www.greywhaleinn.com

LOCATION	One-hundred-and-fifty miles north of San Francisco on Highway 1, two blocks north of downtown Fort Bragg.
OPEN	All year
DESCRIPTION	A 1915 four-story classic revival inn with eclectic furnishings and ocean views.
NO. OF ROOMS	Fourteen rooms with private bathrooms.
RATES	Year-round rates are $90-180 for a single or double. November through March, rates are lower. There is a two-night minimum stay on weekends, three nights during holidays. Cancellation requires seven days' notice with a $10 cancellation fee.
CREDIT CARDS	American Express, Discover, EnRoute, JCB, MasterCard, Visa
BREAKFAST	Full breakfast is served in the dining room and includes a hot entrée, bagels, muffins, homemade coffeecakes and breads, fresh fruit, hot and cold cereal, yogurt, and beverages.
AMENITIES	Telephones, recreation area with TV/VCR and pool table, tidepool explorations, complimentary teas and coffee in the parlor, fruit basket, meeting facilities for 20 to 30 people.
RESTRICTIONS	No smoking, children over 12 are welcome (limited accommodations for younger children).
REVIEWED	America's Favorite Inns, B&Bs, & Small Hotels; Fodor's California; Frommer's California; America's Wonderful Little Hotels & Inns

Grey Whale Inn, Fort Bragg

MEMBER	California Association of Bed & Breakfast Inns, Professional Association of Innkeepers International, Independent Innkeepers Association
RATED	AAA 3 Diamonds, ABBA 3 Crowns, Mobil 3 Stars
AWARDS	Mayor's Well Done award for outstanding landscaping

JUGHANDLE BEACH COUNTRY BED & BREAKFAST

32980 Gibney Lane, Fort Bragg, CA 95437   707-964-1415
Shannon & Jean LaTourre, Resident Owners   800-964-9957
WEBSITE www.jughandle.com   FAX 707-961-1473

LOCATION	Five miles north of the village of Mendocino, three miles south of Fort Bragg.
OPEN	All year
DESCRIPTION	An 1883 two-story Swedish farmhouse with country and antique furnishings.
NO. OF ROOMS	Four rooms with private bathrooms. Try room 3.
RATES	Year-round rates are $79-189 for a single or double. There is a two-night minimum stay over Saturday and cancellation requires seven days' notice.
CREDIT CARDS	MasterCard, Visa

BREAKFAST	Full gourmet breakfast is served in the dining room.
AMENITIES	Coffee service in the rooms, old-fashioned radios, wood stove and classical music in the parlor, spa tubs.
RESTRICTIONS	No smoking, no pets, children welcome. The blind Siberian husky is named Tank.

THE LODGE AT NOYO RIVER

500 Casa del Noyo Drive, Fort Bragg, CA 95437   707-964-8045
WEBSITE *www.mcn.org/a/noyoriver/*

KUDOS/COMMENTS   "Cozy, romantic lodge located at the mouth of the Noyo River."

OLD STEWART HOUSE INN

511 Stewart Street, Fort Bragg, CA 95437   707-961-0775
Darrell Galli, Innkeeper   800-287-8392
Italian spoken
EMAIL *darrell@oldstewarthousinn.com*
WEBSITE *www.oldstewarthouseinn.com*

LOCATION	If entering Fort Bragg from the south, cross the Green Bridge (Noyo) and go through four stop lights. Then go two more blocks, turn left on Pine Street, and go one block.
OPEN	All year
DESCRIPTION	An 1876 three-story Victorian inn built by the owner and founder of the first lumber mill in Fort Bragg.
NO. OF ROOMS	Five rooms with private bathrooms.
RATES	Year-round rates are $65-99 for a single or double. There is a minimum stay during weekends and holidays, and cancellation requires seven days' notice.
CREDIT CARDS	American Express, MasterCard, Visa
BREAKFAST	Full breakfast is served in the dining room or guestrooms and includes coffee, tea, fruit, juice, cereal, pastry, eggs, fried potatoes, sausage, and toast.
AMENITIES	Wine and cheese at 6 p.m.; library with card and board games; phone and data port; TV room; Jacuzzi for two; deck for sunsets and whale-watching; ocean views over the rooftops.

RESTRICTIONS	Two cottages permit children and pets. Lady is the resident sheltie, and Saphire is the Siamese/calico mix.
REVIEWED	The Official Guide to American Historic Inns
MEMBER	California Association of Bed & Breakfast Inns

PUDDING CREEK INN

700 North Main Street, Fort Bragg, CA 95437 707-964-9529
Walt & Jacque Woltman, Innkeepers 800-227-9529
EMAIL pudcreek@jps.net FAX 707-964-9529

LOCATION	At the north end of Fort Bragg on Highway 1.
OPEN	All year
DESCRIPTION	Two 1884 two-story Victorian homes connected by an enclosed garden court and listed on the National Historic Register.
NO. OF ROOMS	Ten rooms with private bathrooms. Count's Room is the best in the house.
RATES	June through September, rates are $75-135 for a single or double. Ask about discounts. There is a two-night minimum stay during weekends and cancellation requires five days' notice.
CREDIT CARDS	American Express, Discover, MasterCard, Visa
BREAKFAST	Full breakfast, served in the dining room, includes an egg dish, fruit, yogurt, coffeecake, cereals, and beverages. Special meals are available on request.
AMENITIES	Flowers, candy, newspaper, social hour, wine in your room, game room, TVs in some rooms, feather beds, fireplaces in some rooms, enclosed garden court, laundry service, fax.
RESTRICTIONS	No smoking, no pets. Children are welcome.
REVIEWED	America's Wonderful Little Hotels & Inns, Bed & Breakfast California, Bed & Breakfasts and Country Inns, Recommended Country Inns—West Coast
MEMBER	National Bed & Breakfast Association, California Association of Bed & Breakfast Inns, Mendocino County Innkeepers Association
RATED	Mobil 3 Stars

Rendezvous Inn & Restaurant

647 North Main Street, Fort Bragg, CA 95437   707-964-8142
Rose & Lionel Jacobs, Resident Owners   800-491-8142
Spanish spoken

LOCATION	Two blocks north of downtown on the ocean side.
OPEN	All year
DESCRIPTION	A 1904 Edwardian inn with Shaker furnishings.
NO. OF ROOMS	Six rooms with private bathrooms.
RATES	Please call for rates and cancellation information.
CREDIT CARDS	Discover, MasterCard, Visa
BREAKFAST	Continental plus is served in the dining room and includes muffins, fresh fruit, omelets, granola parfaits, and beverages.
AMENITIES	No TV or phones to disturb guests, queen-size beds.
RESTRICTIONS	No smoking, no pets
MEMBER	California Lodging Industry Association

Riverview House

220 Riverview Drive, Fort Bragg, CA 95437   707-964-5236
www.mcn.org/b/riverview

Todd Farmhouse Country Bed & Breakfast

100 Highway 20, Fort Bragg, CA 95437   707-964-6575
Judy Haun & Bruce Johanson, Resident Owners

LOCATION	In the city limits of Fort Bragg, 15 miles from Mendocino.
OPEN	March 1 through December 1
DESCRIPTION	An 1898 two-story farmhouse and dairy cabin furnished with antiques and offering ocean views.
NO. OF ROOMS	Two rooms and one cottage with private bathrooms.

RATES	April through October, rates are $75-100 for a double or suite and $85 for the cottage. Off-season rates are 10 percent less. Seven days cancellation notice required.
CREDIT CARDS	MasterCard, Visa
BREAKFAST	Continental breakfast, served in the dining room, includes fresh apple pie, fruit, yogurt, granola, muffins, and beverages.
RESTRICTIONS	No smoking, no pets. There are resident ducks and chickens.

Fort Jones

Enjoy a wealth of outdoor recreation here in the Marble Mountain Wilderness Area and on the Scott River. Also worth seeing is the Fort Jones Christmas Parade. Fort Jones is about 15 miles southwest of Yreka on scenic Highway 3.

The Wild Goose Victorian Bed & Breakfast

11624 Main Street, Fort Jones, CA 96032   530-468-2735
Terry & Cindy Hayes, Innkeepers
EMAIL *wildgoose@sisqtel.net*

LOCATION	In Yreka, exit I-5 onto Highway 3 and drive an easy 16.2 miles to the B&B.
OPEN	Closed December 23 through 27
DESCRIPTION	An 1890 two-story country Victorian lodge decorated with family heirlooms, local art, and treasures from the past. Rambling wisteria, lilacs, and fragrant bouquets line a path to the large handcrafted original door.
NO. OF ROOMS	Two rooms with private bathrooms.
RATES	Year-round rates are $69 for a single or double. There is a minimum stay during weekends, holidays, and special events. Cancellation requires seven days' notice, 30 days during events and holidays.
CREDIT CARDS	No
BREAKFAST	Full gourmet breakfast is served in the dining room and includes French-roast coffee and fresh juice.
AMENITIES	Fresh flowers in season, evening turndown, sunset views over the Siskiyou Mountains from the upstairs veranda, stemwear available upon request.

RESTRICTIONS	No smoking, no pets, no children. "Our rooms are best suited for adults." The resident cats are an Abyssinian named Lino'l and a Bengal named Cheetah. "They are politely curious, enjoy helping at check-in, and adore entertaining upon request."
REVIEWED	Northern California Best Places

FREESTONE

GREEN APPLE INN

520 Bohemian Highway, Freestone, CA 95472   707-874-2526
Rosemary Hoffman, Resident Owner

FREMONT

This city was created in 1956 by the incorporation of five San Francisco Bay communities and their agricultural lands. Points of local interest include Fremont Central Park and its Lake Elizabeth, Ardenwood Historic Farms, Mission San Jose, San Francisco Bay National Wildlife Refuge, and Coyote Hills Regional Park. Fremont is across south San Francisco Bay via Highway 101 and the Dumbarton Bridge, or north of San Jose on I-680.

LORD BRADLEY'S INN

43344 Mission Boulevard, Fremont, CA 94539   510-490-0520
Susie & Steve Wilson, Resident Owners   FAX 510-490-3015
WEBSITE www.lordbradleysinn.com

LOCATION	Take the Mission San Jose exit from Highway 680 and go 0.5 mile south on Mission Boulevard. The inn is in the Mission San Jose District, adjacent to the Mission.
OPEN	All year
DESCRIPTION	An 1868 two-story Victorian inn with Victorian furnishings.
NO. OF ROOMS	There are eight rooms with private bathrooms.
RATES	Year-round rates are $75-125 for a single or double. There is no minimum stay and cancellation requires 24 hours' notice.
CREDIT CARDS	Discover, MasterCard, Visa

BREAKFAST	Continental plus is served in the dining room.
AMENITIES	High tea is available with reservations, Jacuzzi in the bridal suite, gardens and patio available for meetings. The inn can handle weddings and receptions for up to 150 people.
RESTRICTIONS	No smoking, no pets
MEMBER	California Lodging Industry Association

FRENCH GULCH

Time stands still in this historic mining town, which is on the high road to Trinity Lake (part of the awesome Whiskeytown-Shasta-Trinity National Recreation Area). Nearby Whiskeytown Lake is among the best for boating, swimming, fishing, and camping. French Gulch is on Trinity Mountain Road, 17 miles west of Redding via Highway 299.

FRENCH GULCH HOTEL

14138 Main Street, French Gulch, CA 96033   916-359-2112
Andrew Bouchard & Carol Jandrall, Innkeepers

LOCATION	From Redding, take Highway 299 west three miles to French Gulch.
OPEN	From April 1 through December 31
DESCRIPTION	An 1885 two-story gold mining-era hotel with historic interior furnishings and listed on the National Historic Register.
NO. OF ROOMS	One room with a private bathroom and six rooms share two bathrooms.
RATES	Year-round rates are $65-80 for a single or double with a private bathroom and $50-60 for a single or double with a shared bathroom. There is no minimum stay and cancellation requires seven days' notice with a $10 cancellation fee.
CREDIT CARDS	American Express, MasterCard, Visa
BREAKFAST	Full breakfast is served in the dining room and includes coffee, juice, assorted fruit plate, and a main entrée. Dinner and special meals are available in the restaurant.
AMENITIES	Very authentic furnishings, programs on the California Gold Rush Sesquentennial offered, owner Andrew Bouchard is a certified chef.
RESTRICTIONS	No smoking, no pets, and children over 12 are welcome.

MEMBER	National Bed & Breakfast Association, American Culinary Federation—Northern California Chapter
KUDOS/COMMENTS	"Nice rooms, well-kept grounds, excellent food in their full restaurant."

GARDEN VALLEY

Hidden in Gold Country with hardly a word written about it, Garden Valley is nevertheless part of the mythic Mother Lode—and very handy to Coloma's Marshall Gold Discovery State Historic Park. It is located on Highway 193, east of Sacramento via Highways 50 and 49.

MOUNTAINSIDE BED & BREAKFAST

5821 Spanish Flat Road, Garden Valley, CA 95633   530-626-0983
Paul & Mary Ellen Mello, Resident Owners   800-237-0832

LOCATION	Located 7.5 miles from Placerville, north on Spanish Flat Road off Highway 193. Look for our sign on Spanish Flat Road.
OPEN	All year
DESCRIPTION	A 1929 two-story country inn with 1920s decor, on 80 acres.
NO. OF ROOMS	Four rooms with private bathrooms. Mary Ellen suggests the Honeymoon Room.
RATES	Year-round rates for a double are $75-85. The attic, which sleeps up to eight, is $80 per couple; each additional person is $15. Cancellation requires seven days' notice, plus a $5 fee.
CREDIT CARDS	MasterCard, Visa
BREAKFAST	Full breakfast is served in the dining room or breakfast room, or on the deck, and includes fruit, juice, meat, egg dish, muffins or apple skillet cake, a potato dish, and baked tomatoes or Belgian waffles.
AMENITIES	Robes, lots of decks, outdoor hot tub, piano, and fireplace in parlor.
RESTRICTIONS	No smoking in the house, no pets. Outside resident pets include Tawny, a yellow Lab, and Fred the cat.
MEMBER	Historic Country Inns of El Dorado County

GAZELLE

HOLLYHOCK FARM BED & BREAKFAST

18705 Old Highway 99, Gazelle, CA 96034   530-435-2627

GEORGETOWN

When the tent city located here burned in 1852, this mountain town was rebuilt with much wider streets, which are now graced by a few noteworthy old buildings: I.O.O.F. Hall (at Main Street and Highway 193), Georgetown Hotel (6260 Main Street), and the American River Inn, which had an earlier life as a boardinghouse. In the spring, spectacular displays of wild Scotch broom cover the Georgetown hillsides.

AMERICAN RIVER INN

Main and Orleans, Georgetown, CA 95634   530-333-4499
Will & Maria Collin, Innkeepers   800-245-6566
EMAIL ari@pcweb.net   FAX 530-933-9253
WEBSITE www.pcweb.net/ari

LOCATION	Turn east from Highway 193. The inn is 2.5 blocks down on the north side of the street.
OPEN	All year
DESCRIPTION	A restored 1853 three-story Victorian miner's boarding house decorated with antiques.
NO. OF ROOMS	Seventeen rooms have private bathrooms, ten rooms have shared bathrooms.
RATES	Year-round rate for a single or double with a private bathroom is $95. A single or double with shared bathroom is $85, and a honeymoon suite is $115. Cancellation requires 10 days' notice, 20 days on holiday weekends, with a $10 fee.
CREDIT CARDS	American Express, Diners Club, Discover, MasterCard, Visa
BREAKFAST	Full breakfast, served in the dining room, includes apple crepes, fresh fruit, muffins, and beverages. Catering is available for groups.
AMENITIES	Flowers, bikes, driving range and putting green, croquet, two rooms are handicapped accessible, afternoon wine and hors d'oeuvres, conference center for 15–40 people, catering.
RESTRICTIONS	Children over five are welcome.

REVIEWED	*Weekends for Two in Northern California: 50 Romantic Getaways in California; Karen Brown's California Country Inns & Itineraries*
MEMBER	California Association of Bed & Breakfast Inns, El Dorado Historic Inns

GEYSERVILLE

Geyserville is a tiny town surrounded by grapes at the foot of Geyser Peak. The town's Fall Color Tour on the last Sunday in October is a good time to see grape leaves in a blaze of color. Lake Sonoma Recreation Area is a great place to be for fishing, boating, or camping.

CAMPBELL RANCH INN

1475 Canyon Road, Geyserville, CA 95441   707-857-3476
Jerry & Mary Jane Campbell, Resident Owners   800-959-3878
WEBSITE *www.campbellranchinn.com*

LOCATION	At Geyserville, take the Canyon Road exit off Highway 101 and travel 1.6 miles west.
OPEN	All year
DESCRIPTION	A two-story 1968 California country inn with traditional furnishings, on 35 acres.
NO. OF ROOMS	Five rooms with private bathrooms. Try the cottage.
RATES	Year-round rates are $125-225 for a single or double, and the cottage is $225. There is a two-day minimum stay when Saturday is included, three days on holiday weekends. Cancellation requires three days' notice.
CREDIT CARDS	American Express, MasterCard, Visa
BREAKFAST	Full breakfast is served in the dining room or on the outside terrace. Guests may choose from a full menu.
AMENITIES	Evening dessert of homemade pie or cake, tea or coffee, robes, flowers, all king-size beds, four rooms with balconies, swimming pool, pro tennis court, hot tub, bicycles, cottage with private hot tub and fireplace.
RESTRICTIONS	No smoking, no pets, children over 12 are welcome. Maggie, the Border collie, fetches tennis balls for guests.
REVIEWED	*Bed & Breakfast USA*
MEMBER	Professional Association of Innkeepers International
RATED	ABBA 3 Crowns

Campbell Ranch Inn, Geyserville

KUDOS/COMMENTS   "Comfortable ranch-style home, great cooking, wonderful setting high on a hilltop."

Hope-Merrill House & Hope-Bosworth House

21253 and 21238 Geyserville Avenue 707-857-3356
Geyserville, CA 95441 800-825-4233
Ron & Cosette Scheiber, Resident Owners FAX 707-857-4673
Spanish spoken
WEBSITE www.hope-inns.com

LOCATION	From Highway 101, take the Geyserville exit and go north into town; the inns are on the west side of the road.
OPEN	All year
DESCRIPTION	Two separate Victorian buildings romantically restored and beautifully furnished with antiques. Listed on the State Historic Register.
NO. OF ROOMS	Twelve rooms with private bathrooms.
RATES	Year-round rates are $111-147 for a single or double and $174 for a suite. There is a two-night minimum stay on weekends and holidays. Cancellation requires seven days' notice with a $10 fee.
CREDIT CARDS	American Express, Discover, MasterCard, Visa
BREAKFAST	Full breakfast is served in the dining room.

AMENITIES	Heated swimming pool, private Jacuzzi, gardens and gazebo, handicapped accessible, meeting facilities for small groups, garden available for weddings.
RESTRICTIONS	No smoking, no pets
REVIEWED	Bed & Breakfast California, The Old House Lover's Guide to Inns and Bed & Breakfast Guest Houses, Historic Country Inns of California, Feather Beds and Flapjacks
MEMBER	California Association of Bed & Breakfast Innkeepers, Wine Country Inns of Sonoma County
RATED	Mobil 2 Stars
AWARDS	1989, American Home Award for Bed and Breakfast, National Trust for Historic Preservation

Isis Oasis

20889 Geyserville Avenue, Geyserville, CA 95441   707-857-3524
WEBSITE www.isisoasis.org

Glen Ellen

This is Jack London country, so don't miss the Jack London State Historic Park. The Bouverie Audubon Preserve is worth exploring as well. In late summer, the Art Farm Festival of Classical Music gets underway. Glen Ellen is north of San Francisco via Highways 101 and 121.

Above the Clouds Inn

3250 Trinity Road, Glen Ellen, CA 95442   707-996-7371
Claude & Betty Ganaye, Resident Owners   800-736-7894
EMAIL abovetheclouds@vom.com   FAX 707-938-5348
WEBSITE www.sonomabb.com

LOCATION	Eight miles north of Sonoma on Highway 12, turn right onto Trinity Road and travel three miles up the mountain road.
OPEN	February 12 through October
DESCRIPTION	An 1854 three-story California colonial host home with hardwood floors, lace curtains, French doors, and antiques, located on 25 acres.
NO. OF ROOMS	Three rooms with private bathrooms

RATES	April through October, rates are $155-175 for a single or double. February and March, rates are $135-155 for a single or double. There is a minimum stay during weekends and cancellation requires seven days' notice.
CREDIT CARDS	American Express, Discover, JCB, MasterCard, Visa
BREAKFAST	Full breakfast is served in the dining room and includes poached pears, baked apples or fruit salad, coffee, tea, juice, French crepes, blintzes, and quiche Lorraine or spinach pain perdue.
AMENITIES	Flowers, robes, wine upon arrival, outdoor Jacuzzi in meadow, air conditioning and ceiling fans, concierge service, handicapped accessible.
RESTRICTIONS	No smoking, no pets, no children
MEMBER	Bed & Breakfast Association of Sonoma Valley
KUDOS/COMMENTS	"Marvelous view, wonderful hosts, quiet, delicious food."

GLENELLY INN

5131 Warm Springs Road, Glen Ellen, CA 95442   707-996-6720
Kristi Hallamore Jeppesen, Innkeeper   FAX 707-996-5227
Norwegian and Spanish spoken
EMAIL glenelly@vom.com
WEBSITE www.glenelly.com

LOCATION	From Arnold Drive in Glen Ellen, head west 0.33 mile on Warm Springs Road.
OPEN	All year
DESCRIPTION	A 1916 two-story French colonial inn decorated with antiques and country furnishings. The inn consists of two structures with a flagstone patio and an extensive garden, built into a wooded hillside.
NO. OF ROOMS	Eight rooms with private bathrooms. Try the Vallejo Room.
RATES	Year-round rates are $115-150 for a single or double. There is a minimum stay during weekends and cancellation requires seven days' notice.
CREDIT CARDS	MasterCard, Visa
BREAKFAST	Full breakfast is served buffet style in the common room, on the flagstone patio beneath oak trees, or in guestrooms on request. Breakfast always includes fresh-squeezed orange juice or other juice blends, Starbucks coffee, assorted teas and cocoas, home-baked bread, coffeecake or muffins, a seasonal fruit dish, and a hot entrée that changes daily, such as salsa Jack soufflé, hashbrown decadence, or leek tart.

Glenelley Inn, Glen Ellen

AMENITIES	Robes and extra big bath towels; Scandinavian down comforters; ceiling fans; Jacuzzi in the rose garden; massage and spa services available on premises; hammock and swing under 200-year-old oak tree; homemade cookies, lemonade, sun tea, and hot beverages always available; concierge service.
RESTRICTIONS	No smoking, no pets, children are welcome. Hershey is the resident chocolate Lab/Doberman mix, and Nutmeg and Mungojerrie are the cats. Mungojerrie is the official greeter.
REVIEWED	*America's Favorite Inns, B&Bs, & Small Hotels; The Best Places to Kiss in Northern California; Bed & Breakfast in California; Karen Brown's California Country Inns & Itineraries; Northern California Best Places; Northern California Wine Country Access; Frommer's Pocket Guide; Fodor's*
MEMBER	California Association of Bed & Breakfast Inns

JACK LONDON LODGE

13740 Arnold Drive, Glen Ellen, CA 95442   707-938-8510
Elaine & Alan Nealley, Resident Managers   FAX 707-939-9642
WEBSITE *www.jacklondonlodge.com*

LOCATION	From San Francisco, take Highway 121 to Arnold Drive and go straight for 10 to 15 minutes. From Sonoma or Santa Rosa, take Highway 12 to the Glen Ellen sign at Arnold Drive. Turn west and go five minutes to the center of town.
OPEN	All year

DESCRIPTION	A 1960 two-story California country-style lodge on tree-lined Sonoma Creek. The Jack London Saloon is a historic 1905 brick Chauvet-designed building.
NO. OF ROOMS	Twenty-two rooms with private bathrooms.
RATES	May to November, rates are $100 for a single or double. Rates for the remainder of the year are $60-87 for a single or double. There is a two-night minimum stay from May to November and cancellation requires 72 hours' notice, 10 days during holidays.
CREDIT CARDS	MasterCard, Visa
BREAKFAST	Continental breakfast is served from May through November. Lunch and dinner is available at Calabaza's Creek Café.
AMENITIES	Phone and TV in rooms, pool with view of the creek.
RESTRICTIONS	No pets
REVIEWED	The Berkeley guides, *Northwest Budget Travelers Guide*

TANGLEWOOD HOUSE

250 Bonnie Way, Glen Ellen, CA 95442   707-996-5021
John & Mary Field, Resident Owners

LOCATION	From the village of Glen Ellen, take Arnold Drive 0.5 mile to Dunbar Road, turn left, and drive 0.5 mile to Bonnie Way. The host home is at the intersection of Dunbar Road and Bonnie Way.
OPEN	All year
DESCRIPTION	A 1963 country ranch host home with country pine decor and antique furnishings.
NO. OF ROOMS	One-bedroom suite with private bathroom.
RATES	Year-round rate for a single or double is $115. There is a two-night minimum stay during spring and summer, and on fall weekends. Cancellation requires 48 hours' notice.
CREDIT CARDS	No
BREAKFAST	Full breakfast, served in the guest room, includes hot dishes such as eggs or pancakes, plus fresh fruit, juice, muffins, and coffee.
AMENITIES	A bottle of wine, cheese and crackers, cable TV, an acre of secluded gardens with a pool and gazebo.
RESTRICTIONS	No smoking, no pets, children over 12 are welcome. The resident collies are Cleo and Austin.
MEMBER	Bed & Breakfast Association of Sonoma Valley

GLENHAVEN

Another quiet little gem on the southeast shore of Clear Lake. Look for wineries in the vicinity. On Highway 20 southeast of Fort Bragg and Highway 101.

KRISTALBERG BED & BREAKFAST

715 Pearl Court, Glenhaven, CA 95443   707-274-8009
Merv Myers, Resident Owner
German, Spanish, and French spoken
WEBSITE *www.innformation.com/ca/kristalberg*

LOCATION	Four miles east of Lucerne, 0.5 mile off Highway 20, turn left on Bruner Drive, go to the end, and turn left on Pearl Court.
OPEN	All year
DESCRIPTION	A 1987 three-story Cape Cod with European and Victorian antique furnishing.
NO. OF ROOMS	Two rooms with private bathrooms and one room shares one bathroom. Merv likes the Master Suite.
RATES	May through October, rates are $90 for a single or double with a private bathroom, $60 for a single or double with a shared bathroom, and $150 for the suite. November through April, rates are $80 for a single or double with a private bathroom, $55 for a single or double with a shared bathroom, and $125 for the suite. There is no minimum stay and cancellation requires seven days' notice.
CREDIT CARDS	American Express, Discover, MasterCard, Visa
BREAKFAST	Full breakfast is served in the dining room and includes fruit with yogurt and granola, quiche, blackberry shortcake, oatmeal and raisins with fruit, egg custard, or cornbread fruit compote. Dinner is also available.
AMENITIES	Flowers, TV, live organ music, whirlpool tub in master suite, after-dinner sherry, afternoon refreshment, hot tub, balconies on lake side of house.
RESTRICTIONS	Smoking outside, no pets. The resident Australian shepherd is called Lassie.
MEMBER	California Association of Bed & Breakfast Inns

Goodyears Bar

Helm's St. Charles Inn

459 Mountain House Road, Goodyears Bar, CA 95944   530-289-0910

Grass Valley

This town's place in history is marked by the billion dollars in gold that was mined from its hard rock. Check it all out at the 784-acre Empire Mine State Historic Park. June is a good time to be here, for the Cornish Miners' Picnic, the Bluegrass Festival, and Music in the Mountains Summer Festival (a two-week shared event with Nevada City). Grass Valley is located at the gateway to Tahoe National Forest and the Yuba–Donner Scenic Byway and offers handy access to Englebright Lake State Recreation Area. From Sacramento, drive 60 miles northeast via I-80 and Highway 49.

Elam Biggs Bed & Breakfast

220 Colfax Avenue, Grass Valley, CA 95945   530-477-0906
Peter & Barbara Franchino, Innkeepers
WEBSITE www.virtualcities.com

LOCATION	Four blocks from downtown Grass Valley at the eastern edge of the Grass Valley Historic District.
OPEN	All year
DESCRIPTION	An 1892 three-story Queen Anne Victorian inn with country decor and Victorian antiques, surrounded by shade trees and a rose-covered picket fence.
NO. OF ROOMS	Five rooms with private bathrooms. Peter and Barbara say the Empire Room is their favorite.
RATES	Year-round rates are $70-110 for a single or double with a private bathroom. There is a minimum stay on holiday weekends and during the County Fair. Cancellation requires seven days' notice.
CREDIT CARDS	MasterCard, Visa
BREAKFAST	Full country breakfast is served family style in the dining room and includes orange juice, coffee, tea, muffins, breads, fruit, hot dishes, and cereal.

AMENITIES	Air conditioning, seasonal flowers, refreshments, cookies, magic performed at breakfast on request.
RESTRICTIONS	No smoking, no pets. Ask about children. Charlie is the resident cat.
MEMBER	Historical Inns of Grass Valley and Nevada City
RATED	AAA 3 Stars

Golden Ore Bed & Breakfast Inn

448 South Auburn Street, Grass Valley, CA 95945   530-272-6872

The Holbrooke

212 West Main, Grass Valley, CA 95945   530-273-1353
EMAIL holbrool@nccn.net

Murphy's Inn

318 Neal Street, Grass Valley, CA 95945   530-273-6873
Tom & Sue Myers, Resident Owners   FAX 916-273-6873

LOCATION	From Highway 49, take the Colfax 174 exit. Go left on South Auburn and left again on Neal Street.
OPEN	All year
DESCRIPTION	An 1866 two-story wood-frame inn with period decor.
NO. OF ROOMS	Eight rooms with private bathrooms.
RATES	Please call for rates and cancellation information.
CREDIT CARDS	American Express, MasterCard, Visa
BREAKFAST	Full breakfast, served in the dining room, includes an entrée, fruit, muffin, and beverages.
AMENITIES	In-room phone service on request; TV in all rooms; carriage rides on Friday, Saturday, and Sunday (for an additional fee).
RESTRICTIONS	No smoking, no pets
REVIEWED	Karen Brown's California Country Inns & Itineraries
MEMBER	California Association of Bed & Breakfast Inns

PEACOCK INN

439 S Auburn Street, Grass Valley, CA 95945   530-477-2179
WEBSITE *www.virtualcities.com*

SWAN-LEVINE HOUSE

328 South Church Street, Grass Valley, CA 95945   530-272-1873
Howard & Peggy Levine, Resident Owners   FAX 530-272-5720
EMAIL *swlevine@nccn.net*

LOCATION	Two blocks from downtown Grass Valley. Exit Highway 49 at the Colfax-Downtown Grass Valley exit, go left (north), and left again onto 1st Street. Then take Neal Street up the hill to Church Street. Take a left onto Church and go one-and-a-half blocks.
OPEN	All year
DESCRIPTION	An 1867 four-story Queen Anne Victorian inn decorated with eclectic Victorian furnishings, fine art, and family heirlooms. The inn was a hospital for 68 years.
NO. OF ROOMS	Four rooms with private bathrooms. Howard and Peggy suggest the suite with the fireplace.
RATES	Year-round rates are $76 for a single or double. Call about the minimum-stay policy.
CREDIT CARDS	Discover, MasterCard, Visa
BREAKFAST	Full breakfast, served in the dining room, might include Mano quesadilla with fruit or tequila sunrise French toast.
AMENITIES	Badminton court, exercise pool, printmaking demonstration, tour of the carriage house press art studio.
RESTRICTIONS	No smoking. The resident cats live outside.
REVIEWED	*Northern California Best Places, Traveling with Man's Best Friend, The Best Places to Kiss in Northern California*
MEMBER	California Association of Bed & Breakfast Inns, Historic Inns of Grass Valley and Nevada City

GROVELAND

This former mining town lies on scenic Highway 120 on the road to Yosemite's western entrance. Check out the Yosemite Mountain Sugar Pine Railroad for an old-fashioned thrill.

BERKSHIRE INN

19950 Highway 120, Groveland, CA 95321 209-962-6744
Bob & Dody Yates, Resident Owners

THE GROVELAND HOTEL, AN HISTORIC COUNTRY INN

18767 Main Street, Groveland, CA 95321 209-962-4000
Peggy A. & Grover Mosley, Resident Owners 800-273-3314
Some Spanish spoken FAX 209-962-6674
EMAIL peggy@groveland.com WEBSITE www.groveland.com

LOCATION	Two hours from San Francisco. Take Highway 80 east to Highway 580 east and go to Highway 120 east, which heads right through Groveland. The hotel is on Highway 120 (Main Street) on the east end of town.
OPEN	All year
DESCRIPTION	An 1849 two-story Monterey colonial hotel and a 1914 Queen Anne with Victorian antiques.
NO. OF ROOMS	Seventeen rooms with private bathrooms.
RATES	Year-round rates are $115-135 for a double and $195 for a suite. There is no minimum stay and cancellation requires 24 hours' notice with a $10 fee.
CREDIT CARDS	American Express, Diners Club, Discover, MasterCard, Visa
BREAKFAST	Continental plus includes fresh muffins, breads, cereals, and beverages. For groups, lunch and dinner are available with advance notice.
AMENITIES	Robes, phones, down comforters, evening wine, TV in the parlor, verandas, courtyard dining in the summer. Suites have fireplaces, spa tubs, and "teddy bear adoption services." Conference room is available.
RESTRICTIONS	No smoking

MEMBER	Professional Association of Innkeepers International, American Bed & Breakfast Association, California Association of Bed & Breakfast Inns, Independent Innkeepers Association

Hotel Charlotte

PO Box 787, Groveland, CA 95321 209-962-6455
Ruth Kraenzel, Resident Owner

Inn at Sugar Pine Ranch

21250 State Highway 120, Groveland, CA 95321 209-962-7823
Elaine & Craig Maxwell, Innkeepers 888-800-7823
WEBSITE www.bizware.com/sugarpine FAX 209-962-7823 (call first)

LOCATION	Three hours east of San Francisco, four miles east of Groveland on Highway 120.
OPEN	All year
DESCRIPTION	An 1860 two-story New England country-style inn with a farmhouse and cottages, located on a 60-acre ranch.
NO. OF ROOMS	Twelve rooms with private bathrooms.
RATES	Year-round rates are $110-150 for a single or double. There is a three-night minimum stay on holiday weekends and cancellation requires five days' notice.
CREDIT CARDS	MasterCard, Visa
BREAKFAST	Full breakfast is served in the dining room.
AMENITIES	Pool, hiking paths, piano in lobby, air conditioners, some rooms have fireplaces and whirlpool tubs.
RESTRICTIONS	No smoking anywhere on the property, no pets, children over six are welcome. The innkeepers have one dog and several cats.
REVIEWED	Pam Lanier's Complete Guide to B&Bs, Inns, and Guesthouses
MEMBER	California Association of Bed & Breakfast Inns, Gold Country Bed & Breakfast Association

GUALALA

An old lumber town on the Gualala (Wah-LA-la) River and at the south end of the rugged Mendocino Coast, this is one of the best whale-watching spots on the north coast. Del Mar Landing, an ecological reserve of virgin coastline, seals, and tidepools, can be reached via Gualala Point County Park.

INN AT GETCHELL COVE

36101 S Highway 1, Gualala, CA 95445 707-884-1936
WEBSITE *www.getchellcove.com*

NORTH COAST COUNTRY INN

34591 South Highway 1, Gualala, CA 95445 707-884-4537
Loren & Nancy Flanagan, Innkeepers 800-959-4537
Spanish spoken

LOCATION	Four miles north of Gualala at the intersection of Highway 1 and Fish Rock Road, which is identified by a highway sign and milepost 5.12.
OPEN	All year
DESCRIPTION	A rustic multistory California redwood country inn with American and French country furnishings, located near the Pacific Ocean.
NO. OF ROOMS	Six rooms with private bathrooms. Nancy recommends the Evergreen Room.
RATES	Year-round rates are $150-195 for a single or double. There is a two-night minimum stay on weekends, three nights on holidays. Cancellation requires five days' notice.
CREDIT CARDS	American Express, Discover, MasterCard, Visa
BREAKFAST	Full breakfast, served in the new common room, includes seasonal fruit, hot entrée, a variety of baked goods, coffee, tea, and juice.
AMENITIES	Hillside hot tub under the pines, garden gazebo and courtyard, coffee and juice in guestrooms, evening sherry and snacks, library, gift shop, parking. Facilities for small meetings available. The inn has two new guestrooms and a common room, completed in May 1998.
RESTRICTIONS	No smoking, no pets, no children. The inn has two cats, Sam and Sally. Sam is the "official greeter and room inspector."

North Coast Country Inn, Gualala

REVIEWED	*The Complete Guide to Bed & Breakfasts, Inns, and Guesthouses; Karen Brown's California Country Inns & Itineraries*
MEMBER	California Association of Bed & Breakfast Inns, North American Association of Bed & Breakfasts, American and Canadian Association of Bed & Breakfasts
RATED	AAA 2 Diamonds, ABBA 2 Crowns, Mobil 2 Stars

THE OLD MILANO HOTEL

38300 Highway 1, Gualala, CA 95445   707-884-3256
Leslie Linscheid, Resident Owner   FAX 707-884-4249
EMAIL *lll@mcn.org*   WEBSITE *www.cristalen.com/oldmilano*

LOCATION	One mile north of Gualala on the west side of Highway 1.
OPEN	All year
DESCRIPTION	A 1905 two-story Victorian with authentic Victorian period decor, on three acres of ocean-front property. Listed on the National Historic Register.
NO. OF ROOMS	Six cottages and a master suite with private bathrooms and six rooms share two bathrooms.
RATES	April through October, rates are are $135-210 for a double with a private bathroom and $80-115 for a double with a shared bathroom. Cottages are $135-210. November through March (except weekends and holidays), rates are 25 percent less. There is a minimum stay on Saturdays and a three-day cancellation policy.
CREDIT CARDS	MasterCard, Visa
BREAKFAST	Complete country breakfast is served in the dining room or guestrooms.

AMENITIES	Outdoor hot tub perched on the cliffside overlooking the ocean; award-winning restaurant.
RESTRICTIONS	No smoking, no pets, children over 14 are welcome.
REVIEWED	*The Official Guide to America's Historic Inns, Best Choices on the California Coast, Recommended Country Inns—West Coast*
KUDOS/COMMENTS	"Comfortable old-style hotel by the ocean. Very good food, outstanding breakfast." "Spectacular setting, quaint rooms."

SAINT ORRES

36601 South Highway 1, Gualala, CA 95445   707-884-3303
Eric Black, Ted Black, & Rosemary Campiformio, Resident Owners
WEBSITE www.saintorres.com   FAX 707-884-1840

LOCATION	On the south coast of Mendocino County, three miles north of Gualala.
OPEN	All year
DESCRIPTION	A 1970 two-story hotel, with two copper onion domes, and cottages, on 42 acres.
NO. OF ROOMS	Twelve private cottages with private bathrooms and eight rooms share three bathrooms.
RATES	Year-round rates are $85-225 for a single or double or a cottage with a private bathroom and $60-75 for a single or double with a shared bathroom. Suites rent for $270 and a three-bedroom suite rents for $400. A minimum stay is required on weekends and holidays and cancellation requires 72 hours' notice.
CREDIT CARDS	MasterCard, Visa
BREAKFAST	Full breakfast is served in the hotel dining room or delivered to cottages and includes a rotating main dish such as fritatta, rice pudding, waffles, fruit, breakfast breads, granola, and beverages. The dining room is open to the public for dinner.
AMENITIES	Some hotel rooms include ocean views, fireplaces, decks; cottages share spa, hot tub, and sun deck.
RESTRICTIONS	No smoking in public areas, no pets
REVIEWED	*The Best Places to Kiss in Northern California, Bed & Breakfast California, Country Inns of the Far West*

WHALE WATCH INN

35100 Highway 1, Gualala, CA 95445　　　　707-884-3667
Jim & Kazuko Popplewell, Resident Owners　　800-942-5342
Spanish spoken
WEBSITE www.whale-watch.com

LOCATION	Approximately three hours north of San Francisco on Highway 1, four miles north of Gualala on the ocean side of the highway.
OPEN	All year
DESCRIPTION	A 1985 contemporary country inn with sweeping ocean views.
NO. OF ROOMS	Eighteen rooms with private bathrooms. The most popular room is the Bath Suite.
RATES	Year-round rates for a single or double are $170-270. A two-night stay is required on weekends, three nights on holidays. No cancellation penalty is imposed with five days' notice.
CREDIT CARDS	American Express, MasterCard, Visa
BREAKFAST	Full breakfast, served in guestrooms, includes fresh fruit and juices, homemade bread, hot entrée, and beverages. Snack baskets are available that include cheese, crackers, fruit, cookies and wine.
AMENITIES	All rooms have private decks, fireplaces, queen-size beds, down comforters; Saturday evening social hour includes appetizers, wine, and assorted beverages; eight rooms have two-person whirlpool tubs; four rooms have single whirlpool tubs.
RESTRICTIONS	No smoking, no pets
REVIEWED	Weekends for Two in Northern California: 50 Romantic Getaways, The Best Places to Kiss in Northern California, The Best of San Francisco
KUDOS/COMMENTS	"Extraordinary views from every room."

GUERNEVILLE

Pronounce it GURN-ville, never mind that the founder's name is pronounced Gurn-ee. This is the "big city" of the Russian River area, the place for tubing, canoeing, and rafting. The Russian River Jazz Festival in September is a major event. The Crab Feed in February is worth trying, but you may want to skip the Slug Fest in March that honors the forest-dwelling banana slug. Guerneville is located at the south entrance of Armstrong Redwoods State Reserve via Highways 1 and 116.

APPLEWOOD

13555 Highway 116, Guerneville, CA 95446   707-869-9093
James Caron & Darryl Notter, Resident Owners
EMAIL stay@applewoodinn.com   WEBSITE www.applewoodinn.com

LOCATION	Applewood is 0.75 mile south of downtown Guerneville at the intersection of River Road and Highway 116 in Pocket Canyon.
OPEN	All year
DESCRIPTION	A 1922 three-story California mission revival on 6 wooded acres.
NO. OF ROOMS	Sixteen rooms with private bathrooms. Try the Slavianka Suite.
RATES	Year-round rates for a double are $135-300. There is a minimum stay on weekends and holidays. Cancellation requires 10 days' notice with a $15 fee.
CREDIT CARDS	American Express, Discover, MasterCard, Visa
BREAKFAST	Full breakfast is served in the dining room. Dinner is also available.
AMENITIES	Swimming pool; flowers; phones; TV; some rooms have fireplaces and/or Jacuzzis, private patios or balconies; handicapped accessible; meeting rooms available.
RESTRICTIONS	No smoking, no pets. The inn is not suitable for children.
REVIEWED	*Northern California Best Places, The Napa & Sonoma Book, Karen Brown's California Country Inns & Itineraries, Country Inns of the Far West*
RATED	Mobil 3 Stars
KUDOS/COMMENTS	"Posh, very nice, good restaurant." "A charming and elegant revival mansion. Tastefully decorated; stupendous dinners served five nights a week (Tuesday through Saturday)." "The most luxurious accommodations on the Russian River." "Exceptional country estate property."

Creekside Inn & Resort

16180 Neeley Road, Guerneville, CA 95446
Lynn Crescione, Resident Owner
Spanish spoken
WEBSITE *www.creeksideinn.com/innkeep*

707-869-3623
800-776-6586
FAX 707-869-1417

LOCATION	North of Santa Rosa on Highway 101, take the River Road exit and drive west 15 miles to the four-way intersection in Guerneville. Turn left onto Highway 116, continue across the bridge to Neeley Road, turn right, and go 0.2 mile.
OPEN	All year
DESCRIPTION	A 1930s Tudor inn surrounded by 10 cottages.
NO. OF ROOMS	Two rooms with private bathrooms, four rooms share two bathrooms, and ten cottages with kitchens.
RATES	Year-round rates are $60-80 for a single or double, suites are $149, and cottages with kitchens are $75-200. There is a minimum stay from June through September and cancellation requires seven days' notice.
CREDIT CARDS	Discover, MasterCard, Visa
BREAKFAST	Continental plus is served in the dining room and includes beverages, seasonal fruit, and an egg or cheese dish.
AMENITIES	Pool, rose gardens, flowers, pool table, table tennis, badminton, video games, large lounge with TV/VCR, meeting room for 20, wheelchair access to the inn, one handicapped accessible cottage.
RESTRICTIONS	No smoking, pets are OK with prior arrangements.
REVIEWED	*Northern California Handbook, Best Places to Stay in Northern California, Weekend Adventures for City Weary People*

Ridenhour Ranch House Inn

12850 River Road, Guerneville, CA 95446
Diane & Fritz Rechberger, Resident Owners
German spoken
EMAIL *frechberge@aol.com*

707-887-1033
888-877-4466
FAX 707-869-2967

LOCATION	Seventy-five minutes from San Francisco, 12 miles from Highway 101 west. Four miles east of Guerneville and 500 yards from the Korbel Champagne Cellar.
OPEN	All year

DESCRIPTION	A 1906 farmhouse decorated with an eclectic mix of English and American antiques and situated on 2.25 acres.
NO. OF ROOMS	Eight rooms with private bathrooms.
RATES	Year-round rates are $95-145. There is a two-night minimum stay on weekends and cancellation requires seven days' notice.
CREDIT CARDS	American Express, MasterCard, Visa
BREAKFAST	Full breakfast, served in the dining room or country kitchen, includes fruit, breads, cakes, and an egg dish.
AMENITIES	Flowers, robes, hot tub, cookies and fruit in the afternoon, sherry and port always available, one room with handicapped access.
RESTRICTIONS	No smoking, no pets. Resident dogs and cats include Hildegard, a Corgi mix, who loves to challenge guests to a soccer match.
REVIEWED	Northern California Best Places, Bed & Breakfast and Country Inns, Access California Wine Country
MEMBER	Redwood Empire Association, Wine Road Association, Wine Country Inns of Sonoma County

Santa Nella House

12130 Highway 116, Guerneville, CA 95446   707-869-9488
Robyn & Fred Santos, Resident Owners   FAX 707-869-0355
EMAIL webechefs@aol.com   WEBSITE www.santanella.com

LOCATION	From Highway 101 north, above Petaluma, take exit 116 (Sebastopol). Travel west through Sebastopol on to the next village, Forestville. Go 4.5 miles west of Forestville; the inn is on the left side.
OPEN	All year
DESCRIPTION	A circa 1865 two-story Victorian Italianiate farmhouse, with a veranda and Victorian furnishings. The farmhouse is nestled in the redwoods.
NO. OF ROOMS	Four rooms with private bathrooms.
RATES	Year-round rates are $100-110 for a single or double. There is a minimum stay on weekends and holidays, and cancellation requires seven days' notice.
CREDIT CARDS	American Express, Carte Blanche, Diners Club, Discover, MasterCard, Visa
BREAKFAST	Full four-course gourmet breakfast, created by chefs, is served in the dining room and changes daily. Wine dinners are available by prior arrangement.

AMENITIES	Hot tub under the redwoods, wood-burning fireplace in every room, weddings, catering, wine dinners.
RESTRICTIONS	No smoking inside, no pets

HALF MOON BAY

Old Victorian houses and small boutiques line downtown Half Moon Bay, the oldest city in San Mateo County, while produce stands, U-pick farms, and well-stocked nurseries ring its perimeter (artichokes, broccoli, and pumpkins are the town's prime crops). There are plenty of good beaches nearby, too. For the best tide pools, explore the Fitzgerald Marine Reserve at nearby Moss Beach. Every October, thousands of Bay Area families make their yearly pilgrimage to this picturesque seacoast town in search of the ultimate Halloween pumpkin. The Half Moon Bay Pumpkin Festival features all manner of squash cuisine and crafts, as well as the World Heavyweight Pumpkin Championship. During the spring and summer months, the weekend flower market is a big draw.

CYPRESS INN ON MIRAMAR BEACH

407 Mirada Road, Half Moon Bay, CA 94019   650-726-6002
Dan Floyd & Suzie Lankes, Innkeepers   800-832-3224
French and German spoken   FAX 650-458-0989
EMAIL lodging@cypressinn.com   WEBSITE www.cypressinn.com

LOCATION	Off Highway 1 between Princeton Harbor and Half Moon Bay. Take Medio toward the ocean to the corner of Medio and Mirada on Miramar Beach.
OPEN	All year
DESCRIPTION	A 1988 three-story contemporary beach house furnshed with contemporary decor and folk art.
NO. OF ROOMS	Twelve rooms with private bathrooms. Suzie recommends Las Nubes.
RATES	Year-round rates for a single or double are $170-275. There is a minimum stay required over Saturday night and cancellation requires ten days' notice.
CREDIT CARDS	American Express, Discover, Visa
BREAKFAST	Full breakfast includes orange juice, fresh-baked breads, seasonal fruits, cereals, yogurt parfait, beverages, and entrées such as peaches-and-cream French toast or mushroom quiche.
AMENITIES	Fireplaces, TV/VCR, a few steps to the beach, conference facilities for up to 20 people, on-site massage, robes, wine, hors d'oeuvres, desserts, feather beds, hair dryers, some rooms have spa tubs and ironing boards.

RESTRICTIONS	No smoking, no more than two people per room.
MEMBER	Half Moon Bay Bed & Breakfast Association, California Association of Bed & Breakfast Inns, Professional Association of Innkeepers International
RATED	AAA 3 Diamonds

HARBOR HOUSE

346 Princeton Avenue, Half Moon Bay, CA 94019 650-726-1572
Chris Mickelsen, Innkeeper FAX 650-728-8271
WEBSITE www.harborhousebandb.com

LOCATION	Four miles north of Half Moon Bay in the fishing village of Princeton-by-the-Sea.
OPEN	All year
DESCRIPTION	A 1996 two-story Cape Cod inn decorated with pine and wicker furniture and located directly on the water in scenic Princeton Harbor.
NO. OF ROOMS	All rooms with private bathrooms.
RATES	Rates are year-round. There is a two-night minimum stay during weekends.
CREDIT CARDS	American Express, MasterCard, Visa
BREAKFAST	Continental breakfast is delivered to the guestrooms and includes pastries, fresh fruit, bagels, orange juice, muffins.

Harbor House, Half Moon Bay

AMENITIES	Fresh flowers, coffee, tea, soda, bottled water, down comforters, fireplace in each room, deck, patio, TV, microwave, refrigerator, direct-dial phone.
RESTRICTIONS	No smoking
REVIEWED	*Frommer's*

MILL ROSE INN

615 Mill Street, Half Moon Bay, CA 94019   415-716-9794
WEBSITE *www.millroseinn.com*   800-829-1794

KUDOS/COMMENTS   "Beautiful gardens, comfortable rooms."

OLD THYME INN

779 Main Street, Half Moon Bay, CA 94019   650-726-1616
Rick & Kathy Ellis, Innkeepers   800-720-4277
Some French spoken   FAX 650-726-6394
EMAIL *innkeeper@oldthymeinn.com*   WEBSITE *www.oldthymeinn.com*

LOCATION	From San Francisco, take Highway 101 south for four miles to Highway 92 west. Follow Highway 92 approximately 10 miles over the coastal mountains into Half Moon Bay. Turn left at the first stoplight onto Main Street (Shell gas station on the corner) and go seven blocks.
OPEN	All year
DESCRIPTION	A fully restored 1899 two-story spindle-post Queen Anne Victorian inn furnished with antiques and fine art. Listed on the State Historic Register.
NO. OF ROOMS	Seven rooms with private bathrooms. Try the Garden Room.
RATES	Year-round rates are $90-220 for a single or double with a private bathroom. There is a minimum stay during weekends and cancellation requires 14 days' notice with a 10 percent fee.
CREDIT CARDS	American Express, Discover, MasterCard, Visa
BREAKFAST	Full breakfast is served in the dining room. A typical breakfast starts with a selection of teas or fresh-ground gourmet coffee, fruit juice, and fresh fruit, plus an entrée such as orange-pecan French toast, chile rellenos casserole, basil feather-bed eggs, cherry blintzes, scrambled egg tortilla with salsa, island eggs Benedict, orange or blueberry pancakes, or our popular John Wayne corn casserole. Your piping hot main course will likely be accompanied

	by home-baked bread, delicious muffin creations (maple-bran and raspberry-almond are favorites), scones, or Kathy's rosemary-lemon or apricot crumb cake, garnished with flowers (often edible) and herbs from the garden.
AMENITIES	TV/VCRs, cozy fireplaces, and/or luxurious double whirlpool tubs are available in four guestrooms; three rooms have old-fashioned clawfoot tubs; the romantic Garden Suite (honeymoon suite) has a private entrance off the garden, cathedral ceiling, skylights, a four-poster canopy bed, fireplace, two-person whirlpool tub, TV/VCR, stereo, and refrigerator; bottle of wine or champagne upon arrival.
RESTRICTIONS	No smoking, no pets, children over are 10 welcome. Jenny and Kerry are the resident dogs. "Jenny is a real 'people dog'—she takes her duties as official greeter very seriously."
MEMBER	California Association of Bed & Breakfast Inns, Professional Association of Innkeepers International, California Lodging Industry Association
RATED	AAA 2 Diamonds, Mobil 2 Stars, Best Places to Kiss 2.5 Lips
KUDOS/COMMENTS	"Good place to stay, friendly hosts." "Charming Queen Anne Victorian with fragrant English herb garden, fireplaces, whirlpool, tubs, and quiet downtown location."

PACIFIC VICTORIAN BED & BREAKFAST

325 Alameda Avenue, Half Moon Bay, CA 94019   650-712-3900

SAN BENITO HOUSE

356 Main Street, Half Moon Bay, CA 94019   650-726-3425

THE ZABALLA HOUSE BED & BREAKFAST

324 Main Street, Half Moon Bay, CA 94019   650-726-9123
Kerry Pendergast, Innkeeper   FAX 650-726-3921
EMAIL zaballa@coastside.net   WEBSITE www.whistler.com/zaballa

LOCATION	In beautiful downtown Half Moon Bay, one block south of Highway 92 and four blocks east of Highway 1.
OPEN	All year

DESCRIPTION	An 1859 two-story Victorian, decorated with Victorian furnishings and surrounded by gardens.
NO. OF ROOMS	Twenty-three rooms with private bathrooms, including three suites with private entrances.
RATES	Year-round rates are $75-170 for a single or double and $140-210 for a suite; midweek rates are slightly less. There is no minimum stay and cancellation requires 72 hours' notice.
CREDIT CARDS	American Express, Discover, MasterCard, Visa
BREAKFAST	Full breakfast is served buffet style in the dining room.
AMENITIES	Fresh flowers in all rooms, wine and cheese served in the parlor in the evenings, some rooms have two-person whirlpool tubs and fireplaces.
RESTRICTIONS	No smoking, children and pets are welcome.
REVIEWED	Bed, Breakfast and Bike—Northern California; Northern California Best Places; Karen Brown's California Country Inns & Itineraries; The Best Places to Kiss in Northern California; Country Inns and Backroads: California
MEMBER	Professional Association of Innkeepers International, California Lodging Industry Association
RATED	Mobil 2 Stars

HEALDSBURG

This is one tourist town whose charm seems completely unforced. Boutiques and bakeries surround a pretty, tree-lined plaza where you can sit and read the newspaper while munching on pastries from the marvelous Downtown Bakery & Creamery. In the summer, nothing beats paddling down the glorious Russian River past vineyards and secret swimming holes. If you're in need of a respite from your hectic day trips, catch a flick at the Raven Theater, the Wine Country's best movie house for new releases and art films. About 70 miles north of San Francisco via Highway 1. Be here for the main event: Russian River Wine Festival in mid-May.

BELLE DE JOUR INN

16276 Healdsburg Avenue, Healdsburg, CA 95448 707-431-9777
Tom & Brenda Hearn, Resident Owners FAX 707-431-7412
WEBSITE www.belledejourinn.com

LOCATION	On Highway 101 north of San Francisco, take the Dry Creek Road exit, turn right and go to the second traffic light, turn left on Healdsburg Avenue and continue one mile. The Simi Winery visitor center is on the left. Turn right up the tree-lined drive.

OPEN	All year
DESCRIPTION	An 1870s Italianate farmhouse, cottages, and carriage house with California country furnishings, located on 6 acres.
NO. OF ROOMS	Five rooms with private bathrooms. Brenda recommends the Carriage House.
RATES	Year-round rates are $150-200 for a single or double and a suite is $275. There is a two-night minimum stay when a Saturday is included, three nights on major holidays. Cancellation requires 14 days' notice with a $20 fee.
CREDIT CARDS	American Express, MasterCard, Visa
BREAKFAST	Full breakfast is served in the farmhouse dining room and includes house-blend coffee, latte, cappuccino, tea, juice, fresh fruit, home-baked breads and sweets, quiche, frittatas, omelets, tarts, and specialty dishes.
AMENITIES	Flowers, robes, stereos, hair dryers, telephone, refrigerators, bottled water, candy, gas fireplaces, whirlpool tubs for two, steam shower, hammocks, picnic table.
RESTRICTIONS	No smoking, no pets, children are not encouraged. The resident cats are Beast, Zubie, and Ivan.
REVIEWED	*Fodor's B&B California; Northern California Wine Country Access; Karen Brown's California Country Inns & Itineraries; Bed & Breakfast Guide California; Away for the Weekend; The Best Places to Kiss in Northern California; The Napa & Sonoma Book; Weekends for Two in Northern California; The Best Places to Kiss in Northern California*
MEMBER	California Association of Bed & Breakfast Inns
KUDOS/COMMENTS	"Four very nice cottage-type accommodations." "Immaculate surroundings, friendly innkeepers, and excellent homemade food."

CALDERWOOD INN

25 West Grant Street, Healdsburg, CA 95448   707-431-1110
Jennifer & Paul Zawodny, Resident Owners
WEBSITE *www.calderwoodinn.com*

LOCATION	Exactly 65 miles north of the Golden Gate Bridge. Off Highway 101 north, take the Central Healdsberg exit, go exactly one mile north on Healdsberg Avenue to Grant Street, turn right (west), and go one block.
OPEN	All year

DESCRIPTION	A 1902 three-and-a-half-story Queen Anne Victorian inn with elegant yet comfortable Victorian decor, large porches with wicker rockers and swings, lush gardens, fountains, koi ponds, and ancient cypress and redwood trees.
NO. OF ROOMS	Six rooms with private bathrooms. Jennifer and Paul recommend the Springkell Room.
RATES	Year-round rates are $135-185 for a single or double. There is a minimum stay of two nights on weekends and three nights on holiday weekends. Cancellation requires seven days' notice.
CREDIT CARDS	No
BREAKFAST	Full breakfast is served in the dining room and includes house specialties accompanied by fresh-baked goods, fresh fruit dishes, house-blend coffees, and teas.
AMENITIES	Air-conditioned rooms with either clawfoot or whirlpool tubs; sunny, plush window seats; overstuffed chairs; four-poster beds and fireplaces in some rooms; player piano; appetizers; wine and port in the evenings.
RESTRICTIONS	No smoking, no pets. Blue is the resident Lab/husky mix.
REVIEWED	*The Best Places to Kiss in Northern California*
MEMBER	California Lodging Industry Association, California Association of Bed & Breakfast Inns

CAMELLIA INN

211 North Street, Healdsburg, CA 95448　　　707-433-8182
Del, Ray, & Lucy Lewand, Resident Owners　　800-727-8182
WEBSITE *www.camelliainn.com*　　　　　　　　FAX 707-433-8130

LOCATION	Take Highway 101 north to the Central Healdsburg exit. At the fourth traffic light, turn right on North Street; the inn is two-and-a-half blocks on the left.
OPEN	All year
DESCRIPTION	An 1869 two-story Victorian Italianate inn with antique furnishings.
NO. OF ROOMS	Nine rooms with private bathrooms. The most popular room is the Tower West.
RATES	Year-round rates are $80-175 for a single or double; the suite is $145. There is a minimum stay when Saturday is involved and cancellation requires seven days' notice.
CREDIT CARDS	American Express, MasterCard, Visa

HEALDSBURG

BREAKFAST	Full breakfast is served in the dining room and includes beverages, fresh fruit, yogurt, juice, cereal, fresh sourdough goods, and a main dish such as quiche.
AMENITIES	Fresh flowers, afternoon beverages and snacks by the swimming pool in the summer, evening beverages in the winter, tubs for two and fireplaces in several rooms, special events such as a Robert Burns Dinner.
RESTRICTIONS	No smoking indoors, no pets
REVIEWED	America's Wonderful Little Inns & Hotels; The Best Places to Kiss in Northern California; Weekends for Two in Northern California: 50 Romantic Getaways
MEMBER	Professional Association of Innkeepers International, California Association of Bed & Breakfast Inns, Wine Country Inns of Sonoma
KUDOS/COMMENTS	"Beautiful rooms with fireplaces, whirlpool tubs, and lovely gardens"

FRAMPTON HOUSE

489 Powell Avenue, Healdsburg, CA 95448　　　　　707-433-5084

THE GEORGE ALEXANDER HOUSE

423 Matheson Street, Healdsburg, CA 95448　　　　707-433-1358
Phyllis & Christian Baldenhofer, Resident Owners　　800-310-1358
WEBSITE *www.georgealexanderhouse.com*　　　　FAX 707-433-1367

LOCATION	Take the Central Healdsburg exit off Highway 101 and drive 0.5 mile to the third traffic light. Turn right onto Matheson Street.
OPEN	All year; closed Thanksgiving through Christmas
DESCRIPTION	A 1905 two-story late Queen Anne with Victorian furnishings.
NO. OF ROOMS	Four rooms with private bathrooms.
RATES	Please call for current rates and cancellation information.
CREDIT CARDS	MasterCard, Visa
BREAKFAST	Full breakfast is served in the dining room and includes beverages, fresh fruit, homebaked breads, a main dish, plus side dishes such as potatoes with baked eggs.

AMENITIES	Robes, mineral water, juice in the refrigerator, bathroom basket, and two guest parlors.
RESTRICTIONS	No smoking, no pets, resident cats are Moose and Magic.
REVIEWED	Bed & Breakfast California, America's Wonderful Little Hotels & Inns
MEMBER	California Association of Bed & Breakfast Inns
KUDOS/COMMENTS	"Beautifully restored Victorian with exceptional baths. Exceptionally creative breakfasts."

GRAPE LEAF INN

539 Johnson Street, Healdsburg, CA 95448 707-433-8140
Terry & Karen Sweet, Resident Owners FAX 707-433-3140
WEBSITE www.grapeleafinn.com

LOCATION	From Highway 101 take the Healdsburg exit. Grape Leaf is on the corner of Johnson and Grant Streets.
OPEN	All year except Christmas Eve and Christmas Day.
DESCRIPTION	A beautifully restored turn-of-the-century Queen Anne Victorian home decorated with classic, comfortable period furnishings.
NO. OF ROOMS	Seven rooms have private bathrooms.
RATES	Year-round rates are $95-165 for a double. There is a minimum stay of two nights on most weekends. Cancellation requires seven days' notice.
CREDIT CARDS	Discover, MasterCard, Visa
BREAKFAST	Full breakfast, served in the dining room, includes egg dishes, breakfast meats, roasted red potatoes, fresh breads, muffins, and coffee.
AMENITIES	Wraparound porch, five rooms with whirlpool baths for two, complimentary selection of Sonoma County wines served each evening with an assortment of cheeses and French bread.
RESTRICTIONS	No smoking, no pets. Children over 11 are welcome. A tribe of lovable Labradors includes Smokey and Jasmine (a.k.a. "Jazzy Girl").
REVIEWED	Bed & Breakfast in California, America's Wonderful Little Hotels & Inns, Where to Stay in Northern California, Recommended Country Inns—West Coast
MEMBER	California Association of Bed & Breakfast Inns, California Lodging Industry Association

HAYDON STREET INN

321 Haydon Street, Healdsburg, CA 95448
Richard & Joanne Claus, Resident Owners
Some Spanish spoken
WEBSITE www.haydon.com

707-433-5228
800-528-3703
FAX 707-433-6637

LOCATION	Take Highway 101 north to the Central Healdsburg exit. Take Healdsburg Avenue to Matheson and turn right. Go three blocks to Fetch, turn right, drive two blocks, and turn left onto Hayden.
OPEN	All year except December 15 through January 1
DESCRIPTION	A 1912 two-story Victorian Craftsman inn and cottage furnished with antiques.
NO. OF ROOMS	Eight rooms with private bathrooms.
RATES	Year-round rates are $95-170 for a double.
CREDIT CARDS	MasterCard, Visa
BREAKFAST	Full country breakfast is served in the dining room.
AMENITIES	Wine and cheese in the parlor, large front porch with wicker furniture, ceiling fans, whirlpool tubs for two under skylights.
RESTRICTIONS	No smoking, no pets. The resident dog is named Cody.
MEMBER	California Association of Bed & Breakfast Inns

HEALDSBURG INN ON THE PLAZA

110 Matheson Street, Healdsburg, CA 95448
Genny Jenkins, Innkeeper
WEBSITE www.healdsburginn.com

707-433-6991
800-431-8663
FAX 707-433-9513

LOCATION	Located on the south side of the Healdsburg town square. From San Francisco, take Highway 101 across the Golden Gate Bridge and continue north about 70 miles. Take the Central Healdsburg exit, go north to the third stoplight, and turn right on Matheson Street. The inn is the third building on the right.
OPEN	All year
DESCRIPTION	A 1900 two-story Victorian inn with Victorian furnishings. The hotel is on both the National and State Historic Registers.
NO. OF ROOMS	Ten rooms with private bathrooms. Pick Song of the Rose.

RATES	Weekend rates are $185-255 for a single or double. Midweek rates are $115-195 for a single or double. There is a minimum stay from July through November and during holiday weekends. Rooms must be guaranteed with a credit card and cancellation requires three days' notice.
CREDIT CARDS	MasterCard, Visa
BREAKFAST	Full breakfast is served in the dining room and includes cereal and milk, yogurt, breads for toasting, muffins, hot egg and cheese dish, potatoes or sausage, juice, fresh seasonal fruit, and beverages.
AMENITIES	Afternoon wine and popcorn, bottomless cookie jar, soft drinks, bottled water, central heat and air conditioning, video library, fireplaces in nine rooms, TV/VCR in all rooms, room telephones, old-fashioned tubs for two, fluffy towels, rubber duckies.
RESTRICTIONS	No smoking, no pets, children over seven are welcome in certain rooms by prior arrangement.
REVIEWED	*Karen Brown's California: Charming Inns & Itineraries; America's Favorite Inns, B&Bs, & Small Hotels*
MEMBER	Professional Association of Innkeepers International, California Association of Bed & Breakfast Inns, California Lodging Industry Association, California Hotel and Motel Association

Honor Mansion

14891 Grove Street, Healdsburg, CA 95448　　　　707-433-4277
WEBSITE *www.honormansion.com*

Madrona Manor

1001 Westside Road, Healdsburg, CA 95448　　　　707-433-4231
John & Carol Muir, Resident Owners　　　　800-258-4003
Spanish spoken　　　　FAX 707-433-4003
WEBSITE *www.madronamanor.com*

LOCATION	From Highway 101, take the Central Healdsburg exit and travel north on Healdsburg Avenue. Where three streets come together—Healdsburg Avenue, Vine, and Mill—turn sharply left onto Mill. Less than one mile from town, you'll see the arches.
OPEN	All year
DESCRIPTION	An 1881 three-story Gothic Victorian with eclectic furnishings, located on 8 landscaped, wooded acres.

NO. OF ROOMS	Twenty-one rooms with private bathrooms.
RATES	Year-round rates are $165-230 for a single or double. Suites are $225-265. A minimum stay is required from April through November. There is a five-day cancellation policy, plus a $10 cancellation fee.
CREDIT CARDS	American Express, Diners Club, Discover, MasterCard, Visa
BREAKFAST	Full breakfast, served in the dining room, includes fresh juices, hot cereal, homemade granola, eggs, cheeses, meats, pastries, coffee, and tea. Sunday brunch is served and dinner is available seven nights a week.
AMENITIES	Fresh flowers, robes, swimming pool, fresh-baked chocolate chip cookies, champagne for anniversary guests, handicapped accessible, meeting facilities, air conditioning, phones.
RESTRICTIONS	No smoking, no pets
REVIEWED	*Karen Brown's California Country Inns & Itineraries*, *The Best Places to Kiss in Northern California*, *Elegant Small Hotels*
MEMBER	Professional Association of Innkeepers International, Independent Innkeepers Association
KUDOS/COMMENTS	"Beautiful grounds, lovely manor house, excellent restaurant."

THE RAFORD HOUSE

10630 Wohler Road, Healdsburg, CA 95448   707-887-9573
Carole & Jack Vore, Resident Owners   FAX 707-887-9597

LOCATION	Three miles north of Santa Rosa, take the River Road exit from Highway 101 and drive west 7.5 miles to Wohler Road.
OPEN	All year except Christmas weekend
DESCRIPTION	An 1880s two-story Victorian summer house on 4 acres, surrounded by rose gardens and towering palm trees. Listed on the Sonoma County Historic Register.
NO. OF ROOMS	Five rooms with private bathrooms and two rooms share a bathroom. The Bridal Suite is a gem.
RATES	Please call for current rates and cancellation information.
CREDIT CARDS	American Express, Discover, MasterCard, Visa
BREAKFAST	Full breakfast is served in the dining room.
AMENITIES	Two rooms have fireplaces, evening refreshments and local wines served in the common area.
RESTRICTIONS	No smoking, no pets, children are not encouraged.

REVIEWED	Country Inns of America—California; Bed and Breakfast California; The Official Guide to American Historic Bed & Breakfast Inns and Guesthouses
MEMBER	Professional Association of Innkeepers International, California Association of Bed & Breakfast Inns

VILLA MESSINA

316 Burgundy Road, Healdsburg, CA 95448 707-433-6655
Jerry Messina, Resident Owner FAX 707-433-4515
WEBSITE *www.villamessina.com*

LOCATION	Take Highway 101 to the Dry Creek Road exit. Go east to the second stoplight and turn left on Healdsburg Avenue. Go one block after the first stoplight and turn left on Chiquita Road. Proceed under the freeway and take the first right on Burgundy Road. At the divide, turn left; the villa is the second driveway on the right.
OPEN	All year
DESCRIPTION	A 1987 two-story villa with antique and contemporary furnishings.
NO. OF ROOMS	Six rooms with private bathrooms. The Master Bedroom Suite is the best in the house.
RATES	Year-round rates for a double are $150-280. There is a two-night minimum stay on weekends and seven days' notice is required for cancellation.
CREDIT CARDS	American Express, Diners Club, Discover, MasterCard, Visa
BREAKFAST	Full breakfast is served.
AMENITIES	Flowers, robes, telephones, TV in rooms, meeting facilities, afternoon snack.
RESTRICTIONS	No smoking, no pets. The resident critters are a Rottweiler, Max; Jucinda the potbellied pig; and llamas Cancun and Zorba.
MEMBER	California Association of Bed & Breakfast Inns
KUDOS/COMMENTS	"Spectacular house and views; fun, gregarious innkeepers."

HOPE VALLEY

SORENSEN'S RESORT

14255 Highway 88, Hope Valley, CA 96120 530-694-2203
WEBSITE *www.virtualcities.com* 800-423-9949

HOPLAND

If you're heading through inland Mendocino County, stop here for a respite. This may be wine country, but teeny Hopland—named for the hops once grown in the area—offers a good brew. Head over to the Hopland Indian Rancheria for high-stakes bingo. Located on Highway 101, Hopland is 13 miles south of Ukiah.

THATCHER INN AND RESTAURANT, AN 1890 BED & BREAKFAST

13401 South Highway 101, Hopland, CA 95449   707-744-1890
Don & Marlena Sacca, Innkeepers   800-266-1891
EMAIL info@thatcherinn.com   FAX 707-744-1219
WEBSITE www.thatcherinn.com

LOCATION	One hundred miles north of San Francisco on Highway 101.
OPEN	All year
DESCRIPTION	An 1890 three-story Victorian country inn with Victorian furnishings, located in Mendocino's wine country.
NO. OF ROOMS	Twenty rooms with private bathrooms.
RATES	April through December, rates are $130 for a single or double and $150-180 for a suite. January through March, rates are $95-110 for a single or double and $130-150 for a suite. There is a minimum stay on high-season weekends and on holidays. Cancellation requires one week's notice (two weeks for holidays).
CREDIT CARDS	American Express, MasterCard, Visa
BREAKFAST	Full breakfast is served in the dining room and includes seasonal fruit, fruit juice, coffee, tea, eggs, meats, and breads. Dinner and special meals are available in the restaurant.
AMENITIES	Monogrammed robes, swimming pool (summer only), air conditioners and swamp coolers, 4,000-volume English library, lobby bar with a large selection of single-malt Scotch whiskey, private parties for up to 75 may be arranged, meeting area for up to 35.
RESTRICTIONS	No smoking, no pets
REVIEWED	*Complete Guide to Bed & Breakfast Inns and Guesthouses*
MEMBER	California Association of Bed & Breakfast Inns, American Bed & Breakfast Association
RATED	AAA 2 Diamonds, ABBA 4 Crowns

INVERNESS

Inverness is on the Point Reyes Peninsula and Tomales Bay, at the entrance to the most stunning part of Point Reyes National Seashore. Explore the half-moon beach and secret coves of the Bay and visit the oyster farms, for which the town is noted. From San Francisco, head north on Highway 1 and Point Reyes Road.

THE ARK

180 Highland Avenue, Inverness, CA 94937　　　415-663-9338
Jim Van der Ryn, Resident Owner　　　800-808-9338
Spanish spoken
EMAIL rosemarybb@aol.com
WEBSITE www.rosemarybb.com

LOCATION	From Highway 101, take the San Anselmo/Sir Francis Drake Boulevard exit. Go west 25 miles to Olema. Turn north on Highway 1, go one block, and turn left on Bear Valley Road. Go 2.3 miles to the end of the road and turn left at the stop sign onto Sir Francis Drake Boulevard. Go three miles to Inverness, turn left, go three blocks, and turn left onto Highland Avenue.
OPEN	All year
DESCRIPTION	A 1971 rustic cottage furnished with an eclectic collection of original art and weavings.
NO. OF ROOMS	Two-bedroom cottage with private bathroom. The cottage sleeps six.
RATES	Year-round rate for a double is $142 ($21 per additional person up to four). Discount of 20 percent during midweek from November through May. Cancellation requires 10 days' notice with a $20 fee.
CREDIT CARDS	No
BREAKFAST	The cottage is stocked with fresh seasonal fruit, granola, yogurt, local organic milk, home-raised eggs, pastries, home-baked bread, homemade jam, and beverages.
AMENITIES	Flowers, phone, TV, wood-burning stove, fireplace, kitchen, picnic and barbecue area, stereo, small book collection, games.
RESTRICTIONS	No smoking indoors
REVIEWED	Bed & Breakfast California
MEMBER	California Association of Bed & Breakfast Inns

BAYSHORE COTTAGE

12732 Sir Francis Drake Boulevard, Inverness, CA 94937   415-669-1148
Mare M. Hansen, Resident Owner
French spoken
WEBSITE *www.innformation.com/ca/bayshore*

LOCATION	Three-quarters-of-a-mile south of Inverness, directly on Tomales Bay. It is 3.1 miles northwest of the intersection of Sir Francis Drake Boulevard and Highway 1 at Point Reyes Station.
OPEN	All year
DESCRIPTION	A 1988 Cape Cod cottage with painted knotty pine walls and hardwood floors, located in a garden setting on Tomales Bay.
NO. OF ROOMS	One cottage with private bathroom.
RATES	Year-round rate for the cottage is $125. There is a two-night minimum stay on weekends and cancellation requires ten days' notice with a $15 fee.
CREDIT CARDS	No
BREAKFAST	Cottage kitchen is stocked with a variety of juices, fresh fruit basket, hot and cold cereal, pancake mix, yogurt, eggs, bagels, English muffins, and beverages.
AMENITIES	Down quilts and pillows, flowers, candles, outdoor hot tub, pier and gazebo, sherry, adjacent library with TV/VCR, books, binoculars.
RESTRICTIONS	No smoking, no pets

BLACKTHORNE INN

266 Vallejo Avenue, Inverness, CA 94956   415-663-8621
Susan Wigert, Resident Owner
WEBSITE *www.blackthorneinn.com*

KUDOS/COMMENTS   "Very interesting and unusual. Excellent hospitality. Romantic."

Dancing Coyote Beach

12794 Sir Francis Drake Boulevard, Inverness, CA 94937   415-669-7200
Bobbi Stumpf & Sherry King, Resident Managers   FAX 415-663-8275

LOCATION	Just south of the village of Point Reyes Station, turn off Highway 1 onto Sir Francis Drake Boulevard and go four miles to the village of Inverness. The inn is at the north end of Inverness on the right.
OPEN	All year
DESCRIPTION	Four 1972 two-story cottages with cathedral ceilings, contemporary furnishings, and views of Tomales Bay.
NO. OF ROOMS	Four cottages with private bathrooms.
RATES	Year-round rates are $100-135 for a single or double. There is a two-night minimum stay on weekends and cancellation requires 10 days' notice with a $20 fee.
CREDIT CARDS	No
BREAKFAST	Each cottage kitchen is stocked with food, including eggs, yogurt, granola, breakfast butter, jams, and beverages.
AMENITIES	Private beach on Tomales Bay, beach furniture, picnic tables, barbecue on beach, robes, each cottage has a fireplace, skylight, deck, and fully equipped kitchen.
RESTRICTIONS	No smoking in cottages, pets welcome with prior arrangement. Josephine the cat chooses a cottage to stay in each night.
REVIEWED	*The Best Places to Kiss in Northern California*, *Northern California Best Places*

Fairwinds Farm Cottage

82 Drake's Summit, Inverness, CA 94937   415-663-9454
Joyce H. Goldfield, Resident Owner   FAX 415-663-1787
Sign language

LOCATION	From Point Reyes Station, turn right over the green bridge and take the next immediate right (sign reads "Inverness"). Go one mile and when the road curves to the right, start looking on your left for two white houses and a school bus stop. Turn left up Balboa and go two miles to the dead end. The Fairwinds Farm Cottage driveway is directly to your right.
OPEN	All year
DESCRIPTION	A 1964 carriage house furnished with oak antiques and surrounded by 75,000 acres of wilderness.

NO. OF ROOMS	One large cottage with a private bathroom.
RATES	Year-round rate for the entire cottage is $135 for a double ($25 for each additional person). Stay for seven nights and pay for six. There is a two-night minimum stay on weekends and cancellation requires 14 days' notice.
CREDIT CARDS	No
BREAKFAST	Full breakfast is stocked in the cottage kitchen. Provisions include muffins, breads, scones, bacon, eggs, cheese, onions, garlic, herbs, waffles, and beverages.
AMENITIES	Evening snacks provided, flowers, robes, hot tub with ocean view, TV/VCR, over 400 movies, stereo, garden with giant pine trees, two-person swing, ponds with fish and waterfalls, separate child's playhouse filled with toys, large library, musical instruments.
RESTRICTIONS	No smoking, no pets, children of all ages welcome. Resident animals include donkeys, horses, dogs, cats, and an Angora goat.
MEMBER	Coastal Lodging Association

HOTEL INVERNESS

25 Park Avenue, Inverness, CA 94937　　　　　　　　415-669-7393
Susie & Tom Simms, Innkeepers　　　　　　　　FAX 415-669-1702
EMAIL desk@hotelinverness.com　　WEBSITE www.hotelinverness.com

LOCATION	Enter Inverness heading north on Sir Francis Drake Boulevard. Turn left on the second road (careful; they're both named Inverness Way). Go half-a-block to Park Avenue and turn right. The hotel is beyond the library and museum at the corner. Parking is provided in front.
OPEN	All year
DESCRIPTION	A 1906 two-story shingle-style hotel with California eclectic decor, located on parklike grounds in the historic section of this coastal village.
NO. OF ROOMS	Five rooms with private bathrooms.
RATES	Year-round rates are $110-175 for a single or double. There is a minimum stay during weekends and holidays, and cancellation requires seven days' notice plus a $10 fee.
CREDIT CARDS	MasterCard, Visa
BREAKFAST	Continental plus is served in the guestrooms or outside on the deck and includes coffee or tea, fruit juice, fresh-baked muffins or an egg dish (varies daily), and fresh fruit.

RESTRICTIONS	No smoking, no pets
REVIEWED	The Best Places to Kiss in Northern California
MEMBER	California Association of Bed & Breakfast Inns

LAUREL RIDGE COTTAGE INN

217 Laurel Street, Inverness, CA 94937   415-663-9584
Irwin Segal & Janet Attard, Innkeeper
Fluent Spanish spoken

LOCATION	Laurel Street is a private road two miles from Point Reyes Station, west on Sir Francis Drake Boulevard. Our cottage is 0.5 mile to the west of Drake Boulevard on Inverness Ridge.
OPEN	All year
DESCRIPTION	A 1992 contemporary rustic cottage decorated with antique furnishings.
NO. OF ROOMS	One room with a private bathroom.
RATES	The cottage rents for $150-160 per day and includes kitchenette, living area, bedroom, and bathroom.
CREDIT CARDS	No
BREAKFAST	Continental plus is brought to the cottage and includes rolls, eggs, cereals, and beverages.
AMENITIES	Fresh fruit, hot tub, daily maid service, flowers, robes, cable TV and stereo, lounge chairs on two decks overlooking a canyon, wood-burning stove.
RESTRICTIONS	No smoking, no pets

MARSH COTTAGE BED & BREAKFAST

PO Box 1121, Point Reyes Station, CA 94956   415-669 7168
WEBSITE www.marshcottage.com

INVERNESS

PATTERSON HOUSE

12847 Sir Francis Drake Boulevard, Inverness, CA 94937   415-669-1383
Rosalie Patterson, Resident Owner
Spanish, French, and German spoken
WEBSITE *www.visitormags.com/patterson/*

LOCATION	Across from the Inverness Yacht Club and Tomales Bay.
OPEN	All year
DESCRIPTION	A 1916 Craftsman inn with comfortable furnishings, antiques, and porches and decks overlooking Tomales Bay.
NO. OF ROOMS	Five rooms with private bathrooms. Room 1 features the best view.
RATES	Year-round weekend rates are $135-185 for a single or double and $75-125 during midweek. There is a two-night minimum on weekends and during holidays. Ask about a cancellation policy.
CREDIT CARDS	Discover, MasterCard, Visa
BREAKFAST	Full breakfast is served on weekends and continental plus on weekdays. Breakfast is served in the dining room and might include fresh seasonal fruit, waffles, pancakes, eggs, quiche, bacon, ham, croissants, pastries, and beverages. The menu changes daily.
AMENITIES	Fresh flowers, hot tub on deck, clawfoot bathtubs, two rooms with private porches, king- and queen-size beds, phone and fax, common room with stone fireplace.
RESTRICTIONS	No smoking inside, no pets, children over 10 are welcome on weekdays.

ROSEMARY COTTAGE

75 Balboa Avenue, Inverness, CA 94937   415-663-9338
Suzanne Storch, Resident Owner   800-808-9338
Spanish spoken
EMAIL *rosemarybb@aol.com*
WEBSITE *www.rosemarybb.com*

LOCATION	From Highway 101, take the San Anselmo-Sir Francis Drake Boulevard exit. Drive west 25 miles to Olema. Turn right (north) onto Route 1, turn left onto Bear Valley Road, and drive 2.3 miles to the stop sign. Turn left, go one block, and turn left onto Balboa Avenue.
OPEN	All year

DESCRIPTION	A 1987 French country cottage with some antiques and oriental rugs.
NO. OF ROOMS	A two-room cottage with a private bathroom.
RATES	Year-round rate for a double is $192 ($21 per extra person). Twenty percent discount available during Sunday through Thursday from November through May. Cancellation requires 10 days' notice with a $20 fee.
CREDIT CARDS	No
BREAKFAST	Continental plus provisions are stocked in the cottage including fresh fruit, granola, home-raised eggs, yogurt, pastries, home-baked bread, homemade jam, and beverages.
AMENITIES	Flowers, herb garden, wood-burning stove, telephone, TV, AM/FM radio and tape player, games, small book collection, binoculars, hot tub, barbecue and picnic area, large deck, well-equipped kitchen.
RESTRICTIONS	No smoking inside. Fluffy is the resident outdoor cat.

SANDY COVE INN

12990 Sir Francis Drake Boulevard, Inverness, CA 94937   415-669-2683
Kathy & Gerry Coles, Resident Owners   800-759-2683
Spanish, German, and Italian spoken   FAX 415-669-7511
EMAIL innkeeper@sandycove.com   WEBSITE www.sandycove.com

LOCATION	One mile past the town of Inverness on Tomales Bay.
OPEN	All year
DESCRIPTION	A 1986 two-story beachfront Cape Cod inn with Nantucket Island ambiance and original artwork.
NO. OF ROOMS	Three rooms with private bathrooms.
RATES	June through October, rates are $185-250 for a single or double. November through January, rates are $145-250 for a single or double. Midseason is February through May; call for specific rates during midseason. There is a minimum stay during weekends and high season, and cancellation requires 14 days' notice with a $15 per night fee.
CREDIT CARDS	American Express, Diners Club, Discover, JCB, MasterCard, Visa
BREAKFAST	Full breakfast is served with a morning paper in front of the fire, in the guestrooms, or in the solarium, and might include organic apple pancakes, strawberry frappé, and fresh-baked goods. Breakfast is prepared using herbs and organic produce from the garden. Menu varies with the season. Dietary restrictions are respected and picnic baskets are available if ordered in advance.

AMENITIES	Terry robes and slippers, private telephones, cheese and complimentary beverages, fresh flowers and fruit, chilled champagne and chocolates on arrival, CD player, tapes, radio, library and fireplace in room, private deck, fluffy beach towels, beach chairs, backpacks, walking sticks, sitting area in each room, massage available, stocked refrigerator.
RESTRICTIONS	No smoking anywhere, no pets, children under one are welcome. Spots is the resident cat, Chewy is the quarter horse, Truffles is the Shetland pony, Bummer and Beed are are Dorset sheep. They are "great for reducing blood pressure."
REVIEWED	*The Best Places to Kiss in Northern California; Karen Brown's California Country Inns & Itineraries; Adventure Guide to Northern California; Recommended Bed & Breakfasts California; Hidden San Francisco and Northern California; America's Favorite Inns, B&Bs, & Small Hotels*
MEMBER	Professional Association of Innkeepers International, California Association of Bed & Breakfast Inns
RATED	Mobil 2 Stars, Best Places to Kiss in Northern California 4 Lips
AWARDS	Made the cover of the California Association of Bed & Breakfast Inns Directory for 1999

TEN INVERNESS WAY

10 Inverness Way, Inverness, CA 94937   415-669-1648
Teri Mowery, Resident Owner   FAX 415-669-7403
WEBSITE *www.teninvernessway.com*

LOCATION	From Olema, turn right on Highway 1, then left on Bear Valley Road. Drive three miles to the stop sign. Turn left and drive four miles to Inverness. Turn left at the second sign for Inverness Way and look for the inn's sign on the right.
OPEN	All year
DESCRIPTION	A 1904 two-story California redwood shingle decorated with antiques.
NO. OF ROOMS	Five rooms with private bathrooms. Check out the Garden Suite.
RATES	Year-round rates are $125-165 for a single or double. There is a two-night minimum stay on weekends and a seven-day cancellation policy.
CREDIT CARDS	MasterCard, Visa
BREAKFAST	Full breakfast is served in the dining room.
AMENITIES	Fresh flowers, robes, homemade cookies, hot tub in the garden.

RESTRICTIONS	No smoking, no pets, children of all ages are welcome.
REVIEWED	Karen Brown's California Country Inns & Itineraries, Recommended Country Inns—West Coast
MEMBER	Professional Association of Innkeepers International
KUDOS/COMMENTS	"Comfortable, homey, relaxing atmosphere and simple comforts."

THE TREE HOUSE

73 Drake Summit, Inverness, CA 94937
Lisa Patsel, Innkeeper
Italian spoken

415-663-8720
FAX 415-663-8720

LOCATION	Exactly 1.5 miles off the main road, three miles from the center of town.
OPEN	All year
DESCRIPTION	A 1975 contemporary host home located on Inverness Ridge.
NO. OF ROOMS	Three rooms with private bathrooms and one two-bedroom cottage. Lisa likes the Queen's Quarters.
RATES	Year-round rates are $110-145 for a single or a double, and $165 for the cottage. There is a midweek discount and a minimum stay. Cancellation requires five days' notice.
CREDIT CARDS	MasterCard, Visa
BREAKFAST	Continental plus is served in the dining room and includes juices, coffee, fresh seasonal fruit, croissants, muffins, jams, toast, eggs, and bacon.
AMENITIES	Telephones, TV, candy, hot tub in garden, homemade wine, deck with views of Point Reyes Station and surrounding hills.
RESTRICTIONS	No smoking. There are all sorts of resident critters including three cats, three dogs, and two parrots.

IONE

This tiny Gold Country town is home to the new Mule Creek State Prison. The gloomy Preston School of Industry, now an historic monument (and appropriately condemned), was the state's first reform school. Ione is close to Jackson and in the vicinity of Camanche and Pardee Reservoirs and Lake Amador. It is southeast of Sacramento via Highways 16 and 124.

THE HEIRLOOM

214 Shakeley Lane, Ione, CA 95640   209-274-4468
Melisande Hubbs & Patricia Cross, Resident Owners   888-628-7896
WEBSITE www.theheirloominn.com

LOCATION	At the intersection of Highway 124 and Highway 104, go west on Shakeley Lane (Highway 124 becomes Shakeley Lane). The B&B is about 500 feet down on the left.
OPEN	All year except Thanksgiving, Christmas Eve, and Christmas Day
DESCRIPTION	An 1863 two-story Southern antebellum Greek revival inn with columns and balconies, dedicated as an Historic Landmark by California Native Sons of the Golden West.
NO. OF ROOMS	Four rooms with private bathrooms and two rooms with a shared bathroom. Melisande recommends the Winter Room.
RATES	Year-round rates are $85-98 for a single or double with a private bathroom and $65 for a single or double with a shared bathroom. The two-room adobe cottage rents for $95 for each room. Ask about a minimum stay. Cancellation requires 72 hours' notice.
CREDIT CARDS	American Express, MasterCard, Visa
BREAKFAST	Full breakfast is served in the dining room, on the balcony, or in the garden and includes fresh-squeezed orange juice and other beverages, fresh seasonal fruit, breads, and hot entrées such as soufflés, crepes, or eggs Benedict. Dietary restrictions are accommodated on request.
AMENITIES	Afternoon refreshments, gardens with glider and hammocks, croquet, fireplaces and wood-burning stoves, flowers, fruit and candy in rooms, grand piano, bath sheets.
RESTRICTIONS	No smoking, no pets
REVIEWED	*Recommended Country Inns—West Coast; Best Places to Stay in Northern California; The National Trust Guide to Historic Bed & Breakfasts, Inns, and Small Hotels; Bed & Breakfast USA; The Best Places to Kiss in Northern California*
MEMBER	California Association of Bed & Breakfast Inns, Bed & Breakfast Innkeepers of Amador County

KUDOS/COMMENTS "Gracious hospitality, conscientious innkeepers, excellent breakfast." "Innkeepers Pat and Melisande are the heart of their lovely home—great cooks, delightful hosts." "Probably the most comfortable place we have ever stayed." "Southern antebellum circa 1863 offers spacious serenity, English garden, fireplaces, balconies, creative cuisine, and historic area with golf and wineries."

JACKSON

Just beyond an enormous Georgia Pacific lumber mill lies Jackson, the seat of Amador County. Jackson hides most of its rowdy past behind modern facades, but old-timers know the town (once called "Little Reno") as the last place in California to outlaw prostitution. A sight Gold Rush buffs shouldn't miss is the Amador County Museum, which has scale models of the local hard-rock mines. There's also Kennedy Tailing Wheels Park, site of the Kennedy and Argonaut Mines, the Mother Lode's deepest. The park is home to the white, picturesque St. Sava's Servian Orthodox Church, built in 1894 and surrounded by a cemetery.

COURT STREET INN

215 Court Street, Jackson, CA 95642　　209-223-0416
Nancy & David Butow, Resident Owners　　800-200-0416
WEBSITE www.courtstreetinn.com　　FAX 209-223-5429

LOCATION	Two blocks west on Court Street from the center of Main Street.
OPEN	All year
DESCRIPTION	An 1872 two-story Victorian farmhouse and guesthouse furnished with American antiques. Listed on the State and National Historic Registers.
NO. OF ROOMS	Seven rooms with private bathrooms.
RATES	Year-round rates are $95-150 for a single or double. The suite is $135 and the cottage is $150. Rates are lower Sunday through Thursday. There is no minimum stay.
CREDIT CARDS	American Express, Discover, MasterCard, Visa
BREAKFAST	Full breakfast is served in the dining room or guestroom and includes a main entrée, potato dish, meat, fresh fruit, and beverages. Picnic baskets are also available.
AMENITIES	Fresh flowers, terry robes, outdoor hot tub, TV available for each room, iron and ironing board, afternoon refreshments (cookies and tea), fireplaces, 61-inch TV/VCR and stereo in cottage, private decks, pond with waterfall.

RESTRICTIONS	No smoking, no pets
REVIEWED	Bed & Breakfast California, Northern California Best Places, The Best Places to Kiss in Northern California
MEMBER	Professional Association of Innkeepers International, California Association of Bed & Breakfast Inns, Amador County Bed & Breakfast Association

GATE HOUSE INN

1330 Jackson Gate Road, Jackson, CA 95642
Keith & Gail Sweet, Resident Owners

209-223-3500
800-841-1072
FAX 209-223-1299

LOCATION	The inn is located 1.3 miles north of the center of Jackson. Take Main Street, which becomes Jackson Gate, and the inn is on the right side of the road just past Teresa's Restaurant.
OPEN	All year
DESCRIPTION	A 1902 two-story Victorian and cottage with Victorian furnishings throughout. Listed on the State Historic Register.
NO. OF ROOMS	Five rooms with private bathrooms.
RATES	Year-round rates are $100-145 for a single or double, $95 for a suite, and $145 for the guesthouse. There is a minimum stay on weekends when a Saturday is involved and cancellation requires seven days' notice with a $10 charge.
CREDIT CARDS	American Express, Discover, MasterCard, Visa
BREAKFAST	Full breakfast is served in the dining room or guestrooms and includes hot drinks, juices, breads, fruit, meat, and a main dish.
AMENITIES	Fresh flowers in rooms, fresh fruit, homemade cookies, candy available in all public rooms, afternoon tea and hors d'oeuvres, turndown service with chocolate, pool and patio with barbecue facilities, Ping-Pong, exercise room.
RESTRICTIONS	No smoking, children over 12 are welcome.
MEMBER	Professional Association of Innkeepers International, Amador County Bed & Breakfast Association, California Association of Bed & Breakfast Inns
RATED	AAA 3 Diamonds

THE WEDGEWOOD INN

11941 Narcissus Road, Jackson, CA 95642
Vic & Jeannine Beltz, Innkeepers
EMAIL vic@wedgewoodinnn.com
WEBSITE www.wedgewoodinn.com

209-296-4300
800-933-4393
FAX 209-296-4301

LOCATION	From Jackson, take Highway 88 east 6.5 miles and turn right onto Irishtown Road. Take an immediate right again onto Clinton Road, drive 0.75 mile to Narcissus Road, turn left, and go 0.25 mile to the Wedgewood driveway, on your left.
OPEN	All year
DESCRIPTION	A 1987 three-story Victorian-style inn decorated with antique furnishings and located on wooded acreage.
NO. OF ROOMS	Six rooms with private bathrooms. Jeannine says the suite is her most popular room.
RATES	Year-round rates are $110-175 for a single or double. There is a minimum stay on holiday weekends and for special events. Cancellation requires seven days' notice and a $10 fee. If reservations are cancelled with less notice, your deposit (less the $10 fee) will be returned only if the room is rebooked.
CREDIT CARDS	American Express, Discover, MasterCard, Visa

The Wedgewood Inn, Jackson

BREAKFAST	A multiple-course gourmet breakfast is served by candlelight in the dining room on bone china. Breakfast may be delivered to select guestrooms by request.
AMENITIES	Afternoon refreshments, flowers, robes and Jacuzzi in suites, air conditioning, wood-burning stoves, close to over 20 wineries and many outdoor attractions.
RESTRICTIONS	No smoking, no pets, not appropriate for small children. The resident long-haired miniature dachshund is named Wags More.
REVIEWED	*Karen Brown's California Country Inns & Itineraries, Recommended Inns of the West Coast, Fodor's, The Best Places to Kiss in Northern California*
MEMBER	Professional Association of Innkeepers International, California Association of Bed & Breakfast Inns
RATED	AAA 3 Diamonds, Mobil 3 Stars
AWARDS	1991, selected as one of the Top 50 inns in America, Inn-Ovations by *Inn Times*

JAMESTOWN

Jamestown has been preoccupied with gold since the first fleck was taken out of Woods Creek in 1848. For a fee, you can pan for gold at troughs on Main Street or go prospecting with a guide. But gold isn't Jamestown's only claim to fame. For decades, this two-block town lined with picturesque buildings has been Hollywood's favorite Western movie set: scenes from famous flicks like *Butch Cassidy and the Sundance Kid* were shot here, and vintage railway cars and steam locomotives used in such TV classics as *Little House on the Prairie*, *Bonanza*, and *High Noon* are on display at the Railtown 1897 State Historic Park.

THE NATIONAL HOTEL

18183 Main Street, Jamestown, CA 95327 209-984-3446
Stephen Willey, Innkeeper 800-894-3446
German and Spanish spoken FAX 209-984-5620
EMAIL info@national-hotel.com WEBSITE www.national-hotel.com

LOCATION	On Main Street in the center of town.
OPEN	All year
DESCRIPTION	An 1859 two-story Victorian Gold Rush hotel and restaurant with original antique furnishings. Listed on the State Historic Register.
NO. OF ROOMS	Nine rooms with private bathrooms. Stephen suggests room 1.

RATES	Year-round rates are $80-100 for a single or double and $800 for the entire inn. There is a minimum stay during major holidays and cancellation requires 72 hours' notice.
CREDIT CARDS	American Express, Carte Blanche, Diners Club, Discover, MasterCard, Visa
BREAKFAST	Continental plus is served in the dining room and includes fresh muffins, toast, cereal, sliced and whole fruit, hard-boiled eggs, fruit juices, coffee, tea, and milk. Lunch and dinner are also available.
AMENITIES	Fresh flowers, brass beds, patchwork quilts, robes, cable TV on request, meeting facilities, air conditioning, award-winning Gold Country wine list, a friendly resident ghost.
RESTRICTIONS	Children over eight are welcome. Smoking is OK on balcony only. Garfield is the resident cat.
REVIEWED	*Recommended Country Inns—West Coast; Northern California Best Places; Best Bed & Breakfasts and Country Inns; Country Inns of the Far West; Weekend Adventures for City Weary People*
MEMBER	National Bed & Breakfast Association, California Association of Bed & Breakfast Inns, Gold Country Inns of Tuolumne County
RATED	AAA 3 Diamonds, Mobil 3 Stars
KUDOS/COMMENTS	"Historic, clean, good breakfast, great old bar, friendly hosts. The place has character." (1999)

THE PALM HOTEL BED & BREAKFAST

10382 Willow Street, Jamestown, CA 95327   209-984-3429
Rick & Sandy Allen, Resident Owners
WEBSITE *www.palmhotel.com*

LOCATION	One block off Main Street.
OPEN	All year
DESCRIPTION	A turn-of-the-century two-story Victorian mansion with eclectic and Victorian furnishings.
NO. OF ROOMS	Eight rooms with private bathrooms.
RATES	Year-round rates are $85-145 for a single or double. There is no minimum stay and cancellation requires five days' notice.
CREDIT CARDS	American Express, MasterCard, Visa
BREAKFAST	Full breakfast is served in the dining room or lobby, or on the porch, and includes eggs, potatoes, breads, fruits, beverages, and the specialty: baked apple crisp.

AMENITIES	Flowers, robes, TV, local candy on every pillow, handicapped accessible, soda fountain.
RESTRICTIONS	No smoking, no pets
REVIEWED	Historic Inns of California's Gold Country Cookbook and Guide

Royal Hotel

18239 Main Street, Jamestown, CA 95327 209-984-5271
Nancy & Bob Bosich, Resident Owners FAX 209-984-1675

LOCATION	Downtown, across from the community park and gazebo.
OPEN	All year
DESCRIPTION	A 1922 two-story Victorian hotel and cottages surrounded by landscaped grounds.
NO. OF ROOMS	Ten rooms with private bathrooms and nine rooms with shared bathrooms. Pick the Honeymoon Cottage.
RATES	Please call for current rates and cancellation information.
CREDIT CARDS	American Express, MasterCard, Visa
BREAKFAST	Continental plus is served in the parlor and includes seasonal fruit, granola, yogurt, muffins, bread, coffee, and tea.
AMENITIES	Balconies, barbecues, air conditioning, fireplace, bookshop, community kitchen, laundry facilities, RV parking.
RESTRICTIONS	No smoking, no pets

Jenner

About 16 miles north of Bodega Bay on Highway 1 is what seems to be every Northern Californian's "secret" getaway spot: Jenner. Built on a bluff rising from the mouth of the Russian River, the tiny seaside town's best attraction is its location—it's two hours closer than Mendocino to the Bay Area, yet has the same spectacular coastal scenery and a far better selection of beaches. One of the major highlights of the Jenner area is beautiful Goat Rock Beach, a popular breeding ground for harbor seals. Pupping season begins in March and lasts until June.

Jenner Inn

10400 Coast Highway 1, Jenner, CA 95451 707-865-2377
Richard & Sheldon Murphy, Resident Owners 800-732-2377
WEBSITE www.jennerinn.com FAX 707-865-0829

LOCATION	From Highway 101, take the Central Petaluma exit west to Highway 1, then go north to Jenner. Don't blink or you'll miss us.
OPEN	All year
DESCRIPTION	This seaside resort includes a redwood lodge and seven traditional coastal cottages, built in 1895 and 1948 respectively. Furnishings are either country Victorian or rustic and woodsy.
NO. OF ROOMS	Thirteen rooms or cottages with private bathrooms. The Rosewater Cottage is the best of the bunch.
RATES	Year-round rates are $75-215 for a double room, suite or cottage. There is a 15 percent midweek discount in winter and a two-night minimum stay on weekends, three nights on holidays. Cancellation requires seven days' notice with a $10 fee.
CREDIT CARDS	American Express, MasterCard, Visa
BREAKFAST	Continental plus, served in the lodge parlor, includes fresh fruit, warm pastries and muffins, granola, and beverages.
AMENITIES	Most rooms have private decks or porches with water views; fireplaces, kitchens, and hot tubs available; teas; apéritifs; games, books, and magazines; small boat launch with river estuary; conferences and retreats accommodated; full wedding and reception services.
RESTRICTIONS	Smoking allowed on decks, no pets. The surrounding area includes a wildlife sanctuary.
MEMBER	California Association of Bed & Breakfast Inns

KLAMATH

The Klamath River is one of the finest salmon and steelhead streams in the world. The scenery around the river is extraordinary: smack in the middle of Redwood National Forest, the area has some incredible coastal drives and trails that even the timid and out-of-shape can handle with aplomb. Stretch your legs at the lofty Klamath Overlook, which stands about 600 feet above an estuary at the mouth of the Klamath River. A short but steep trail leads down to a second overlook that's ideal for whale-watching and taking photographs. To get there, take the Requa Road turnoff from Highway 101, north of the Klamath River bridge.

KLAMATH INN

151 Requa Road, Klamath, CA 95548   707-482-1425
Paul & Donna Hamby, Innkeepers
EMAIL auction2@gte.net
WEBSITE www.home1.gte.net/auction2/

LOCATION	One mile west off Highway 101 on Requa Road in Klamath.
OPEN	All year
DESCRIPTION	A 1914 two-story Craftsman hotel overlooking the Klamath River and furnished with antiques.
NO. OF ROOMS	Ten rooms with private bathrooms.
RATES	Year-round rates are $59-95 for a single or double and $800 for the entire inn. There is no minimum stay and cancellation requires 24 hours' notice.
CREDIT CARDS	Discover, MasterCard, Visa
BREAKFAST	Full breakfast is served in the dining room and includes bacon, ham, or sausage, hot cakes, eggs, toast, fruit, hot or cold cereal, juice, milk, coffee, or tea. Guests get their choice of three items plus drinks. Dinner is also available.
AMENITIES	Large lobby with fireplace; some rooms have clawfoot bathtubs.
RESTRICTIONS	No smoking, no pets

RHODE'S END BED & BREAKFAST

115 Trobitz Road, Klamath, CA 95548   707-482-1654

KNEELAND

Prepare for some remote country here. From Kneeland, the nearest community is Eureka, some 25 miles to the west.

ABE'S OCEAN VIEW REDWOODS WILDERNESS CHALET

Star Route Box 20-A, Kneeland, CA 95549   707-442-5594
Doug & Lily Vieyra, Innkeepers   FAX 707-442-5594

LOCATION	Because of its remote location, please ask for directions during booking.
OPEN	May through October
DESCRIPTION	An 1882 one-story Swiss–Tyrolian alpine chalet with Bavarian–Austrian decor. The chalet is perched atop a 3,000-foot mountain, surrounded by 1,000 square miles of forested wilderness with panoramic views.

NO. OF ROOMS	One room with a private bathroom and two rooms share one bathroom.
RATES	Rates are $300 for a double with a private or shared bathroom. There is a three-day minimum stay. Ask about the cancellation policy.
CREDIT CARDS	MasterCard, Visa
BREAKFAST	Continental breakfast is served in the dining room or on the deck and includes cereals, fruits, juices, teas, coffee. A full kitchen is available for guest use.
AMENITIES	Deck with vast panoramic views, horseshoe pit, kites, incredible views of sunsets over the Pacific Ocean. "We offer complete and absolute peace and quiet, solitude, and nature."
RESTRICTIONS	No smoking, no pets except horses (corral on site), children over 13 are welcome. There are cattle and abundant wildlife on the property.
KUDOS/COMMENTS	"A deluxe wilderness retreat on a mountaintop."

LA PORTE

GOLD COUNTRY

2140 Main Street, La Porte, CA 95981   530-675-2322

LAKE ARROWHEAD

CARRIAGE HOUSE BED & BREAKFAST

472 Emerald Drive, Lake Arrowhead, CA 92352   909-336-1400

LAKE TAHOE

Lake Tahoe is North America's largest alpine lake and the eighth deepest lake in the world. If completely drained, Lake Tahoe would cover the entire state of California with 14 inches of water. The South Shore area is the most populous and urban, where you'll hear all those slot machines ringing and coins tinkling. If you'd rather steer clear of the one-armed bandits, head for the North Shore. There you'll find fewer casinos (and tourists) and more of everything else, including Tahoe's best alpine and cross-country ski resorts and first-rate restaurants.

CHANEY HOUSE

4725 Westlake Boulevard, Tahoe City, CA 96145 530-525-7333
Gary & Lori Chaney, Innkeepers FAX 530-525-4413
EMAIL gary@chaneyhouse.com WEBSITE *www.chaneyhouse.com*

LOCATION	Located five miles south of Tahoe City on Highway 89 (Westlake Boulevard).
OPEN	All year
DESCRIPTION	A 1928 two-story native-stone home with pine accents, 18-inch-thick stone walls, gothic arches, and a massive stone fireplace; located on the west shore of Lake Tahoe.
NO. OF ROOMS	Four rooms with private bathrooms. Lori recommends the Honeymoon Hideaway.
RATES	June through Labor Day, rates are $140-195 for a single or double. Low season rates are $110-175 for a single or double. There is a minimum stay on weekends and cancellation requires two weeks' notice, one month for holidays.
CREDIT CARDS	MasterCard, Visa
BREAKFAST	Full breakfast, served in the dining room or on the patio, includes beverages, coffeecakes, and egg dishes or French toast with blackberry sauce and crème fraiche.
AMENITIES	Three patios, private pier, TV/VCR, CD player, close to all Tahoe outdoor activities.
RESTRICTIONS	Smoking outside only, no pets, children over 12 are welcome. Sierra is the resident golden retriever.
REVIEWED	*Northern California Best Places; Bed & Breakfast California; Fodor's Bed & Breakfasts; Country Inns and Other Weekend Pleasures*
MEMBER	California Association of Bed & Breakfast Inns

Cottage Inn at Lake Tahoe

1690 W Lake Boulevard, Tahoe City, CA 96145   530-581-4073

Mayfield House

236 Grove Street, Tahoe City, CA 96145   530-583-1001
Colleen McDevitt & Stan Scott, Resident Owner   FAX 530-581-4104
WEBSITE www.mayfieldhouse.com

LOCATION	From Highway 28, one-and-a-half blocks north of the center of town.
OPEN	All year
DESCRIPTION	A 1932 two-story English country Tudor with "early Tahoe" furnishings.
NO. OF ROOMS	Three rooms with private bathrooms and two rooms share a bathroom. There is a cabin in the back with a private bathroom.
RATES	Year-round rates are $110-175 for a single or double or the cabin. Holiday rates are slightly more; midweek rates are less. There is a two-night minimum stay during weekends, three nights' during holidays. Cancellation requires two weeks' notice, 30 days during holidays.
CREDIT CARDS	American Express, MasterCard, Visa
BREAKFAST	Full breakfast is served in the dining room or on the patio.
AMENITIES	Flowers, robes, TV in main room, afternoon snack, collection of books in each room, Jacuzzi in one suite, steam bath.
RESTRICTIONS	No smoking, no pets, children over 15 are welcome.
MEMBER	Professional Association of Innkeepers International

Norfolk Woods Inn

6941 Westlake Boulevard, Tahoma, CA 96142   530-525-5000
Al & Patty Multon, Innkeepers   FAX 530-525-5266
Spanish, French, and Italian spoken
EMAIL norfwds@sierra.net
WEBSITE www.tahoecountry.com/wslodging/nw.html

LOCATION	Exit Highway 80 at Truckee at the Lake Tahoe exit, proceed 15 miles to Tahoe City, and turn right at the first light on Highway 89. Drive 7.5 miles toward Emerald Bay. The inn is in the heart of Tahoma.
OPEN	All year
DESCRIPTION	A 1940s three-story Tahoe-style country inn with country furnishings and a restaurant.
NO. OF ROOMS	Seven rooms with private bathrooms, five private cottages, and two rooms share a bathroom. Pick Amy's Cottage, a century-old log cabin.
RATES	Rates are $100 for a single or double with a private bathroom and $90 for a single or double with a shared bathroom. The suite is $160 and the cottages are $150-160. There is no minimum stay. A deposit is required and cancellations require two weeks' notice and a $15 fee.
CREDIT CARDS	American Express, MasterCard, Visa
BREAKFAST	Full breakfast is served in the dining room and includes a choice of French toast, bacon and eggs, omelet of the day, pancakes, and beverages. Cottage guests get a discount in the restaurant. Lunch and dinner are available and special allergy-free meals and prix fixe dinners for groups are available by prior arrangement.
AMENITIES	Telephones, cable TV in cottages, heated swimming pool and spa (seasonal), gift shop, espresso/ice cream shop, expert mountain biking, fishing, and skiing advice, hiking, close to world-class skiing, award-winning restaurant.
RESTRICTIONS	No smoking, children are welcome. Extra charge for pets.
REVIEWED	*Lake Tahoe—The Complete Guide, What Shall We Do Tomorrow at Lake Tahoe*
MEMBER	California Association of Bed & Breakfast Inns
RATED	AAA 2 Diamonds
AWARDS	1994 and 1995, Best Food, Autumn Food and Wine Festival; 1994 and 1995, Best Marriage of Wine and Food, Autumn Food and Wine Festival

RIVER RANCH LODGE

PO Box 197, Tahoe City, CA 96145   530-583-4264

ROCKWOOD LODGE

5295 West Lake Boulevard, Homewood, CA 96141 530-525-5273
WEBSITE *www.rockwoodlodge.com* FAX 916-525-5949

THE SHORE HOUSE AT LAKE TAHOE

7170 North Lake Boulevard, Tahoe Vista, CA 96148 (530) 546-7270
Barb & Marty Cohen, Innkeepers 800-207-5160
Swedish spoken FAX 530-546-7130
EMAIL *shorehse@inntahoe.com* WEBSITE *www.inntahoe.com*

LOCATION	On the north shore of Lake Tahoe, eight miles north of Tahoe City.
OPEN	All year
DESCRIPTION	A 1958 two-story mountain lodge with knotty pine walls and log furniture.
NO. OF ROOMS	Nine rooms with private bathrooms. Barb suggests the Honeymoon Cottage.
RATES	Weekday rates from June through September are $175-190 for a single or double and $190-255 for a suite. Weekend rates are $15 more. Weekday rates from October through May are $135-150 for a single or double and $200-205 for a suite. Weekend rates are $25 more. Holiday rates are $190-255. There is a two-night minimum stay on weekends, three nights during holidays. Cancellation requires 14 days' notice for a full refund less a $25 fee.
CREDIT CARDS	Discover, MasterCard, Visa
BREAKFAST	Full breakfast is served in the dining room or outside on the lakefront lawn and includes pears poached with apricot nectar and grapes, stuffed French toast, New England maple syrup, and chicken apple sausages.
AMENITIES	Fresh flowers and baked treats in rooms; robes to wear to lakefront hot tub; afternoon wine; coffee, tea, or hot chocolate served anytime; chocolate kisses by the bed each night; gas log fireplaces in every room; full concierge service.
RESTRICTIONS	No smoking, no pets. The inn's Australian shepherd is named Fuzzball.
REVIEWED	*The Complete Guide to B&Bs, Inns, and Guesthouses; Recommended B&Bs of California; Fodor's Bed & Breakfasts, Country Inns, and Other Weekend Pleasures; Frommer's*

MEMBER	California Association of Bed & Breakfast Inns, Professional Association of Innkeepers International, Lake Tahoe Bed & Breakfast Association
RATED	AAA 3 Diamonds, ABBA 3 Crowns
AWARDS	1997, first place breakfast entrée in the ABBA and Jones Dairy Farm Cook-Off

THE STANFORD ALPINE CHALET

1980 Chalet Road, Tahoe City, CA 96145   530-583-4625
Some French and Spanish spoken   FAX 530-583-2082
EMAIL *chalet@lelend.stanford.edu*   WEBSITE *www.tahoeguide.com*

LOCATION	From I-80, take the 89 South/Squaw Valley exit. Drive south (past the last gas station) for nearly 10 miles. Pass the entrance to Squaw Valley USA and turn right onto Alpine Meadows Road. Climb to the top of the road where it widens to become the bottom of the parking lot for Alpine Meadows Ski Area. Take the first left (Ginzton Access Road) and wind around to the left. The chalet is the first building on the left.
DESCRIPTION	A 1963 newly renovated three-story Swiss chalet located at the doorstep of Alpine Meadows Ski Area and surrounded by mountain peaks and ponderosa pine.
NO. OF ROOMS	Fourteen rooms with private bathrooms.
RATES	Rates are $100-180 for a single or double. The entire inn rents for a minimum of $1,400. There is a minimum stay during Christmas and cancellation requires two weeks' written notice.
CREDIT CARDS	American Express, MasterCard, Visa
BREAKFAST	Full breakfast is served in the dining room and includes meats, eggs, something sweet, fruit dishes, plus a buffet with cereal, breads, jam, yogurt, coffee, tea, and hot chocolate. Dinner is also available.
AMENITIES	Ski shuttle, daily après-ski with wine and cheese in front of the wood-burning fireplace, hot tub in the snow under the stars, large heated pool (summer only), volleyball court, crouquet, basketball court, horseshoe pit in the pines, tennis pass available, exceptional hiking and biking, horseback riding, minutes away from Lake Tahoe.
RESTRICTIONS	No smoking, no pets. "Part of the beauty of the Sierra is seeing wild animals nearby like bears, deer, marmots, and coyotes."

Tahoma Meadows Bed & Breakfast

6821 W Lake Boulevard, Tahoma, CA 94142   530-525-1553

Lakehead

The Pacific Crest Trail crisscrosses this remote area 25 miles north of Redding. Fish or pan for gold in mountain rivers and streams, ski Mount Shasta, or just enjoy the beautiful scenery around Lake Shasta.

Lake Shasta's True Bed & Breakfast

215 Lake Boulevard, Suite 215, Lakehead, CA 96003   530-238-2388
Susan True, Innkeeper   800-744-8783
WEBSITE www.lakeshasta-inn.com

LOCATION	About 25 miles north of Redding.
DESCRIPTION	A secluded inn nestled into Fall Creek Canyon on over 80 acres.
NO. OF ROOMS	Custom designed rooms featuring nautical, Camelot, and outdoor themes.
RATES	Please call for current rates and cancellation information.
CREDIT CARDS	American Express, MasterCard, Visa
BREAKFAST	Full gourmet breakfast is served on weekends; continental is served during the week.
AMENITIES	Romantic candles, chocolates, spa, chilled sparkling cider, fresh flowers, robes and slippers, decks, barbecue, complimentary movies, books and magazines, romance packages.
KUDOS/COMMENTS	"Beautifully decorated and includes several grand amenities." (1999)

LAKEPORT

Escape from wine country madness to the western shore of spring-fed Clear Lake, which is full of bass—bring your rod and reel. The area is also known for its mineral and hot springs and famous for Barlett Pears. The Historic County Courthouse and Museum are worth a visit. Check out the Pear Blossom Festival in April, Boat and Ski Races in August, and Celebrity Pro-Am Bass Tourney in October. Lakeport is north of San Francisco on Highways 101 and 175, with handy access to Cow Mountain Recreation Area.

ARBOR HOUSE INN

150 Clearlake Avenue, Lakeport, CA 95453   707-263-6444
Lori Bacci, Innkeeper

LOCATION	Take the Eleventh Street exit off Highway 29 and turn east to Main Street. Turn north, go one block to Clearlake Avenue, turn west, and park in front.
OPEN	All year
DESCRIPTION	An 1880s Victorian inn.
NO. OF ROOMS	Five rooms with private bathrooms. Lori likes the Courtyard Suite.
RATES	Year-round rates are $79-109 for a single or double and the entire B&B rents for $375. There is a minimum stay on major holidays and cancellation requires 48 hours' notice.
CREDIT CARDS	American Express, MasterCard, Visa
BREAKFAST	Full three-course breakfast is served in the dining room and includes fresh fruit, homemade muffins, hashbrowns, an entrée of the day, juice, coffee, and tea.
AMENITIES	Private outdoor entrances to all rooms; parlor room for conversation; library with historical literature; outdoor garden spa; wine and cheese reception; some rooms have double Jacuzzi tubs, fireplaces, and wet bars.
RESTRICTIONS	No smoking, no pets, children over 10 are welcome.
MEMBER	California Hotel and Motel Association

THE FORBESTOWN BED & BREAKFAST INN

825 Forbes Street, Lakeport, CA 95453 707-263-7858
Wally & Pat Kelley, Innkeepers FAX 707-263-7878
EMAIL *forbestowninn@zapcom.net* WEBSITE *www.innaccess.com/fti*

LOCATION	In downtown Lakeport, one block west of Main Street between 8th and 9th Streets.
OPEN	All year
DESCRIPTION	An 1863 two-story clapboard farmhouse furnished with American oak antiques.
NO. OF ROOMS	Two rooms with private bathrooms and two rooms with one shared bathroom.
RATES	Year-round rates for a single or double with a private or shared bathroom are $75-110. Cancellation requires one weeks' notice.
CREDIT CARDS	American Express, Diners Club, Discover, MasterCard, Visa
BREAKFAST	Full breakfast is served in the dining room.
AMENITIES	Flowers, robes, TV/VCR in shared living area, hot tub, swimming pool, wine and hors d'oeuvres, tea and baked goods, turndown service, bikes. Weddings, reunions, and other special events held in the garden.
RESTRICTIONS	No smoking, no pets, children over 12 years old welcome. Rusty is the resident poodle.
REVIEWED	*Northwest Best Places*
MEMBER	California Association of Bed & Breakfast Inns
KUDOS/COMMENTS	"Great full breakfast; warm hospitality and comfort."

THE THOMPSON HOUSE

3315 Lakeshore Boulevard, Lakeport, CA 95453 707-263-4905
William & Jan Thompson, Innkeepers FAX 707-263-6276
EMAIL *anthonys@zapcom.net*
WEBSITE *www.lakecountyrandr.com/thompson.shtml*

LOCATION	Exactly one mile north of Lakeport on Lakeshore Boulevard, across the street from Clearlake just north of Parkway. From Highway 29, take the Parkway turnoff and go east about one mile, where it will dead end at Lakeshore Boulevard. Turn left and you will see the sign on the left.

OPEN	All year
DESCRIPTION	A 1900 Spanish-style ranch house decorated in the style of an English manor, located on two acres with large shade trees and vine-covered arbors.
NO. OF ROOMS	One room with a private bathroom.
RATES	Year-round rates are $95 for a single or double. There is no minimum stay and cancellation requires 72 hours' notice with a 15 percent charge.
CREDIT CARDS	American Express, Discover, Visa
BREAKFAST	Continental plus is served in the dining room and includes hot pastries, granola, fruit dish, juice, and coffee.
AMENITIES	Bath robes; complimentary bottle of wine; complimentary juices and soft drinks (in-room fridge); fireplace; in-room coffee, chocolate, and tea; horseshoe pit, croquet, badminton; ceiling fans; private entrance; library; sitting room; meeting room.
RESTRICTIONS	No smoking, no pets, no children. Sparky is the resident mutt. Damn Bird is the chicken.
MEMBER	Lake County Resort & Restaurant Association

THE WOODEN BRIDGE BED & BREAKFAST

1441 Oakwood Court, Lakeport, CA 95453 707-263-9125
Don & Ginny Carmody, Resident Owners

LOCATION	From north Highway 29, exit at Park Way Hill Road. Turn left over the freeway to Hill Road, then turn left and go 0.75 mile to the B&B.
OPEN	All year except Christmas and New Year's Day
DESCRIPTION	A 1991 English manor with country French decor, located on 5 oak-covered acres.
NO. OF ROOMS	Two rooms with private bathrooms.
RATES	Please call for current rates and cancellation information.
CREDIT CARDS	No
BREAKFAST	Full breakfast is served in the dining room.
AMENITIES	Robes, bicycles, stocked refrigerator, afternoon refreshments.
RESTRICTIONS	No smoking, no pets, children are not encouraged.
MEMBER	California Association of Bed & Breakfast Inns

LEWISTON

A fishing paradise on Lake Lewiston, and a great base camp for access into the stunning Trinity Alps Wilderness and Trinity Lake. Make time for a tour of the Trinity River Fish Hatchery (salmon and steelhead) just south of the dam. Northwest of Redding via Highway 299 and Road 105.

OLD LEWISTON INN

Deadwood Road, Historic District, Lewiston, CA 96052   530-778-3354
Connor & Mary Nixon, Resident Owners   800-286-4441
Spanish spoken   FAX 530-778-0309
EMAIL nixons@snowcrest.com

LOCATION	Beside the Trinity River in the historic section of Lewiston, 500 feet from the historic Lewiston Bridge. Lewiston is 35 miles west of Redding and four miles off Highway 299.
OPEN	All year
DESCRIPTION	A fully restored 1875 two-story Gold Rush-style inn decorated with mining era antiques, situated along the Trinity River and surrounded by gardens. Listed on the National and State Historic Registers.
NO. OF ROOMS	Five rooms with private bathrooms and two rooms share one bathroom. Connor suggests the Deadwood Room.
RATES	Year-round rates for a double with a private bathroom are $85. There is a two-night minimum stay weekends from May to September and cancellation requires seven days' notice.

Old Lewiston Inn, Lewiston

CREDIT CARDS	American Express, MasterCard, Visa
BREAKFAST	Full breakfast is served in the main dining room or on the decks and includes cereal, juice, fresh fruit, French toast, two eggs, and sausage.
AMENITIES	Air conditioning; in-room phone; individual heating; cable TV; refrigerators; soft drinks, beer, and wine; hot tub by the river; hiking and biking maps; handicapped accessible; decks overlooking the river; meeting facilities.
RESTRICTIONS	No smoking
MEMBER	Shasta Cascade Wonderland Association

LITTLE RIVER

Don't miss this place. Founded as a lumber town by settlers from Maine, this is picture-postcard New England. A good reason to be here is Van Damme State Park, one of the finer things along this stretch of the coast. Divers love it here, too. Most notable: the 2.5-mile Fern Canyon Trail and the fairy-like Pygmy Forest, where rhododendrons nearly dwarf the trees! Little River is on the rugged north central coast, just south of Mendocino.

THE BLANCHARD HOUSE

8141 Pacific Coast Highway 1, Little River, CA 95456   707-937-1627
WEBSITE www.mcn.org/c/blanchardhouse

GLENDEVEN

8221 North Highway 1, Little River, CA 95456   707-937-0083
WEBSITE www.glendeven.com

KUDOS/COMMENTS	"One of the finest inns on the Mendocino coast." "Large rooms with fireplace and picture window. Very inviting. Wonderful breakfast. Friendly innkeeper."

HERITAGE HOUSE

5200 North Highway 1, Little River, CA 95456   707-937-5885

Heritage House, Little River

Candace Prairie, Innkeeper 800-235-5885
WEBSITE *www.innaccess.com/hhi/* FAX 707-937-0318

LOCATION	Five miles south of Mendocino on the ocean side of Highway 1.
OPEN	Open Valentines Day week until the Sunday after New Year's
DESCRIPTION	An 1877 two-story New England country inn, surrounded by 37 acres of spectacular gardens overlooking the Pacific Ocean.
NO. OF ROOMS	Sixty-six rooms with private bathrooms. Try the Juliet Room.
RATES	May through October and all weekends, rates are $150-300 for a single or double and $225-350 for a suite. November through April, excluding weekends and holidays, rates are $125-275 for a single or double and $200-300 for a suite. There is a minimum stay during Saturdays and holidays and cancellation requires 72 hours' notice with a $10 fee.
CREDIT CARDS	MasterCard, Visa
BREAKFAST	Full country breakfast is served à la carte in the dining room and includes eggs Benedict, vegetable omelets, smoked salmon with bagels and cream cheese. Dinner is also available.
AMENITIES	Afternoon tea and pastries, robes, split of local chardonnay, in-room coffee, some rooms with whirlpool tubs, many rooms with fireplaces, most rooms have ocean views, dining rooms and bar/lounge with ocean views, cliffside gazebo.
RESTRICTIONS	No pets. There are several resident cats.
REVIEWED	*The Best Places to Kiss in Northern California, California Coast Getaways*

MEMBER   California Lodging Industry Association

AWARDS   1996, Award of Excellence, *Wine Spectator*; 1992, California Grand Hotel Award for most beautiful location, *San Francisco Focus* magazine.

Rachel's Inn

8200 N Highway 1, Little River, CA 95456   707-937-0088
WEBSITE *www.rachelsinn.com*

KUDOS/COMMENTS "So intimate."

The Seafoam Lodge

6751 N Highway 1, Little River, CA 95456   707-937-1827
WEBSITE *www.seafoamlodge.com*

Victorian Farmhouse Bed & Breakfast

7001 N Highway 1, Little River, CA 95456   707-937-0697
WEBSITE *www.victorianfarmhouse.com*

Livermore

Purple Orchid Inn Resort & Spa

4549 Cross Road, Livermore, CA 94550   925-606-8855

KUDOS/COMMENTS "Set below an olive grove; majestic; wonderful pool and spa; well-appointed." (1999)

LODI

WINE & ROSES COUNTRY INN

2505 West Turner Road, Lodi, CA 95242
WEBSITE www.winerose.com

209-334-6988
FAX 209-334-6570

LOLETA

SOUTHPORT LANDING

444 Phelan Road, Loleta, CA 95551

707-733-5915

LOOMIS

EMMA'S BED & BREAKFAST

3137 Taylor Road, Loomis, CA 95650

916-652-1392

OLD FLOWER FARM BED & BREAKFAST

4150 Auburn Folsom Road, Loomis, CA 95650

916-652-4200

LOTUS

GOLDEN LOTUS

1006 Lotus Road, Lotus, CA 95651

530-621-4562

LOWER LAKE

The southernmost town near Clear Lake's shore, Lower Lake is worth a stop. From here, you can reach Anderson Marsh State Historic Park and John Still Anderson Ranch House (the park's headquarters). Anyone with an archaeological bent will love this area. Check out the Blackberry Festival in August—and wineries anytime. Take the scenic route north through Napa Valley on Highway 29.

BIG CANYON INN

11750 Big Canyon Road, Lower Lake, CA 95457   707-928-5631
John & Helen Wiegand, Resident Owners   707-928-4892
German spoken
EMAIL *jetsetjohn@jps.net*
WEBSITE *www.go-natives.com/Inns/0110.html*

LOCATION	From Lower Lake, head north on Highway 20 for one mile and turn left on Seigler Canyon Road. Go 5 miles and turn left on Big Canyon Road. Go 0.2 mile, turn left, and go 0.3 mile. Turn right and go 0.2 mile to the driveway, on the left.
OPEN	All year
DESCRIPTION	A two-story host home on 12 wooded acres.
NO. OF ROOMS	Two rooms with private bathrooms.
RATES	Year-round rate is $70 for a single or double. Cancellation requires 24 hours' notice.
CREDIT CARDS	No
BREAKFAST	Continental breakfast is served in the guestrooms and includes fruit and pastry.
RESTRICTIONS	No smoking, no pets, children are welcome.

MAMMOTH LAKES

At the base of 11,053-foot Mammoth Mountain are nearly a dozen alpine lakes and the sprawling town of Mammoth Lakes. Ever since founder Dave McCoy mortgaged his motorcycle for $85 in 1938 to buy his first ski lift, folks have been coming here in droves (particularly from Southern California) to carve turns and navigate the moguls at one the best downhill areas in the United States. In addition to skiing, this section of the eastern Sierra Nevada has been famous for decades for its fantastic fishing holes. In fact, the trout is king here, and several fishing derbies celebrate its royal status. This natural kingdom is no longer the exclusive domain of anglers and skiers, however. Word has gotten out about Mammoth's charms, attracting every kind of outdoor enthusiast and adventurer to this spectacular region in the heart of the High Sierra.

SNOW GOOSE INN

57 Forest Trail, Mammoth Lakes, CA 93546 760-934-2260
Scott & Denise Robertson, Resident Owners 800-874-7368
WEBSITE www.snowgoose-inn.com FAX 760-934-5655

LOCATION	From Highway 395, exit onto Highway 203 to Mammoth Lakes. In town, go through one traffic light and turn right on Forest Trail.
OPEN	All year
DESCRIPTION	A 1969 two-story mountain lodge with antique and European furnishings.
NO. OF ROOMS	Nineteen rooms with private bathrooms.
RATES	Mid-November to mid-April, rates are $78-98 for a single or double and suites are $148-168. Mid-April to mid-November, rates are $58-78 for a single or double and suites are $98-108. There is a three-day minimum stay on holiday weekends.
CREDIT CARDS	Discover, MasterCard, Visa
BREAKFAST	Full breakfast, served in the dining room, includes fresh-baked muffins, coffeecakes, fresh fruit, frittatas, quiche, and beverages.
AMENITIES	Hot tub, evening appetizers and wine, telephone, TV in rooms.
RESTRICTIONS	No smoking, no pets
MEMBER	California Association of Bed & Breakfast Innkeepers
RATED	AAA 2 Diamonds, Mobil 2 Stars

The White Horse Inn

2180 Old Mammoth Road, Mammoth Lakes, CA 93546   619-924-3656
Lynn Criss, Manager   800-982-5657
Some Spanish and French spoken
WEBSITE www.mammoth-realestate.com

LOCATION	From Highway 395, take the Mammoth Lakes/Highway 203 exit. Follow Highway 203 to the first traffic signal in town (Old Mammoth Road). Turn left and drive for almost three miles. The inn is on the right.
OPEN	All year
DESCRIPTION	A 1963 two-story contemporary inn.
NO. OF ROOMS	Three rooms with private bathroms and two rooms share one bathroom. The Emperor's Room is recommended.
RATES	Mid-November through April, rates are $100-150 for a single or double and $150 for a suite. May through mid-November, rates are $65-105 for a single or double and $120 for a suite. The deposit is forfeited if cancellations are made within 30 days, unless the room is rebooked.
CREDIT CARDS	American Express, Diners Club, Discover, MasterCard, Visa
BREAKFAST	Full breakfast, served in the dining room, includes fresh fruit, fresh-baked goods, omelets, waffles, soufflés, and fresh-ground coffee.
AMENITIES	Afternoon hors d'oeuvres and refreshments, robes in each room, paperback library, TV/VCRs, movie channel, pool room, kitchen for guests, fireplaces in living rooms, safe for storing valuables.
RESTRICTIONS	No smoking, no pets. Rosie the Australian shepherd and the cats, Fatso and Thomas, are "delightful and friendly—no fleas in the mountains."
MEMBER	Professional Association of Innkeepers International

Manchester

Victorian Gardens

14409 S Highway 1, Manchester, CA 95459   707-882-3606

MARIPOSA

This peaceful and woodsy southwestern gateway into Yosemite National Park is a nifty surprise. Meander the unmarked ghost towns in the hills nearby or just hang out and take in the local offerings: Old Mariposa Jail, County Courthouse (check out the second floor), and the excellent State Mining and Mineral Exhibit. Drop in on the wonderful wineries and sample fine chardonnays, cabernets, and merlots. Mariposa is north of Fresno via Highway 99 and west of Merced on Highway 140.

5TH STREET INN

4990 5th Street, Mariposa, CA 95338   209-966-6048

BOULDER CREEK BED & BREAKFAST

4572 Ben Hur Road, Yosemite—Mariposa, CA 95338   209-742-7729
Nancy & Michael Habermann, Resident Owners
German spoken
WEBSITE www.mariposa.yosemite.net/boulder_creek/

LOCATION	Two miles from Mariposa on Highway 49 south, make a right turn onto Ben Hur Road. The host home is 0.25 mile on the left.
OPEN	All year
DESCRIPTION	A 1988 Swiss chalet decorated with contemporary and antique furnishings.
NO. OF ROOMS	Three rooms with private bathrooms. Try the Bridal Room.
RATES	Year-round rates are $85 for a single or double. The entire chalet rents for $235. There is no minimum stay and cancellation requires 72 hours' notice with a $10 fee
CREDIT CARDS	MasterCard, Visa
BREAKFAST	Full breakfast is served in the dining room or on the redwood deck and includes spinach soufflé, fresh-baked bread, orange or banana smoothie, fresh fruit, jam, and coffee. Vegetarians are welcome and special meals are available.
AMENITIES	Spa, gazebo, flower gardens, trails, complimentary refreshments.
RESTRICTIONS	No smoking inside, children over 12 are welcome. The outdoor cat is Peggy Sue, "who loves to go on the trail out back with the guests."
REVIEWED	*The Best of the Sierra Nevada, The Best of the Gold Country*
MEMBER	Yosemite—Mariposa Bed & Breakfast Association

Dubord's Restful Nest

4274 Buckeye Creek Road, Mariposa, CA 95338 209-742-7127
Huguette Dubord, Resident Owner
French spoken

LOCATION	Near the western edge of Yosemite National Park in Mariposa. Please call for directions.
OPEN	All year
DESCRIPTION	A 1984 two-story country ranch on 11 acres.
NO. OF ROOMS	Three rooms have private bathrooms.
RATES	Please call for current rates and cancellation information.
CREDIT CARDS	American Express, Discover, MasterCard, Visa
BREAKFAST	Full breakfast, served in the dining room, includes French toast, beignets, casseroles, fancy Jello, crepes, quiche, homemade jam and muffins from "the little French lady who is always cooking."
AMENITIES	Private entrances, fishing pond, swimming pool, TV in rooms, phone, snacks, movies.
RESTRICTIONS	No smoking inside, children are welcome. The resident Lab and poodle love children and are very gentle.
MEMBER	California Association of Bed & Breakfast Inns, Yosemite Bed & Breakfast Association
KUDOS/COMMENTS	"Warm, friendly hosts; nice grounds; good breakfast"

Finch Haven

4605 Triangle Road, Mariposa, CA 95338 209-966-4738

Granny's Garden

7333 Highway 49 North, Mariposa, CA 95338 209-377-8342

HIGHLAND HOUSE

6308 Jerseydale Road, Mariposa, CA 95338 209-966-3737
WEBSITE www.moriah.com/highland

MARIPOSA HOTEL & INN

5029 Highway 140, Mariposa, CA 95338 209-966-4676
Sal & Sharon Maccarone, Innkeepers 800-317-3244
Italian spoken FAX 209-742-5963
EMAIL sal@sierratel.com WEBSITE www.yosemitehotel.com

LOCATION	On Highway 140 (Main Street) between 5th and 6th Streets.
OPEN	All year
DESCRIPTION	A restored 1901 two-story Victorian stage stop with antique furniture; listed on both the National and State Historic Registers.
NO. OF ROOMS	Five rooms with private bathrooms. Sal likes Evelyn and Carmelo's Room.
RATES	Year-round rates are $84-107 for a single or double. There is no minimum stay; cancellation requires two days' notice.
CREDIT CARDS	American Express, Discover, MasterCard, Visa
BREAKFAST	A healthy continental breakfast is served in the vestibule and includes seasonal fruit and a variety of muffins, bagels, and breads.

Mariposa Hotel & Inn, Mariposa

AMENITIES	Cable TV, tape players, radios, clocks, hair dryers, in-room coffee/tea, garden veranda with resident population of 50 hummingbirds, bird-watching, wine tasting, seasonal horse and buggy stop at front door, air conditioning, refreshments, history museum in lobby, gold panning.
RESTRICTIONS	Smoking on the veranda only, no pets, children over four are welcome. Resident pets include Lola the parrot and several tropical fish.
REVIEWED	*The Complete Guide to Bed & Breakfasts, Inns, and Guesthouse; The Best of the Gold Country; Northern California Best Places; Northern California Handbook*
MEMBER	Mariposa County Bed & Breakfast Association
RATED	AAA 2 Diamonds

MARIPOSA MEADOWS RANCH

3972 Guadalupe Creek Road, Mariposa, CA 95338   209-966-2239

MEADOW CREEK RANCH BED & BREAKFAST INN

2669 Triangle Road, Mariposa, CA 95338   209-966-3843
Some Spanish spoken

LOCATION	From Mariposa, 11.5 miles from the Highway 140 turnoff. Visible from Highway 49 south at the corner of Triangle Road.
OPEN	All year
DESCRIPTION	An 1858 two-story ranch house and cottage furnished with American and European antiques.
NO. OF ROOMS	One room has a private bathroom and three rooms share three bathrooms. The Country Cottage is a favorite.
RATES	Inquire about rates and cancellation information.
CREDIT CARDS	American Express, Discover, MasterCard, Visa
BREAKFAST	Full breakfast is served in the dining room.
AMENITIES	Library, old water wheel, and porch.
RESTRICTIONS	No smoking in buildings, no pets, children over 12 are welcome.

REVIEWED	Bed & Breakfast California, The Best of the Gold Country, Northern California Best Places
MEMBER	Yosemite—Mariposa Bed & Breakfast Association

THE PELENNOR BED & BREAKFAST

3871 Highway 49 South, Mariposa, CA 95338   209-966-2832
Dick & Gwen Foster, Resident Owners
EMAIL pelennor@yosemite.net

LOCATION	From Mariposa, go south on Highway 49 for 5.5 miles and turn right into the drive directly across from the Bootjack Volunteer Fire Station, and follow signs.
OPEN	All year
DESCRIPTION	A 1986 two-story "box" decorated with "very basic Scottish tartans" and situated on 15 wooded acres.
NO. OF ROOMS	Four rooms share two bathrooms.
RATES	Year-round rate is $35-45 for a single or double. There is no minimum stay and cancellation requires 24 hours' notice.
CREDIT CARDS	No
BREAKFAST	Full breakfast is served in the main house and includes meat, eggs, English muffins, cereal, fruit, orange juice or other juices, hashbrowns, and beverages.
AMENITIES	Both of the owners play bagpipes; darts and bumper pool in the common area; spa, lap pool, and sauna outside; walking and jogging paths.
RESTRICTIONS	Smoking outside only
MEMBER	Yosemite—Mariposa Bed & Breakfast Association

POPPY HILL

5218 Crystal Aire Drive, Mariposa, CA 95338   209-742-6273
Tom & Mary Ellen Kirn, Resident Owners

ROCKWOOD GARDENS

5155 Tip Top Road, Mariposa, CA 95338   209-742-6817

SHANGRI LA BED & BREAKFAST

3085 Wild Dove Lane, Mariposa, CA 95338   209-966-2653

SHILOH BED & BREAKFAST

3265 Triangle Park Road, Mariposa, CA 95338   209-742-7200

SIERRA HOUSE BED & BREAKFAST

4981 Indian Peak Road, Mariposa, CA 95338   209-966-3515
Libby & Norm Murrell, Innkeepers   800-496-3515
EMAIL sierrabb@yosemite.net   FAX 209-966-3515

LOCATION	From Mariposa, go south on Main Street (Highway 140) to Highway 49. Take Highway 49 for four miles to Indian Peak Road and turn right. Go 200 yards and turn right again.
OPEN	All year
DESCRIPTION	A 1974 California/Spanish ranch-style host home set on 2 acres with a terra cotta roof and an eclectic interior decor.
NO. OF ROOMS	Three rooms with private bathrooms. Try the Middle East Room.
RATES	April through September, rates are $75-85 for a single or double. October through March, rates are $65-75 for a single or double. There is no minimum stay and cancellation requires 48 hours' notice for a full refund.
CREDIT CARDS	Discover, MasterCard, Visa
BREAKFAST	Full breakfast is served in the dining room. Coffee and tea are served outside the guestrooms one hour before breakfast.
AMENITIES	Robes; air conditioning; front porch; waterfall; close to Yosemite National Park; four miles from an old gold-mining town; 2 acres of trees; hiking.

Sierra House Bed & Breakfast, Mariposa

RESTRICTIONS   No smoking, no pets. The dog and cat are both outside pets.
MEMBER   Yosemite—Mariposa Bed & Breakfast Association

VILLA MONTI BED & BREAKFAST

4990 8th Street, Mariposa, CA 95338   209-966-2439

MCCLOUD

A company-built mill town, McCloud bills itself as "the quiet side of Mount Shasta." And true to its motto, this is a relatively sleepy place that attracts a lot of anglers, hikers, and other nature lovers. Whatever your attraction to this neck of the woods, you can introduce yourself to the area in style by hopping aboard the Shasta Sunset Dinner Train, which follows a historic turn-of-the-century logging route over steep grades, sharp curves, and across a unique switchback at Signal Butte. As you nosh on a very good dinner in your railcar, you'll be treated to views of Mount Shasta, Castle Crags, and the Trinity Alps. In the summer, you can watch—or, better yet, join—the McCloud locals as they kick up their heels every weekend from May to September in the town's two air-conditioned dance halls. Dancing—especially square dancing—is a favorite pastime here.

MCCLOUD RIVER INN

325 Lawndale Court, McCloud, CA 96057   530-964-2130
WEBSITE *www.riverinn.com*

Stoney Brook Inn

309 West Colombero Drive, McCloud, CA 96057   530-964-2300
WEBSITE *www.touristguide.com/b&b/ca/stoneybrook*

Meadow Valley

Haskins Valley Inn

10206 Bucks Lake Road, Meadow Valley, CA 95956   530-283-2262

Mendocino

The grande dame of Northern California's coastal tourist towns, this refurbished replica of a New England-style fishing village—complete with a white-spired church—has managed to retain more of its charm and allure than most North Coast vacation spots. Motels, fast-food chains, and anything hinting of development are strictly forbidden here, resulting in the almost-passable illusion that Mendocino is just another quaint little coastal community. Mendocino Headlands State Park, the small grassy stretch of land between the village of Mendocino and the ocean, is one of the town's most popular sites. The park's flat, three-mile trail winds along the edge of a heather-covered bluff, providing spectacular sunset views and good lookout points for seabirds and California gray whales.

Agate Cove Inn

11201 Lansing Street, Mendocino, CA 95460   707-937-0551
Betsy & Scott Buckwald, Resident Owners   800-527-3111 (CA only)
WEBSITE *www.agatecove.com*

LOCATION	From Highway 1 north at Mendocino, take the first Lansing Street exit. The inn is 0.5 mile north.
OPEN	All year
DESCRIPTION	An 1863 farmhouse and cottages with country decor, on a bluff above the Pacific Ocean.
NO. OF ROOMS	Ten rooms with private bathrooms.

RATES	April through October rates are $109-250 for a double. November through March rates are discounted 20 percent. There is a two-night minimum stay on weekends, three nights on holidays. Cancellation requires seven days' notice and a $15 fee.
CREDIT CARDS	American Express, Discover, MasterCard, Visa
BREAKFAST	Full breakfast, served in the dining room, includes fresh fruit with yogurt; homemade breads; eggs Benedict, French toast, or omelets; coffee and tea.
AMENITIES	Fresh flowers and a a decanter of sherry in guest rooms, newspaper delivered each morning; all but one room have TV, fireplace, and deck.
RESTRICTIONS	No smoking, no pets. Resident critters include lovable Wheadon terriers, Sadie and Willi Wonka, and a tabby cat, Lulu.
REVIEWED	*Country Inns and Back Roads: California; America's Wonderful Little Hotels & Inns; Northern California Wine Country Access; The Best Places to Kiss in Northern California; Recommended Country Inns—West Coast*
MEMBER	Professional Association of Innkeepers International, California Association of Bed & Breakfast Inns
RATED	AAA 2 Diamonds
KUDOS/COMMENTS	"Complete privacy, comfortable rooms with wood-burning stoves, and a path to the beach right outside your room. Delicious breakfast."

BLAIR HOUSE INN

45110 Little Lake Street, Mendocino, CA 95460   707-937-1800
Shay Forest, Manager   800-699-9296
WEBSITE *www.blairhouse.com*   FAX 707-937-2444

LOCATION	In the heart of Mendocino on the corner of Ford and Little Lake Streets, three blocks from the ocean.
OPEN	All year
DESCRIPTION	An 1888 two-story Victorian furnished with antiques and Persian rugs. This was Jessica Fletcher's home on the TV series *Murder, She Wrote*.
NO. OF ROOMS	Three rooms with private bathrooms and two rooms share one bathroom.
RATES	Year-round rates are $85-165 for a single or double. There is a two-night minimum stay on weekends, and three nights on holiday weekends. Cancellation requires five days' notice.

CREDIT CARDS	MasterCard, Visa
BREAKFAST	Continental breakfast is served at the Mendocino Bakery down the street. The inn gives each guest a $3.50 ticket to use at the bakery.
AMENITIES	Complimentary bottle of wine.
RESTRICTIONS	No smoking
MEMBER	Professional Association of Innkeepers International

BREWERY GULCH INN

9350 North Coast Highway 1, Mendocino, CA 95460   707-937-4752
Authur Ciancutti, Owner
WEBSITE www.mcn.org/e/brewery

LOCATION	One mile south of town.
OPEN	All year
DESCRIPTION	An 1862 country inn with gardens and Victorian furnishings.
NO. OF ROOMS	Three rooms with private bathrooms and two rooms share two bathrooms.
RATES	May through October, rates are $85-110 for a single or double with a private bathroom and $110-130 for a suite. November through April (excluding holidays), rates are $75-95 for a single or a double and $95-115 for a suite. There is a two-night minimum stay on the weekends and cancellation requires five days' notice.
CREDIT CARDS	MasterCard, Visa
BREAKFAST	Full breakfast is served in the dining room and includes quiche, scones, banana pancakes, fruit, orange juice, and coffee.
AMENITIES	Wine and port on Saturday night, limited handicapped access.
RESTRICTIONS	No smoking, children over 15 are welcome. The resident dog is Cindy and the Manx cat is Mickey.
REVIEWED	*America's Wonderful Little Hotels & Inns*, *The Best Places to Kiss in Northern California*

CAPTAIN'S COVE INN

44781 Main Street, Mendocino, CA 95460   707-937-5150
WEBSITE www.innaccess.com/cci/   800-780-7905

THE HEADLANDS INN

Corner of Howard & Albion Streets, Mendocino, CA 95460   707-937-4431
Gail Erickson, Resident Owners   800-354-4431
WEBSITE *www.headlandsinn.com*

LOCATION	Turn into the village of Mendocino at the stoplight (Little Lake Road), go west two blocks, turn left onto Howard, and go two blocks to the corner of Howard and Albion.
OPEN	All year
DESCRIPTION	A 1868 three-story New England Victorian saltbox furnished with "casual" antiques.
NO. OF ROOMS	Six rooms with private bathrooms.
RATES	Year-round rates are $100-195 for a single or double. Weekday rates from December through May are reduced. There is a two-night minimum stay on the weekends, three nights on holiday weekends. Cancellation requires 14 days' notice with a $15 fee.
CREDIT CARDS	American Express, Carte Blanche, Diners Club, MasterCard, Visa
BREAKFAST	Full breakfast, served in guestrooms, includes a hot entrée that changes daily, fresh-baked bread, fresh fruit, and a choice of beverage.
AMENITIES	Afternoon tea with mineral waters, cookies, nuts, breads; fresh-cut flowers; some rooms have robes; feather beds; down comforters; European reading pillows; wood-burning fireplaces in rooms; phone; fresh fruit and candy in parlor; English garden; ocean views.
RESTRICTIONS	No smoking, no pets, children over 12 are welcome.
REVIEWED	*Weekends for Two in Northern California: 50 Romantic Getaways; The Best Places to Kiss in Northern California; Karen Brown's California Country Inns & Itineraries; Bed & Breakfast California; Country Inns West Coast; Country Inns and Back Roads: California*
MEMBER	California Association of Bed & Breakfast Inns, California Lodging Industry Association
KUDOS/COMMENTS	"Excellent location, in-room breakfast."

JOHN DOUGHERTY HOUSE

571 Ukiah Street, Mendocino, CA 95460   707-937-5266
David & Marion Wells, Resident Owners   800-486-2104
EMAIL *jdhbmw@mcn.org*

LOCATION	In Mendocino village center, 175 miles northwest of San Francisco.
OPEN	All year
DESCRIPTION	An 1867 two-story New England saltbox furnished with early American period decor and antiques. Listed on the National Historic Register.
NO. OF ROOMS	Eight rooms with private bathrooms. Check out the Captain's Room.
RATES	July through October and weekends, rates are $105-205 for a single or double and $175 for a suite. January through June and November and December, rates are $95-175 for a single or double. There is a two-night minimum stay during weekends, three nights during holidays. Cancellation requires 15 days' notice.
CREDIT CARDS	Discover, MasterCard, Visa
BREAKFAST	Full gourmet breakfast is served in the dining room and includes a hot dish, fruits, cereals, and scones.
AMENITIES	Wine, box of chocolates on weekends, ocean views.
RESTRICTIONS	No smoking, no pets, children over 12 are welcome. Three cats—Basil, Coriander, and Tristan—roam the gardens.
REVIEWED	*Northern California Best Places*
MEMBER	California Association of Bed & Breakfast Inns
RATED	AAA 2 Diamonds

JOSHUA GRINDLE INN

44800 Little Lake Road, Mendocino, CA 95460   707-937-4143
Jim & Arlene Moorehead, Innkeepers   800-474-6353
EMAIL stay@joshgrin.com   WEBSITE www.joshgrin.com

LOCATION	From San Francisco, take Highway 101 just past Cloverdale to the Mendocino/Highway 128 West exit. Travel west on Highway 128 to Highway 1 and go north 10 miles to Mendocino. After crossing the bridge into Mendocino, take the second left, at the stoplight, onto Little Lake Road. The inn is the first large white Victorian home on the hillside to your right. Travel time from San Francisco is approximately 3.5 hours, unless you choose to enjoy coastal Highway 1 all the way, which takes approximately 5 hours.
OPEN	All year
DESCRIPTION	An 1879 two-story New England Victorian farmhouse with early American Shaker decor. The inn is located on a 2-acre estate overlooking the Pacific Ocean, Mendocino Bay, and the quaint village of Mendocino. Listed on the National Historic Register.

NO. OF ROOMS	Ten rooms with private bathrooms. Jim and Arlene suggest the master room with the four-poster queen bed, fireplace, whirlpool bath, and separate stall shower.
RATES	June through October, rates are $105-205 for a single or double and $200-250 for the guesthouse. November though May and midweek, rates are $100-185 for a single or double and $200-250 for the guesthouse. There is a minimum stay during weekends and in August; cancellation requires seven days' notice.
CREDIT CARDS	MasterCard, Visa
BREAKFAST	Full breakfast is served in the dining room or on the veranda and includes oven-fresh muffins or scones, a savory frittata or quiche, cereals and seasonal fruits, yogurt, locally roasted coffee, and herbal teas. "Breakfast is a time to enjoy conversation with new acquaintances around the circa 1830 pine harvest table while savoring selections from our cookbook, *Mendocino Mornings*. Every morning brings new treats."
AMENITIES	Fresh-cut flowers or live orchids in each room; complimentary afternoon sherry, mineral water, tea, and biscotti in parlor.
RESTRICTIONS	No smoking, no pets, children over 12 are welcome. Basil and Sybil are the resident Siamese cats. "Sybil is 'Head Inncat' and wrote the chapter 'The Real Owners of the Inn' in our new cookbook, *Mendocino Mornings*."
REVIEWED	*Weekends for Two in Northern California: 50 Romantic Getaways; Fodor's America's Best B&Bs; Frommer's; Northern California Wine Country Access; Quick Escapes from San Francisco*
MEMBER	Independent Innkeepers Association, California Association of Bed & Breakfast Inns, Professional Association of Innkeepers International, Mendocino County Lodging Association
RATED	AAA 3 Diamonds, Mobil 2 Stars
AWARDS	1985, Inn of the Year, *Pamela Lanier's Complete Guide to B&Bs, Inns, and Guesthouses*
KUDOS/COMMENTS	"A very nice inn." "The best in Mendocino, comfortable, not intrusive" "Upscale. Great breakfast."

MACCALLUM HOUSE INN

42150 Albion Street, Mendocino, CA 95460 707-937-0289
Joe & Melanie Reding, Innkeepers 800-609-0492
EMAIL *machouse@mcn.org* FAX 707-937-3076
WEBSITE *www.maccallumhouse.com*

LOCATION	Take the Main Street Mendocino exit off Coast Highway 1, go one mile, take a right turn onto Lansing, then take the first left onto Albion Street.

OPEN	All year
DESCRIPTION	An 1882 two-story Victorian inn furnished with Victorian antiques and situated in the heart of historic Mendocino village, surrounded by English gardens, and listed on the State Historic Register.
NO. OF ROOMS	Nineteen rooms with private bathrooms. Try the Upper Barn Loft.
RATES	Year-round rates are $100-190 for a single or double. There is a minimum stay during weekends from May through December and during holiday weekends year-round. Cancellation requires seven days' notice.
CREDIT CARDS	American Express, Visa
BREAKFAST	Continental breakfast includes homemade granola, fresh juices, fine baked goods, and coffee from locally roasted beans. Dinner is also available.
AMENITIES	Fine restaurant on premises (chef is a graduate of the Culinary Institute of America), flowers and wine for special occasions, handicapped access and remodeled Greenhouse Cottage for disabled, clawfoot tubs for two, fireside dining.
RESTRICTIONS	No smoking, no pets
REVIEWED	*The Complete Guide to Bed & Breakfast Inns & Guest Houses*, *The Best Places to Kiss in Northern California*, *Hidden Coast of California*, *Non-Smokers Guide to Bed & Breakfasts*

MENDOCINO FARMHOUSE

43410 Comptche-Ukiah Road, Mendocino, CA 95460   707-937-0241
Margie Kamb, Innkeeper   800-475-1536
EMAIL mkamb@mcn.org   FAX 707-937-2932
WEBSITE www.mendocinofarmhouse.com

LOCATION	From Highway 1, turn east onto Comptche-Ukiah Road. Travel 1.7 miles and turn left onto Olson Lane. Go to the end of the road and look for the sign.
OPEN	All year
DESCRIPTION	A 1976 two-story farmhouse with wall-papered walls, oak floors, and antique furnishings. The home is surrounded by tall redwoods and beautiful flower gardens.
NO. OF ROOMS	Five rooms with private bathrooms. Margie suggests the Jim or Cedar Rooms.
RATES	Year-round rates are $85-130 for a single or double. There is a minimum stay during weekends and holidays and cancellation requires seven days' notice.

CREDIT CARDS	MasterCard, Visa
BREAKFAST	Full hearty breakfast is served in the dining room. Breakfast changes daily but always includes fresh fruit, a main dish, and lots of coffee.
AMENITIES	Fresh flowers from our garden, lots of quiet.
RESTRICTIONS	No smoking, no pets, children over 10 are welcome. Molly is the resident yellow Lab, Bunny is the Manx cat, and Bubba is the tabby.
REVIEWED	Karen Brown's California Country Inns & Itineraries, Frommer's Northern California, Northern California Coast Best Places
MEMBER	California Association of Bed & Breakfast Innkeepers, Mendocino Coast Innkeepers Association

MENDOCINO VILLAGE INN

44860 Main Street, Mendocino, CA 95460　　707-937-0246
Wendy Blum, Resident Manager　　　　　　800-882-7029
WEBSITE www.mendocinoinn.com

LOCATION	About 0.25 mile west of Highway 1 across from the Presbyterian Church.
OPEN	All year
DESCRIPTION	An 1892 three-story Queen Anne Victorian with an eclectic mix of Victorian and early California furnishings. Listed on the State Historic Register.
NO. OF ROOMS	Eleven rooms with private bathrooms and two rooms share one bathroom.
RATES	Year-round rates are $75-175 for a single or double with a private or shared bathroom. There is two-night minimum stay on weekends, three nights during holidays. Cancellation requires one weeks' notice and a $15 fee.
CREDIT CARDS	No
BREAKFAST	Full breakfast is served in the dining room and includes a soufflé, blue cornmeal pancakes, omelets or other hot dishes, fresh fruit, homemade baked goods, yogurt, and beverages.
AMENITIES	Fresh flowers throughout the inn, sun deck, evening wine and snacks, daily newspaper, guest refrigerator, one room handicapped accessible.

RESTRICTIONS	No smoking, no pets, children over 10 are welcome, "shirts and shoes in all common areas please." There are many outside "panhandler" cats and eight cockatiels who have formed a kind of glee club.
REVIEWED	*The Best Places to Kiss in Northern California*, *Fodor's Northern California*.

REED MANOR

44950 Little Lake Road, Mendocino, CA 95460   707-937-5446
WEBSITE *www.mcn.org/a/reedmanor/rmrlrpg1.htm*

SEA GULL INN

44960 Albion, Mendocino, CA 95460   707-937-5204
Marlene McIntyre & Bill Yearous, Managers

KUDOS/COMMENTS	"Very helpful hostess."

SEA ROCK BED & BREAKFAST INN

11101 Lansing Street, Mendocino, CA 95460   707-937-0926
Andy & Susie Plocher, Resident Owners
Some Spanish spoken

LOCATION	One-half mile north of the village of Mendocino, on Lansing Street.
OPEN	All year
DESCRIPTION	Country cottages overlooking the ocean and surrounded by lawns, gardens, and century-old cypress trees.
NO. OF ROOMS	Fourteen cottages with private bathrooms.
RATES	Please call for current rates and cancellation information.
CREDIT CARDS	MasterCard, Visa
BREAKFAST	Continental plus is served in the dining room or outside, or may be carried back to your cottage.
AMENITIES	Mountain spring water in all rooms; TV/VCR; flowers; down pillows; comforters and some feather beds; fireplaces; some kitchens.

RESTRICTIONS	No smoking, no pets, children welcome.
REVIEWED	Bed & Breakfast in California, Hidden Coast of California, The Best Places to Kiss in Northern California

STANFORD INN BY THE SEA—BIG RIVER LODGE

Coast Highway 1 and Comptche-Ukiah Road 707-937-5615
Mendocino, CA 95460 800-331-8884
Joan & Jeff Stanford, Resident Owners FAX 707-937-0305
Spanish, Japanese, and German spoken
EMAIL stanford@stanfordinn.com

LOCATION	At the intersection of Highway 1 and Comptche-Ukiah Road, 0.25 mile south of the historic village of Mendocino, across the Big River Bridge.
OPEN	All year
DESCRIPTION	An elegant 1968 redwood country inn, refurbished in 1996, overlooking Mendocino and the Pacific Ocean, with organic gardens and a solarium. The inn is decorated with traditional furnishings and antiques.
NO. OF ROOMS	Thirty-three rooms with private bathrooms. Try the Bishop Pine Suite.
RATES	Year-round rates are $215-265 for a single or double, $275-365 for suites, and $275 for the guesthouse. There is a minimum stay on weekends and cancellation requires seven days' notice.
CREDIT CARDS	American Express, Diners Club, Discover, MasterCard, Visa
BREAKFAST	Full breakfast, served in the dining room, is cooked to order and includes egg dishes, French omelets, vegan garden scramble, blue-corn waffles, freshly squeezed juices. Vegetarian and vegan dietary needs are accommodated. "We use cage-free eggs."
AMENITIES	Vegetarian dining in restaurant; workout room; in-room massage; complimentary use of mountain bikes; canoeing and kayaking; home of California certified organic Big River nurseries; coffee-makers, organic coffees and teas; refrigerators; TV/VCRs; extensive video library; some units handicapped accessible; meeting and wedding facility for up to 100; organic gardening and health seminars; wood-burning fireplaces.
RESTRICTIONS	No smoking. There are 40 resident critters, including three dogs, 12 llamas, and two horses.

REVIEWED	Best Places to Stay in California; Northern California Best Places; Fodor's California; America's Wonderful Little Hotels & Inns; Weekend for Two in Northern California: 50 Romantic Getaways; Dog Lover's Companion; The Best Places to Kiss in Northern California; Country Inns and Backroads: California
MEMBER	California Association of Bed & Breakfast Innkeepers, California Historic Country Inns
RATED	AAA 4 Diamonds
AWARDS	1998, Five Star Award for Best Inn or Bed & Breakfasts, North American Travel Journalists Association

WHITEGATE INN BED & BREAKFAST

499 Howard Street, Mendocino, CA 95460　　　　707-937-4892
George & Carol Bechtoff, Resident Owners　　　　800-531-7282
Spanish spoken　　　　　　　　　　　　　　　FAX 707-937-1131
EMAIL staff@whitegateinn.com　　　WEBSITE www.whitegateinn.com

LOCATION	Turn west off Highway 1 at Little Lake, go to Howard Street, and turn left on Ukiah.
OPEN	All year
DESCRIPTION	An 1883 two-story Victorian with guesthouse furnished in French and Victorian antiques and listed on the National and State Historic Registers.
NO. OF ROOMS	Six rooms with private bathrooms. George recommends the French Rose Room.
RATES	June through December, rates are $119-229 for a single or double. Off season and midweek rates are $20 less. There is a two-night minimum stay on weekends and cancellation requires 14 days' notice with a $25 charge.
CREDIT CARDS	American Express, Discover, MasterCard, Visa
BREAKFAST	Full breakfast, served in the dining room, includes egg soufflé, carmel apple French toast, muffins or scones, fresh fruit, and beverages.
AMENITIES	Victorian tea, flowers, welcome basket, garden or ocean views, fireplaces, TVs, afternoon wine and hors d'oeuvres, English gardens surround the deck and gazebo.
RESTRICTIONS	No smoking, no pets, children over 10 are welcome (younger children welcome in the cottage). There are two colorful cats: Oliver, who roams the grounds, and Violet, who will curl up with you in the house.

REVIEWED	Country Inns and Back Roads: California; The Best Places to Kiss in Northern California; Weddings in Style; Bed & Breakfasts and Country Inns
MEMBER	Professional Association of Innkeepers International, California Association of Bed & Breakfast Inns
RATED	Mobil 3 Stars
KUDOS/COMMENTS	"Great decor and breakfast."

MERCED

RAMBLING ROSE BED & BREAKFAST

436 West 20th Street, Merced, CA 95340   209-723-4084

MI WUK VILLAGE

CHRISTMAS TREE INN

24685 State Highway 108, Mi Wuk Village, CA 95346   209-586-1005

MILL VALLEY

This Bay Area residential community had the good sense to locate at the base of triple-peaked Mount Tamalpais in affluent Marin County, where ecological diversity is a pride and joy. In town, visit Old Mill Park and the remains of the old sawmill for which the town was named. The main event is the Mill Valley Film Festival. Mount Tamalpais State Park, six miles west, covers 6,233 acres of coastal hill country, with endless hiking and biking trails winding to the summit. To reach Mill Valley, cross the Golden Gate Bridge onto Highway 1.

MILL VALLEY BED & BREAKFAST

20 Sunnyside Avenue, Mill Valley, CA 94941   415-389-4040

MILL VALLEY INN

165 Throckmorton Avenue, Mill Valley, CA 94941　　　415-389-6608
WEBSITE *www.millvalleyinn.com*

MOUNTAIN HOME INN

810 Panoramic Highway, Mill Valley, CA 94941　　　415-381-9000
Lynn Saggese, Manager　　　FAX 415-381-3615
Spanish spoken

LOCATION	Heading north on Highway 101, take the Stinson Beach exit. After 0.66 mile, turn left at the light, staying on Highway 1. After 2.6 miles, turn right onto Panoramic Highway (signs say Mount Tamalpais). Go 0.8 mile at a four-way intersection, take the high road, Panoramic. After 1.8 miles the inn is on the right.
OPEN	All year
DESCRIPTION	A 1985 three-story rustic inn with "rustic-elegant" furnishings and cathedral ceilings and featuring spectacular views of the Marin Hills across the East Bay.
NO. OF ROOMS	Ten rooms with private bathrooms. Lynn suggests the Canopy Room.
RATES	Year-round rates are $139-259 for a single or double. There is no minimum stay and a five-day cancellation policy.
CREDIT CARDS	American Express, MasterCard, Visa
BREAKFAST	Full breakfast is served in the dining room and includes a choice of spinach and mushroom omelet, French toast, eggs any style, muffins, yogurt, and fruit. Lunch and dinner are also available.
AMENITIES	Phones in rooms, meeting facilities, handicapped accessible, decks, fresh flowers.
RESTRICTIONS	Some smoking rooms, no pets
REVIEWED	*Recommended Country Inns*

MODESTO

VINEYARD VIEW

2837 Michigan Avenue, Modesto, CA 95358   209-523-9009

MOKELUMNE HILL

MOKELUMNE RIVER LODGE

10704 Highway 49, Mokelumne Hill, CA 95245   209-286-1000
WEBSITE *www.mokeriverlodge.com*

MONTARA

Montara State Beach offers great bird- and whale-watching where the land juts out to form the San Mateo coastline. Beachcombing and walking the shoreline are reasons enough to visit. Montara is south of San Francisco on Highway 1.

GOOSE & TURRETS BED & BREAKFAST

835 George Street, Montara, CA 94037   650-728-5451
Raymond & Emily Hoche-Mong, Innkeepers   FAX 650-728-0141
Fluent French spoken
EMAIL *rhmgt@montara.com*
WEBSITE *www.montara.com/goose.html*

LOCATION	Montara is 23 miles south of downtown San Francisco, 15 miles east of San Francisco airport, and eight miles north of Half Moon Bay. In Montara, turn east on 2nd Street, right on Main Street, left on 3rd Street, and go 0.5 mile to the inn on the left (3rd Street changes to Kanoff and then to George; ignore the signs).
OPEN	All year
DESCRIPTION	A 1908 two-story Italianate villa decorated with antiques and art, located 0.5 mile from the beach amidst quiet gardens.

NO. OF ROOMS	Five rooms with private bathrooms. Try the Hummingbird or Whale Rooms.
RATES	Year-round rates are $100-135 for a single or double and $682 for the entire B&B. There is no minimum stay and cancellation requires 72 hours' notice.
CREDIT CARDS	American Express, Diners Club, Discover, MasterCard, Visa
BREAKFAST	Full four-course breakfast is served in the dining room. Breakfast changes daily, but may include cream cheese and smoked salmon on baby bagel, Southwest pancakes with sour cream and salsa, and handmade fresh blackberry sorbet.
AMENITIES	Down comforters; towel warmers; afternoon tea with savories and sweets; expert advice on birding and hiking; quiet gardens with fountains, swing, hammock, and boccie ball; the inn caters to readers, nature lovers, pilots, and enthusiastic eaters.
RESTRICTIONS	No smoking, no pets
REVIEWED	*Northern California Handbook; Recommended Country Inns— West Coast; Fodor's California and San Francisco; Frommer's B&Bs in California; America's Favorite Inns, B&Bs, & Small Hotels; Bay Area Backroads; Bed & Breakfast California*
MEMBER	Professional Association of Innkeepers International, California Lodging Industry Association
RATED	AAA 2 Diamonds, Mobil 2 Stars

MONTE RIO

Essentially an old resort town, Monte Rio is home of the infamous Bohemian Grove, the elite all-male playground of San Francisco's Bohemian Club, founded in the 1920s by such literary anarchists as Jack London and Ambrose Bierce. In July, the Bohos arrive by private helicopters, stretch limos, or in the dark of night. Monte Rio is just north of Bodega Bay via Highway 1 and 116.

HIGHLAND DELL INN

21050 River Boulevard, Monte Rio, CA 95462
Glenn Dixon & Anthony Patchett, Innkeepers
EMAIL highland@netdex.com
WEBSITE www.highlanddellinn.com

707-865-1759
800-767-1759
FAX 707-865-4128

LOCATION	From Highway 101, take the River Road exit west and go for 21 miles to the Monte Rio stop sign. Go straight under the "Monte Rio Vacation Wonderland" sign and turn left onto Bohemian Highway. The inn is the first left across the bridge over the Russian River.

OPEN	April through November
DESCRIPTION	A restored 1906 three-story Germanic redwood lodge on the Russian River, decorated with a blend of antiques and contemporary furnishings.
NO. OF ROOMS	Eight rooms with private bathrooms. Try the New Bohemian Suite.
RATES	Year-round rates are $100-125 for a single or double with a private bathroom, $140-190 for a suite, and $1200 for the entire inn. There is a two-night minimum stay and cancellation requires five days' notice with a $15 fee, 30 days' notice required during holidays.
CREDIT CARDS	American Express, Discover, JCB, MasterCard, Visa
BREAKFAST	Full breakfast is served buffet-style in the dining room and includes homemade baked goods, omelets, egg casseroles, Dutch babies, bacon, Glenn's homemade peach pork sausage, seasonal fruits, Anthony's orange/guava-blend juice, and cereals. Vegetarian diets are accommodated by request.
AMENITIES	Telephones, data ports, voice mail, faxes, and TVs in all rooms; suites additionally have VCRs; candies and chocolates throughout (grandmother's touch); afternoon tea and coffee service; conference rooms with special catering available; Great Room with comfortable seating areas and river-rock fireplace.
RESTRICTIONS	No smoking, no children. Call for pet restrictions. Sparky is the resident golden retriever and Lady is the golden mix. Sport is the weimeraner mix. "Lady was featured on CNN during a flood, being rescued off our roof."
REVIEWED	Bed, Breakfast & Bike—Northern California; Hidden Secrets North of San Francisco; Fodor's Gay USA; Fodor's Gay San Francisco
RATED	Mobil 2 Stars
AWARDS	Out & About Travel Newsletter, rated One of the 50 Most Romantic Places for Gays and Lesbians in the World.

HOUSE OF A THOUSAND FLOWERS

PO Box 369, Monte Rio, CA 95462   707 632-5571

HUCKLEBERRY SPRINGS COUNTRY INN & SPA

8105 Old Beedle Road, Monte Rio, CA 95462   707-865-2683
Suzanne Greene & Rebecca Goehring, Innkeepers   800-822-2683
Spanish and Italian spoken
EMAIL *mail@huckleberrysprings.com*
WEBSITE *www.huckleberrysprings.com*

LOCATION	Take the "Russian River Resorts" exit west from Santa Rosa and travel 23 miles to Monte Rio. Turn left across the bridge, then take an immediate right on Main Street. Travel one mile to Tyrone, turn right, go 0.5 mile, and look for the sign.
OPEN	March 1 to December 1
DESCRIPTION	A 1987 California country inn and cottages located on 56 acres in the coastal hills. The lodge is filled with art and the cottages have modern furnishings.
NO. OF ROOMS	Four cottages with private baths. Ask for the Barrel Cottage—it's a refurbished maraschino cherry curing barrel!
RATES	Rates are $125-155 for a single or double. The entire inn rents for $600. There is a minimum stay and cancellation requires two weeks' notice.
CREDIT CARDS	Discover, MasterCard, Visa
BREAKFAST	Full breakfast is served in the dining room and includes meat, fruit, juice, coffee, and tea, and may include fresh blueberry pancakes, poached eggs on grits with pan-seared ham and red pepper cream sauce, French toast, or Mexican scrambles with black beans. Four-course dinners are available on Wednesday and Saturday nights.
AMENITIES	Hillside spa in a landscaped gazebo, private massage cottage in redwood grove (additional charge for massage), swimming pool, sun deck, fresh flowers in lodge and cottages, chocolates, VCRs in cottages, 250 videos, cassette players, hair dryers, coffee-makers.
RESTRICTIONS	No smoking, no pets, no children. The resident pets are Brava, a Jack Russell terrier, Maggie, a terrier mix, and Peaches, a cockatiel. Brava "provides escort service to Barrel Cottage and back and picks apples from apple trees—to be used in lieu of balls for games of fetch with guests."
REVIEWED	*Northern California Best Places; Recommended Country Inns—West Coast; Frommer's Wonderful Weekends from San Francisco; Offbeat Overnights; Bay Area Backroads*
RATED	AAA 3 Diamonds, Mobil 2 Stars

Monterey

Old Monterey Inn

500 Martin Street, Monterey, CA 93940   831-375-8284
WEBSITE *www.oldmontereyinn.com*   FAX 831-375-6730

KUDOS/COMMENTS   "Every detail is perfect: the rooms, breakfast, fireplaces, hors d'oeuvres." (1999)

Moraga

In the hills behind Oakland, some amazing natural wonders here invite exploration. Chief among them are the serene and wonderful Redwood and Chabot Regional Parks and Sibley Volcanic Preserve. San Francisco and Berkeley are easily accessed from Moraga.

Hallman Bed & Breakfast

309 Constance Place, Moraga, CA 94556   925-376-4318
Virginia Hallman, Innkeeper

LOCATION	Five miles south of the Orinda exit off Highway 24. Drive south on Moraga Way to the dead end. Turn right on Canyon Road, go 0.75 mile, and turn right on Constance Place.
OPEN	All year
DESCRIPTION	A 1970 California ranch home with contemporary furnishings. One room is furnished with antiques.
NO. OF ROOMS	Two rooms share one bathroom.
RATES	Year-round rates are $60 for a single or double. If a family takes both rooms, the rate is $90. There is no minimum stay and cancellation requires three days' notice
CREDIT CARDS	No
BREAKFAST	Full breakfast is served in the dining room and includes fresh fruit, choice of eggs, cereal, pancakes, or French toast, with juice, muffins, and coffee.
AMENITIES	TV and private telephones in rooms, robes, large stall shower, books, hot tub and swimming pool available in season. Host only rents both rooms to one family or party.
RESTRICTIONS	No smoking, no pets

Hallman Bed & Breakfast, Moraga

REVIEWED Bed & Breakfast North America, Complete Guide to American B&Bs, The Non-Smokers Guide to Bed & Breakfasts, Bed & Breakfast Homes: Best of the West Coast

MOSS BEACH

Named for the moss that adorns the sea rocks at low tide. A significant reason to be here is James V. Fitzgerald State Park and Marine Reserve. Its 30 acres of tidepools make it one of the state's most diverse intertidal regions. Low tide is the best time to explore. On the San Mateo Coastline via Highway 1.

SEAL COVE INN

221 Cypress Avenue, Moss Beach, CA 94038 650-728-7325
Karen Brown Herbert & Rick Herbert, Resident Owners 800-995-9987
Spanish, French, and German spoken FAX 650-728-4116
EMAIL sealcove@coastside.net WEBSITE www.sealcoveinn.com

LOCATION	Take Highway 1 from Half Moon Bay and turn west on Cypress Avenue. Travel 0.5 mile to the inn, which is on the right.
OPEN	All year except Christmas
DESCRIPTION	A 1991 two-story inn styled after an English country home with a traditional interior of antiques and original art. The inn sits on a hillside overlooking the ocean.
NO. OF ROOMS	Ten rooms with private bathrooms. Karen recommends the Fitzgerald Room.
RATES	Year-round rates are $190-210 for a double and $270 for a suite. There is a minimum stay on holiday weekends, and cancellation requires seven days' notice and a $20 fee. Reservations must be guaranteed with a credit card.

Seal Cove Inn, Moss Beach

CREDIT CARDS	American Express, Discover, MasterCard, Visa
BREAKFAST	Full breakfast is served in the dining room and includes fresh fruit, juice, and a hot entrée that varies daily such as French toast, egg soufflé, etc. Guests may choose to have continental breakfast in their rooms.
AMENITIES	Evening buffet of wine and hors d'oeuvres. Each room has a refrigerator stocked with wine and soft drinks, TV/VCR, wood-burning fireplaces, phones, excellent reading lights, movie library with 200 videos, popcorn, fresh flowers, daily newspapers, turndown service, evening chocolates, conference room, one guestroom with handicapped access.
RESTRICTIONS	No smoking and no pets. You may see Molly, the owners' Portuguese water dog, on the grounds, but she is not allowed in the inn.
REVIEWED	*Northern California Best Places; America's Wonderful Little Hotels & Inns; Hidden Coast California; The Best Places to Kiss in Northern California; Recommended Country Inns—West Coast; Karen Brown's California Charming Inns & Itineraries; Weekends for Two in Northern California: 50 Romantic Getaways; Frommer's*
MEMBER	California Association of Bed & Breakfast Inns, Independent Innkeepers Association
RATED	AAA 4 Diamonds, Mobil 4 Stars
AWARDS	1993, Best US Bed & Breakfasts, *Andrew Harper Hideaway Report*
KUDOS/COMMENTS	"Special breakfast and lots of outside areas to explore." "Lovely location, great service, so close to San Francisco."

MOUNT SHASTA

At the foot and always in the shadows of towering Mount Shasta, the largest volcano (by mass) in the contiguous 48 states. Shasta is a dormant volcano; it's sleepy, not dead. Though an eruption may seem long overdue, fear not; geologists constantly monitor movement within the volcano and claim they will be able to predict an eruption early enough for you to pack your bags and skeedaddle. From here, head to the Sisson Fish Hatchery and Park and outdoor recreation at Lake Siskiyou. North of Redding via I-5.

DREAM INN BED & BREAKFAST

326 Chestnut Street, Mount Shasta, CA 96067 530-926-1536
David Ream & Lonna Smith, Innkeepers 877-375-4744
Spanish spoken FAX 530-926-1536
EMAIL dreaminn@worldnet.att.net WEBSITE home.att.net/~dreaminn

LOCATION	From I-5, take the Central Mount Shasta City exit. Head toward the mountain on Lake Street and turn left on Chestnut; the inn is five doors down on your right.
OPEN	All year
DESCRIPTION	A restored 1904 two-story Victorian with Victorian antiques and rose gardens.
NO. OF ROOMS	One room with a private bathroom, and four rooms share two bathrooms. Lonna recommends room 1.
RATES	June through September, rates are $90 for a single or double with a private bathroom, $70 for a single or double with a shared bathroom, and the entire inn rents for $370. October through May, rates are $10 less and the entire inn rents for $320. There is no minimum stay and cancellation incurs a $20 fee.
CREDIT CARDS	American Express, Discover, MasterCard, Visa
BREAKFAST	Full breakfast, served in the dining room, includes juice, coffee, fruit, waffles, pancakes, and eggs any style. The inn offers vegetarian breakfast options.
AMENITIES	Front porch complete with classic swing and rocking chairs; flowers; robes; back patio with "enchanted" lily pond; fireplace in dining room; clawfoot bathtubs and shower; facilities for small weddings, seminars, and retreats.
RESTRICTIONS	No smoking. Noel, a black Lab and the inn's "official greeter," loves children and other dogs.
MEMBER	California Association of Bed & Breakfast Inns
AWARDS	First Place and Judges' Award for Best Landscaping and Flower Boxes, Mount Shasta Garden Club

Mount Shasta Ranch Bed & Breakfast

1008 W. A. Barr Road, Mount Shasta, CA 96067 530-926-3870
Bill & Mary Larsen, Resident Owners FAX 916-926-6882
EMAIL alpinere@snowcrest.net
WEBSITE www.travelassist.com/req/ca121s.html

LOCATION	Southwest 1.5 miles from Mount Shasta City, off I-5. Follow the signs to Lake Siskiyou. The inn is on the corner of Ream Avenue and W. A. Barr Road.
OPEN	All year
DESCRIPTION	A 1923 two-story ranch house with Dutch gambrel roof, carriage house, and cottage with Victorian furnishings.
NO. OF ROOMS	Four rooms with private bathrooms and five rooms share five bathrooms. There is also a two-bedroom cottage.
RATES	Year-round rates are $80-95 for a single or double with a private bathroom, $50-70 for a single or a double with a shared bathroom, and $95-125 for the cottage rents. There is a minimum stay on holidays and summer weekends, and cancellation requires 72 hours' notice.
CREDIT CARDS	American Express, Discover, MasterCard, Visa
BREAKFAST	Full country-style breakfast, served in the dining room, includes juice, fresh fruit, entrée, meat, breads, and beverages.
AMENITIES	Drinks and snacks, game room with piano, Ping-Pong, and pool tables, outside spa, robes available for spa, TV, meeting room in dining room.
RESTRICTIONS	No smoking. The resident critters include a talking parrot named Ahab and a dog, Sadie.
REVIEWED	Bed, Breakfast & Bike—Northern California
KUDOS/COMMENTS	"Spacious, beautiful views, sumptuous breakfasts, gracious hosts." "Quiet, great for groups and retreats."

Wagon Creek Inn

1239 Woodland Park Drive, Mount Shasta, CA 96067 530-926-0838
Kim Smith, Resident Owner

LOCATION	Two-and-a-half miles from Mount Shasta City; 1.5 miles north of the fish hatchery on Old State Road.
OPEN	All year

DESCRIPTION	A 1984 two-story log home with southwestern decor and mountain-lodge atmosphere.
NO. OF ROOMS	One room with a private bathroom and two rooms share two bathrooms.
RATES	Year-round rates are $95 for a single or double with a private bathroom and $75-85 for a single or double with a shared bathroom. There is no minimum stay and cancellation requires 48 hours' notice.
CREDIT CARDS	American Express, Diners Club, Discover, MasterCard, Visa
BREAKFAST	Breakfast includes baked items, an egg dish, cereal, and fruit.
AMENITIES	Robes, mini-refrigerator, VCR and movie collection.
RESTRICTIONS	No smoking, children are welcome. Jekel, the resident cat, loves water.
REVIEWED	Lonely Planet

WARD'S BIG FOOT RANCH

1530 Hill Road, Mount Shasta, CA 96067   530-926-5170
Phil & Barbara Ward, Resident Owners   800-926-1272

LOCATION	Two miles from downtown Mount Shasta. Take the Central Mount Shasta exit, go west 0.5 mile, and turn north onto North Old Stage Road. Go exactly one mile from the fish hatchery, turn left (west), and go 0.3 mile.
OPEN	All year
DESCRIPTION	A 1960 ranch-style home with English and French country furnishings and some antiques.
NO. OF ROOMS	Two rooms with private bathrooms.
RATES	Please call for current rates and cancellation information.
CREDIT CARDS	No
BREAKFAST	Full breakfast is served in the dining room.
AMENITIES	Flowers, robes, phone available, hot tub on deck, baby grand piano and stereo in living room, cheese and crackers, horse boarding by arrangement.
RESTRICTIONS	No smoking inside, no pets
REVIEWED	Best Places to Stay in California, Northern California Guide
MEMBER	International Bed & Breakfast Exchange, California Association of Bed & Breakfast Inns

KUDOS/COMMENTS "Super setting that is peaceful with a creek meandering through the property and super Mount Shasta view." "Great hosts; nice cottage for romantic couple; they go out of their way to make the place very comfortable and romantic." "Friendly hosts; a relaxing, woodsy atmosphere."

MUIR BEACH

THE PELICAN INN

10 Pacific Way, Muir Beach, CA 94965 415-383-6000
WEBSITE www.pelicaninn.com

MURPHYS

Gingerbread Victorian homes peek from behind white picket fences and tall locust trees border the streets of Murphys, a former trading post set up by brothers Dan and John Murphy in cooperation with local Native Americans (John married the chief's daughter). It's worth taking the detour off Highway 49 just to stroll down Murphys' tree-lined Main Street. Eighteen miles northeast of Murphys on Highway 4 is Calaveras Big Trees State Park, a popular summer retreat that offers swimming, hiking, and fishing along the Stanislaus River. Many of the numerous caverns in the area were discovered in the mid-1800s by gold prospectors and can now be toured.

DUNBAR HOUSE, 1880

271 Jones Street, Murphys, CA 95247 209-728-2897
Bob & Barbara Costa, Innkeepers 800-692-6006
EMAIL innkeep@dunbarhouse.com FAX 209-728-1451
WEBSITE www.dunbarhouse.com

LOCATION	From Highway 4, turn left on Main Street. The inn is across from the Milliaire Winery.
OPEN	All year
DESCRIPTION	An 1880 two-story Italianate inn with country Victorian furnishings, a century-old rose garden, and a secluded cottage. Listed on the State Historic Register.

NO. OF ROOMS	Five rooms with private bathrooms. Barbara recommends the Cedar Room or the Garden Cottage.
RATES	Year-round rates are $125-225 for a single or double. There is a minimum stay on weekends and cancellations require five days' notice.
CREDIT CARDS	American Express, MasterCard, Visa
BREAKFAST	Full gourmet breakfast is served by candlelight in the dining room or guestrooms, or in the rose garden, and includes a crab specialty dish, fresh fruit, specialty cakes, fresh fruit juice, and edible floral garnishes.
AMENITIES	Fresh flowers, fireplaces, two-person Jacuzzi, TV/VCR, classic video library, personal refrigerators stocked with complimentary local wine, phones, hair dryers, appetizers, down comforters and pillows, makeup mirrors.
RESTRICTIONS	No smoking, no pets, children over 10 are welcome. Cody is the inn's smiling cocker spaniel.
REVIEWED	*Northern California Best Places; Karen Brown's California Country Inns & Itineraries; Country Inns and Back Roads: California; The Best Places to Kiss in Northern California; Best Places to Stay in Northern California*
MEMBER	Professional Association of Innkeepers International, California Association of Bed & Breakfast Inns
RATED	ABBA 3 Crowns, Best Places to Kiss 4 Lips
AWARDS	1984 Calaveras Historical Society Award of Architectural Merit

THE REDBUD INN

402 Main Street, Murphys, CA 95247 209-728-8533
Pam & Steve Hatch, Innkeepers 800-827-8533
Spanish spoken FAX 209-728-9123
EMAIL info@redbudinn.com

LOCATION	Eight miles off Highway 49 on Main Street (Highway 4) in the center of Murphys.
OPEN	All year
DESCRIPTION	A 1994 two-story rustic inn—a new building made to look 100 years old but with all the luxuries of today.
NO. OF ROOMS	Thirteen rooms with private bathrooms. Try the Anniversary Suite.
RATES	Year-round rates are $95-125 for a single or double and the suite is $135-235. The two bedroom/two bathroom guesthouse is $245. There is a two-night minimum stay on weekends and cancellation requires seven days' notice.

CREDIT CARDS	Discover, MasterCard, Visa
BREAKFAST	Full breakfast is served in the dining room and includes a buffet of pastries, fruits, breads, cereals, and bread pudding, followed by a hot entrée that changes daily. Catered meals are available in the conference room.
AMENITIES	Evening wine and hors d'oeuvres, robes in suites, cookies in room, full concierge service.
RESTRICTIONS	No smoking, no pets. Magnum is the resident Lab/Akita mix. "Magnum's the town mascot. He never met a treat he didn't like."
REVIEWED	Lanier's, Fodor's, The Best Places to Kiss in Northern California, Best Places to Stay
MEMBER	California Association of Bed & Breakfast Inns, Professional Association of Innkeepers International
RATED	Mobil 4 Stars
KUDOS/COMMENTS	"Delightful." "Charming inn with interesting rooms on historic main street." (1999)

MYERS FLAT

MYERS COUNTRY INN

12913 Avenue of the Giants, Myers Flat, CA 95554   707-943-3259
WEBSITE www.northcoast.com/myersinn

NAPA

Wine Country starts here, at the southeast end of the fertile Napa Valley. Once a silver lode, it's now the county's agricultural hub. Victorians still stand in the old neighborhoods and the Opera House is a restored showpiece. There's always action and special events at the Town Center. Major local events include the Chili Ball and Cookoff and the County Fair in July, and Concours d'Elegance in June.

ARBOR GUEST HOUSE

1436 G Street, Napa, CA 94559   707-252-8144
James & Andrea Chadwick, Resident Owners   800-457-0007
WEBSITE www.arborguesthouse.com

LOCATION	Take the Lincoln Avenue exit off Highway 29 in Napa. Go east to the second signal, turn right onto Jefferson Street, go three short blocks to G Street, and turn right. The inn is in two blocks, on the right.
OPEN	All year
DESCRIPTION	A 1906 two-story colonial inn and carriage house.
NO. OF ROOMS	Five rooms with private bathrooms. Winter Haven and Autumn Harvest are the best rooms.
RATES	April through November, rates for a single or double are $130-200. There are special rates from December through March; call for details. There is a two-night minimum stay during weekends and holidays. Cancellation requires 72 hours' notice.
CREDIT CARDS	MasterCard, Visa
BREAKFAST	Full gourmet breakfast is served in the dining room, carriage house, guestrooms, or patio areas. Breakfast includes fresh fruits, crustless quiche, French toast, chicken sausages, muffins, croissants, scones, coffee, and tea,.
AMENITIES	Fireplaces, spa tubs, TV on request, handicapped accessible room available.
RESTRICTIONS	No smoking, pets OK, children over 10 are welcome.
MEMBER	Professional Association of Innkeepers International, Bed & Breakfast Inns of Napa Valley

BEAZLEY HOUSE

1910 First Street, Napa, CA 94559
Carol & Jim Beazley, Innkeepers
Spanish and French spoken
EMAIL Innkeeper@beazleyhouse.com

707-257-1649
800-559-1649
FAX 707-257-1518
WEBSITE www.beazleyhouse.com

LOCATION	In the historic Old Town section of Napa. Take the Downtown Napa/First Street exit off Highway 29 at California Street, turn right, and go to Second Street. Turn left on Second Street and go 0.3 mile to Warren Street. Turn left on Warren and go to First Street.
OPEN	All year
DESCRIPTION	A 1902 three-story colonial revival shingle-style inn and carriage house furnished with turn-of-the-century antiques and nestled on a half-acre of lawns and gardens. Listed on the State Historic Register.
NO. OF ROOMS	Eleven rooms with private bathrooms. Carol and Jim suggest the West Loft.

RATES	Year-round rates are $125-235 for a single or double. There is a two-night minimum stay during weekends and cancellation requires seven days' notice.
CREDIT CARDS	American Express, MasterCard, Visa
BREAKFAST	Full breakfast is served in the dining room and includes fresh fruits, inn-baked breads and muffins, a daily hot dish, fresh fruit juice, and house-blend coffee.
AMENITIES	Soft drinks, cheese, sherry, chocolate chip cookies, personalized wine-touring itineraries, restaurant reservations and guidance.
RESTRICTIONS	No smoking. Sissy is the resident golden retriever, who will allow you to rub her belly "and will fetch tennis balls until your arm falls off."
REVIEWED	*Country Inns of America: California*
MEMBER	Professional Association of Innkeepers International, California Association of Bed & Breakfast Innkeepers
RATED	Mobil 3 Stars
KUDOS/COMMENTS	"Oldest and very popular inn in the valley."

BLUE VIOLET MANSION

443 Brown Street, Napa, CA 94559   707-253-2583
Bob & Kathy Morris, Resident Owners   800-799-2583
EMAIL bviolet@napanet.net   FAX 707-257-8205
WEBSITE www.bluevioletmansion.com

LOCATION	Take Highway 29 north to the Imola exit. Turn right and then left onto Coombs. Go 0.5 mile and turn right on Laurel Street. Drive one block and turn left on Brown Street.
OPEN	All year
DESCRIPTION	An 1886 two-story Queen Anne Victorian with Victorian furnishings, listed on the National Historic Register.
NO. OF ROOMS	Fourteen rooms with private bathrooms. Try the Blue Violet Room.
RATES	Seasonal rates range from $159-289 for a double. There is a 10 percent midweek discount and low-season rates are 20 percent lower on the weekend and 40 percent lower midweek. There is a minimum stay and cancellation requires 10 days' notice.
CREDIT CARDS	American Express, JCB, MasterCard, Visa
BREAKFAST	Full breakfast is served in the dining room or guestrooms and includes freshly ground coffee, fruit juice, cakes, beverages, and a main course such as quiche, French toast, or waffles. Candlelight champagne dinners are available.

AMENITIES	Three rooms with spas; two with balconies; five with fireplaces; all rooms have robes, iron, ironing board, silver wine goblets, and books; TV in sun room; dessert buffet in the evenings; wine at check in; concierge; garden gazebo.
RESTRICTIONS	No smoking, no pets, children welcome in the suite.
REVIEWED	*The Best Places to Kiss in Northern California*
MEMBER	California Association of Bed & Breakfast Inns, Bed & Breakfast Inns of Napa, Bed & Breakfast Inns of Napa Valley
AWARDS	1993, Napa County Landmarks Award of Merit for Historic Preservation
KUDOS/COMMENTS	"Beautifully restored mansion with all the little extra touches and warm, wonderful host and hostess." "Fabulous place!"

THE CANDLELIGHT INN

1045 Easum Drive, Napa, CA 94558   707-257-3717
Johanna & Wolfgang Brox, Resident Owners   FAX 707-257-3762
EMAIL *mail@candlelightinn.com*   WEBSITE *www.candlelightinn.com*

LOCATION	Sixty miles west of San Francisco, 1.3 miles west of downtown Napa.
OPEN	All year
DESCRIPTION	A 1929 two-story English Tudor inn on the bank of Napa Creek.
NO. OF ROOMS	Ten rooms with private bathrooms.
RATES	Year-round rates are $110-235 for a single or double. There is a two-night minimum stay on weekends and cancellation requires seven days' notice and a $10 fee.
CREDIT CARDS	American Express, Discover, MasterCard, Visa
BREAKFAST	A three-course gourmet breakfast is served in the breakfast room. Favorite dishes include crepes, peach waffles, and rosemary potatoes.
AMENITIES	Wine, hors d'oeuvres, coffee, tea, cake, port and sherry in the evening, homemade truffles and cookies, large pool, Jacuzzi, fireplaces in rooms, beautiful grounds and gardens.
RESTRICTIONS	No pets, children over 12 are welcome.
REVIEWED	*Napa Valley Guide*
MEMBER	California Association of Bed & Breakfast Inns

Cedar Gables Inn

486 Coombs Street, Napa, CA 94559 707-224-7969
Margaret & Craig Snasdell, Resident Owners 800-309-7969
EMAIL info@cedargablesinn.com FAX 707-224-4838
WEBSITE www.cedargablesinn.com

LOCATION	Four blocks south of downtown Napa on the corner of Oak and Coombs streets.
OPEN	All year except December 22–27
DESCRIPTION	An 1892 three-story Old English-style country inn designed by English architect Ernest Coxhead and decorated with Victorian antiques.
NO. OF ROOMS	Six rooms with private bathrooms. Try Count Bonzi's Room.
RATES	High-season rates (April 15 through November 15) are $139-199 for a single or double. November 16 through April 14, rates are $139-189 for a single or a double. There is a minimum stay on Saturday nights and cancellation requires seven days' notice.
CREDIT CARDS	American Express, Discover, MasterCard, Visa
BREAKFAST	Full breakfast is served in the dining room or sun room and includes muffins, scones, fresh fruit, and an entrée such as French toast with sausage, frittata, crepes, or pancakes, plus beverages. Special needs may be accommodated with prior notice.

Cedar GAbles Inn, Napa

AMENITIES	Fireplace, robes, and whirlpool tubs in four rooms; fresh flowers in common areas and guestrooms; complimentary wine and cheese social hour; downstairs parlor with big-screen TV/VCR and huge wood-burning fireplace.
RESTRICTIONS	None
REVIEWED	*Frommer's, The Best Places to Kiss in Northern California, Recommended Bed & Breakfasts: California*
MEMBER	California Association of Bed & Breakfast Inns, Professional Association of Innkeepers International, American Bed & Breakfast Association
RATED	ABBA 3 Crowns, Best Places to Kiss 3 Lips
AWARDS	1992, Napa County Landmarks Inc., Award of Merit
KUDOS/COMMENTS	"Great old house. Hospitality is superb." "Country English manor. Very elegant. Services are the best, as is the atmosphere."

CHURCHILL MANOR BED & BREAKFAST

485 Brown Street, Napa, CA 94559　　　707-253-7733
Joanna Guidotti & Brian Jensen, Innkeepers　　　FAX 707-253-8836
Spanish spoken
WEBSITE *www.churchhillmanor.com*

LOCATION	In beautiful downtown Napa, at the corner of Oak and Brown in the Abajo Historic District.
OPEN	Closed December 24 and 25
DESCRIPTION	An 1889 three-story Second Empire mansion with Victorian furnishings and original carved redwood columns, located on a full acre of gardens. Listed on the National Historic Register.
NO. OF ROOMS	Ten rooms with private bathrooms.
RATES	Year-round rates are $95-205 for a single or double. There is two-night minimum stay when a Saturday is involved and cancellation requires five days' notice.
CREDIT CARDS	Discover, MasterCard, Visa
BREAKFAST	Full breakfast is served in the dining room or on the veranda and includes fresh fruits, homemade nutbreads and muffins, croissants, made-to-order omelets or French toast, and fresh-ground coffee.
AMENITIES	Fresh flowers in the common areas and guestrooms, cookies and refreshments at check-in, wine and cheese reception in the evening, tandem bicycles, grand piano, facilities for weddings, games, TV/VCR in common room, nine fireplaces (seven wood-burning), four two-person soaking tubs, three two-person showers.

RESTRICTIONS	No smoking, no pets, children over 12 are welcome. Blackie is the resident cat.
REVIEWED	America's Wonderful Little Hotels & Inns; The Best Places to Stay in California; The Best Places to Kiss in Northern California; Weekends for Two in Northern California: 50 Romantic Getaways
MEMBER	Professional Association of Innkeepers International, American Bed & Breakfast Association, Napa Bed & Breakfast Inns
RATED	ABBA 3 Crowns

COUNTRY GARDEN INN

1815 Silverado Trail, Napa, CA 94558
Lisa & George Smith, Resident Owners
WEBSITE www.countrygardeninn.com

707-255-1197
FAX 707-255-3112

LOCATION	From Highway 29 south, take Trancas east to the fork in the road. Take the right-hand fork to Napa; the inn is in 0.75 mile, on the right.
OPEN	All year
DESCRIPTION	An 1850 carriage house with English country antique furnishing.
NO. OF ROOMS	Ten rooms with private bathrooms. Lisa likes a room called Hedgerow.
RATES	Year-round rates are $150-185 for a single or double and the suite is $225. There is a two-night minimum stay on weekends and cancellation requires 72 hours' notice with a 10 percent fee.
CREDIT CARDS	American Express, MasterCard, Visa
BREAKFAST	Full breakfast is served in the dining room and includes beverages, fruit, homemade coffeecake, scones, and a hot entrée such as buttermilk French toast with fresh strawberries.
AMENITIES	Large aviary with over 40 species of birds, afternoon tea, happy hour with international cheese desserts.
RESTRICTIONS	No smoking, no pets, children over 16 are welcome. The outdoor cat is called Tigger and the dogs are Missee and Amber.
REVIEWED	*Country Inns of America: California; Recommended Country Inns—West Coast*
MEMBER	Professional Association of Innkeepers International, California Association of Bed & Breakfast Inns
RATED	Mobil 3 Stars

CROSSROADS INN

6380 Silverado Trail, Napa, CA 94558　　　　　　　707-944-0646
WEBSITE www.crossroadsnv.com

THE ELM HOUSE

800 California Boulevard, Napa, CA 94559　　　　707-255-1831
Cecil Lale, Resident Manager　　　　　　　　　　　800-528-1234
Spanish spoken　　　　　　　　　　　　　　　FAX 707-255-8609
EMAIL elmhouse@webtv.net　　　　　WEBSITE www.bestwestern.com

OPEN	All year
DESCRIPTION	A 1987 Queen Anne with French country furnishings.
NO. OF ROOMS	Seventeen rooms with private bathrooms. Christopher suggests room 207.
RATES	April through November 14, rates are $139-169 for a single or double and $159-189 for a suite. November 15 through March, rates are $99-139 for a single or double and suites are $119-139. There is a minimum stay from April through November 14 and cancellation requires 24 hours' notice.
CREDIT CARDS	American Express, Carte Blanche, Diners Club, Discover, MasterCard, Visa
BREAKFAST	Continental plus is served in the dining room and includes fresh fruits in season, bagels, hot scones, granola, pastries, muffins, croissants, banana bread, hard-cooked eggs, and beverages. Arrangements can be made for catered meals.
AMENITIES	Cable TV, telephones, honor bar, refrigerator, one handicapped-accessible room, hot tub on private patio.
RESTRICTIONS	No smoking, no pets
MEMBER	California Lodging Industry Association

HENNESSEY HOUSE

1727 Main Street, Napa, CA 94559　　　　　　　　707-226-3774
Gilda & Alex Feit, Innkeepers　　　　　　　　FAX 707-226-2975
Portuguese, Spanish, and French spoken
EMAIL hennessey@cwix.com
WEBSITE www.hennesseyhouse.com

LOCATION	Take Highway 29 to the Lincoln Avenue exit. Go east on Lincoln to the third traffic light and turn right onto Main Street. The inn is three blocks down on the right.
OPEN	All year
DESCRIPTION	An 1889 two-story Queen Anne Victorian inn tastefully decorated with European antiques with marble bathroom floors and antique brass fixtures. Listed on the National Historic Register.
NO. OF ROOMS	Ten rooms with private bathrooms. Filda and Alex suggest the Foxes Den.
RATES	May through October, rates are $105-190 for a single or double and $190-230 for the guesthouse. November through April, rates are $85-190 for a single or double and $170-230 for the guesthouse. There is a minimum stay when a Saturday is included. Cancellation requires seven days' notice with a $15 charge.
CREDIT CARDS	American Express, Discover, MasterCard, Visa
BREAKFAST	Full gourmet breakfast is served in the dining room and includes fresh fruit, a main dish such as blueberry stuffed French toast or eggs Florentine, a side dish, plus homemade granola, fresh-baked muffins, a special house blend of coffee, yogurt, and juice.
AMENITIES	Wine and cheese in the evening, tea and cookies or cake in the afternoon; warm, friendly, knowledgeable hosts; a peaceful garden fountain; sauna; in-room sherry and chocolates; flowers in the garden and throughout the inn; lots of books and information about the Napa Valley; discount packages for the Wine Train, hot air balloon rides, golf, and in-room massages; meeting areas for up to 20 people; rooms air conditioned and heated; some rooms with two-person whirlpool tubs, fireplaces, featherbeds, or four poster canopy beds, private patios, vaulted ceilings with skylights, and robes.
RESTRICTIONS	No smoking, no pets, children are welcome. Ralphina is the resident cat. "Ralphina is very friendly and spends time outside or in the basement. She does not have full run of the house."
REVIEWED	*Access California Wine Country, Frommer's*
MEMBER	Professional Association of Innkeepers International, American Bed & Breakfast Association
RATED	ABBA 3 Crowns

HILLVIEW COUNTRY INN

1205 Hillview Lane, Napa, CA 94558
Al & Susie Hasenpusch, Resident Owners
WEBSITE *www.hillviewinnnapa.com*

707-224-5004
FAX 707-224-6422

LOCATION	From Highway 29 north, turn left at Darms Lane, then right on Solano Avenue. Go about half-a-block and turn left at the Hillview Country Inn gate.
OPEN	All year
DESCRIPTION	A newly remodeled two-story country farmhouse built in the 1800s.
NO. OF ROOMS	Four rooms with private bathrooms. Sample the Vineyard Room.
RATES	May through September, rates for a double are $160-185. October through January, rates for a double are $135-175. There is a two-night minimum stay on weekends (there is some flexibility) and cancellation requires seven days' notice with a $15 charge per night.
CREDIT CARDS	American Express, Diners Club, Discover, JCB, MasterCard, Visa
BREAKFAST	Full country breakfast is served in the dining room.
AMENITIES	Pool, vineyard views, dessert wines and brandy, hors d'oeuvres, some TVs and fireplaces in rooms, meeting facilities.
RESTRICTIONS	No smoking. Little Guy and Max are the resident cats.

INN ON RANDOLPH

411 Randolph, Napa, CA 94559   707-257-2886
Deborah Coffee, Resident Owner   FAX 707-257-8756
Only English spoken ("just ask my college Spanish teacher")

LOCATION	Within blocks of downtown Napa.
OPEN	All year
DESCRIPTION	An 1860 two-story Gothic revival inn with a blend of antiques and comfortable furniture.
NO. OF ROOMS	Five rooms with private bathrooms. Deborah suggests the Autumn Room.
RATES	Please ask about current rates and cancellation information.
CREDIT CARDS	American Express, MasterCard, Visa
BREAKFAST	Full breakfast is served in the dining room or sun room, or on the garden deck, and is varied with "a southern accent." Breakfast includes fresh fruit, freshly baked breads, a hot entrée, and usually a side dish. Special meals and picnic baskets are available.
AMENITIES	Two rooms with fireplaces, two-person tubs and balconies, in-room telephone jacks, baby grand piano in dining room, refreshment bar and refrigerator, small meeting facilities, wine, champagne, in-room massage available.

RESTRICTIONS	No smoking, no pets
MEMBER	Professional Association of Innkeepers International, Bed & Breakfast Innkeepers of Napa Valley

LA BELLE EPOQUE

1386 Calistoga Avenue, Napa, CA 94559 707-257-2161
Georgia Jump, Innkeeper 800-238-8070
EMAIL innkeeper@labelleepoque.com FAX 707-226-6314

LOCATION	Take the First Street exit from Highway 29, go right to 2nd Street, left on 2nd to Jefferson, left on Jefferson to Calistoga, and right one block on Calistoga to Seminary.
OPEN	All year
DESCRIPTION	An 1893 two-story Queen Anne Victorian with stained glass, crafted interiors, Victorian furnishings, and oriental carpets.
NO. OF ROOMS	Six rooms with private bathrooms. Try the Champagne Suite.
RATES	April through November and holidays, rates are $159-209 for a single or double. December through March, rates are $149-199. There is a minimum stay on weekends and holidays; cancellation requires 72 hours' notice with a $25 charge.
CREDIT CARDS	American Express, Discover, MasterCard, Visa
BREAKFAST	Full breakfast is served in the dining room and includes La Belle grapes in honeydew with a rosemary and wine syrup, chile egg puff with sour cream, sauté of heirloom tomatoes, beef tenderloin in merlot sauce, and double cornbread.

La Belle Epoque, Napa

AMENITIES	Twenty-four-hour guest hospitality buffet, robes, TV/VCR and over 200 videos, evening wine and hors d'oeuvres served in the wine-tasting room, wine cellar, air conditioning, sherry and snacks in each guestroom, fireplaces, whirlpool, meeting facilities and accommodations for small weddings, pocket gardens.
REVIEWED	*Bed & Breakfast California, The Best Places to Kiss in Northern California, The Napa and Sonoma Book, Best of Wine Country, Bed & Breakfast in California*
MEMBER	American Bed & Breakfast Association, Napa Bed & Breakfast Association, California Association of Bed & Breakfast Inns, Professional Association of Innkeepers International, Urban Inns, Napa Valley Bed & Breakfast Association

LA RESIDENCE COUNTRY INN

4066 St. Helena Highway, Napa, CA 94558   707-253-0337
David Jackson & Craig Claussen, Resident Owners   FAX 707-253-0382

LOCATION	When traveling north, take the first right turn after the intersection of Highway 29 and Salvador. When traveling south on Highway 29, take the first left after the intersection of Highway 29 and Oak Knoll.
OPEN	All year
DESCRIPTION	An 1870 three-story Gothic revival home with American antiques, plantation shutters, and chandeliers; and a two-story French barn with antiques and French country decor. Both are located in a wooded, gardenlike setting.
NO. OF ROOMS	Twenty rooms with private bathrooms. Craig says his best room is the Deluxe Suite.
RATES	Year-round rates are $165-195 for a single or double, and suites are $235-300. There is a two-night minimum stay on Saturdays and holidays. Cancellation requires at least 11 days' notice.
CREDIT CARDS	American Express, Diners Club, MasterCard, Visa
BREAKFAST	Breakfast is served in three courses: juice and beverage, fresh fruit, and entrée such as blueberry pancakes or scrambled eggs, and caramel nut rolls. Catered lunches and dinners may be arranged for special occasions or meetings.
AMENITIES	Hot tub, heated pool, wine and cheese hour every evening (often with a local winery pouring), phones in rooms, meeting room for up to 15 people, one room is handicapped accessible.

La Residence Country Inn, Napa

RESTRICTIONS	No smoking, no pets
REVIEWED	Fodor's Wine Country, Karen Brown's California Country Inns & Itineraries, The Best Places to Kiss in Northern California, Northern California Best Places, Access California Wine Country
RATED	Mobil 3 Stars

McCLELLAND–PRIEST BED & BREAKFAST

569 Randolph Street, Napa, CA 94559   707-224-6875

THE NAPA INN

1137 Warren Street, Napa, CA 95449   707-257-1444
Brooke & Jim Boyer, Resident Owners   800-435-1144
EMAIL info@napainn.com   FAX 707-257-0251
WEBSITE www.napainn.com

LOCATION	Exit 1st Street off Highway 29, turn left on California, go right on Clay, then left on Warren.
OPEN	All year
DESCRIPTION	A turn-of-the-century three-story Queen Anne Victorian furnished with antiques and located on a quiet street in downtown Napa.
NO. OF ROOMS	Seven rooms with private bathrooms.
RATES	June through November, rates are $140-155 for a single or double and suites are $185. December through May, rates are 10 to 20 percent less. There is a two-night minimum stay on weekends and seven days' notice is required for cancellation.
CREDIT CARDS	American Express, Carte Blanche, Diners Club, Discover, MasterCard, Visa

BREAKFAST	Full gourmet breakfast is served in the dining room.
AMENITIES	Evening dessert and liqueurs, TV/VCR and movies, phones, two rooms with two-person tubs, fireplaces in three suites, fireplace and library in the parlor, gardens and patio area, close to the wine train, hot air balloon rides, wineries, spas, on-site therapeutic massages.
RESTRICTIONS	No smoking, no pets
MEMBER	Napa Bed & Breakfast Association

OAK KNOLL INN

2200 Oak Knoll Avenue, Napa, CA 94559   707-255-2200
Barbara Passino & John Kuhlmann, Innkeepers   FAX 707-255-2296
French and Spanish spoken
WEBSITE www.virtualcities.com

LOCATION	North on Highway 29, take the second right after the Salvador Avenue traffic light onto Oak Knoll Avenue. Turn left at Big Ranch Road, then right onto Oak Knoll again. Go 0.5 mile.
OPEN	All year
DESCRIPTION	A 1984 one-story country French stone building with rustic stone walls, French windows, and vaulted ceilings, surrounded by 600 acres of vineyard.
NO. OF ROOMS	Four rooms with private bathrooms.
RATES	April through November, rates are $350-395 for a single or double. December, January, and midweek rates are $285-350 for a single or double. There is a minimum stay on Saturdays and during holidays, and cancellation requires seven days' notice.
CREDIT CARDS	MasterCard, Visa
BREAKFAST	Full breakfast is served in the dining room or guestrooms and includes fresh-squeezed juice, a fruit course, and a main course such as chocolate tacos filled with fresh berries, followed by Anaheim chile quiche served with fresh salsa, black beans, and corn muffins.
AMENITIES	Nightly wine and cheese parties (winemakers frequently in attendance), fresh flowers, robes, bottle of wine, bottled water and soft drinks, binoculars, current books and magazines, air conditioning, wood-burning fireplaces, reservations and full itineraries prepared, pool, Jacuzzi.
RESTRICTIONS	No smoking, no pets, children over 14 are welcome. There are four resident cats: Nolan Oaks, Sahara Hot Stuff, Alexandria the Tiny, and Francesca the Fat. Nolan appears promptly at 6 p.m. to greet guests at the wine and cheese party.

REVIEWED	*The Best Places to Kiss in Northern California; Karen Brown's California Country Inns & Itineraries; More Weekends for Two in Northern California; Northern California Wine Country Access; Northern California Best Places*

OLD WORLD INN

1301 Jefferson Street, Napa, CA 94559 707-257-0112
Sam Van Hoeve, Resident Owner 800-966-6624
WEBSITE *www.oldworldinn.com* FAX 707-257-0118

LOCATION	From Highway 29, take the Lincoln Street exit. Head east, then turn right onto Jefferson Street. The inn is 0.25 mile down Jefferson.
OPEN	All year except Christmas Eve and Christmas Day
DESCRIPTION	A 1906 two-story Victorian inn with country European decor. Listed on the State Historic Register.
NO. OF ROOMS	Ten rooms with private bathrooms. Sam recommends the Cottage.
RATES	Year-round rates for a single or double are $125-170 and the cottage rents for $215-225. There is a two-night minimum stay on weekends. The cancellation policy requires seven days' notice and a $10 per room, per day cancellation fee.
CREDIT CARDS	American Express, Discover, MasterCard, Visa
BREAKFAST	Full breakfast, served in the dining room, includes a hot egg dish, fresh fruit, nut breads, homemade muffins, croissants, coffeecake, and juices.
AMENITIES	Outdoor spa, air conditioning, carafe of wine in room, afternoon wine and cheese, evening chocolate-lover's desserts, parlor with fireplace, some rooms have robes.
RESTRICTIONS	No smoking indoors, no pets, maximum of two people per room. The resident cats are Miko and Precious.
REVIEWED	*The Best Places to Kiss in Northern California; Bed and Breakfast California; Best Places to Stay in Northern California; Country Inns and Back Roads: California; Recommended Country Inns—West Coast; The Complete Guide to Bed & Breakfasts, Inns, and Guesthouses; The Official Guide to American Historic Inns; Complete Guide to American B&Bs; The National Trust Guide to Historic B&Bs, Inns, and Small Hotels; The Non-Smokers Guide to Bed & Breakfasts; The Inn Guide; Bed & Breakfast U.S.A.; Havens, Retreats, and Hideaways North of San Francisco*
MEMBER	California Association of Bed & Breakfast Inns, Napa Bed & Breakfast Inns
RATED	AAA 2 Diamonds, Best Places to Kiss 2 Lips, Mobil 2 Stars

ON MAYACAMAS

1565 Partrick Road, Napa, CA 95449   707-259-2920

STAHLECKER HOUSE BED & BREAKFAST, COUNTRY INN, AND GARDENS

1042 Easum Drive, Napa, CA 94558   707-257-1588
Ron & Ethyl Stahlecker, Innkeepers   800-799-1588
WEBSITE www.stahleckerhousebnb.com   FAX 707-224-7429

LOCATION	Take Highway 29 to Napa. Exit at First Street/Downtown Napa, stay to the left, then exit west on First Street. Drive six blocks to Easum Street and turn right. The inn is at the end of the street, on the right.
OPEN	All year
DESCRIPTION	A 1947 one-story country inn furnished with heirloom antiques and located on 1.5 manicured acres.
NO. OF ROOMS	Four rooms with private bathrooms. Ethel's favorite room is Kaitlyn's Karousel.
RATES	Year-round rates are $135 for a single or double (extra person $50) and $185 for the suite. The minimum stay is two nights on weekends and three nights on holidays.

Stahlecker House Bed & Breakfast, Country Inn, and Gardens, Napa

CREDIT CARDS	American Express, MasterCard, Visa
BREAKFAST	Full breakfast is served by candlelight in the dining room and includes juice, coffee, tea, fruit, and a main course such as quiche, waffles, or pancakes.
AMENITIES	Fireplaces in all bedrooms, fireplaces in gathering rooms, air conditioning, flowers in rooms, robes, sun deck with antique refrigerator full of soft drinks, ice machine, evening coffee, tea, and chocolate chip cookies.
RESTRICTIONS	No pets, smoking allowed on outside deck only, well-behaved children welcome. There are two outside pets: Nolan, a yellow Lab, and Percy, a fluffy cat. Nolan is a retired guide dog for the blind.
REVIEWED	*Bed & Breakfast Inns and Guesthouses, Historic Inns, Bed & Breakfast Country Inns, The Official Guide to American Historic Inns*
MEMBER	California Association of Bed & Breakfast Inns, California Lodging Industry Association, Bed & Breakfast Inns of Napa Valley

TALL TIMBERS CHALETS

1012 Darms Lane, Napa, CA 94558 707-252-7810
Mary Montes, Resident Owner

KUDOS/COMMENTS	"Each squeaky clean 1940s cottage is surrounded by fresh flowers and big trees."

TRUBODY RANCH BED & BREAKFAST

5444 St. Helena Highway, Napa, CA 94558 707-255-5907
Jeff & Mary Page, Resident Owners FAX 707-255-7254
WEBSITE www.napanet.net/~trubody/

LOCATION	Six miles north of Highway 29 and Trancas. Turn right on Washington Street, go north 0.5 mile, and turn right on Trubody Lane.
OPEN	All year except Thanksgiving and Christmas
DESCRIPTION	An 1872 Gothic Victorian farmhouse furnished with antiques and listed on the California Historic Register. The B&B is located on a 127-acre family vineyard, which also houses 19th-century barns, a watertower, a cottage, and a blacksmith shop.
NO. OF ROOMS	Three rooms with private bathrooms. The top Watertower Room is recommended.

RATES	April 15 through November 15, rates are $115-225 for a single or double. Off-season rates are 15 percent less. Call about a minimum-stay policy.
CREDIT CARDS	American Express, MasterCard, Visa
BREAKFAST	Expanded continental breakfast includes a fruit platter, home-baked muffins and coffeecakes, and beverages.
AMENITIES	Fresh-cut flowers from the garden, 360-degree view of surrounding valley, vineyard walks. The guesthouse has a telephone, a fireplace, and a soaking tub.
RESTRICTIONS	No smoking, no pets. Resident pets include two cats, Daisy and Pearl, and designer chickens.
MEMBER	Inns of Napa Valley

NEVADA CITY

Established in 1849, when miners found gold in Deer Creek, Nevada City occupies one of the most picturesque sites in the Sierra foothills. When the sugar maples blaze in autumn, the town resembles a small New England village, making it hard to believe this was once the third-largest city in California. To understand the lay of the land, put on your walking shoes and pick up a free walking-tour map at the chamber of commerce. A town highlight is the white, cupola-topped Firehouse Number 1 Museum, featuring Gold Rush memorabilia, a fine Chinese altar from a local 1860s joss house, and relics from the infamous and ill-fated Donner Party. Sixteen miles north of Nevada City, up the steep and winding North Bloomfield Road, is the 3,000-acre Malakoff Diggins State Historic Park, home of the world's largest hydraulic gold mine and a monument to mining's devastating results.

DEER CREEK INN

116 Nevada Street, Nevada City, CA 95959　　　530-265-0363
Chuck & Elaine Matroni, Resident Owners　　　800-655-0363
Italian spoken　　　FAX 530-265-0980
EMAIL deercreek@gv.net　　　WEBSITE www.gv.net/~histinns/deer.htm

LOCATION	From Highway 49 north, exit at Broad Street in Nevada City. The inn is at the edge of town.
OPEN	All year
DESCRIPTION	An 1860 three-story Queen Anne Victorian nestled amongst the trees, with porches and verandas overlooking Deer Creek.
NO. OF ROOMS	Five rooms with private bathrooms.

RATES	Year-round rates for a single or double are $98-145. There is a two-night minimum on Saturdays and cancellation requires ten days' notice.
CREDIT CARDS	American Express, MasterCard, Visa
BREAKFAST	Full gourmet breakfast, served in the dining room or on the veranda overlooking the creek, includes fresh beverages, fruit cup, and entrée choices such as eggs Florentine, French toast, and onion-baked potato.
AMENITIES	Wine and hors d'oeuvres each evening, wine or champagne for individual guests on special occasions, brownies, cookies, chocolates, candies, fresh flowers in rooms, telephone available, some rooms with private balconies and/or patios, 30-channel uninterrupted music, cable TV in main parlor only, small meeting facilities.
RESTRICTIONS	No smoking indoors. You will be greeted by Murphy the sheltie.
REVIEWED	*The Best Places to Kiss in Northern California*
MEMBER	Historical Inns of Grass Valley and Nevada City
AWARDS	1993, Stan Halls Architectural Award

Downey House Bed & Breakfast

517 West Broad Street, Nevada City, CA 95959   530-265-2815

Emma Nevada House

528 East Broad Street, Nevada City, CA 95959   530-265-4415
Ruth Ann & Richard Riese, Innkeepers   800-916-3662
Some Japanese spoken   FAX 530-265-4416
EMAIL emmanev@nevadacityinns.com
WEBSITE www.nevadacityinns.com

LOCATION	Turn left onto Broad Street from Highway 49. Go up the hill and take the right fork at the Y in the road.
OPEN	All year
DESCRIPTION	An 1856 two-story Victorian cottage with traditional decor, antiques, and fine linens.
NO. OF ROOMS	Six rooms with private bathrooms. Try the Empress's Chamber.

RATES	Rates are $100-160 for a single or double. Rates are slightly higher from Thanksgiving through December. There is a minimum stay during weekends from April through December and cancellation requires seven days' notice.
CREDIT CARDS	American Express, Diners Club, MasterCard, Visa
BREAKFAST	Full breakfast is served in the dining room and includes quiches with fresh-baked scones or minimuffins; or orange French toast with sausage, fresh fruit plate, and Emma's special cobbler; plus juice, fresh-brewed coffee, and teas.
AMENITIES	Tea and home-baked cookies, creekside garden, air conditioning, robes, fresh flowers throughout, a perfect rose for anniversary couples, Jacuzzi and clawfoot tubs, fireplaces.
RESTRICTIONS	No smoking, no pets, children over eight are welcome. Taffy, the resident dog, is always outside.
REVIEWED	*Karen Brown's California Country Inns & Itineraries, Northern California Best Places, Frommer's, The Best Places to Kiss in Northern California, Fodor's*
MEMBER	Professional Association of Innkeepers International, California Association of Bed & Breakfast Inns, Historic Inns of Grass Valley & Nevada City
RATED	AAA 3 Diamonds, ABBA 3 Crowns

FLUME'S END

317 South Pine Street, Nevada City, CA 95959 916-265-9665
Terrianne Straw & Steve Wilson, Resident Owners 800-991-8118

LOCATION	Take I-80 to Auburn, then 50 miles to Nevada City. The B&B is two blocks from the center of town on Pine Street.
OPEN	All year
DESCRIPTION	An 1861 three-story Victorian mansion surrounded by trees, flowers, and a creek.
NO. OF ROOMS	Six rooms with private bathrooms. The Master Room is the best in the house.
RATES	Year-round rates for a double are $80-140. There is a two-night minimum stay on weekends and holidays. Ask about a cancellation policy.
CREDIT CARDS	MasterCard, Visa
BREAKFAST	Full breakfast is served in the dining room or on the terrace and includes homemade breads, granola, fruit, yogurt, hot entrée, and beverages.

AMENITIES	Piano and other musical instruments, phone and TV in sitting room, games, robes, homemade cookies and fudge, guest refrigerator stocked with beverages, off-street parking.
RESTRICTIONS	No smoking, no pets. Terrianne's goldie guide dog, Roanna, shares the mansion with guests.
MEMBER	Professional Association of Innkeepers International, California Association Bed & Breakfast Inns, California Lodging Industry Association
KUDOS/COMMENTS	"Very different and pleasant; unique rooms, excellent breakfasts (made-to-order)."

GRANDMERE'S INN

449 Broad Street, Nevada City, CA 95959 530-265-4660
Ruth Ann Riese, Innkeeper FAX 530-265-4416
EMAIL grandmere@nevadacityinns.com
WEBSITE www.nevadacityinns.com

LOCATION	From Highway 49, turn left onto Broad Street and go up the hill.
OPEN	All year
DESCRIPTION	An 1856 three-story colonial revival, built by U. S. Senator Aaron Sargent, and decorated with elegant, country French furnishings. Listed on the National Historic Register.
NO. OF ROOMS	Six rooms with private bathrooms. Try the Master Suite.
RATES	Rates are $110-175 for a single or double. Rates are slightly higher from Thanksgiving through December. There is a minimum stay during weekends from April through December and holidays. Cancellation requires seven days' notice.
CREDIT CARDS	American Express, MasterCard, Visa
BREAKFAST	Full breakfast is served in the dining room and includes one of grandmere's quiches with cornbread or muffins; or our special stuffed French toast with sausage, fresh fruit, and a baked dessert such as mountain berry cobbler.
AMENITIES	Tea and home-baked cookies in the pantry; large formal gardens with year-round blooms; complete air conditioning; garden weddings and meeting facilities for small groups.
RESTRICTIONS	No smoking, no pets, children are welcome.
REVIEWED	Northern California Best Places, Fodor's California, Frommer's Northern California, The Best Places to Kiss in Northern California

MEMBER	Professional Association of Innkeepers International, California Association of Bed & Breakfast Inns, Historic Inns of Grass Valley & Nevada City
RATED	AAA 3 Diamonds, Best Places to Kiss 3 Lips

THE KENDALL HOUSE

534 Spring Street, Nevada City, CA 95959   530-265-0405
Jan & Ted Kendall, Resident Owners   888-647-0405
WEBSITE www.virtualcities.com   FAX 530-265-0405 (call first)

LOCATION	From Highway 49, take the Broad Street exit, turn left, and go three blocks through town to Bennett. Turn left on Bennett, right on Spring, and go one block to the inn.
OPEN	All year
DESCRIPTION	An 1860s two-story California farmhouse with eclectic ("but it all works") furnishings.
NO. OF ROOMS	Five rooms with private bathrooms, including the guesthouse (the Barn).
RATES	Year-round rates are $105-125 for a single or double and $150-210 for the guesthouse. There is a two-night minimum stay on weekends from April through December and during all holidays. Cancellation requires seven days' notice, sometimes 14 days, with a $15 fee.
CREDIT CARDS	Discover, MasterCard, Visa
BREAKFAST	Full breakfast is served in the dining room and includes juice, fruit plate, and entrée.
AMENITIES	Heated swimming pool, wood-burning stove in Barn, air conditioning where needed, gas fireplace in master bedroom, cookies, soft drinks, mineral water, multilevel decks, off-street parking, limited handicapped access.
RESTRICTIONS	No smoking, no pets, ask about children. The dog, Kelsey, plays with the cats, Gracie and Buddy.
REVIEWED	Northern California Best Places, The Definitive Northern California Bed & Breakfast Touring Guide
MEMBER	Historic Inns of Grass Valley/Nevada City

MARSH HOUSE

254 Boulder Street, Nevada City, CA 95959   530-265-5709
WEBSITE www.marshmansion.com

THE PARSONAGE BED & BREAKFAST

427 Broad Street, Nevada City, CA 95959   530-265-9478
Deborah Dane, Resident Owner   FAX 530-265-8147
WEBSITE www.gv.net/~histinns/pars.htm

LOCATION	Look for the first white picket fence on the left at the top of Broad Street.
OPEN	All year
DESCRIPTION	An 1865 two-story Victorian cottage with traditional furnishings and antiques.
NO. OF ROOMS	Six rooms with private bathrooms.
RATES	Year-round rates are $70-135 for a double. Midweek rates are a bit less. There is a two-night minimum stay if a Saturday or a holiday is included, and cancellation requires seven days' notice.
CREDIT CARDS	MasterCard, Visa
BREAKFAST	Full breakfast is served in the dining room or guestrooms and includes juices, home-baked breads, homemade jams, yogurt, cream cheese, fresh fruit platter, an egg and meat dish, and beverages.
AMENITIES	Flowers, telephones, TV in rooms.
RESTRICTIONS	No smoking, children are welcome in the Mouse House.

PIETY HILL INN

523 Sacramento Street, Nevada City, CA 95959   530-265-2245
Joan & Steve Oas, Innkeepers   800-443-2245
WEBSITE www.firsttravelerschoice.com

LOCATION	Exit Highway 49 at Sacramento Street, turn left, and go 0.33 mile up hill. Look to your left for the inn, behind a white picket fence.
OPEN	All year

NEVADA CITY

DESCRIPTION	English cottages built in 1930, decorated with antiques and memorabilia, and situated on 1 acre with huge trees and gardens.
NO. OF ROOMS	Nine rooms with private bathrooms. Pick the Apple Blossom Room.
RATES	Year-round rates are $75 for a single or double with a private bathroom and $100-135 for a suite. There is a minimum stay over Saturdays and cancellation requires seven days' notice, 14 days for holidays.
CREDIT CARDS	American Express, MasterCard, Visa
BREAKFAST	Full breakfast is served in the cottages and includes homemade breads, fresh fruit plate, a main entrée, and orange juice. Special meals are also available.
AMENITIES	TV, coffee, tea, hot chocolate, apple cider, sodas, phones, refrigerators, one large cottage for meetings, one cottage has cooking facilities, one cottage has a wood-burning stove.
RESTRICTIONS	No smoking, no pets

RED CASTLE INN, HISTORIC LODGINGS

109 Prospect Street, Nevada City, CA 95959   530-265-5135
Mary Louise & Conley Weaver, Resident Owners   800-761-4766
WEBSITE *www.g.v.net/~histinns/red.htm*

LOCATION	From Highway 49 east, exit onto Sacramento Street, turn right onto Adams, left onto Prospect Street, and proceed one block. From Highway 20 west, turn left onto Coyote Street to Broad, left onto Sacramento, right onto Adams, and left onto Prospect.
OPEN	All year
DESCRIPTION	An 1857 four-story brick Gothic revival mansion furnished with the owner's art collection, period pieces, and historic memorabilia. Listed on the California Historic Register.
NO. OF ROOMS	Seven rooms with private bathrooms. Guests like the Rose Room.
RATES	April through December, rates are $110-145 for a single or double and suites are $100-150. January through March, rates are $90-125 for a single or double and suites are $90-130. There are special midweek and business-traveler rates during low season. There is a two-night minimum stay from April through December when a Saturday is involved. Cancellation requires seven to 30 days' advance notice.
CREDIT CARDS	MasterCard, Visa

BREAKFAST	Full buffet breakfast is served in the foyer. Christmas dinner is served.
AMENITIES	Air conditioning, visits from "Mark Twain," down comforters, triple sheeting, turndown service, afternoon refreshments.
RESTRICTIONS	No smoking, no pets, children over six are welcome. Foxy and Beau, the resident host cats, are "available as lap warmers. They receive almost as much fan mail as we do."
REVIEWED	Fodor's California; Recommended Romantic Inns of America; Frommer's California; Fifty Romantic Weekends for Two in Northern California; Johansen's Recommended Hotels and Inns North America; Northern California Best Places; Best Places to Stay in Northern California; The Best Places to Kiss in Northern California; America's Favorite Inns, B&Bs, & Small Hotels
MEMBER	Professional Association of Innkeepers International, American Historic Inns, California Association of Bed & Breakfast Inns, Historic Bed & Breakfast Inns of Grass Valley and Nevada City
RATED	1992, Grand Hotel—Best Bed & Breakfast, San Francisco Focus

U. S. HOTEL BED & BREAKFAST

233 Broad Street B, Nevada City, CA 95959   530-265-7999

NICE

Nice is located along scenic Highway 20 on the northern bank of Clear Lake, California's largest freshwater lake and the bass capitol of the West.

GINGERBREAD COTTAGES BED & BREAKFAST

4057 East Highway 20, Nice, CA 95464   707-274-0200
Buddy & Yvonne Lipscomb, Innkeepers

LOCATION	On Highway 20, 120 miles north of San Francisco and 110 miles northwest of Sacramento.
OPEN	February through November
DESCRIPTION	Ten one-story lakefront gingerbread cottages with antique and wicker furnishings. The cottages are located on Clear Lake, the largest natural lake in the state.

Gingerbread Cottages Bed & Breakfast, Nice

NO. OF ROOMS	Ten cottages with private bathrooms. Choose Cinderella's Cottage.
RATES	Year-round rates are $125-250 for a cottage. Weekday discounts are available (holidays excluded). Reservations are required. There is a minimum stay and cancellation requires one week's notice and a $10 fee per day.
CREDIT CARDS	American Express, Discover, MasterCard, Visa
BREAKFAST	Continental breakfast is served in the cottages and includes muffins, fruit, juice, coffee, and tea. Picnic lunches are also available.
AMENITIES	Beach, dock, gardens, picnic/barbecue grounds, pool, special scheduled events, themed cottages, stereo and romantic tapes, microwave, air conditioning, cable TV/VCR, whirlpool tubs, fireplaces, kichenettes with cooking equipment, basket of gourmet snacks, ceiling fans.
RESTRICTIONS	No smoking, no pets, children over 12 are welcome.
MEMBER	Professional Association of Innkeepers International

O'BRIEN

O'Brien Mountain Inn

PO Box 27, O'Brien, CA 96070   530-238-8026
WEBSITE *www.obrienmtn.com*

Oakhurst

Oakhurst is a dozen miles from the southern entrance to Yosemite National Park on Highway 41. Check out Friday Nite Jazz on the Lake at nearby Bass Lake. The Peddlars Fair is held during both Memorial and Labor Day weekends.

Chateau du Sureau

48688 Victoria Lane, Oakhurst, CA 93644   209-683-6800
Erna Kubin-Clanin, Resident Owner   FAX 209-683-0800
Spanish, French, and German spoken

LOCATION	Located in the town of Oakhurst, 0.25 mile south of the intersection of Highways 49 and 41.
OPEN	Closed January 1 through January 21
DESCRIPTION	A 1991 two-story French chateau surrounded by gardens.
NO. OF ROOMS	Nine rooms with private bathrooms.
RATES	Year-round rates for a double are $315-515. There is a two-night minimum stay on weekends, three nights during some holidays, and cancellation requires 14 days' notice for a refund less 10 percent.
CREDIT CARDS	American Express, MasterCard, Visa
BREAKFAST	Full breakfast is served in the breakfast room and includes fruit frappe, quiche, Black Forest ham, brioche, and croissants.
AMENITIES	Flowers, robes, phones, TV available, wine and hors d'oeuvres, pool, slippers, house bar, life-size chess court, fireplaces in rooms, deep soaking tubs for two in five rooms.
RESTRICTIONS	No smoking, no pets, no children under nine.
REVIEWED	*The Best Places to Kiss in Northern California; Karen Brown's California Country Inns & Itineraries; Country Inns and Back Roads: California*

MEMBER	Relais and Chateaux
RATED	AAA 5 Diamonds, Mobil 5 Stars

CHINA CREEK

49522 Road 426, Oakhurst, CA 93644 209-642-6248
WEBSITE *www.bbhost.com/chinacreek/*

HOUND'S TOOTH INN

42071 Highway 41, Oakhurst, CA 93644 209-642-6600
Bill & Anna Williams and 888-642-6610
Rob & Lisa Kiehlmeier, Innkeepers FAX 209-658-2946

LOCATION	On Highway 41, 2.5 miles north of the junction of Highways 41 and 49, in the town of Oakhurst, on the left.
OPEN	All year
DESCRIPTION	A 1997 two-story Victorian-style inn.
NO. OF ROOMS	Twelve rooms with private bathrooms. The Hound's Tooth Room is Anna's favorite.
RATES	Year-round rates are $95-180 for a single or double, $180-250 for the suites, and $250 for the guesthouse. There is a minimum stay on major holidays and cancellation requires three days' notice.
CREDIT CARDS	American Express, Discover, MasterCard, Visa
BREAKFAST	Full breakfast is served in the dining room and includes juice, cereals, assorted breads with jam and cream cheese, fresh fruit, sweet roll, quiche or egg dish, coffee, and tea.
AMENITIES	Handicapped accessible, patio sitting areas, air conditioning, afternoon wine, evening cookies, fax, some rooms have fireplaces or Jacuzzi tubs for two, all rooms have phones and TVs, future meeting facilities, wine and flowers for special occasions.
RESTRICTIONS	No smoking. The resident cat is named H. T.
REVIEWED	*Rough Guide*
MEMBER	California Association of Bed & Breakfast Inns, Professional Association of Innkeepers International, California Lodging Industry Association
RATED	AAA 3 Diamonds

Pine Rose Inn

41703 Road 222, Oakhurst, CA 93644   209-642-2800

Oakland

Redwood and oak-covered hills rise above the city, and the weather is fair year-round, even when San Francisco is dreary. This big city across the bay is almost one with Berkeley and has enough scenic, cultural, and entertainment offerings to compete with its two higher-profile neighbors. For starters, Redwood and Anthony Chabot Regional Parks are worth exploring. The Oakland Jazz Festival gets its groove going in August.

Bedside Manor

612 Valle Vista Avenue, Oakland, CA 94610   510-452-4550
Deborah Stevenson, Resident Owner
Spanish spoken

LOCATION	Located near downtown Oakland in the Piedmont Manor district. Exit Highway 580 at Grand Avenue. The manor is two blocks from the freeway, near the Rose Garden.
OPEN	All year
DESCRIPTION	A 1924 two-story Moorish inn with hardwood floors and stained-glass windows.
NO. OF ROOMS	Two suites with private bathrooms. Deborah recommends the Master Suite.
RATES	Please call for current rates and cancellation information.
CREDIT CARDS	No
BREAKFAST	Continental plus is served in the dining room and includes juice, fruit salad, breakfast breads, hot or cold cereal, and beverages. Guests are welcome to prepare family meals in the kitchen. Lunches and picnic baskets are available upon request.
AMENITIES	Outside deck with a fountain; Master Suite with phone, sitting room, TV/VCR, and small sweets.
RESTRICTIONS	No smoking

DOCKSIDE BOAT & BED

77 Jack London Square, Oakland, CA 94607 510-444-5858
WEBSITE www.boatandbed.com

TUDOR ROSE BED & BREAKFAST

316 Modoc Avenue, Oakland, CA 94618 510-655-3201
Corinne Edmonson, Resident Owner

THE WASHINGTON INN

495 10th Street, Oakland, CA 94607 510-452-1776
WEBSITE www.thewashingtoninn.com

OLEMA

The main gateway into the Point Reyes National Seashore, Olema boasts a 74,000-acre park of marshes, sandy beaches, dunes, and forests. Explore Bear Valley Trail's Fivebrooks Pond, the wetlands of Limantour, tidepools, and estuaries. Venture out to the Point Reyes Lighthouse and watch for gray whales. On a clear day, look south to the Point Reyes–Farallon Islands National Wildlife Refuge and Marine Sanctuary, now part of the UNESCO Biosphere Reserve. Make time for the Point Reyes Bird Observatory. Oh, yes—Olema was the epicenter for the 1906 earthquake (just a thought to ponder). From San Francisco, drive north on Highway 1.

BEAR VALLEY INN

88 Bear Valley Road, Olema, CA 94950 415-663-1777
Ron Nowell, Innkeeper FAX 415-663-9000

DESCRIPTION	An 1899 two-story Victorian ranch house surrounded by gardens and adjoining the Point Reyes National Seashore.
NO. OF ROOMS	Three rooms with private bathrooms.

RATES	Year-round weekday rates are $80-90 for a single or double. Weekend and holiday rates are $90-105. Ask about a cancellation policy.
CREDIT CARDS	American Express, Discover, MasterCard, Visa
BREAKFAST	Continental breakfast is served in the dining room.
RESTRICTIONS	No smoking
MEMBER	Inns of Point Reyes

OLEMA INN

10000 Sir Francis Drake Boulevard, Olema, CA 94950   415-663-9559
WEBSITE www.olemainn.com

POINT REYES SEASHORE LODGE

10021 Highway 1, Olema, CA 94950   415-663-9000
Jeff & Nancy Harriman, Owners   800-404-5634
Spanish and some French spoken   FAX 415-663-9030
WEBSITE www.pointreyesseashore.com

LOCATION	In the center of Olema, one block north of Sir Francis Drake Boulevard.
OPEN	All year
DESCRIPTION	A 1988 Victorian-style lodge that adjoins Point Reyes National Seashore on Olema Creek.
NO. OF ROOMS	Twenty-two rooms with private bathrooms.
RATES	April through October and all weekends and holidays, rates are $115-195 for a single or double and the guesthouse is $250. November through March, rates are $85-160 for a single or double and the guesthouse is $195. Cancellation requires five days' notice.
CREDIT CARDS	American Express, Discover, MasterCard, Visa
BREAKFAST	Continental plus, served in the dining room or guestrooms, includes fresh fruit, pastries, cereals, juices, and yogurt.
AMENITIES	Wine and champagne, snack baskets, telephones in rooms, antique pool table, library, fireplace, 2 acres of gardens. Suites include whirlpool tubs, robes, and coffee-makers.
RESTRICTIONS	No smoking, no pets

REVIEWED   The Best Places to Kiss in Northern California

MEMBER   Professional Association of Innkeepers International, California
               Association of Bed & Breakfast Innkeepers, California Lodging
               Industry Association

Ridgetop Inn & Cottages

9876 Sir Francis Drake Boulevard, Olema, CA 94950   415-663-1500
WEBSITE www.ridgetopinn.com

Roundstone Farm Bed & Breakfast

9940 Sir Francis Drake Boulevard, Olema, CA 94950   415-663-1020
WEBSITE www.roundstonefarm.com

Orland

Orland offers handy access to Black Butte Lake to the west and Woodson Bridge State Recreation Area to the north. It is located only 10 miles east of Chico via Highway 32, and 50 miles south of Redding on the I-5 corridor.

Inn at Shallow Creek Farm

4712 Road DD, Orland, CA 95963   530-865-4093
Kurt & Mary Glaeseman, Resident Owners   800-865-4093
German, French, and Spanish spoken   FAX 530-865-4093

LOCATION	Take the Chico/Orland exit from I-5. Go west 2.5 miles. Turn right (north) onto Road DD. Proceed 0.5 mile, cross the concrete bridge, and turn into the next driveway on the right.
OPEN	All year
DESCRIPTION	A 1900 two-story country farmhouse and cottage furnished with antiques and located amid orange orchards.
NO. OF ROOMS	Two rooms with private bathrooms and two rooms share one bathroom. Mary suggests the Penfield Suite.

RATES	Year-round rates are $75-85 for a single or double with a private bathroom and $65 for a single or double with a shared bathroom. There is no minimum stay and cancellation requires six days' notice.
CREDIT CARDS	MasterCard, Visa
BREAKFAST	Continental plus is served in the dining room and includes home-baked breads and muffins, fresh fruit and juice from the orchard.
AMENITIES	Guest refrigerator; cottage has a fully equipped kitchen and wood-burning stove; phones, books, games, piano, and TV in the common room; hosts are birders.
RESTRICTIONS	No smoking, no pets, the inn is "not particularly suitable for children." The resident calico cats are Monkey Business and Moonshine.
REVIEWED	*Best Places to Stay in Northern California, America's Wonderful Little Hotels & Inns, Northern California Best Places, The Birder's Guide to Bed & Breakfasts*
MEMBER	Professional Association of Innkeepers International

OROVILLE

This foothills Gold Rush town has a wild past. Now, it's the gateway into Lake Oroville Dam and State Recreation Area. The Feather River Fish Hatchery is great fun to visit, especially during spawning season (October and November). Don't miss the Temple of Assorted Deities, built by the town's Chinese population in 1863. From Chico, drive 26 miles south on Highway 149.

JEAN'S RIVERSIDE BED & BREAKFAST

1142 Cabana Drive, Oroville, CA 95965   530-533-1413
Jean Pratt, Resident Owner
WEBSITE *www.oroville-city.com/jeans/*

LOCATION	Entering Oroville, turn west on Oroville Dam Boulevard, cross Feather River, turn right on Middlehoff Lane, and turn right at the sign.
OPEN	All year
DESCRIPTION	A 1936 two-story cedar country inn with upscale country antiques, on 6 waterfront acres.
NO. OF ROOMS	Ten rooms with private bathrooms.
RATES	Year-round rates are $65-125 for a single or double. Cancellation requires one week's notice with a 10 percent fee.

CREDIT CARDS	Diners Club, MasterCard, Visa
BREAKFAST	Full goldminer's breakfast is served in the dining room.
AMENITIES	Flowers in room, wine or other refreshment on arrival, TV, phones as requested, fishing, gold panning, horseshoes, Ping-Pong, croquet, serious bird-watching, docks, decks, six rooms with private Jacuzzis and wood-burning stoves on brick hearths.
RESTRICTIONS	No smoking, no pets, children OK in cottage depending on availability.
REVIEWED	*Perfect Places: Northern California: The Most Outstanding Locations for Parties, Special Events, and Business Functions*

LAKE OROVILLE BED & BREAKFAST

240 Sunday Drive, Oroville, CA 95916 530-589-0700
Ronald & Cheryl Damberger, Resident Owners 800-455-5253

LOCATION	From Route 70, take Oroville Dam Boulevard east for 1.7 miles. Turn right at Olive Highway (Route 162) and continue 13.5 miles around Lake Oroville. Cross two bridges and look for the sign to Foreman Creek Recreation Area. Take the next left, onto Bell Ranch Road, drive 0.6 mile, and bear right to Sunday Drive. Continue 0.75 mile to the big yellow house.
OPEN	All year
DESCRIPTION	A 1991 two-story Victorian furnished with period antiques and located on 40 acres.
NO. OF ROOMS	Six rooms with private bathrooms. Cheryl recommends the Victorian Room.
RATES	Please inquire about rates and cancellation information.
CREDIT CARDS	American Express, Discover, MasterCard, Visa
BREAKFAST	Full breakfast served in the dining room.
AMENITIES	Telephones, radio with cassettes, TV/VCR upon request, whirlpool tubs in bedrooms, game room with billiard table, soft drinks, snack basket, sun room with books and reading chairs, 2,000-square-foot covered porches with private entrance to bedrooms. Meeting, wedding, retreat facilities; children's play room and sitter service; handicapped accessible.
RESTRICTIONS	Smoking permitted only on the patio.
REVIEWED	*The Official Guide to American Historic Inns*
MEMBER	Professional Association of Innkeepers International, California Association of Bed & Breakfast Inns

Palo Alto

Stanford University and all things cultural and creative come together here. Tour the splendid campus and historic downtown, and check out the Baylands Nature Preserve. Palo Alto is located at the southwest terminus of San Francisco Bay.

Hotel California

2431 Ash, Palo Alto, CA 94306 650-322-7666
WEBSITE *www.hotelcalifornia.com*

The Victorian on Lytton

555 Lytton Avenue, Palo Alto, CA 94301 650-322-8555
Maxwell & Susan Hall, Resident Owners FAX 650-322-7141
WEBSITE *www.virtualcities.com*

LOCATION	From San Francisco, go south on Highway 101 to the University Street exit. Turn west, go about two miles, turn right on Middlefield, then turn left on Lytton. Park in the rear.
OPEN	All year
DESCRIPTION	A 1985 two-story Victorian with English decor, listed on the National Historic Register. A Victorian garden with over 1,200 perennials.
NO. OF ROOMS	Ten rooms with private bathrooms.
RATES	Year-round rates for a single or double are $143-240. There is no minimum stay and a 10-day cancellation policy.
CREDIT CARDS	American Express, MasterCard, Visa
BREAKFAST	Continental breakfast, served in the guestrooms, includes fresh juice and fruit, homemade muffins and croissants, coffee, and tea.
AMENITIES	Flowers, robes, TV, radio, voicemail.
RESTRICTIONS	No smoking, no pets, children over 13 are welcome.
REVIEWED	*Karen Brown's California Country Inns & Itineraries*

PESCADERO

"The fishing place" is off the San Mateo Coast just inland of Highway 1 and Pescadero State Beach. Pescadero Creek runs through it. Check out the Año Nuevo State Elephant Seal Reserve. The Pescadero Arts and Fun Festival kicks off in mid-August.

OLD SAW MILL LODGE

700 Ranch Road West, Pescadero, CA 94060
Tom & Annie Hines, Innkeepers
German spoken
EMAIL innkeepers@oldsawmill.com

650-879-0111
800-596-6455
FAX 650-879-0656
WEBSITE www.oldsawmill.com

LOCATION	From Half Moon Bay, go 15 miles south on Highway 1 to Pescadero Road. Go 2.5 miles east on Pescadero Road to Cloverdale Road. Turn south (toward the state park) and go 0.8 mile to Ranch Road West. Call for the access code to the private gate.
OPEN	All year
DESCRIPTION	A 1994 two-story wood-frame lodge with open-beamed ceilings and comfortable "masculine" lodge decor.
NO. OF ROOMS	Five rooms with private bathrooms. Try the Head Bullmaster's Room.
RATES	Year-round rates are $105-175 for a single or double. There is no minimum stay. Ask about a cancellation policy.
CREDIT CARDS	American Express, MasterCard, Visa
BREAKFAST	Full country-gourmet breakfast, all made from scratch, is served in the dining room and includes fresh or baked fruit, a main egg entrée, bacon, sausage, or ham, home fries, sweet breads, muffins or coffeecakes, yogurt, cereal, coffee, tea, and juice.
AMENITIES	Complimentary robes and slippers; indoor pool; Jacuzzi; fresh flowers in rooms; in-room TV/VCR with complimentary movie library; 60 wooded acres with private trails and maps; handicapped accessible; conference facility with copier, fax, overhead projector, and big-screen TV with data port (full luncheon catering with rental of conference facility); complimentary soft drinks, bottled water, and juices.
RESTRICTIONS	No smoking, no pets. Rooms are single or double occupancy only.
REVIEWED	Quick Escapes from San Francisco, The Complete Guide to B&B Inns & Guesthouses, Inns & Wineries of California's Northern Coast

Old Saw Mill Lodge, Pescadero

MEMBER   California Association of Bed & Breakfast Inns, Professional Association of Innkeepers International, California Lodging Industry Association

RATED   AAA 3 Diamonds

Pescadero Creek Inn Bed & Breakfast

393 Stage Road, Pescadero, CA 94060   650-879-1898

Petaluma

Chicks and cows are big here—dairy farming and poultry ranching are the major industries. There's more to do than you can shake a feather at: tour the Petaluma River, the cheese factory, and Petaluma Adobe State Historic Park, among other things. Petaluma is on Highway 101 just north of San Francisco.

Cavanagh Inn

10 Keller Street, Petaluma, CA 94952   707-765-4657
Ray & Jeanne Farris, Resident Owners   888-765-4658
Spanish spoken   FAX 707-769-0466
EMAIL info@cavanaghinn.com   WEBSITE www.cavanaghinn.com

Cavanagh Inn, Petaluma

LOCATION	Exit Highway 101 in Petaluma onto Washington Street. Proceed west to Old Town. Cross Petaluma Boulevard and Kentucky Street, then turn left onto Keller Street.
OPEN	All year
DESCRIPTION	A 1902 three-story Georgian revival mansion and a 1910 two-story California Craftsman inn. Both buildings have rare redwood paneling and are furnished with antiques.
NO. OF ROOMS	Five rooms with private bathrooms and two rooms share one bathroom. Ray and Jeanne recommend the Sterling Rose Room.
RATES	Year-round rates are $120-130 for a single or a double with a private bathroom and $85 for a single or a double with a shared bathroom. There is a two-night minimum stay during holidays and cancellation requires 10 days' notice.
CREDIT CARDS	American Express, MasterCard, Visa
BREAKFAST	Full breakfast is served in the dining room. Chef Jeanne Farris prepares a full sit-down breakfast that includes poached pears in cardamon syrup, lemon poppyseed muffins, Jeanne's breakfast stack with three-pepper sauces, juice, and coffee. Lunch and dinner are also available.
AMENITIES	Sonoma wines in evening, turndown service with sweets, well-stocked library, meeting room for up to 10, garden with large trees and many roses, TV, telephones, piano.
RESTRICTIONS	No smoking, no pets, children over 12 are welcome. Billie is the resident spoiled cat.

REVIEWED	Karen Brown's California Country Inns & Itineraries, The Complete Guide to Bed & Breakfast Inns and Guesthouses, Bed & Breakfasts and Country Inns
MEMBER	California Association of Bed & Breakfast Inns
RATED	AAA 3 Diamonds
KUDOS/COMMENTS	"Comfortable rooms, beautiful woodwork, knowledgeable hosts, fabulous breakfast!"

PETROLIA

This sleepy hamlet lies in the Mattole Valley, a remote area known as the Lost Coast. The ocean is close at hand, as is the Kings Range National Conservation Area.

THE LOST INN

1610 Mattock Road, Petrolia, CA 95558   707-629-3394
Phil & Gail Franklin, Innkeepers   FAX 707-629-3668
Spanish spoken

LOCATION	One block from the only store in the hamlet of Petrolia. A one-hour drive south from Ferndale, or six hours north of San Francisco. Please call for exact directions.
OPEN	All year
DESCRIPTION	A large 1938 two-story Craftsman bungalow with pecan paneling, wainscoting, and original art, located five miles from the ocean.
NO. OF ROOMS	One room with a private bathroom.
RATES	April through October, a single or double is $95. November through March, a single or double is $90. There is a minimum stay on weekends. Ask about a cancellation policy.
CREDIT CARDS	No
BREAKFAST	Full breakfast is served "as you like it" in the dining room or guestrooms and may include croissants, omelets, or pancakes. Special meals are prepared upon request.
AMENITIES	Fresh fruits and veggies from gardens, fresh eggs, large two-room guest suite with separate kitchenette and porch, vast pastoral view, library, stereo.
RESTRICTIONS	No smoking inside the guest suite. Sasha is the resident schnauzer terrier, Bear is the black cat, and there are a dozen chickens on the property.
REVIEWED	Northern California Best Places, Exploring the North Coast, Northern California Handbook

PHILO

PHILO POTTERY INN

8550 Route 128, Philo, CA 95466   707-895-3069
WEBSITE *www.innaccess.com/phi/*

PINOLI RANCH COUNTRY INN

3280 Clark Road, Philo, CA 95466   707-895-2550

PINE GROVE

DRUID HOUSE BED & BREAKFAST

13887 Druid Lane, Pine Grove, CA 95665   209-296-4156

PLACERVILLE

One of the first camps settled by miners who branched out from Coloma, Placerville initially was dubbed Dry Diggins because of the lack of water. Its name was changed to Hangtown in 1849 after a series of grisly lynchings; it became Placerville in 1854 to satisfy local pride. A dangling dummy marks the location of the town's infamous hanging tree. A mile north of downtown Placerville is Gold Bug Park, home of the city-owned Gold Bug Mine; guided tours of the mine lead you deep into the lighted shafts. El Dorado County Historical Museum showcases Pony Express paraphernalia and mining-era relics.

CHICHESTER-MCKEE HOUSE

800 Spring Street, Placerville, CA 95667   530-626-1882
Doreen & Bill Thornhill, Innkeepers   800-831-4008
EMAIL *inn@innercite.com*   WEBSITE *www.innercite.com/~inn/*

LOCATION	One-and-a-half blocks from historic downtown Placerville, half a block north of Highway 50 on Spring Street (Highway 49).
OPEN	All year
DESCRIPTION	An 1892 two-story Queen Anne Victorian with period furnishings, built by local lumber baron D. W. Chichester.
NO. OF ROOMS	Three rooms with private half-bathrooms.
RATES	Year-round rates for a single or double are $80-90. Cancellation requires five days' notice with a $10 fee.
CREDIT CARDS	American Express, Discover, MasterCard, Visa
BREAKFAST	Full breakfast is served in the dining room.
AMENITIES	Solarium/conservatory, gardens, air conditioning/heating, robes, fireplaces, soft drinks, Doreen's delicious caramel brownies, meeting facilities (with brunch) available for up to 10.
RESTRICTIONS	Smoking restricted to designated areas, no pets. Heidi, a miniature dachshund, performs math tricks at breakfast.
REVIEWED	*The Best of the Gold Country; Bed, Breakfast and Bikes—Northern California; Complete Guide to American Bed and Breakfasts; Bed & Breakfast in California; Northern California Best Places*
MEMBER	California Association of Bed & Breakfast Inns, Historic Country Inns of El Dorado County

COMBELLACK BLAIR HOUSE

3059 Cedar Ravine Road, Placerville, CA 95667   530-622-3764
Loren & Marlene DeLaurenti, Innkeepers

LOCATION	Located in downtown Placerville. Take the Historic Main Street exit and go to the end of Main. Turn right on Cedar Ravine and go half a block to the inn, on the right.
OPEN	All year
DESCRIPTION	An 1895 two-story Queen Anne stick Victorian with extensive gingerbread trim, listed on the National Historic Register.
NO. OF ROOMS	Three rooms with private bathrooms. Ask for the Combellack Room or the Blair Room.
RATES	Year-round rate for a single or double is $110. There is no minimum stay and cancellation requires one week's notice and a $10 fee.
CREDIT CARDS	MasterCard, Visa
BREAKFAST	Full breakfast is served and includes fresh juice, baked apple, scrambled eggs Florentine, ham, country potatoes, and muffins; or strawberry/walnut French toast, sausage, and peach smoothie.

AMENITIES	Fresh flowers in every room, robes and slippers in the Kinkade Room, sherry in the front parlor, evening treats with turndown. Inn features cupola and gardens with a gazebo and rose arbor.
RESTRICTIONS	No smoking, no pets, no children
REVIEWED	*America's Painted Ladies*
MEMBER	California Association of Bed & Breakfast Inns, Historic Inns of El Dorado County

FITZPATRICK WINERY & LODGE

7740 Fair Play Road, Fair Play, CA 95684　　530-620-3248
Brian & Diana Fitzpatrick, Innkeepers　　800-245-9166
EMAIL *brian@fitzpatrickwinery.com*　　FAX 530-620-6838
WEBSITE *www.fitzpatrickwinery.com*

LOCATION	Eighteen miles southeast of Placerville, 18 miles east of Plymouth, about an hour east of Sacramento. Get directions ahead of time or call from Placerville.
OPEN	All year
DESCRIPTION	A 1986 hand-built log lodge decorated with comfortable country Irish pine furnishings and situated on 40 acres.
NO. OF ROOMS	Five rooms with private bathrooms. Diana recommends the Winemaker's Suite.
RATES	Year-round rates for a single or double are $79-130. A two-night stay required on holidays; call about a cancellation policy.
CREDIT CARDS	MasterCard, Visa
BREAKFAST	Full made-to-order breakfast is served in the dining room. Vegetarians are welcome. Plowman's lunch is served on weekends.
AMENITIES	Hot tub on the deck; beverages; award-winning organic winery in the cellar; wine tasting and complimentary beverage of your choice; air-conditioned rooms; large Great Room with fireplace; candy in rooms; 25-meter lap pool; meeting, reunion, or wedding facilities available.
RESTRICTIONS	No smoking, no pets. Outdoor pets include a golden retriever named Corky, a cockatiel called Danny Boy, and three cats Mama, Gay Boy, and Ting Ting.
REVIEWED	*Northern California Best Places*
MEMBER	California Association of Bed & Breakfast Inns, Historic Inns of El Dorado County

River Rock

1756 Georgetown Drive, Placerville, CA 95667   530-622-7640

The Seasons Bed & Breakfast

2934 Bedford Avenue, Placerville, CA 95667   530-626-4420
Eric & Catalina McElwain, Innkeepers
Spanish, Italian, and Hungarian spoken
WEBSITE www.bbonline.com/ca/seasons

LOCATION	Two-tenths of a mile north of Highway 50. Turn left on Bedford Avenue if coming from Sacramento—turn right if coming from Lake Tahoe.
OPEN	All year
DESCRIPTION	An 1859 three-story pre-Victorian home and two cottages filled with art and architectural treasures in a parklike setting, within walking distance of downtown Placerville. The inn is on the El Dorado County Historic Register.
NO. OF ROOMS	Four rooms with private bathrooms. Eric and Catalina recommend the Cottage.
RATES	Year-round rates are $95-125 for a single or double. There is no minimum stay and cancellation requires at least seven days' notice.
CREDIT CARDS	MasterCard, Visa
BREAKFAST	Full breakfast is served in the dining room and includes hot dishes, fresh-baked goods, and fresh fruit.
AMENITIES	Bottle of local wine and refreshments, gazebo, fountain, waterfall, wraparound porch, certified massage therapist available by appointment, all rooms have individual heat and air conditioning.
RESTRICTIONS	No smoking. The resident cats are Tigger, Zoe, and Anise; Tigger greets each guest individually.
REVIEWED	*Fodor's Best California B&Bs*
MEMBER	California Association of Bed & Breakfast Inns
AWARDS	1996, Historic Preservation Award, El Dorado County Chamber of Commerce

SHADOWRIDGE RANCH & LODGE

3500 Fort Jim Road, Placerville, CA 95667　　530-295-1000
Jim & Carlotta Davies, Innkeepers　　800-644-3498
EMAIL shadowridge@inforum.net　　FAX 530-626-5613
WEBSITE www.shadowridgeranch.com

LOCATION	Take Highway 50 two exits east of Placerville (Pt. View Drive/Newtown Road) and exit to the stop sign. Turn right. There will be another stop sign for the frontage road (Newtown Road). Turn left, go three miles to Fort Jim Road, turn right and go just under 2 miles, and you will see the signs guiding you to the parking area. Note: Don't go by street numbers as they are in no logical order.
OPEN	Open April through December
DESCRIPTION	One-story hand-hewn log cabins with turn-of-the-century decor.
NO. OF ROOMS	Four rooms with private bathrooms. Try Betty's Cabin.
RATES	Call for year-round rates. There is a minimum stay during weekends and cancellation requires 72 hours' notice.
CREDIT CARDS	American Express, MasterCard, Visa
BREAKFAST	Full ranch-style breakfast is served in the dining room or outdoors and includes bacon, eggs, sausage, muffins, juices, and fruits.
AMENITIES	Wine and hors d'oeuvres in the afternoon; fresh-baked goodies at bedtime; cozy main lodge with fireplace and board game area; fireplace in dining room; each suite has a river-rock fireplace, wood-burning stove, air conditioning, and refrigerator; robes; suites include complimentary soft drinks, spring water, and coffee-makers; suites with queen-size beds.
RESTRICTIONS	No smoking, no pets. Louie is the resident cat. "We have daily visits from herds of wild turkeys and deer. At night we are visited by raccoons, opossum, and other nighttime critters."
REVIEWED	*Historic Country Inns of California*
MEMBER	California Association of Bed & Breakfast Inns

THE SHAFSKY HOUSE BED & BREAKFAST INN

2942 Coloma Street, Placerville, CA 95667　　530-642-2776
Joy & Nobi Tsumura, Innkeepers　　FAX 530-642-2109
Japanese spoken
EMAIL shafsky@directcon.net
WEBSITE www.shafsky.com

LOCATION	Two blocks from downtown Placerville.
OPEN	All year
DESCRIPTION	An elegant 1902 two-story Queen Anne Victorian inn decorated with Victorian antiques and reproductions.
NO. OF ROOMS	Three rooms with private bathrooms. Try the Sapphire Suite.
RATES	Year-round rates are $95 for a single or double and $120 for a suite. There is no minimum stay and cancellation requires five days' notice.
CREDIT CARDS	MasterCard, Visa
BREAKFAST	Full breakfast is served in the dining room or guestrooms. The menu changes daily, but a typical breakfast will include fresh fruit, home-baked goods, and a sumptuous hot dish such as a frittata or quiche. Breakfast is served when the guest requests it.
AMENITIES	Complimentary snack upon arrival, self-service cold beverages, in-room coffee, fresh flowers, slippers, feather beds, goose-down comforters, individually controlled heating and air conditioning.
RESTRICTIONS	No smoking, no pets, children over 12 are welcome.
MEMBER	California Association of Bed & Breakfast Inns, Historic Country Inns of El Dorado County

PLEASANTON

With 17 wineries to its credit, the Livermore Valley is establishing itself as the state's second-most important wine country. The Scottish Games are held in Pleasanton each Labor Day Weekend, as is the National Good Guys Show of vintage cars. Old-town Pleasanton is great for antiquing.

EVERGREEN

9104 Longview Drive, Pleasanton, CA 94588
Jane & Clay Cameron, Innkeepers
German spoken
EMAIL Jane@Evergreen-Inn.com
WEBSITE www.evergreen-inn.com

925-426-0901
FAX 925-426-9568

LOCATION	Take Highway 680 to Bernal Avenue West. Turn left and left again onto Foothill Road. Travel 0.25 mile south and turn right onto Longview Drive.
OPEN	All year
DESCRIPTION	A 1988 three-story contemporary inn with modern interior and antiques, in a secluded natural setting surrounded by oak trees.
NO. OF ROOMS	Four rooms with private bathrooms. Try the Grandview Room.

RATES	Year-round rates are $135-250 for a single or double. There is no minimum stay and cancellation requires seven days' notice.
CREDIT CARDS	American Express, MasterCard, Visa
BREAKFAST	Full breakfast buffet is served in the dining room and includes fresh fruit, juice, cereals, homemade granola, muffins, coffeecake, breads, eggs any style, omelets, French toast, fresh-brewed coffee, and assorted teas.
AMENITIES	Snacks and homemade cookies, robes, fresh flowers, wine and cheese, champagne for special occasions, English soaps, cable TV, private phone lines, refrigerators, fabulous views, hair dryers, great library, outdoor hot tub and deck.
RESTRICTIONS	No smoking, no pets, children over 12 are welcome. Babe and Scottie are the resident Border collies. There is also a cat on the premises. "The collies love to play ball. They are very smart and a lot of fun."
REVIEWED	*The Best Places To Kiss In Northern California; America's Favorite Inns, B&B's, and Small Hotels; Recommended Bed & Breakfasts: California*
MEMBER	Professional Association of Innkeepers International, California Association of Bed & Breakfasts
RATED	AAA 3 Diamonds, Mobil 2 Stars

PLUM TREE INN

262 West Angela, Pleasanton, CA 94566   925-426-9588

PLYMOUTH

A dozen fine vintners flourish in Plymouth; tours and tastings are always available. Events abound here including the Music at the Wineries Festival in May, which benefits the Amador County Arts Council; the Sierra Showcase of Wines, also in May; the Wine Festival in June; the Bluegrass Festival in August; and the Gold Country Jubilee in September. Plymouth is located 35 miles southeast of Sacramento on Highways 16 and 49.

AMADOR HARVEST INN

12455 Steiner Road, Plymouth, CA 95669   209-245-5512
Bobbie Deaver, Resident Owner
WEBSITE *www.amadorharvest.com*

LOCATION	Five miles southeast of Plymouth off Highway 49. Take the E16 exit and go one mile on Steiner Road.
OPEN	All year
DESCRIPTION	A 1969 ranch-style country inn situated on the edge of a lake and surrounded by vineyards and oak trees.
NO. OF ROOMS	Four rooms with private bathrooms. Try the Zinfandel Room.
RATES	Year-round rates are $85-95 for a single or double, and $110 for a suite. Rates are subject to change; please call. Cancellation requires seven days' notice.
CREDIT CARDS	MasterCard, Visa
BREAKFAST	Full breakfast, served in the dining room, includes an egg dish, meat, various breakfast breads, and beverages.
AMENITIES	Flowers in rooms, hors d'oeuvres and wine, catch-and-release fishing in the lake.
RESTRICTIONS	No smoking, no pets
MEMBER	California Association of Bed & Breakfast Inns, Amador County Bed & Breakfast Association

INDIAN CREEK BED & BREAKFAST

21950 State Highway 49, Plymouth, CA 95669   209-245-4648
Lena Stiward & Steve Noffsinger, Innkeepers   FAX 209-245-3230
Swedish spoken
WEBSITE www.indiancreek.com

LOCATION	Three miles north of Plymouth on Highway 49.
OPEN	All year
DESCRIPTION	A 1932 two-story log lodge decorated with western and Indian artifacts and secluded on 10 wooded acres in the heart of Gold Country at the gateway to the Shenandoah Valley wine region.
NO. OF ROOMS	Four rooms with private bathrooms. Try the Margaret Breen Room.
RATES	Year-round rates are $100-130 for a single or double. There is a two-night minimum stay and cancellation requires 14 days' notice with a $10 charge.
CREDIT CARDS	Discover, MasterCard, Visa
BREAKFAST	Full breakfast is served in the dining room and includes homemade muffins or breads, juice, coffee and tea, fruit with sauce, and a hot entrée such as stuffed French toast and sausage, eggs Benedict and roasted potatoes, quiche, frittata, and baked omelets.

Indian Creek Bed & Breakfast, Plymouth

AMENITIES	Swimming pool and spa under the stars; hammocks at the artesian spring and pond; large covered porch and decks; gold mine; hiking; large goldfish pond; large fireplace; sun room; cowboy bar; 10 wooded acres with creek; air conditioning; dish of chocolates; gift bag with body puff, moisturizer, shaving cream, and body shampoo.
RESTRICTIONS	No smoking, no pets, no children. There is abundant wildlife on the property, including wild turkeys, deer, rabbits, quail, doves, hummingbirds, foxes, otters, beavers, songbirds, and coyotes.
REVIEWED	*The Best Places to Kiss in Northern California*, *Northern California Best Places*, *Fodor's*, *Frommer's*
MEMBER	Bed & Breakfast Inns of Amador County

Plymouth House Inn

9525 Main, Plymouth, CA 95669　　　　　　　　　　　　　　209-245-3298

POINT ARENA

COAST GUARD HOUSE

695 Arena Cove, Point Arena, CA 95468   707-882-2442
www.coastguardhouse.com

POINT ARENA BED & BREAKFAST

300 Main Street Highway 1, Point Arena, CA 95468   707-882-3455

POINT REYES STATION

Just outside the southeast end of Tomales Bay, this only slightly yuppified little town is famous for its Pulitzer Prize-winning newspaper, the *Point Reyes Light*. From here, it's a very short drive to Point Reyes National Seashore. From San Francisco, cross the Golden Gate Bridge and head north on Highway 1.

CARRIAGE HOUSE BED & BREAKFAST

325 Mesa Road, Point Reyes Station, CA 94956   415-663-8627
Felicity Kirsch, Resident Owner   800-613-8351
EMAIL *felicity@nbn.com*   FAX 415-663-8431
WEBSITE *www.carriagehousebb.com*

LOCATION	Turn right at the west end of town onto Highway 1, then turn left at Mesa Road. Go 0.33 mile and turn left at the sign, down the lane.
OPEN	All year
DESCRIPTION	A 1920 two-story old-fashioned country inn decorated with antiques and folk art, with views of Inverness Ridge.
NO. OF ROOMS	Three rooms with private bathrooms
RATES	Year-round rates are $125 for a single or double and $145-160 for a suite. Midweek rates are $110 for a single or double and $130-145 for a suite. There is a two-night minimum stay on the weekend and cancellation requires seven days' notice.
CREDIT CARDS	MasterCard, Visa

Carriage House Bed & Breakfast, Point Reyes Station

BREAKFAST	Continental plus is served in the guestrooms and includes fresh-squeezed juice, fresh fruit, pastries, cereal, yogurt, tea, and coffee.
AMENITIES	Flowers, cookies, a beautiful garden, in-room massage, concierge, fireplace, TV/VCR, fax, babysitting and crib, kitchen or wet bar.
RESTRICTIONS	No smoking, no pets, children are welcome. The resident cats are Mocha, Guido, and Tuxedo, all beautiful long-haired Persian/Siamese mixes.
MEMBER	California Association of Bed & Breakfast Inns, Point Reyes Lodging Association

CRICKETT COTTAGE

PO Box 627, Point Reyes Station, CA 94956 415-663-9139

FERRANDO'S HIDEAWAY AND COTTAGES

12010 Highway 1, Point Reyes Station, CA 94956 415-663-1966
Doris & Greg Ferrando, Innkeepers 800-337-2636
German spoken FAX 415-666-1825
EMAIL ferrando@nbn.com WEBSITE www.ferrando.com

LOCATION	Thirty-four miles north of San Francisco and one mile north of Point Reyes Station, on Highway 1.
OPEN	All year

DESCRIPTION	A 1972 two-story contemporary home and two cottages with country furnishings.
NO. OF ROOMS	Two rooms, one suite, and two cottages with private bathrooms. Alberti Cottage is highly recommended.
RATES	Year-round rates for a single or double are $130-220, the suite is $195, and the cottages are $175-220. Cancellation requires seven days' notice.
CREDIT CARDS	MasterCard, Visa
BREAKFAST	Full breakfast, served in the breakfast room, includes an egg dish made with eggs from the Ferrandos' chickens, fresh fruit, muffins, granola, yogurt, breads, cheeses, and beverages.
AMENITIES	Outdoor shared hot tub, complimentary cookies, and afternoon tea.
RESTRICTIONS	No smoking, no pets, children welcome in cottages.
REVIEWED	*San Francisco and the Bay Area: Romantic Weekends; Inns and Wineries of California's Northern Coast; Complete Guide to B&Bs, Inns, and Guesthouses; Bay Area Backroads*
MEMBER	California Association of Bed & Breakfast Inns
KUDOS/COMMENTS	"Wonderful, clean, gracious accommodations; special hostess." "Very clean; charming host and hostess; beautiful gardens; restful."

HOLLY TREE INN

3 Silverhills Road, Inverness Park, CA 94956   415-663-1554
Tom & Diane Balogh, Resident Owners   800-286-4655
Limited French and Spanish spoken   FAX 415-663-8566
WEBSITE www.hollytreeinn.com

LOCATION	From San Francisco, take Highway 101 north to Larkspur. Exit on Sir Francis Drake Boulevard westbound. At Highway 1 in Olema, head north (right), and take the first right on Bear Valley Road. Go 1.9 miles and turn left on Silverhills Road.
OPEN	Cottages open all year. The inn is closed Christmas Eve and Christmas Day.
DESCRIPTION	Built in 1939, the clapboard inn and cottages are surrounded by 19 acres of valleys, wooded hillsides, and creekside gardens.
NO. OF ROOMS	Four rooms and three cottages with private bathrooms. The best room in the inn is the Laurel Room; the best cottage is the Sea Star.
RATES	Year-round rates are $120-145 for a single or double and $175-250 for a cottage. A two-night stay is required on weekends and cancellation requires seven days' notice with a $15 fee.

CREDIT CARDS	MasterCard, Visa
BREAKFAST	Full breakfast, served in the dining room or in the cottages, includes quiche, frittata, or egg casserole; fresh fruit; scones or pastries; muffins; and beverages.
AMENITIES	Garden hot tub, flowers in rooms, robes, telephones in some cottages, private hot tubs in two cottages, massage available, suitable for small meetings or retreats.
RESTRICTIONS	No smoking. Three cats share the grounds.
REVIEWED	Country Inns, Lodges and Historic Hotels; Northern California Best Places; The Best Places to Kiss in Northern California; America's Wonderful Little Hotels & Inns
MEMBER	Professional Association of Innkeepers International, California Bed & Breakfast Association, Inns of Point Reyes

JASMINE COTTAGE

PO Box 56, Point Reyes Station, CA 94956 415-663-1166
Karen Gray, Resident Owner

KNOB HILL

40 Knob Hill Road, Point Reyes Station, CA 94956 415-663-1784
Janet Schlirr, Resident Owner
WEBSITE www.knobhill.com

LOCATION	From Point Reyes Station, head north on Highway 1. Turn left on Viento just past the school; Viento turns into Knob Hill.
OPEN	All year
DESCRIPTION	A 1989 California redwood cottage.
NO. OF ROOMS	Two rooms with private bathrooms.
RATES	Year-round rates for a single or double are $60-65. The cottage is $95-110. There is a two-night minimum stay over Saturdays and a seven-day cancellation policy.
CREDIT CARDS	No
BREAKFAST	Continental plus is included in the price by arrangement.
AMENITIES	Flowers, crystal, candles, wood-burning stove, access to phone and TV, horse boarding.

RESTRICTIONS	Smoking permitted outside, pets accepted by request. Resident pets include a yellow Lab, Dougal, Patches the cat, and many horses. There are also barn owls.
REVIEWED	*Getting Away for the Weekend*
MEMBER	Coastal Lodging Association

TERRI'S HOMESTAY

83 Sunnyside Drive, Point Reyes Station, CA 94956   800-969-1289
Terri Elaine, Resident Owner   FAX 415-663-1289
Spanish spoken
WEBSITE www.terrishomestay.com

LOCATION	On the Inverness Ridge, 1.1 miles up steep and winding Drake View Drive and between Inverness and Inverness Park.
OPEN	All year
DESCRIPTION	A 1966 contemporary California host home with Central American furnishings.
NO. OF ROOMS	Two rooms with private bathrooms.
RATES	Year-round rates are $95-125 for a single or double. November through March and midweek, rates are lower. There is a minimum stay and cancellation requires seven days' notice.
CREDIT CARDS	No
BREAKFAST	Healthy continental plus is served in the kitchen.
AMENITIES	Flowers and robes, hot tub in the garden, large decks, professional massage by appointment.
RESTRICTIONS	No smoking, no pets

THIRTY-NINE CYPRESS AND REDWING COTTAGE

39 Cypress Road, Point Reyes Station, CA 94956   415-633-1709
Julia Bartlett, Resident Owner   FAX 415-663-9292
French spoken
EMAIL bartlett@sun.net
WEBSITE www.1bbweb.com/39cypress

LOCATION	From Golden Gate Bridge, go nine miles north and turn west on Sir Francis Drake Boulevard. Go 2.5 miles to Route 1, then go north 2.3 miles to Mesa Road. Go one mile, then turn left onto Cypress. Park at the end of the drive (400 yards down on the left).

OPEN	All year
DESCRIPTION	A 1980 contemporary California redwood inn decorated with antique and eclectic furnishings, overlooking a 600-acre cattle ranch.
NO. OF ROOMS	Three rooms with private bathrooms and a three-room garden cottage.
RATES	Year-round rates are $115-150 for a single or double and $150 for the cottage. There is a minimum stay on weekends, and cancellation requires seven days' notice.
CREDIT CARDS	American Express, MasterCard, Visa
BREAKFAST	Full breakfast is served in the dining room and includes orange juice, fruit salad with yogurt, blueberry pan bread, salmon scramble, fresh-ground coffee.
AMENITIES	Flowers; robes; outdoor hot tub with 180-degree view; garden; cozy corner for reading; cottage has kitchen, hot tub, and Franklin stove.
RESTRICTIONS	No smoking, children over five are welcome. Flora Borrealis is the Australian cattle dog and Resca is the Border collie.
MEMBER	Professional Association of Innkeepers International, California Association of Bed & Breakfast Inns, Inns of Point Reyes

WINDSONG COTTAGE

25 McDonald Lane, Point Reyes Station, CA 94956 415-663-9695
Anthony Ragona, Innkeeper 800-663-9695
EMAIL windsong@nbn.com FAX 415-663-1577
WEBSITE www.windsongcottage.com

LOCATION	One mile north of Point Reyes Station.
OPEN	All year
DESCRIPTION	A contemporary yurt (round cottage) with mostly contemporary decor and some antiques. The yurt has a gently sloped ceiling topped with a round skylight that provides great natural light and views.
NO. OF ROOMS	One room with a private bathroom.
RATES	Year-round rates are $125-165 for a single or double. There is a two-night minimum stay during weekends and cancellation requires seven days' notice.
CREDIT CARDS	No
BREAKFAST	Continental plus is stocked in the cottage's kitchen and includes coffee, tea, local pastries, eggs, milk, cereal, juice, butter, and spices.

AMENITIES	Private hot tub in garden, telephone, cable TV/VCR, stereo, flowers, all bedding and towels.
RESTRICTIONS	No smoking, no pets
KUDOS/COMMENTS	"Unique structure, expansive view of Tomales Bay, mellow innkeeper."

PORTOLA

PULLMAN HOUSE BED & BREAKFAST

256 Commercial Street, Portola, CA 96122   530-832-0107

SILVER LADY BED & BREAKFAST

100 Escondido Way, Portola, CA 96122   530-832-1641

PRINCETON-BY-THE-SEA

This is another seaside charmer with a lovely harbor on the San Mateo coast, just north of Half Moon Bay via Highway 1.

PILLAR POINT INN BED & BREAKFAST

380 Capistrano Road, Princeton-by-the-Sea, CA 94018   650-728-7377
Sarah Woodruff, Manager   800-400-8281
Spanish spoken   FAX 415-728-8345
WEBSITE www.pillarpointinn.com

LOCATION	Four miles north of Half Moon Bay on Highway 1. Turn west at the first stoplight onto Capistrano Road. The first building on the right is the Pillar Point Inn.
OPEN	All year
DESCRIPTION	A 1985 two-story contemporary Cape Cod inn with large bay windows, overlooking the harbor and ocean. Grounds include a topiary and herb garden.

NO. OF ROOMS	Eleven rooms with private bathrooms. Room 10 is recommended.
RATES	Year-round rates are $140-175 for a double. A two-night stay is required on weekends from June through October. Cancellation requires three days' notice, five days over holidays.
CREDIT CARDS	American Express, MasterCard, Visa
BREAKFAST	Full breakfast is served in the dining room and includes homemade granola, locally grown fruit, fresh yogurt, home-baked breads, egg strata, organic juices, coffee, and tea.
AMENITIES	Guestrooms include window seats with ocean views, brass and hand-painted enamel feather beds, concealed refrigerators and fireplaces; first floor rooms have steam baths; snacks include fruit, cookies, candy, port, and sherry; telephones, TV/VCRs, and radios in rooms; handicapped accessible.
RESTRICTIONS	No smoking, no pets
REVIEWED	*Weekends for Two in Northern California, The Best Places to Kiss in Northern California, Best Choices in Northern California*
KUDOS/COMMENTS	"Lovely seaside inn with fireplaces and good seafood nearby."

QUINCY

This sleepy little town on scenic Highway 70, in the high hills of the northern Sierra Nevada Mountains, enjoys a steady, mild climate. Take advantage of the weather and partake in any number of the area's attractive outdoor recreational options.

THE FEATHER BED

542 Jackson Street, Quincy, CA 95971   530-283-0102
Bob & Jan Janowski, Innkeepers   800-696-8624
WEBSITE www.innaccess.com/tfb   FAX 530-283-0167

LOCATION	In Quincy, one block south of Highway 70 and behind the County Courthouse.
OPEN	All year
DESCRIPTION	An 1893 two-story Queen Anne inn with country Victorian furnishings, located in the Quincy Historic District.
NO. OF ROOMS	Seven rooms with private bathrooms. Jan recommends the guesthouse.
RATES	Year-round rates are $75-90 for a single or double, $95 for the suite, and $124-130 for the guesthouse. There is a two-night minimum stay during some holidays and cancellation requires six days' notice.

The Feather Bed, Quincy

CREDIT CARDS	American Express, Diners Club, Discover, MasterCard, Visa
BREAKFAST	Full breakfast is served in the dining room or cottage and includes smoothies made from inn-grown berries, seasonal fruit, or apple crisp; a hot entrée such as quiche, egg puff, or frittata; hickory-smoked sausage; and homemade breakfast bread.
AMENITIES	Tea, cocoa, apple cider, lemonade, homemade fudge and cookies available afternoons and evenings, off-street parking, bicycles (including an antique tandem bike), air conditioning, fireplaces. The guesthouse is handicapped accessible.
RESTRICTIONS	No smoking, no pets. Jackson and Cosmo are the resident cats.
REVIEWED	*America's Favorite Inns, B&Bs, & Small Hotels; Northern California Best Places; Fodor's*
MEMBER	California Association of Bed & Breakfast Inns, Professional Association of Innkeepers International
RATED	AAA 2 Diamonds, ABBA 3 Crowns
AWARDS	1997 Jones Dairy Farm B&B Recipe Competition, Second Place (breakfast/brunch)

RED BLUFF

Named for the colored sand and gravel cliffs of the surrounding area, it could also be called Red Hot in summer. In early spring, horse and cattle sales and roundups are major events. Head out to the Salmon Viewing Plaza at Diversion Dam on the Sacramento River, or to the William B. Ide Adobe State Historic Park (remember the Bear Flag Republic?). Red Bluff is just south of Redding on I-5.

THE FAULKNER HOUSE

1029 Jefferson Street, Red Bluff, CA 96080
Harvey & Mary Klinger, Innkeepers
EMAIL *faulknerbb@juno.com*

530-529-0520
800-549-6171
FAX 530-527-4970

LOCATION	One mile west of I-5.
OPEN	All year
DESCRIPTION	An 1890 two-story Queen Anne Victorian inn with original stained-glass windows, ornate molding, eight-foot pocket doors, antiques, and Victorian decor.
NO. OF ROOMS	Four rooms with private bathrooms. Try the Rose Room.
RATES	Year-round rates are $65-90 for a single or double. There is no minimum stay and cancellation requires three days' notice.
CREDIT CARDS	American Express, MasterCard, Visa
BREAKFAST	Full breakfast is served in the dining room and includes French toast, bacon, fresh fruit, fresh-squeezed orange juice, tea, and coffee.

The Faulkner House, Red Bluff

AMENITIES	Flowers; sherry; peanut M&Ms; air conditioning; TV in common room; sparkling water, tea, and coffee upon arrival.
RESTRICTIONS	No smoking, no pets, children over 10 are welcome. There is a resident cat.
REVIEWED	*Complete Guide to Bed & Breakfasts, Inns & Guest Houses; The Official Guide to American Historic Inns; Northern California Best Places*
MEMBER	American Bed & Breakfast Association, California Association of Bed & Breakfast Inns
KUDOS/COMMENTS	"A nicely decorated Victorian with friendly, knowledgeable hosts."

JARVIS MANSION BED & BREAKFAST

1313 Jackson Street, Red Bluff, CA 96080 530-527-6901
Dave & Tina Ebert, Innkeepers 877-527-6901

LOCATION	From I-5, take the Antelope Boulevard exit and head west, crossing the Sacramento River. Antelope becomes Oak Street. Cross the railroad tracks, turn right (north) on Jackson Street, and go five blocks.
OPEN	All year
DESCRIPTION	An 1870 two-story Victorian Italianate inn decorated with period furnishings.
NO. OF ROOMS	Four rooms with private bathrooms. The French Rose Room is the best in the house.
RATES	Year-round rates for a single or double are $65-90. There is no minimum stay and cancellation requires 72 hours' notice.
CREDIT CARDS	MasterCard, Visa
BREAKFAST	Continental plus is served in the dining room and includes seasonal fruit cup, main course, muffins, and beverages.
AMENITIES	Wine and hors d'oeuvres at check-in, TV, phone available, parklike grounds with gazebo.
RESTRICTIONS	No smoking, no pets, children with prior arrangements. The resident dog is Ebony.

JEFFERSON HOUSE

1236 Jefferson Street, Red Bluff, CA 96080 530-527-4133

JETER VICTORIAN INN

1107 Jefferson Street, Red Bluff, CA 96080 530-527-7574
Bill & Mary Dunlap, Innkeepers

LOCATION	Located in the Victorian community of Red Bluff, approximately seven blocks from Historic Downtown Red Bluff. I-5 parallels Jefferson Street three blocks to the east.
OPEN	All year
DESCRIPTION	An 1881 two-story authentic Victorian inn.
NO. OF ROOMS	Three rooms with private bathrooms and three rooms with shared bathrooms. Try the Imperial Room.
RATES	Year-round rates range from $65-85 for a room with a shared bathroom to $140 for the Imperial Suite, with a private bathroom. There is no minimum stay and cancellation requires 72 hours' notice.
CREDIT CARDS	MasterCard, Visa
BREAKFAST	Full breakfast is served in the dining room or in the garden or pavilion.
AMENITIES	Complimentary basket of cookies, candy, and fruit in rooms, evening dessert, robes, TV in some rooms, hot tub in Imperial Suite.
RESTRICTIONS	No smoking, children over 14 are welcome (younger children by special arrangement).
REVIEWED	*Bed & Breakfast Country Inns*, *California Bed & Breakfast Inns*, *Away for the Weekend*

REDDING

This is the main gateway to the splendors of the Shasta–Trinity National Recreation Area and National Forest. The town itself is on the banks of the Sacramento River and its 14 tributaries, and Redding's restored Victorian neighborhoods make for pleasant strolling. Horse lovers can mix with the mustangs at the Shingletown Wild Horse Sanctuary (an up-close experience), about 30 miles southeast of town.

PALISADES PARADISE BED & BREAKFAST

1200 Palisades Avenue, Redding, CA 96003 530-223-5305
Gail Goetz, Innkeeper FAX 530-223-1200
EMAIL bnbno1@jett.net WEBSITE www.jett.net/~bnbno1

LOCATION	From I-5 north, take the Highway 44 exit to the hilltop, go one mile (the road makes a left turn over I-5), and make an immediate left onto Palisades Avenue.
OPEN	All year
DESCRIPTION	A 1977 contemporary host home with contemporary and traditional furnishings.
NO. OF ROOMS	Two rooms with private bathrooms. Try the Sunset Suite.
RATES	Year-round rates are $70-100 for a single or double with a private bathroom. There is no minimum stay and cancellation requires five days' notice.
CREDIT CARDS	American Express, MasterCard, Visa
BREAKFAST	Continental plus is served in the dining room and includes juice, fresh fruit, cereal, pastries, boiled eggs, cheese, and beverages.
AMENITIES	Flowers in season, cable TV in rooms, garden spa overlooking river, bird-watching, nightly chocolates, refreshments on arrival.
RESTRICTIONS	No smoking. Snuggles is the resident pooch.
MEMBER	California Association of Bed & Breakfast Inns
RATED	ABBA 2 Crowns
KUDOS/COMMENTS	"Wonderful setting; pleasant owner; casual newer home; spectacular river view."

REDDING'S BED & BREAKFAST

1094 Palisades Avenue, Redding, CA 96003
Lacy LaMoire, Innkeeper

530-222-2494
FAX 530-221-2878

LOCATION	Located off Redding's main street (Hilltop Drive) on the bluffs with a view of the city lights. A short distance from I-5, Highway 44, and Highway 299.
OPEN	All year
DESCRIPTION	A 1950 three-story "Iowa farmhouse" with country furnishings and antiques.
NO. OF ROOMS	One room with a private bathroom and three rooms share a bathroom. Pick Lacy's Favorite Room.
RATES	Year-round rates are $25-100 for a single or double with a shared bathroom and $50-100 for a double with a private bathroom. There is no minimum stay and cancellation requires seven days' notice.
CREDIT CARDS	American Express, Discover, MasterCard, Visa

BREAKFAST	Full breakfast is served in the guestrooms or on the back deck and includes juice, coffee, strawberries and whipped cream, fruit, pound cake, muffins, French toast, and eggs.
AMENITIES	Fresh roses in rooms, chocolates, candles, sparkling cider, CD player, robes, slippers, one room with private Jacuzzi, hot tub outside on deck with views of city lights, limousine service available.
RESTRICTIONS	No smoking indoors, children over six are welcome. The Jack Russell terrier is named Betty Boop.

TIFFANY HOUSE BED & BREAKFAST INN

1510 Barbara Road, Redding, CA 96003   530-244-3225
Arthur & Roberta Dube, Resident Owners

LOCATION	Take Highway 5 through town to Lake Boulevard and turn left. Drive 0.75 mile to North Market (second stoplight) and turn left. Go to Barbara Road, turn right, and go uphill to the inn.
OPEN	All year
DESCRIPTION	A 1939 late Victorian with Victorian furnishings, nestled under oaks on a hill.
NO. OF ROOMS	Four rooms with private bathrooms. Roberta likes the Wisteria Cottage.
RATES	Please call for current rates and cancellation information.
CREDIT CARDS	American Express, MasterCard, Visa
BREAKFAST	Full breakfast is served in the dining room, country kitchen, or gazebo.
AMENITIES	Fresh flowers in room, robes, spa in cottage, hair dryers, TV in drawing room, fireplaces in drawing room and parlor, swimming pool, gazebo, basketball court, very large deck, evening refreshments. The cottage is handicapped accessible.
RESTRICTIONS	No smoking, no pets, children are welcome.
REVIEWED	*Northern California Best Places, Quick Escapes From San Francisco*
MEMBER	Professional Association of Innkeepers International, California Association of Bed & Breakfast Inns
KUDOS/COMMENTS	" A reputable establishment." "Wonderful Victorian overlooking the city, gracious hosts, excellent food, beautiful decor."

RICHMOND

Across the bay from San Francisco, Richmond offers easy access to the treasures of San Francisco, Berkeley, Oakland, and surrounding natural areas.

EAST BROTHER LIGHT STATION

117 Park Place, Richmond, CA 94801
Pat Diamond, Director
WEBSITE www.ebls.org

510-233-2385
FAX 510-235-5234

LOCATION   On a small rocky island at the north end of San Francisco Bay. Approximately one hour north of San Francisco and 30 minutes from Berkeley. From either direction on I-80, take the San Rafael exit to I-580 west toward the Richmond/San Rafael Bridge. Just before the toll plaza, take the Point Molate exit to the right and follow the signs to Point San Pablo Yacht Harbor.

OPEN   All year

DESCRIPTION   An 1873 two-story Carpenters Gothic light station furnished with period antiques and reproductions and surrounded by a white picket fence. Listed on the National Historic Register.

NO. OF ROOMS   Two rooms with private bathrooms, two rooms share two bathrooms. Pat recommends the San Francisco Room or the Marin Room.

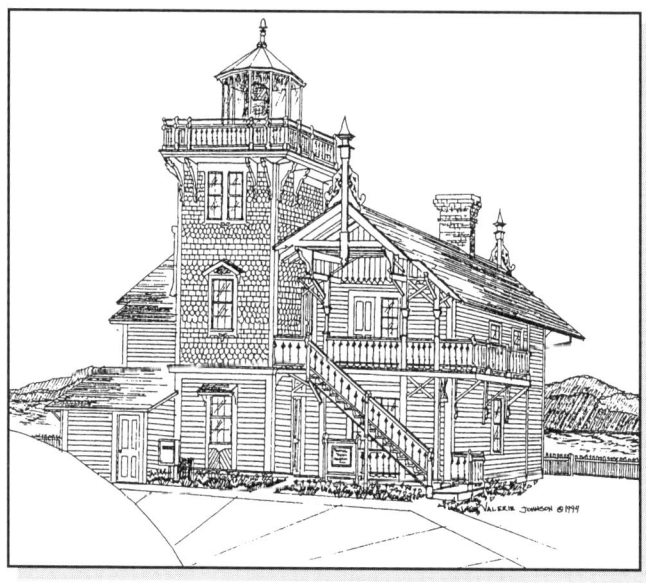

East Brother Light Station, Richmond

RATES	Year-round rates are $305-325 for a single or double with a private bathroom and $295-315 for a single or double with a shared bathroom. All cancellations are subject to a $15 service charge. Cancellations made with less than 30 days' notice will be refunded at 90 percent of the total cost only if the room is rebooked.
CREDIT CARDS	American Express, MasterCard, Visa
BREAKFAST	Full breakfast, served in the dining room, includes homemade waffles, fresh fruit, and beverages. Rates also include a four-course dinner with wine (vegetarian available on request).
AMENITIES	Boat transportation to and from the island; champagne and hors d'oeuvres served before the guided tour of the lighthouse; views of Mount Tamalpais, San Pablo Bay, and nearby islands; one room with a fireplace.
RESTRICTIONS	No smoking, no pets, children OK with prior arrangement.
REVIEWED	*Karen Brown's California: Charming Inns & Itineraries; Weekends for Two in Northern California: 50 Romantic Getaways; America's Wonderful Little Hotels & Inns; By Recommendation Only; Fodor's California; The Complete Guide to Bed & Breakfast Inns in the U.S., Canada, and Worldwide; The Historic Trust Guide to Historic Bed & Breakfasts, Inns, and Small Hotels*
MEMBER	Professional Association of Innkeepers International
KUDOS/COMMENTS	"Cozy; a great escape to nature."

HOTEL MAC

10 Cottage Avenue, Richmond, CA 94801   510-235-0010
WEBSITE www.PointRichmond.com/HotelMac

RUTHEFORD

Winery tours and related activities are the reasons to be here in the heart of Napa County wine country on Highway 29.

RANCHO CAYMUS

1140 Rutheford Road, Rutheford, CA 94573   707-963-1777
Otto Komes, Innkeeper   800-845-1777
Spanish, Russian, and Hungarian spoken   FAX 707-963-5387

LOCATION	From the city of Napa, go north on Highway 29 for 18 miles. Turn right at the junction of Highway 128 and go down the road 100 yards. The inn is on the left.
OPEN	All year
DESCRIPTION	A 1985 Southwest-style hacienda with rustic California furnishings.
NO. OF ROOMS	Twenty-six rooms with private bathrooms. Otto likes room 209.
RATES	April 1 through November, rates are $155-185 for a single or double and suites are $255-325. December 1 to March 31, rates are $145-175 for a single or double and suites are $245-295. There is a two-night minimum stay and cancellation requires 72 hours' notice.
CREDIT CARDS	American Express, MasterCard, Visa
BREAKFAST	Continental plus is served in the dining room and includes homemade granola and muffins, fresh fruit, and beverages. Lunch and dinner are available for private functions.
AMENITIES	Most of the rooms have fireplaces; five suites include Jacuzzi tubs; most rooms have TV, telephone, refrigerator, and wet bar; meeting facilities for 50; two rooms handicapped accessible.
RESTRICTIONS	No pets, children allowed "but not suggested."
REVIEWED	*Weekends for Two in Northern California: 50 Romantic Getaways*
MEMBER	California Association of Bed & Breakfast Inns
RATED	AAA 3 Diamonds, Mobil 3 Stars

SACRAMENTO

A former Gold Rush boomtown, Sacramento sprang up where the American and Sacramento Rivers meet—a tourist area now known as Old Sacramento. Start your tour of the town in Old Sacramento, the historic district. Perched along the Sacramento River, the four-block-long stretch is filled with dozens of restaurants, gift shops, and saloons. An Old Sac highlight is the California State Railroad Museum, a grand monument to the glory days of locomotion and the Big Four, and the largest museum of its kind in the nation. The granddaddy of Old Sac attractions is the Sacramento Dixieland Jubilee, the world's largest Dixieland jazz festival, which attracts thousands each Memorial Day weekend.

ABIGAIL'S BED & BREAKFAST

2120 G Street, Sacramento, CA 95816
Susanne & Ken Ventura, Resident Owners

916-441-5007
800-858-1568
FAX 916-441-0621

LOCATION	From the business I-80 loop, exit onto H Street and turn left, then turn right at the second light. Turn left at G Street. From I-5, take the J Street exit to 21st Street and take a left. Then turn left on G Street.
OPEN	All year
DESCRIPTION	A three-story colonial revival inn with eclectic Edwardian furnishings and original art.
NO. OF ROOMS	Five rooms with private bathrooms. The staff voted the Margaret Room as best.
RATES	Midweek rates are $105-125 for a single and $115-175 for a double. There is a three-night minimum stay during Thanksgiving and Memorial Day weekends. Cancellation requires seven days' notice.
CREDIT CARDS	American Express, Diners Club, Discover, MasterCard, Visa
BREAKFAST	Full breakfast is served in the dining room or guestrooms and includes fruit, yogurt, custard, award-winning zucchini-walnut-sour cream pancakes or sundried tomato quiche.
AMENITIES	Flowers, robes, telephone, TV, late-night snack, early morning coffee outside rooms, refrigerator stocked with cold drinks, hot tub in the garden, gazebo, special offers at local restaurants.
RESTRICTIONS	No smoking in house, no pets, children over five are welcome. The inn is home to two cats, Abigail and Fiona.
REVIEWED	*The Best Places to Kiss in Northern California, Jan Peverille's Inn Places for Bed & Breakfast, The California Bed & Breakfast Book, Bed & Breakfast California, America's Wonderful Little Hotels & Inns, Bay Area Backroads, Best Places to Stay in California*
MEMBER	California Association of Bed & Breakfast Inns
RATED	AAA 3 Diamonds
KUDOS/COMMENTS	"Nicely kept up. Great breakfast."

Amber House Bed & Breakfast Inn

1315 22nd Street, Sacramento, CA 95816　　916-444-8085
Michael & Jane Richardson, Resident Owners　　800-755-6526
EMAIL *innkeeper@amberhouse.com*　　FAX 916-447-1548
WEBSITE *www.amberhouse.com*

LOCATION	Eight blocks east of the State Capitol between Capitol Avenue and 22nd Street.
OPEN	All year

DESCRIPTION	Three side-by-side two-story homes: a 1905 Craftsman, a 1913 Mediterranean, and a newly remodeled historic home. All three are furnished with antiques.
NO. OF ROOMS	Fourteen rooms with private bathrooms. Try the Renoir Room.
RATES	Year-round rates for a single or double are $129-269. There is no minimum stay. Cancellation requires two days' notice for weekdays and seven days' notice for weekends.
CREDIT CARDS	American Express, Diners Club, Discover, MasterCard, Visa
BREAKFAST	Full breakfast is served in the dining room or guestrooms, or on the veranda, and includes beverages, fruit, and a hot entrée such as quiche and potatoes with peppers.
AMENITIES	Flowers, phones, data port, cable TV/VCRs, Jacuzzi, robes, clock radios with tape players in every room.
RESTRICTIONS	No smoking
REVIEWED	*The Best Places to Kiss in Northern California, America's Wonderful Little Hotels & Inns, Recommended Country Inns—West Coast, Northern California Discovery Guide*
MEMBER	American Bed & Breakfast Association, California Association of Bed & Breakfast Inns, Special Places
RATED	ABBA 3 Crowns, Mobil 3 Stars
KUDOS/COMMENTS	"Charming, quality B&B; beautifully appointed rooms and bathrooms; friendly staff; yummy breakfast." "Fantastic. Great bathrooms."

HARTLEY HOUSE BED & BREAKFAST INN

700 22nd Street, Sacramento, CA 95816   916-447-7829
Randy Hartley, Resident Owner   800-831-5806
Spanish spoken   FAX 916-447-1820
EMAIL randy@hartleyhouse.com   WEBSITE www.hartleyhouse.com

LOCATION	From I-5, take the J Street exit downtown, proceed on J Street to 22nd Street, turn left, and drive to the corner of 22nd and G Streets.
OPEN	All year
DESCRIPTION	A 1906 two-story colonial revival with authentic leaded glass, stained-glass windows, historic antiques, and period decor—an elegant, small European hotel located in Historic Boulevard Park.
NO. OF ROOMS	Five rooms with private bathrooms. Dover is the best room in the house.

Hartley House Bed & Breakfast Inn, Sacramento

RATES	Year-round rates for a single or double are $100-165. There is a minimum stay during holiday weekends only.
CREDIT CARDS	American Express, Diners Club, JCB, MasterCard, Visa
BREAKFAST	Full breakfast is served in the dining room or courtyard and includes fresh fruit, egg dish, freshly baked muffins and scones, and beverages. Lunch, dinner, and special meals are available on request.
AMENITIES	Robes, fresh flowers, phones, TV, turndown service, fax, meeting facilities, and catering services.
RESTRICTIONS	No smoking, no pets, children over 12 are welcome.
REVIEWED	*The Best Places to Kiss in Northern California, Best Places to Stay in Northern California, Fodor's California*
MEMBER	California Association of Bed & Breakfast Inns, California Hotel & Motel Association, American Hotel Association
RATED	AAA 3 Diamonds

INN AT PARKSIDE

2116 6th Street, Sacramento, CA 95816　　　　916-658-1818
WEBSITE *www.innatparkside.com*

Moon River Inn

8201 Freeport Boulevard, Sacramento, CA 95816 916-665-6550
WEBSITE *members.aol.com/moonriver1/refmr3.htm*

On the Bluffs

9735 Mira Del Rio Drive, Sacramento, CA 95816 916-591-4114
Mark & Penny Bingham, Innkeepers
EMAIL *otbluffs@aol.com*
WEBSITE *www.usa-411.com/otbluffs.html*

LOCATION	One mile north of Highway 50 on Bradshaw Road, just minutes from downtown Sacramento.
OPEN	All year
DESCRIPTION	A 1980 contemporary host home overlooking the scenic American River and decorated with elegant furnishings, including antiques and collectibles.
NO. OF ROOMS	Two rooms with private bathrooms. The Binghams suggest the River View Room.
RATES	Year-round rates are $80-95 for a single or double. There is no minimum stay and cancellation requires seven days' notice.
CREDIT CARDS	American Express, MasterCard, Visa
BREAKFAST	Full breakfast is served in the dining room or on the decks and includes breads, fruits, soufflés, omelets, pancakes, waffles, and meat.
AMENITIES	Bicycles available, swimming pool, outdoor hot tub, fireplace in public living room.
RESTRICTIONS	No smoking, no pets, children over 14 are welcome. Classy is the resident papillon, Ralph and Alice are the lovebirds.

Savoyard Bed & Breakfast

3322 H Street, Sacramento, CA 95816-4504 916-442-6709
Brus & Pat Ansell, Resident Owners 800-7SA-VOYA
EMAIL *info@savoyard.com* FAX 916-442-6709
WEBSITE *www.savoyard.com*

LOCATION	Two miles east of the State Capitol.
OPEN	All year
DESCRIPTION	A 1925 two-story Italian Renaissance inn with classic Greek columns and eclectic antique furnishings.
NO. OF ROOMS	Four rooms with private bathrooms. Try the Penzance Room.
RATES	Year-round rates are $90-120 for a single or double. There is no minimum stay and cancellation requires three days' notice.
CREDIT CARDS	American Express, Diners Club, Discover, MasterCard, Visa
BREAKFAST	Continental breakfast is served in the dining room and includes coffee or tea, orange juice, fresh fruit cup, and blueberry muffins.
AMENITIES	Air conditioning, TV/VCR, hot tub in garden.
RESTRICTIONS	No smoking, no pets
MEMBER	California Association of Bed & Breakfast Inns

Vizcaya

2019 21st Street, Sacramento, CA 95816   916-455-5243

San Andreas

The Calaveras County Seat is bustling, touristy, and historically colorful. Check out the County Museum, Black Bart's jail cell, or the California Cavers, or head out to the New Hogan Reservoir Recreation Area. San Andreas is southeast of Sacramento on Highway 49.

Courtyard Bed & Breakfast

334 West St. Charles Street, San Andreas, CA 95249   209-754-1518
Lucy Thein, Resident Owner

LOCATION	In greater downtown San Andreas.
OPEN	All year
DESCRIPTION	A 1920 wood-frame host home decorated with country furnishings. The property features a 400-year-old oak tree, gardens, and 55 bird houses.
NO. OF ROOMS	Two rooms with private bathrooms.

RATES	Please call for current rates. Cancellation requires 48 hours' notice and a $25 fee.
CREDIT CARDS	No
BREAKFAST	Coffee is brought to the room and a full two-course breakfast is served in the gardens or breakfast room.
AMENITIES	Redwood hot tub under the trees; hors d'oeuvres served on arrival; the master suite has a fireplace, baby grand piano, stained-glass window over the bathtub, and walk-in closet.
RESTRICTIONS	Smoking outside only, children and dogs are welcome.

THE ROBIN'S NEST

247 West St. Charles Street, San Andreas, CA 95249   209-754-1076
William Konietzny, Innkeeper   888-214-9202
Limited German spoken   FAX 209-754-3975
EMAIL Robins.Nest.Inn@worldnet.att.net
WEBSITE www.touristguide.com/b&b/ca/robinsnest

LOCATION	From the north or west: 0.5 mile southeast of the junction of Highways 12 and 49, on the right side of Highway 49. From the south or east: 0.25 mile northwest of Main Street (center of town), on the left side of Highway 49. The parking lot is off Market Street, which runs parallel to Highway 49 on the south side.
OPEN	All year
DESCRIPTION	An 1895 three-story Queen Ann Victorian mansion with turn-of-the-century decor, including many antiques. The mansion is situated on 1.3 landscaped acres. Listed on the State Historic Register.
NO. OF ROOMS	Seven rooms with private bathrooms and two rooms with one shared bathroom. Try the Carousel Room.
RATES	Year-round rates are $70-110 for a single or double with a private bathroom and $60-70 for a single or double with a shared bathroom. There is a two-night minimum stay on long weekends and holidays, and cancellation requires seven days' notice.
CREDIT CARDS	American Express, Discover, MasterCard, Visa
BREAKFAST	Five-course gourmet breakfast is served in the dining room and may include kiwi strawberry platter, hot biscuits, peaches and cream nectar, eggs Florentine, and creme brulé. Dinner is also available for groups of four or more with advance reservation.

AMENITIES	Eight-person outside hot tub; robes in all rooms; fresh flowers; guest refrigerator stocked with complimentary soft drinks and iced tea; complimentary port, cream sherry, mints, and chocolate kisses; central air conditioning; space for meetings (up to 30) and weddings (up to 36); several patio sets, benches, and picnic tables under shaded awnings; brick draw-well; steel windmill; horseshoe pits; mixed and rose gardens.
RESTRICTIONS	No smoking, no pets, well-behaved children are welcome.
REVIEWED	*Victorian Voyages; The Official Guide to American Historic Inns*
MEMBER	Calaveras Visitors Bureau Association
RATED	AAA 2 Stars
AWARDS	1982, Award for Architectural Excellence, Calaveras County Historical Society
KUDOS/COMMENTS	"Relatively unknown; wonderful innkeepers; lovely B&B with well-appointed rooms." (1999)

THORN MANSION INN

87 West St. Charles Street, San Andreas, CA 95249   209-754-1027

SAN FRANCISCO

In no other city in the country is the meeting of land and sea so spectacular. Add to the city's fabled beauty its exceptional cuisine, art, and culture, and no wonder San Francisco is one of the world's favorite cities.

ABIGAIL HOTEL

246 McAllister Street, San Francisco, CA 94102   415-861-9728

ADELAIDE INN

5 Isadora Duncan Lane, San Francisco, CA 94102   415-441-2261

Alamo Square Inn

719 Scott Street, San Francisco, CA 94117
Wayne Corn & Klaus May, Resident Owners
WEBSITE *www.alamoinn.com*

415-922-2055
800-345-9888

Albion House Bed & Breakfast

135 Gough Street, San Francisco, CA 94102

415-621-0896

Alexander Inn

415 Ofarrell Street, San Francisco, CA 94102

415-928-6800
800-843-8709

The Amsterdam Hotel

749 Taylor Street, San Francisco, CA 94108
Kanti Gopal, Manager
WEBSITE *www.amsterdamhotel.com*

415-673-3277
800-637-3444

Andora Inn

2434 Mission Street, San Francisco, CA 94110
EMAIL *andorasf@aol.com*

415-282-0337
415-282-2608

THE ANDREWS HOTEL

624 Post Street, San Francisco, CA 94109
Italian, French, and Spanish spoken
WEBSITE www.sftrips.com

415-563-6877
800-926-3739
FAX 415-928-6919

LOCATION	Two blocks west of Union Square at Post and Taylor Streets.
OPEN	All year
DESCRIPTION	A 1905 Queen Anne hotel.
NO. OF ROOMS	Forty-eight rooms with private bathrooms. Try a petite suite.
RATES	Year-round rates are $89-132 for a single or double. Petite suites are $125-142. There is a minimum stay when Saturday is involved and cancellation requires 48 hours' notice, seven days for groups that reserve five or more rooms.
CREDIT CARDS	American Express, Carte Blanche, Diners Club, MasterCard, Visa
BREAKFAST	Continental breakfast is served on buffet tables in the hallway and includes fresh fruit, muffins, rolls, croissants, and beverages.
AMENITIES	Telephones, TV, complimentary glass of wine, Italian restaurant and concierge on premises.
RESTRICTIONS	No smoking, no pets
REVIEWED	America's Wonderful Little Hotels & Inns, Frommer's California
RATED	Mobil 2 Stars

ARCHBISHOP'S MANSION

1000 Fulton Street, San Francisco, CA 94117
Rick Janzier, Manager
Spanish spoken
EMAIL abm@jdvhospitality

415-563-7872
800-543-5820
FAX 415-885-3193
WEBSITE www.sftrips.com

LOCATION	From Highway 101, take the Fell/Laguna exit. Go four blocks on Fell Street to Steiner Street and turn right. Go three blocks to Fulton Street and turn left. The mansion is across the street from Alamo Square Park.
OPEN	All year
DESCRIPTION	A 1904 three-story Second French Empire mansion—built for the archbishop—with lots of exposed redwood and antiques.
NO. OF ROOMS	Fifteen rooms with private bathrooms. Try the Don Giovanni Room.

RATES	Year-round rates are $139-219 for a single or double and $229-399 for a suite. There is a two-night minimum stay on weekends and cancellation requires seven days' notice.
CREDIT CARDS	American Express, MasterCard, Visa
BREAKFAST	Continental plus is served in the guestrooms and includes fresh orange juice, muffins and coffeecake, fresh fruit, and granola and yogurt on request.
AMENITIES	Phones and cable TV in all rooms, wine and cheese every afternoon, player piano, VCRs and romantic movies available.
RESTRICTIONS	No smoking in guestrooms, no pets
REVIEWED	*Country Inns of America—California, Birnbaum's Country Inns and Backroads*
MEMBER	Alamo Square Inn Association
RATED	AAA 3 Diamonds, Mobil 3 Stars

ART CENTER BED & BREAKFAST

1902 Filbert Street, San Francisco, CA 94123　　　　　415-567-1526

THE BED & BREAKFAST INN

4 Charlton Court, San Francisco, CA 94123　　　　　415-921-9784

KUDOS/COMMENTS　"Wonderful location, delightful staff."

BLACK STALLION INN

635 Castro Street, San Francisco, CA 94114　　　　　415-863-0131

Bock's Bed & Breakfast

1448 Willard Street, San Francisco, CA 94117
Laurie Bock, Resident Owner
Smattering of French spoken

415-664-6842
FAX 415-664-1109

LOCATION	Located two blocks from the southeast corner of Golden Gate Park in the Parnassus Heights neighborhood. The nearest major intersection is Parnassus and Stanyan Streets.
OPEN	All year
DESCRIPTION	A 1906 three-story Edwardian host home restored to include original redwood and mahogany paneling and floors. Furnishings are "comfortable and casual, with some of antiques."
NO. OF ROOMS	One room with a private bathroom and two rooms with one shared bathroom.
RATES	Year-round rates are $70-80 for a single or double with a private bathroom and $45-65 for a single or double with a shared bathroom. There is a two-night minimum stay and cancellation requires seven days' notice.
CREDIT CARDS	No
BREAKFAST	Continental plus is served in the dining room and includes fresh fruit, granola, a variety of breads, pastries, and beverages.
AMENITIES	Decks, view, access to guest refrigerator and microwave; all rooms have private phones, color TVs, and coffee and tea service.

Bock's Bed & Breakfast, San Francisco

RESTRICTIONS	No smoking, no pets, no nude sunbathing on the deck.
REVIEWED	*Frommer's Guide to San Francisco, Fodor's Guide, Inn Places, Rough Guide to San Francisco*
MEMBER	Professional Association of Innkeepers International

CAROL'S COW HOLLOW INN

2821 Steiner Street, San Francisco, CA 94123 415-775-8295
Carol Blumenfeld, Innkeeper 800-400-8295
French, Spanish, Russian, and German spoken FAX 415-775-8296
EMAIL subtle@ix.netcom.com WEBSITE www.subtleties.com

LOCATION	Six minutes west of Union Square and the center of San Francisco. Three-quarters of a mile from San Francisco Bay, Fisherman's Wharf, and the Palace of Fine Arts.
OPEN	All year
DESCRIPTION	A 1907 three-story Edwardian inn built on a hilltop and decorated with homey, comfortable furnishings.
NO. OF ROOMS	Three rooms with private bathrooms. Carol's favorite is the Emperor Norton Suite.
RATES	March through December, rates are $135-185 for a single or double and $175-265 for the suites. Low season rates (January and

Carol's Cow Hollow Inn, San Francisco

	February) are $100-150 for a single or double and $135-165 for the suites. There is no minimum stay and cancellation requires one weeks' notice.
CREDIT CARDS	MasterCard, Visa
BREAKFAST	Full breakfast includes fresh fruit, fresh orange juice, eggs Benedict, blueberry pancakes with turkey-artichoke sausages, frittatas, omelettes, quiche. Catering is available for special events.
AMENITIES	Flowers, robes, California wines at sunset, special treats on arrival.
RESTRICTIONS	Smoking permitted on balconies and decks only.
REVIEWED	*The Complete Guide to Bed & Breakfasts, Inns, and Guesthouses; The Official Bed & Breakfast Guide USA, Canada, and the Caribbean*

CASA ARGUELLO BED & BREAKFAST

225 Arguello Boulevard, San Francisco, CA 94118   415-752-9482
    FAX 415-681-1400

CASITA BLANCA

330 Edgehill Way, San Francisco, CA 94127   415-564-9339
Joan Bard, Resident Owner   FAX 415-566-4737
Spanish spoken
EMAIL *joan-bard@compuserve.com*

LOCATION	Twenty minutes from San Francisco International Airport, not far from Golden Gate Park. Call for directions.
OPEN	All year
DESCRIPTION	A 1927 Spanish cottage decorated with antiques and eclectic furnishings and nestled into the trees high on a hill near Golden Gate Park.
NO. OF ROOMS	One-room cottage with a private bathroom.
RATES	A single or double is $80 with a two-night minimum stay. Cancellation requires two weeks' notice.
CREDIT CARDS	No
BREAKFAST	Continental breakfast is available in the cottage and includes juice, toast or sweet roll, coffee or tea.

AMENITIES	Private telephone, TV, fireplace, full kitchen.
RESTRICTIONS	No pets. The cottage is for two people only. There are two resident great Pyrenées—Bentley and Nana—and a cat named Oliver.

CHATEAU TIVOLI

1057 Steiner & Golden Gate Avenue 415-776-5462
San Francisco, CA 94115 800-228-1647

CHEZ DUCHENE

1075 Broadway, San Francisco, CA 94133 415-441-3160
Jay Duchene, Innkeeper

LOCATION	Top of Russian Hill.
OPEN	All year
DESCRIPTION	A 1908 three-story Victorian host home with eclectic furnishings.
NO. OF ROOMS	One room with a private bathroom.
RATES	Year-round rates are $100 for a single or double. There is a two-night minimum stay and cancellation requires 48 hours' notice.
CREDIT CARDS	No
BREAKFAST	Continental plus is served in the dining room and includes fresh orange juice, fruit, muffin, pastry, yogurt, cereal, and coffee.
AMENITIES	Flowers, candy, views of Nob Hill and the Bay Bridge.
RESTRICTIONS	No smoking, no pets
REVIEWED	*Bed & Breakfast USA*

CHURCH STREET BED & BREAKFAST

325 Church Street, San Francisco, CA 94114 415-565-6755

CORNELL HOTEL

715 Bush Street, San Francisco, CA 94108   415-421-3154
WEBSITE www.cornellhotel.com

DOCKSIDE BOAT & BED

Pier 39, San Francisco, CA 94133   415-392-5526
WEBSITE www.boatandbed.com

DOLORES PARK INN

3641 17th Street, San Francisco, CA 94114   415-621-0482
Bernie Vielwerth, Resident Owner
Spanish and German spoken

LOCATION	From San Francisco International Airport, take Highway 101 north. Exit at Army Street West and go straight to Dolores Street. Turn right and then left on 17th Street.
OPEN	All year
DESCRIPTION	An 1874 two-story Italianate Victorian with Victorian furnishings. The inn is on the San Francisco Historic Register.
NO. OF ROOMS	One room with a private bathroom and four rooms share three bathrooms. Pick the suite.
RATES	Call for current rates. Ask about cancellation information.
CREDIT CARDS	MasterCard, Visa
BREAKFAST	Full breakfast, served in the dining room, includes eggs, toast, muffins, croissants, cheeses, fresh fruit, cereal, juices, tea, and coffee.
AMENITIES	TV and clock radio in every room; complimentary afternoon coffee, tea, wine, or sherry; free city and Bay Area maps.
RESTRICTIONS	No smoking, no pets
REVIEWED	*The Best of San Francisco*, *San Francisco on a Shoestring*, *The Rough Guide*

Edward II Bed & Breakfast

3155 Scott Street at Lombard, San Francisco, CA 94123   415-922-3000
WEBSITE www.citysearch.com/sfo/edwardiiinn   800-473-2846
FAX 415-931-5784

LOCATION	Ten blocks west of Van Ness Avenue on the corner of Lombard and Scott.
OPEN	All year
DESCRIPTION	A 1915 three-story Edwardian with country furnishings.
NO. OF ROOMS	Seven suites (14 rooms) with private bathrooms and 11 rooms share four bathrooms.
RATES	Year-round rates are $99 for a single or double with a private bathroom, $75-79 for a single or double with a shared bathroom, and $165-225 for the suites. There is a two-night minimum stay on weekends (except for rooms with shared bathrooms) and cancellation requires 72 hours' notice.
CREDIT CARDS	American Express, MasterCard, Visa
BREAKFAST	Continental breakfast is served in the dining room and includes pastries, bagels, English muffins, and beverages.
AMENITIES	Telephone, robes, cable TV in rooms, coffee and tea in the afternoon, sherry in the evening.
RESTRICTIONS	No smoking, no pets, children of any age are welcome.

Golden Gate Hotel

775 Bush Street, San Francisco, CA 94108   415-392-3702
John & Renate Kenaston, Innkeepers   800-835-1118
WEBSITE www.goldengatehotel.com   FAX 415-392-6202

LOCATION	Between Mason and Powell (the main cable-car line), two blocks north of Union Square and two blocks down from the very top of Nob Hill. Bush Street is one way heading east.
OPEN	All year
DESCRIPTION	A 1913 four-story Edwardian urban inn decorated with antiques and old world charm.
NO. OF ROOMS	Fourteen rooms with private bathrooms and 11 rooms share four bathrooms.

RATES	Year-round rates are $109-115 for a single or double with a private bathroom and $72-78 for a single or double with a shared bathroom. There is a two-night minimum stay during busy summer weekends and cancellation requires 48 hours' notice.
CREDIT CARDS	American Express, Diners Club, MasterCard, Visa
BREAKFAST	Breakfast is served in the parlor and includes coffee, real English tea, orange juice, and a variety of croissants or healthy bread.
AMENITIES	Fresh flowers throughout, parlor with fireplace, afternoon tea and cookies, birdcage elevator, cable-car stop on the corner, quilted bedspreads, some rooms with clawfoot tubs.
RESTRICTIONS	No smoking, no pets. Captain Nemo is the resident cat and Humphrey is the golden retriever. "Captain Nemo knows who's missing their own cat and will invariably seek out their company."
REVIEWED	*Frommer's, Let's Go USA, Let's Go California, Fodor's Best of San Francisco, Fodor's Official Guide to American Historic Inns, The Complete Guide to Bed & Breakfast Inns and Guesthouses, Lonely Planet, San Francisco on a Shoestring, Best Places to Stay in California*
MEMBER	California Association of Bed & Breakfast Inns
AWARDS	1996, Frommer's Super Special Value Award

THE HERB'N INN

PO Box 170106, San Francisco, CA 94117   415-553-8542

HILL POINT BED & BREAKFAST

15 Hill Point Avenue, San Francisco, CA 94117   415-753-0393
Bob McCormick, Resident Owner   FAX 415-753-0738
German, French, Italian, and Spanish spoken
WEBSITE *www.citysearch.com/sfo/hillpointinn*

LOCATION	From Highway 1 (19th Avenue), take Judah Street heading east. Hill Point Avenue is the last street on the left before descending down the hill to Stanyan Street.
OPEN	All year
DESCRIPTION	Five 1912 San Francisco Victorians decorated with a combination of modern and antique furnishings and located on a cul-de-sac overlooking Golden Gate Park.

NO. OF ROOMS	Nine rooms with private bathrooms and 16 rooms share four bathrooms.
RATES	Year-round rates are $79-89 for a single or double with a private bathroom and $60-70 for a single or double room with a shared bathroom. Suites are $95-195. Cancellation requires 24 hours' notice.
CREDIT CARDS	American Express, Diners Club, Discover, MasterCard, Visa
BREAKFAST	Continental breakfast, served in the dining room, includes blueberry muffins, apple turnovers, Danish, English muffins, croissants, seasonal fruit, and beverages.
AMENITIES	TV; phones; barbecue; garden; some rooms have views of Golden Gate Park, the ocean, and city.
RESTRICTIONS	No smoking, no pets. Frederick the Great, Elisabeth (the Empress), and Kaiser Franz Jozeph are the resident family of Shih Tzus.
MEMBER	California Lodging Industry Association

HOTEL DAVID

480 Geary Street, San Francisco, CA 94102
WEBSITE www.hoteldavid.com
415-771-1600
800-524-1888

INN 1890

1890 Page Street, San Francisco, CA 94117
WEBSITE www.adamsnet.com/inn1890
415-386-0486

INN ON CASTRO

321 Castro Street, San Francisco, CA 94114
Jan de Gier, Resident Owner
415-861-0321
FAX 415-861-0321 (call first)

LOCATION	In the heart of the Castro district, San Francisco's gay neighborhood, at Market and Castro Streets.
OPEN	All year

DESCRIPTION	An 1889 three-story Edwardian inn with detailing intact, decorated in a modern style with exotic plants and flowers, and large modern oil paintings and sculptures.
NO. OF ROOMS	Seven rooms with private bathrooms and one room with one shared bathroom. Try the Patio Suite.
RATES	Year-round rates are $120-145 for a single or double with a private bathroom, $90-100 for a single or double with a shared bathroom, and $145-175 for a suite. There is a minimum stay and cancellation requires 14 days' notice.
CREDIT CARDS	American Express, MasterCard, Visa
BREAKFAST	Full breakfast is served in the dining room and includes fresh-baked goods, fruits, cereals, eggs, and waffles.
AMENITIES	Robes, brandy for nightcap, private telephone, answering machine, data port, TV, and radio.
RESTRICTIONS	No smoking, no pets, children over 10 are welcome.
REVIEWED	*Out & About; Rough Guide San Francisco; San Francisco Access Guide; Fodor's San Francisco and Fodor's Gay; Frommer's San Francisco; Inn Places*
AWARDS	1994–1998, Best Inn for the Gay Traveler in San Francisco, *Out & About*

INN SAN FRANCISCO

943 South Van Ness Avenue, San Francisco, CA 94110   415-641-0188
WEBSITE *www.innsf.com*   800-359-0913

JACKSON COURT

2198 Jackson Street, San Francisco, CA 94115   415-929-7670
Evelyn Jingco, Resident Manager   FAX 415-929-1405
Spanish spoken
WEBSITE *www.sftrips.com*

LOCATION	Fifteen minutes west of downtown San Francisco. Five blocks from Van Ness, two blocks east of Fillmore, five blocks up the hill south of Union Street. From the south, take Highway 101 north to Golden Gate Bridge. From the north, take Highway 101 south to Lombard Street, turn right, and go eight blocks to Jackson and Buchanan.

OPEN	All year
DESCRIPTION	A 1900 three-story brownstone mansion with antique and contemporary furnishings.
NO. OF ROOMS	Ten rooms with private bathrooms. The Library Room is the best in the house.
RATES	Year-round rates are $150-205 for a single or double. There is a two-night minimum stay on weekends and cancellation requires seven days' notice.
CREDIT CARDS	American Express, MasterCard, Visa
BREAKFAST	Continental plus is served in the dining room and includes fresh fruit, salad, cereals, breads, muffins, bagels, croissant or Danish, and beverages.
AMENITIES	Flowers, telephones, cable TV in rooms, afternoon refreshments next to the fireplace.
RESTRICTIONS	No smoking, children over 12 are welcome.
REVIEWED	America's Wonderful Little Hotels & Inns, Northern California Best Places
MEMBER	San Francisco Bed & Breakfast Association
RATED	ABBA 3 Crowns
KUDOS/COMMENTS	"Elegant; great location—around the corner from fabulous restaurants." (1999)

THE MANSIONS HOTEL

2220 Sacramento Street, San Francisco, CA 94115   415-929-9444
WEBSITE www.themansions.com

KUDOS/COMMENTS   "Delightful, mysterious, haunted, and thoroughly entertaining."

MARINA INN

3110 Octavia Street, San Francisco, CA 94123   415-928-1000
                                                    800-274-1420
                                                 FAX 415-928-5909

Monte Cristo Bed & Breakfast

600 Presidio Avenue, San Francisco, CA 94115　　　415-931-1875
George Yuan, Resident Owner　　　FAX 415-931-6005
Spanish and Chinese spoken

LOCATION	From the San Francisco International Airport, take Highway 101 north, exit at 7th Street, drive past Market Street to Franklin Street, and turn left onto Pine Street. Monte Cristo is between Pine and Push Streets on Presidio Avenue.
OPEN	All year
DESCRIPTION	An 1875 two-story Victorian home with English and American furnishings, originally built as a bordello.
NO. OF ROOMS	Eleven rooms with private bathrooms and three rooms share five bathrooms.
RATES	Year-round rates are $78-98 for a double with a private bathroom, $73 for a double with a shared bathroom, and $118 for a suite. There is a seven-day cancellation policy.
CREDIT CARDS	American Express, Diners Club, Discover, MasterCard, Visa
BREAKFAST	Continental plus, served buffet style in the dining room, includes fresh orange juice, cereal, breads, blueberry muffins, and a variety of fresh fruit and beverages.
AMENITIES	Robes, tea or wine on arrival, phone, TV/VCR.
RESTRICTIONS	No smoking, no pets, children are welcome.
MEMBER	California Lodging Industry Association

No Name Victorian Bed & Breakfast

847 Fillmore Street, San Francisco CA 94117　　　415-479-1913
Richard & Susan Kreibich, Innkeepers　　　800-452-8249
German and Czechoslovakian spoken　　　FAX 415-479-1917
EMAIL bbsf@linex.com　　　WEBSITE www.bbsf.com

LOCATION	Two miles west of downtown, five blocks west of Davies Symphony Halland Opera House, one block from Alamo Square Park.
OPEN	All year
DESCRIPTION	An 1890 three-story Victorian with traditional and antique furnishings.
NO. OF ROOMS	Four rooms with private bathrooms and two rooms share one bathroom.

RATES	Year-round rates are $79-125 for a single or double with a private bathroom, $69-79 for a single or double with a shared bathroom, and $105-125 for a suite. There is a two-night minimum stay at most times and cancellation requires 14 days' notice.
CREDIT CARDS	American Express, MasterCard, Visa
BREAKFAST	Full breakfast is served in the dining room and includes items such as sausages, eggs, fruit, and cereal. Special dietary needs are accommodated.
AMENITIES	Complimentary wine, fireplaces in most rooms, deck and hot tub, sightseeing trips arranged.
RESTRICTIONS	No smoking, no pets
REVIEWED	*Bed & Breakfast USA; Bed & Breakfasts and Country Inns; San Francisco on a Shoestring; Definitive California Bed & Breakfast Touring Guide; The Complete Guide to Bed & Breakfasts, Inns, and Guesthouses; Fodor's*

THE NOB HILL LAMBOURNE

725 Pine Street, San Francisco, CA 94108   415-433-2287
WEBSITE *www.sftrips.com*

NOE'S NEST

3973 23rd Street, San Francisco, CA 94114   415-821-0751
Sheila R. Ash, Innkeeper   888-663-6378
French, a little Hebrew, and Japanese spoken   FAX 415-821-0723
EMAIL *noes@aol.com*   WEBSITE *www.citysearch7.com*

LOCATION	Located in the heart of Noe Valley. From the San Francisco International Airport, take Highway 101 north, exit on Army Street west, drive to Sanchez, and turn right. Go six blocks and turn left onto 23rd; Noe's Nest is between Sanchez and Noe.
OPEN	All year
DESCRIPTION	An 1895 three-story host home remodeled to include seven comfortable, individually styled rooms and suites.
NO. OF ROOMS	Six rooms with private bathrooms and one room with a shared bathroom. Try the Penthouse.

RATES	Year-round rates are $99-160 for a single or double with a private bathroom and $95 for the room with the shared bathroom. The minimum stay is two nights on weekends and three nights on holiday weekends. Cancellation requires at least eight days' notice.
CREDIT CARDS	American Express, Discover, MasterCard, Visa
BREAKFAST	Full breakfast buffet is served.
AMENITIES	Outdoor hot tub; some rooms have decks, fireplaces, brass beds, or refrigerators; video library; complimentary wine for anniversaries, birthdays, or weddings; all rooms have TV/VCR, phone, and fresh flowers.
RESTRICTIONS	No smoking. Potty-trained pets are welcome.
REVIEWED	*Damron Accomodations, Access San Francisco, Hidden San Francisco and Northern California, Romantic Weekends in San Francisco and the Bay Area*
MEMBER	Gay and Lesbian Travel Guide Association

OBRERO HOTEL

1208 Stockton Street, San Francisco, CA 94133   415-989-3960

PARKER HOUSE

520 Church Street, San Francisco, CA 94114   415-621-3222
Bill Boeddiker & Bob O'Hallovan, Innkeepers   888-520-7275
EMAIL parkerhse@aol.com   FAX 415-621-4139
WEBSITE www.members.aol.com/parkerhse/st.html

LOCATION	In the Castro district on Church Street, between 17th and 18th Streets.
OPEN	All year
DESCRIPTION	A 1909 three-story Edwardian minimansion with casual, elegant decor, extensive public rooms, and garden areas.
NO. OF ROOMS	Five rooms with private bathrooms and two rooms share two bathrooms. Try room 24.
RATES	Year-round rates are $119-169 for a single or double with a private bathroom and $99 for a single or double with a shared bathroom. There is a minimum stay during weekends and cancellation requires 14 days' notice.
CREDIT CARDS	American Express, MasterCard, Visa

Parker House, San Francisco

BREAKFAST	Continental plus is served in the dining room.
AMENITIES	Robes, voice mail, data ports, cable TV, library with piano and fireplace, extensive gardens.
RESTRICTIONS	Smoking in outdoor areas only. Parker is the resident pug dog.
REVIEWED	*Fodor's Gay Guide; Access Gay US; Damron Accommodations; Inn Places*
MEMBER	International Gay & Lesbian Travel Association, Professional Association of Innkeepers International
RATED	*Out & About* 5 Palms
AWARDS	1998 Editors Choice Award, *Out & About*

PENSIONE INTERNATIONAL

875 Post Street, San Francisco, CA 94109   415-775-3344

Petite Auberge

863 Bush Street, San Francisco, CA 94108
Celeste Lytle, Manager
French and Spanish spoken
WEBSITE www.foursisters.com

415-928-6000
800-365-3004
FAX 415-775-5717

LOCATION	From Highway 101, take Bush Street east. The inn is between Mason and Taylor, three blocks from Union Square, and one block from the cable cars.
OPEN	All year
DESCRIPTION	An early 1900's Baroque country inn with country French decor and curved bay windows.
NO. OF ROOMS	Twenty-six rooms with private bathrooms.
RATES	Year-round rates are $120-165 for a double and suites are $245. Cancellation requires 24 hours' notice.
CREDIT CARDS	American Express, MasterCard, Visa
BREAKFAST	Full breakfast, served in the dining room, includes homemade breads, fresh seasonal fruit, cereals, muffins, hot dish, juices, tea, and coffee. Room service is optional (with an extra charge).
AMENITIES	Terry robes; unlimited coffee, tea, and soft drinks; afternoon wine and hors d'oeuvres; turndown service; newspaper at door; large basket of amenities; parlor with a fireplace; dining room with view of a small courtyard garden.
RESTRICTIONS	No smoking, no pets
REVIEWED	Karen Brown's California Country Inns & Itineraries, Frommer's B&B North America, Best Places to Stay in California
RATED	AAA 3 Diamonds, Mobil 3 Stars

Queen Anne Hotel

1590 Sutter Street, San Francisco, CA 94109
Steven Bobb, Manager
Spanish, Chinese, German, and Greek spoken

415-441-2828
800-227-3970
FAX 415-775-5212

LOCATION	Heading into downtown San Francisco on Van Ness Avenue (Highway 101), turn right on Sutter and go three blocks to Octavia. The hotel is between Octavia and Laguna Streets.
OPEN	All year

DESCRIPTION	An 1890 four-story Victorian hotel with antique period furnishings.
NO. OF ROOMS	Forty-nine rooms with private bathrooms.
RATES	Please call for current rates and cancellation information.
CREDIT CARDS	American Express, Diners Club, Discover, JCB, MasterCard, Visa
BREAKFAST	Continental breakfast is served in the dining room.
AMENITIES	Moderate and deluxe rooms have fireplaces, afternoon tea and sherry, complimentary limo to downtown, TV, telephone, meeting facilities for 150, rooms with handicapped access.
RESTRICTIONS	Non-smoking rooms available.
RATED	AAA 3 Diamonds, Mobil 3 Stars

RED VICTORIAN BED, BREAKFAST, AND PEACE CENTER

1665 Haight Street, San Francisco, CA 94117   415-864-1978
Sami Sunchild, Innkeeper   FAX 415-863-3293
EMAIL redvic@linex.com   WEBSITE www.redvic.com

LOCATION	Driving from south or east: follow signs to Golden Gate Park and take the Fell Street exit. Left at Masonic, right on Haight. Shuttle vans deliver guests from the airport.
OPEN	All year
DESCRIPTION	A 1904 three-story Victorian inn with San Francisco theme-rooms like Golden Gate Park and Summer of Love.
NO. OF ROOMS	Six rooms with private bathrooms and 13 rooms share five bathrooms. Sami says the Peacock Suite is the finest in the house.
RATES	Year-round rates are $105-185 for a single or double with a private bathroom, $71-115 for a single or double with a shared bathroom, and $200 for the suite. Discounts are available for stays over two days. There is a two-night minimum stay on weekends and cancellation requires 48 hours' notice for a full refund, one week during holidays.
CREDIT CARDS	American Express, MasterCard, Visa
BREAKFAST	Continental plus is served in the art gallery/lounge and includes wholesome, tasty food, "multicultural friendships and creative conversation."
AMENITIES	Meeting space for up to 30 people, meditation room, video library for life enhancement, TV- and smoke-free. "We specialize in taking care of people who are taking care of the world ... loving, creative people."

RESTRICTIONS	No smoking, no pets. "Children with well-behaved parents are welcome." The inn's minipoodle, Angel, receives guests at the front desk at breakfast time. Other resident animals include a cat, Mr. Mouser, and several goldfish.
REVIEWED	Lonely Planet, Let's Go California, Frommer's America on Wheels—California and Nevada, Northern California Handbook, Eyewitness Travel Guides—San Francisco and Northern California
AWARDS	1998, National Association of Women Business Owners Award "in recognition of a woman business owner whose life has been dedicated to communicating the hope of one world living and working together."

SHANNON-KAVANAUGH HOUSE

722 Steiner Street, San Francisco, CA 94117   415-563-2727
WEBSITE www.s-j.com

SHEEHAN HOTEL

620 Sutter Street, San Francisco, CA 94102   415-775-6500
Don Hayden, General Manager   800-848-1529
French and Spanish spoken   FAX 415-775-3271
WEBSITE www.citysearch.com/sfo/sheehanhotel

LOCATION	At the intersection of Sutter and Mason Streets, one block from Powell Street (cable-car route), and two blocks from Union Square in downtown San Francisco's shopping and theatre district.
OPEN	All year
DESCRIPTION	A 1917 multistory Georgian hotel decorated with European antiques.
NO. OF ROOMS	Sixty-five rooms with private bathrooms.
RATES	May 15 through October, rates are $99-129 for a single or double. November through May 15, rates are $89-119. Cancellation requires 24 hours' notice.
CREDIT CARDS	American Express, Diners Club, Discover, JCB, MasterCard, Visa
BREAKFAST	Continental breakfast is served in the dining room and includes homemade muffins, scones, breads, and beverages.
AMENITIES	City's largest indoor pool, exercise room, cable TV, direct dial phones, 300-seat theater, meeting room, beer and wine, afternoon tea, handicapped accessible.

RESTRICTIONS	No pets. Children under 12 are free.
REVIEWED	Let's Go USA, San Francisco on a Shoestring, Best Places to Stay in California
MEMBER	California Lodging Industry Association
RATED	Mobil 1 Star

SPENCER HOUSE

1080 Haight Street, San Francisco, CA 94117   415-626-9205
Jack & Barbara Chambers, Resident Owners   FAX 415-626-9230
WEBSITE www.spencerhouse.com

LOCATION	Eight blocks east of Golden Gate Park in the Haight-Ashbury neighborhood of San Francisco.
OPEN	All year
DESCRIPTION	An 1887 three-story Queen Anne Victorian mansion furnished with antiques, hand-painted wallpapers, and oriental rugs.
NO. OF ROOMS	Six rooms with private bathrooms. The French Room is the best in the house.
RATES	Year-round rates for a single or double are $125-185. There is a two-night minimum stay on weekends, three nights on holidays. Cancellation requires seven days' notice, two weeks' notice during holidays, with a $10 fee.
CREDIT CARDS	American Express, MasterCard, Visa
BREAKFAST	Full breakfast is served in the grand dining room and includes fresh orange juice and coffee, eggs ranchero or Belgian waffles with warm strawberries.
AMENITIES	Robes and telephones in rooms, down mattresses, pillows and duvets, antique linens, antique armoires and beds, decanter of port or sherry.
RESTRICTIONS	No smoking, no pets. The resident critters are an American spaniel, Perry, and Carmen the macaw.
REVIEWED	Karen Brown's California Country Inns & Itineraries; Country Inns and Back Roads: California; The Best Places to Kiss in Northern California; Bed & Breakfast California
MEMBER	Innkeepers of San Francisco
KUDOS/COMMENTS	"Outstanding!" "Without a doubt the finest B&B in San Francisco! Quality restoration of a fabulous Victorian with great hosts." (1999)

Stanyan Park Hotel Bed & Breakfast

750 Stanyan Street, San Francisco, CA 94117 415-751-1000
John Brockenhurst, Innkeeper FAX 415-668-5454
Spanish spoken
EMAIL *info@stanyanpark.com*
WEBSITE *www.stanyanpark.com*

LOCATION	Southwest corner of Golden Gate Park, three miles from downtown San Francisco, a few blocks from the University of San Francisco and the Haight-Ashbury district, across from Kezar Stadium.
OPEN	All year
DESCRIPTION	A restored 1905 three-story Queen Anne Victorian hotel with Victorian decor, listed on the National Historic Register.
NO. OF ROOMS	Thirty-six rooms with private bathrooms. Try the Cupola Queen.
RATES	Year-round rates are $115-300 for a single or double and $225-300 for a suite. There is no minimum stay and cancellation requires 24 hours' notice.
CREDIT CARDS	American Express, Diners Club, Discover, MasterCard, Visa
BREAKFAST	Continental plus is served in the dining room and includes croissants, bagels with cream cheese, muffins, fresh juices, fruit, and fresh-brewed coffee.

Stanyan Park Hotel Bed & Breakfast, San Francisco

AMENITIES	Afternoon tea and cookies in the dining room, all rooms with cable TV and phones with data ports, two rooms are handicapped accessible.
RESTRICTIONS	No pets, no smoking
REVIEWED	Elegant Small Hotels, The Official Guide to American Historic Inns, The Definitive California Bed & Breakfast Touring Guide
MEMBER	California Association of Bed & Breakfast Inns
RATED	AAA 3 Diamonds

SUNSET EDWARDIAN

1471 18th Avenue, San Francisco, CA 94122 　　　　　415-564-8823

TWENTY-FOUR HENRY

24 Henry Street, San Francisco, CA 94114 　　　　　415-864-5686

THE UNION STREET INN

2229 Union Street, San Francisco, CA 94123 　　　　415-346-0424
Jane Bertorelli & David Coyle, Resident Owners 　　FAX 415-922-8046
Spanish and limited French spoken
WEBSITE www.unionstreetinn.com

LOCATION	Located on Union Street between Steiner and Fillmore Streets in the heart of San Francisco.
OPEN	All year
DESCRIPTION	A 1904 two-story Edwardian/Victorian inn and carriage house furnished with period antiques.
NO. OF ROOMS	Six rooms with private bathrooms. The Carriage House is highly recommended.
RATES	Year-round rates for a single or double are $135-245. There is a two-night minimum stay on weekends and a very firm seven-day cancellation policy.
CREDIT CARDS	American Express, MasterCard, Visa
BREAKFAST	Full breakfast is served in the dining room or garden, or on the deck, and includes an egg entrée, homemade muffins and breads, fruit, and beverages.

AMENITIES	Flowers, fruit, chocolates, robes, TV/VCR, down comforters, telephones, welcome baskets.
RESTRICTIONS	No smoking, no pets
MEMBER	California Association of Bed & Breakfast Inns, California Lodging and Industry Association

VICTORIAN INN ON THE PARK

301 Lyon Street, San Francisco, CA 94117 415-931-1830
Lisa & William Benau, Innkeepers 800-435-1967
Spanish, Italian, and Portuguese spoken FAX 415-931-1830
EMAIL vicinn@aol.com WEBSITE www.citysearch.com/sfo/victorianinn

LOCATION	From the San Francisco International Airport, take Highway 101 north to San Francisco. Exit west onto Fell Street, go one mile, and turn right on Lyon. The inn is adjacent to Golden Gate Park.
OPEN	All year
DESCRIPTION	An 1897 four-story Queen Anne Victorian with Victorian furnishings, an open Belvedere turret, silk-screened wallpaper, and intricate mahogany and redwood paneling. Listed on the State Historic Register.
NO. OF ROOMS	Twelve rooms with private bathrooms. Lisa likes the Belvedere Room.
RATES	Year-round rates for a single or a double are $124-174. The suites range from $174-345. There is a two-night minimum stay on weekends, three nights on holiday weekends. Cancellation requires seven days' notice.
CREDIT CARDS	American Express, Diners Club, Discover, MasterCard, Visa
BREAKFAST	Continental plus is served in the dining room or guestrooms and includes assorted fruits and cheeses, fresh-squeezed orange juice, home-baked breads, croissants, scones, coffee, tea, and hot chocolate.
AMENITIES	Complimentary wine and sherry; inn is staffed 24 hours; phones in room; data ports; staff will book tours, airport shuttles, and rental cars; some rooms have fireplaces, decks, views of park, sunken bathtubs, and Roman tubs.
RESTRICTIONS	No smoking, no pets
REVIEWED	*Elegant Small Hotel; American Historic Inns; Bed & Breakfast Guide—Twenty-Eight Great American Cities; Country Inns of America—California; The Best Places to Kiss in Northern California; San Francisco Access; America's Wonderful Little Hotels & Inns*

Victorian Inn on the Park, San Francisco

MEMBER   Professional Association of Innkeepers International, California
                    Association of Bed & Breakfast Innkeepers, San Francisco Bed &
                    Breakfast Innkeepers
RATED   Mobil 3 Stars

WASHINGTON SQUARE INN

1660 Stockton Street, San Francisco, CA 94133   415-981-4220
David Norwitt, Innkeeper   800-388-0220
EMAIL david@wsisf.com   FAX 415-397-7242
WEBSITE www.wsisf.com

LOCATION   In the heart of North Beach at Washington Square.
OPEN   All year
DESCRIPTION   A 1978 three-story country French inn furnished with French and
                    English antiques.
NO. OF ROOMS   Fifteen rooms with private bathrooms.
RATES   Year-round rates are $120-200 for a single or double. There is a
                    two-night minimum stay on weekends, and cancellation requires 48
                    hours' notice.
CREDIT CARDS   American Express, Diners Club, Discover, MasterCard, Visa

SAN FRANCISCO

BREAKFAST	Expanded continental breakfast, served in the dining room, includes three fresh juices, fresh fruit, a variety of cereals, baked goods, tea, and coffee.
AMENITIES	Robes, afternoon wine and hors d'oeuvres, valet parking.
RESTRICTIONS	No smoking, no pets
REVIEWED	Karen Brown's California Country Inns & Itineraries, Frommer's, San Francisco Access
MEMBER	California Association of Bed & Breakfast Inns
RATED	Mobil 3 Stars

WHITE SWAN INN

845 Bush Street, San Francisco, CA 94108   415-775-1755
WEBSITE www.foursisters.com

WILLOWS BED & BREAKFAST INN

710 14th Street, San Francisco, CA 94114   415-431-4770
WEBSITE www.willowsff.com

SAN GREGORIO

The state beach is a good reason to visit this tiny hamlet, south of Half Moon Bay and west of Palo Alto on Highways 1 and 84.

RANCHO SAN GREGORIO

5086 La Honda Road (Hwy 84), San Gregorio, CA 94074   650-747-0810
Bud & Lee Raynor, Resident Owners   888-822-4694
EMAIL rsgleebud@aol.com   FAX 650-747-0184
WEBSITE www.scruznet.com/~prankstr/rancho/home.html

LOCATION	From Half Moon Bay, take Highway 1 south 10 miles to Highway 84 and go east five miles.
OPEN	All year

Rancho San Gregorio, San Gregorio

DESCRIPTION	A 1971 two-story Spanish mission-style inn decorated with early California furnishings, Indian quilts, and pottery. This coastal country retreat sits on 15 wooded acres.
NO. OF ROOMS	Four rooms with private bathrooms.
RATES	Year-round rates for a single or double are $90-150. There is no minimum stay and cancellation requires seven days' notice.
CREDIT CARDS	American Express, Diners Club, Discover, MasterCard, Visa
BREAKFAST	Full breakfast is served in the country kitchen dining area and includes fresh-squeezed orange juice; fresh-ground coffee; a hot entrée (crepes, frittata, waffles, pancakes, etc.); homemade muffins, breads, coffeecake, and jams. Breakfast incorporates ranch-grown products.
AMENITIES	Robes; hair dryers; coffee, tea, soft drinks, candy, cookies; pick-your-own berries and fruit in season; barbecue area; barn for meetings and events; tour information and maps; VCR library; books and games.
RESTRICTIONS	Smoking limited to outside. The resident outdoor critters are Sancho the brown Lab, Duster the Australian shepherd/Border collie mix, Goblin the cat, and Ramchop the ram.
REVIEWED	*Bed, Breakfast and Bike—Northern California; Bed & Breakfast in California; America's Favorite Inns, B&Bs, & Small Hotels; Complete Guide to Bed & Breakfasts*
MEMBER	Professional Association of Innkeepers International, California Association of Bed & Breakfast Innkeepers, California Lodging Association

RATED	AAA 3 Diamonds, Mobil 2 Stars
AWARDS	1998, America's Favorite Inns Award
KUDOS/COMMENTS	"Charming country inn nestled in an apple orchard."

San Jose

First-class restaurants, a state-of-the-art light rail system, a flourishing arts scene, and a dazzling sports arena have all contributed to the city's revitalization, helping it emerge at last from the long cultural shadow cast by San Francisco, its cosmopolitan neighbor to the north. The newly renovated San Jose Museum of Art provides a handsome setting for contemporary European and American art. The Tech Museum of Innovation is a terrific hands-on science museum where adults and kids alike can play with robots, gain insight into gene engineering, or design a high-tech bicycle.

Briar Rose Bed & Breakfast Inn

897 East Jackson Street, San Jose, CA 95112   408-279-5999
Tom & Pat Worthy, Resident Owners
WEBSITE *www.briar-rose.com*

LOCATION	From Highway 280, take a left on 11th Street and a right on Jackson.
OPEN	All year
DESCRIPTION	An 1875 two-story Victorian farmhouse and two-story pump house with American Victorian antiques.
NO. OF ROOMS	Six rooms with private bathrooms.
RATES	Year-round rates are $110-140 for a single or double. There is no minimum stay and cancellation requires 48 hours' notice.
CREDIT CARDS	American Express, Diners Club, Discover, MasterCard, Visa
BREAKFAST	Full breakfast is served in the dining room and includes crepes, quiche, muffins, breads, juice, fruit, and "killer spuds."
AMENITIES	Fresh flowers, robes, large wraparound porch, TV, goodies at night, gardens, meeting facilities.
RESTRICTIONS	No smoking, no pets, children over five are welcome. The dogs are Gertie and Barney and the cats are Ms. Peepers and Wally.
REVIEWED	*The Painted Ladies Guide to Victorian California*

THE HENSLEY HOUSE

456 North Third Street, San Jose, CA 95112 408-298-3537
Ron Evans & Tony Contreras, Resident Owners 800-498-3537
Spanish spoken FAX 408-298-4676
WEBSITE www.hensleyhouse.com

LOCATION	Take Highway 101 from San Francisco to Guadalupe Expressway. Exit at Julian Street, turn left under the freeway, turn left onto Third Street, and go one block to Hensley.
OPEN	All year
DESCRIPTION	A 1884 three-story Queen Anne Victorian with stained-glass windows, crystal and brass chandeliers, 12-foot ceilings, and a "witch's cap" tower. Listed on the National and State Historic Registers.
NO. OF ROOMS	Nine rooms with private bathrooms.
RATES	Year-round rates for a single or double are $125-255. There is no minimum stay and cancellation requires 48 hours' notice.
CREDIT CARDS	American Express, Carte Blanche, Diners Club, Discover, MasterCard, Visa
BREAKFAST	Full gourmet breakfast is served in the dining room and includes fresh juice and fruits, a hot entrée, muffins, croissants, coffee, espresso, and cappuccino.
AMENITIES	TV/VCR, phone, data port, air conditioning, flowers, robes, fireplace and grand piano in the living room, tape library, hors d'oeuvres, afternoon tea by appointment, three rooms have whirlpools and two rooms have fireplaces, complete office services and meeting facilities.
RESTRICTIONS	No smoking, no pets, children over 12 are welcome.
REVIEWED	*Country Inns and Backroads: California, America's Wonderful Little Hotels & Inns*
MEMBER	Professional Association of Innkeepers International, California Association of Bed & Breakfast Inns
RATED	AAA 3 Diamonds, ABBA 3 Crowns

SAN MARTIN

Located on the business stretch of Highway 101 between Gilroy and San Jose, San Martin is a good starting point for excursions to the Monterey Bay area. May brings the Morgan Hill Mushroom Mardi Gras. The Garlic Festival gets underway in July in nearby Gilroy.

COUNTRY ROSE INN BED & BREAKFAST

455 E Fitzgerald Avenue, San Martin, CA 95046   408-842-0441
Rose Hernandez, Resident Owner   FAX 408-842-6646
Spanish spoken
WEBSITE *www.bbonline.com/ca/countryrose/*

LOCATION	From Highway 101, take the northernmost Gilroy exit, Masten Avenue, and go west. Cross Monterey Road and continue for 0.4 mile to the first set of mail boxes. Go right onto a private lane and travel 0.3 mile to the inn.
OPEN	All year
DESCRIPTION	A 1920s two-story Dutch colonial inn with a rose motif interior.
NO. OF ROOMS	Five rooms with private bathrooms.
RATES	Year-round rates are $129 for a single or double and $189 for a suite. There is a minimum stay during festivals and special events and cancellation requires seven days' notice with a $10 fee.
CREDIT CARDS	Diners Club, Discover, MasterCard, Visa
BREAKFAST	Full breakfast is served in the dining room and includes coffee, juice, fruit, and a hot entrée with a California platter. For $10 breakfast will be delivered to guestrooms.
AMENITIES	Fresh flowers, dinner and theater reservations, afternoon tea, steam shower, jetted tub in the suite, wood-burning stove, fireplaces in parlor and garden room, large common areas and porches, parlor with grand piano, 20 minutes from San Juan Bautista, convenient to Silicon Valley.
RESTRICTIONS	No smoking, no pets, children over nine are welcome.
REVIEWED	*Country Inns and Back Roads: California; Bed & Breakfast California; Best Places to Stay in California; Away for the Weekend; Quick Escapes from San Francisco*
MEMBER	California Association of Bed & Breakfast Inns

SAN MATEO

This residential city south of San Francisco offers up some goodies. Make time for a day at Coyote Point Museum and Biopark and at Central Park's Japanese Garden. From here, there's direct access to Half Moon Bay via Highway 92.

COXHEAD HOUSE BED & BREAKFAST

37 East Santa Inez Avenue, San Mateo, CA 94401   650-685-1600
Patricia E. Osborn & Steven G. Cabrera, Innkeepers   FAX 650-685-1684
Spanish spoken
EMAIL coxhead@coxhead.com
WEBSITE www.coxhead.com

LOCATION	Three-and-a-half miles south of the San Francisco International Airport, take exit 3 south (Poplar Avenue). Turn left on Poplar Avenue and left again on Elm Street. Go right on East Santa Inez Avenue. The B&B is 0.6 mile north of San Mateo proper.
OPEN	All year
DESCRIPTION	A restored 1891 two-story Tudor revival country inn with period furnishings and a garden courtyard.
NO. OF ROOMS	Four rooms with private bathrooms. Patricia and Steven recommend the Bernard Maybeck Room.
RATES	Year-round rates are $125-169 for a single or double. Cancellation requires seven days' notice.
CREDIT CARDS	American Express, MasterCard, Visa
BREAKFAST	Full breakfast is served in the dining room and includes assorted fruit juices, muffins, quiches, pancakes, sausages, and cereals.
RESTRICTIONS	No smoking, no pets. Mocha is the resident cat.

Coxhead House Bed & Breakfast, San Mateo

MEMBER	California Association of Bed & Breakfast Inns, Professional Association of Innkeepers International
RATED	AAA 3 Diamonds

THE PALM HOUSE

1216 Palm Avenue, San Mateo, CA 94402   650-573-7256
Alan & Marian Brooks, Innkeepers

LOCATION	Ten miles south of the San Francisco International Airport near Highway 82.
OPEN	All year
DESCRIPTION	A 1907 two-story Craftsman with arts and crafts decor.
NO. OF ROOMS	One room with a private bathroom and two rooms share one bathroom.
RATES	Year-round rates are $75-80 for a single or double with a private bathroom and $70-75 for a single or double with a shared bathroom. There is no minimum stay.
CREDIT CARDS	No
BREAKFAST	Continental breakfast is served in the dining room or on the veranda and includes a home-baked item, juice, fruit, and hot cereal. On Saturday, bacon and eggs are served; Sunday is pancakes day.
AMENITIES	Solarium, sherry or port on arrival, 100-percent cotton sun-dried sheets and towels.
RESTRICTIONS	No pets. Blue is the resident weimaraner. The canary is called Angel.

SAN RAFAEL

The Marin County Seat is noted for its 140-acre Civic Center, Frank Lloyd Wright's last major architectural achievement. Two great places to visit: the California Center for Wildlife Rehabilitation and the Guide Dogs for the Blind campus. San Rafael is north of San Francisco via Highway 101.

GERSTLE PARK INN

34 Grove Street, San Rafael, CA 94901   415-721-7611
WEBSITE www.gerstleparkinn.com

KUDOS/COMMENTS	"Beautiful setting; georgous antiques and decor; marvelous innkeepers." (1999)

Panama Hotel

4 Bayview Street, San Rafael, CA 94901　　　415-457-3993
Dan Miller, Resident Owner　　　　　　　　800-899-3993
Spanish and some French spoken

LOCATION	From Highway 101 north, take the central San Rafael exit. Go two blocks to Third Street, turn left, go 0.5 mile to B Street, and turn left again. Go five blocks to the stop sign; the hotel is a quarter block farther down on the right.
OPEN	All year
DESCRIPTION	Two 1910 two-story vintage Victorian homes connected by a rambling garden patio and restaurant.
NO. OF ROOMS	Nine rooms have private bathrooms and six rooms share two bathrooms. Dan suggests Rosie's Room.
RATES	Year-round rates are $89-145 for a single or double with a private bathroom and $60-65 for a single or double with a shared bathroom. There is a two-night minimum stay on summer weekends and cancellation requires 48 hours' notice.
CREDIT CARDS	Diners Club, Discover
BREAKFAST	Continental plus is served in the dining room and includes fruit, scones, muffins, hot and cold cereals, fresh coffee, and tea. Lunch and dinner are available in the restaurant.
AMENITIES	TVs, telephones, swing music in the dining room on Tuesday nights, room service, Sunday brunch.
RESTRICTIONS	No smoking, no pets

Santa Clara

Madison Street Inn

1390 Madison Street, Santa Clara, CA 95050　　　408-249-5541
Ralph & Theresa Wigginton, Resident Owners　　　800-491-5541
　　　　　　　　　　　　　　　　　　　　　　FAX 408-249-6676

LOCATION	From Highway 101, take the De la Cruz exit and follow De la Cruz until it forks. Take the right fork, which becomes Lewis, toward Santa Clara. Stay on Lewis for approximately six blocks. The inn is at the corner of Lewis and Madison, on the left.

Madison Street Inn, Santa Clara

OPEN	All year
DESCRIPTION	An 1895 one-and-a-half-story Queen Anne Victorian with antique furnishings and landscaped gardens.
NO. OF ROOMS	Four rooms with private bathrooms and two rooms share one bathroom. The Madison Room is the best in the house.
RATES	Year-round rates are $95-115 for a single or double with a private bathroom and $75 for a single or double with a shared bathroom. The suite is $115 and the entire B&B rents for $500. Two days' notice is required for cancellation.
CREDIT CARDS	American Express, Diners Club, Discover, MasterCard, Visa
BREAKFAST	Full breakfast includes an egg dish, meat, fresh fruit, breakfast bread, and beverages.
AMENITIES	Wine, soft drinks, fresh-baked cookies, hot tub in garden, sherry, fax, phones, pool, dry cleaning picked up, meeting facilities for up to 20 people.
RESTRICTIONS	No smoking, no pets. Shadow the beagle likes to play ball.
REVIEWED	*Official Guide to American Historic Inns; Recommended Country Inns—West Coast; The Complete Guide to Bed & Breakfasts, Inns, and Guesthouses*
MEMBER	California Association of Bed & Breakfast Inns
RATED	Mobil 2 Stars

SANTA CRUZ

First inhabited by the Ohlone and later by Junipero Serra and his missions, today's Santa Cruz is a nice, easy, middle-class tourist and university town that loves its Boardwalk and beaches. And for good reason. Make time for the redwood-cloistered University of California campus overlooking the Bay; Natural Bridges State Park and its many tidepools, and the mythic monarch butterflies; and an up-close tour of the seals and sea lions of Año Nuevo State Reserve. Try the Monarch Migration Festival and the Clam Chowder Cookoff in February, and the Shakespeare Festival in August. Downtown is still rebuilding from the devastation of the 1989 earthquake, so stick with the beach areas.

BABBLING BROOK BED & BREAKFAST

1025 Laurel Street, Santa Cruz, CA 95060　　　　　408-427-2437
　　　　　　　　　　　　　　　　　　　　　　　FAX 408-427-2457

CHATEAU VICTORIAN, A BED & BREAKFAST INN

118 First Street, Santa Cruz, CA 95060　　　　　831-458-9458
Alice June, Resident Owner
WEBSITE *www.travelguides.com/bb/chateauvictorian*

LOCATION	Please call for directions.
OPEN	All year
DESCRIPTION	An 1880s two-story Queen Anne Victorian inn with Victorian furnishings, located one block from the beach.
NO. OF ROOMS	Seven rooms with private bathrooms.
RATES	Year-round rates for a single or double are $110-140. There is no minimum stay and cancellation requires 48 hours' notice.
CREDIT CARDS	American Express, MasterCard, Visa (prefer cash or check)
BREAKFAST	Continental plus is served in the dining room or on the decks or brick patio.
AMENITIES	Pump organ and guitar in the living room for those who play; hostess will make reservations and direct guests to fine dining and cultural events; evening refreshments.
RESTRICTIONS	No smoking. "We are unable to accommodate children or pets."
REVIEWED	*Bed & Breakfast North America, Bed & Breakfast California, Weekend Adventures for City Weary People, Hidden San Francisco and Northern California, The Complete Guide to B&B Inns and Guesthouses*

MEMBER	Bed & Breakfast Innkeepers of Santa Cruz County, California Association of Bed & Breakfast Inns

CLIFF CREST BED & BREAKFAST INN

407 Cliff Street, Santa Cruz, CA 95060   831-427-2609
Bruce & Sharon Taylor, Resident Owners   800-427-2609
WEBSITE *www.cliffcrestinn.com*   FAX 831-427-2710

LOCATION	From Highways 17 or 1 northbound, take the Ocean Street exit and drive to the end. Turn right on San Lorenzo Boulevard and go to the stop light at Riverside, turn left, and cross the bridge. Take an immediate right turn onto Third Street and go uphill to the second house on the right.
OPEN	All year
DESCRIPTION	An 1887 two-story Queen Anne Victorian with family antiques and stained-glass windows. Listed on the State Historic Register.
NO. OF ROOMS	Five rooms with private bathrooms.
RATES	Year-round rates are $95-150 for a single or a double. There is a two-night minimum stay on weekends and holidays, and cancellation requires three days' notice.
CREDIT CARDS	American Express, Discover, MasterCard, Visa
BREAKFAST	Full breakfast is served in the dining room or in the garden and includes fresh juice, fresh fruit in season, an egg dish, coffeecake, muffins, French toast, pancakes, and sausage.
AMENITIES	Flowers, wine and cheese, soft drinks, lots of books, robes, games and puzzles, telephone in parlor, candy dishes, TV available, small meeting room, solarium.
RESTRICTIONS	No smoking, no pets, children are discouraged. Murphy is the resident tabby.
REVIEWED	*Bed & Breakfast California, Recommended Country Inns—West Coast. Hidden Coast of California, Country Inns and Backroads*
MEMBER	California Association of Bed & Breakfast Inns, Professional Association of Innkeepers International, Bed & Breakfast Innkeepers of Santa Cruz County
KUDOS/COMMENTS	"One feels at home and significant the moment Sharon or Bruce Taylor answer the phone. A feeling of comfort and belongingness permeates the inn."

The Darling House, a Bed & Breakfast Inn by the Sea

314 West Cliff Drive, Santa Cruz, CA 95060 831-458-1958
Darrell & Karen Darling, Resident Owners 800-458-1958
Spanish spoken
WEBSITE www.infopoint.com/darlinghouse

LOCATION	South on Highway 17 to Highway 1 north (Mission Street). Turn left on Bay, then right on West Cliff, and go two blocks. Turn right on Gharkey.
OPEN	All year
DESCRIPTION	A 1910 two-story Spanish mission revival with Prairie School influences, furnished with American antiques.
NO. OF ROOMS	One room with a private bathroom, six rooms share three bathrooms.
RATES	Year-round rates are $260 for a single or double with a private bathroom, $95-170 for a single or double with a shared bathroom, and $430 for the suite. There is a minimum stay when Saturday or a long weekend is involved and cancellation requires five days' notice.
CREDIT CARDS	American Express, Discover, MasterCard, Visa
BREAKFAST	Continental plus is served in the dining room and includes espresso or cappuccino, breads, croissants, and fresh fruit. A caterer is on call for special meals.
AMENITIES	Orchids or roses in each room, hot tub in garden, telephones in rooms, complimentary gourmet dinner on weekdays from September through May.
RESTRICTIONS	No smoking, no pets
REVIEWED	*Recommended Country Inns—West Coast; Northern California Best Places; Country Inns, Lodges & Historic Hotels; Northern California Handbook*
MEMBER	California Lodging Industry Association, Santa Cruz County Lodging Association
AWARDS	Santa Cruz Historical Society Landmark Award

HUMMINGBIRD HILL BED & BREAKFAST

420 Woodland Drive, Scotts Valley, CA 95066   831-439-8632
Lynn & Jane Dreeszen, Innkeepers   FAX 831-439-8173
EMAIL hummingbird@bonk.com   WEBSITE www.bonk.com/hummingbird

LOCATION	Take Highway 17 to the Glenwood Cutoff exit, then go 0.5 mile west to Woodland Drive.
OPEN	All year
DESCRIPTION	A 1960s one-story pitched-roof cabin decorated with "semirustic" and antique furnishings.
NO. OF ROOMS	One room with a private bathroom.
RATES	May through December, rates are $120 for Friday and Saturday nights and $100 midweek for a single or double. January through April, rates are $100 for Friday and Saturday nights and $80 midweek. There is a two-night minimum stay and cancellation requires five days' notice for a full refund.
CREDIT CARDS	MasterCard, Visa
BREAKFAST	Continental breakfast is served in guestroom and includes coffee or tea, fresh juice, fresh fruit in season, scones or pastries, butter, and jelly.
AMENITIES	Innkeepers take photographs of guests as mementos of their visit; fresh flowers in the cottage; welcome chocolates.
RESTRICTIONS	No smoking, no pets, no children. The resident pets include Doc, a Dandie Dinmont terrier, and several cockatoos. The innkeepers breed three species of cockatoos, and say that "the birds do not disturb the guests."

INN AT PASATIEMPO

555 Highway 17, Santa Cruz, CA 95060   408-423-5000
WEBSITE www.innatpasatiempo.com

PLEASURE POINT INN

3665 East Cliff Drive, Santa Cruz, CA 95062   408-475-4657
Barbara & Gary Pasquini, Resident Owners
WEBSITE www.innaccess.com/pp//

Santa Rosa

Santa Rosa has more than its share of offbeat museums. Botanists, gardeners, and other plant lovers will want to make a beeline to the popular gardens and greenhouse at the Luther Burbank Home & Gardens; while pop culture fans will get a kick out of Snoopy's Gallery & Gift Shop, a "Peanuts" cartoon museum with the world's largest collection of Snoopy memorabilia. The tacky but fun Robert L. Ripley Memorial Museum is filled with wacky displays and information about the late Santa Rosa resident who created the world-famous "Ripley's Believe It or Not" cartoon strip. The wildly successful Thursday Night Farmers Market on downtown Santa Rosa's Fourth Street draws folks from far and near from Memorial Day through Labor Day. Another local crowd-pleaser is the annual Sonoma County Harvest Fair, a wine-tasting, food-gorging orgy held at the fairgrounds from late July to early August.

The Gables Inn

4257 Petaluma Hill Road, Santa Rosa, CA 95404   707-585-7777
Mike & Judy Ogne, Resident Owners   800-422-5376
WEBSITE *www.thegablesinn.com*   FAX 707-584-5634

LOCATION	From Highway 101, exit at Rohnert Park Expressway and turn right. Travel 2.5 miles to Petaluma Hill Road. Turn left and travel four miles to the inn.
OPEN	All year
DESCRIPTION	An 1877 Victorian inn listed on the National and State Historic Registers—a restored Gothic mansion with a sun deck and a separate Victorian honeymoon cottage, set on 3.5 acres in the center of Sonoma wine country.
NO. OF ROOMS	Eight rooms with private bathrooms
RATES	Year-round rates are $135-225 for a single or double. There is a minimum stay of two nights on weekends and three nights on holiday weekends.
CREDIT CARDS	American Express, Diners Club, Discover, MasterCard, Visa
BREAKFAST	Four-course breakfast is served in the dining room.
AMENITIES	Classical CDs and player, fresh flowers, casual afternoon refreshments, central air conditioning, hair dryers, irons and ironing boards. Hospitality area with tea, coffee, cold drinks, and homemade cookies. Full concierge service to arrange for winery tours, dinner, or hot air ballooning. Meeting space for up to 16. Handicapped accessible.
RESTRICTIONS	No smoking, no pets. Three resident cats roam the premises, affectionately named Barn Cats 1, 2, and 3.

REVIEWED	Bed & Breakfast California; The Best Places to Kiss in Northern California; Karen Brown's California Country Inns & Itineraries; Bed & Breakfast Guide: California
MEMBER	Wine Country Inns of Sonoma County
KUDOS/COMMENTS	"Beautifully done country mansion. The hospitality of Michael and Judy Ogne ensure a memorable stay." "It is elegant yet welcoming to weary travelers. They are gracious hosts."

MELITTA STATION INN

5850 Melitta Road, Santa Rosa, CA 95409   707-538-7712
Diane Crandon & Vic Amstadter, Resident Owners   800-504-3099
WEBSITE www.melittastation.com

LOCATION	From Highway 101, take the Highway 12 exit east in Santa Rosa. Follow Highway 12 (Sonoma Highway) to Melitta Road just past Calistoga Road, turn right on Melitta and go 0.9 mile; the inn is on the right across from Annadel State Park.
OPEN	All year
DESCRIPTION	An 1880 railroad station furnished with American country decor and antiques.
NO. OF ROOMS	Four rooms with private bathrooms and two rooms share one bathroom.
RATES	Year-round rates for a single or double with a private or shared bathroom are $95-120, and a two-room suite is $160.
CREDIT CARDS	MasterCard, Visa
BREAKFAST	Full breakfast is served in the Great Room or on the balcony and includes fruit, fresh juice, breads, muffins, cakes, a main egg dish, and beverages.
AMENITIES	Fresh flowers in the rooms; wine, cheese, and crackers served in the afternoon.
RESTRICTIONS	No smoking, no pets, children are welcome with prior approval.
REVIEWED	Non-Smokers Guide to Bed & Breakfasts, The Official Guide to American Historic Bed & Breakfasts, Inns, and Guesthouses, Northern California Best Places
MEMBER	Wine Country Inns of Sonoma County, Bed & Breakfast Association of Sonoma Valley

PYGMALION HOUSE

331 Orange Street, Santa Rosa, CA 95407   707-526-3407

KUDOS/COMMENTS   "Great full breakfast, warm hosts."

VINTNERS INN

4350 Barnes Road, Santa Rosa, CA 95403   707-575-7350
John & Cindy Duffy, Innkeepers   800-421-2584
Spanish spoken   FAX 707-575-1426
WEBSITE *www.vintnersinn.com*

LOCATION	Sixty miles north of the Golden Gate Bridge. From Highway 101 take the River Road exit, go left on River Road, and take the first immediate left onto Barnes Road.
OPEN	All year
DESCRIPTION	A 1984 two-story Mediterranean-style hotel decorated with country French furnishings. Four stucco buildings with red-tile roofs on a working 45-acre vineyard.
NO. OF ROOMS	Forty-four rooms with private bathrooms.
RATES	Year-round rates are $148-198 for a single or double and $185-225 for a suite. There is a two-night minimum stay when a Saturday night is included. Cancellation requires 72 hours' notice.
CREDIT CARDS	American Express, Diners Club, MasterCard, Visa
BREAKFAST	Continental plus is served in the dining room and includes homemade breakfast breads, pastries, savories, fruits, cereals, juices, beverages, waffles. Lunch and dinner are available in the restaurant.
AMENITIES	Phones, air conditioning, vineyard views, patios, balconies, Jacuzzi, sun deck, newspapers, evening turndown and concierge services, local maps, robes, cable TV, meeting facilities, fireplaces, refrigerators, data ports, handicapped accessible.
RESTRICTIONS	No smoking, no pets. The resident cats are Gracie and Jester; Rascal is the shepherd/Lab mix.
REVIEWED	*Away for the Weekend; Northern California Best Places; The Best Places to Kiss in Northern California; Fodor's; Elegant Small Hotels; The Napa and Sonoma Book; City Guide; A Guide to America's Finest Small Hotels; America's Favorite Inns, B&Bs, & Small Hotels; Best Places to Stay in California; Frommer's California*
RATED	AAA 4 Diamonds, Mobil 3 Stars

SAUSALITO

This little hillside hamlet is a prime getaway destination for San Franciscans. Houses cling precariously to the hills, and bohemian and marine influences blend nicely between the artists' colony, houseboat community, and gorgeous yacht harbor. Plan a cruise over to Angel Island State Park.

CASA MADRONA HOTEL

801 Bridgeway, Sausalito, CA 94965   415-332-0502
John W. Mans, Resident Owner   800-567-9524
Spanish, French, Portugese, Vietnamese spoken   FAX 415-332-2837
EMAIL casa@casamadrona.com   WEBSITE www.casamadrona.com

LOCATION	In downtown Sausalito, a 15-minute drive from San Francisco across the Golden Gate Bridge—or a 30-minute ferry ride from San Francisco.
OPEN	All year
DESCRIPTION	An 1885 blend of Victorian hotel and New England-style inn, surrounded by gardens and bay views and listed on the National Historic Register
NO. OF ROOMS	Thirty-four rooms with private bathrooms. The Rose Chalet is the best room.
RATES	Year-round rates for a single or double are $138-260. There is a two-night minimum stay on weekends and cancellation requires 48 hours' notice.
CREDIT CARDS	American Express, Diners Club, Discover, MasterCard, Visa
BREAKFAST	Full breakfast, served in the dining room, includes fresh fruit, toast, homemade muffins and scones, waffles, and a hot egg dish. Lunch and dinner are also available; brunch is served on Sunday.
AMENITIES	Five cottages have wood-burning stoves; most rooms offer fireplaces, views, and decks; wine and cheese social hour every evening; phones; robes; outdoor Jacuzzi; wet bar in some rooms; room service available during restaurant hours; valet parking; turndown service; business and concierge services; one room is handicapped accessible.
RESTRICTIONS	No pets
REVIEWED	Weekends for Two in Northern California: 50 Romantic Getaways; Karen Brown's California Country Inns & Itineraries
RATED	AAA 3 Diamonds, Mobil 3 Stars

GABLES INN SAUSALITO

40 Princess, Sausalito, CA 94965   415-289-1100

SEBASTOPOL

One hour northwest of San Francisco on Highway 116, Sebastopol is situated in the wine mecca of Sonoma County. Be sure to check out Fort Ross, a restored Russian outpost.

GRAVENSTEIN INN

3160 Hicks Road, Sebastopol, CA 95472   707-829-0493
EMAIL *gravensteininn@metro.net*
WEBSITE *www.metro.net/gravensteininn*

KUDOS/COMMENTS   "So lovely. Gracious hostess and host."

VINE HILL INN BED & BREAKFAST

3949 Vine Hill Road, Sebastopol, CA 95472   707-823-8832
Ann Deichmann, Innkeeper   FAX 707-824-1045
EMAIL *vhiadmin@vine-hill-inn.com*   WEBSITE *www.vine-hill-inn.com*

LOCATION	Twelve miles west of Highway 101 (north of San Francisco) off Highway 116 west, four miles outside of Sepastopol.
OPEN	All year
DESCRIPTION	An 1897 two-story Victorian country inn with comfortable farm decor, set amongst pines next to a vineyard.
NO. OF ROOMS	Four rooms with private bathrooms. Try the Sage Room.
RATES	Year-round rates are $125-150 for a single or double. There is no minimum stay and cancellation requires seven days' notice.
CREDIT CARDS	American Express, MasterCard, Visa
BREAKFAST	Full breakfast is served in the dining room and includes fresh juice, fruit, an egg dish, pancakes, waffles, or French toast, with sausage or bacon, coffee, and tea.

AMENITIES	Robes in rooms, fresh flowers, air conditioning, choice of whirlpool or clawfoot tubs, two rooms with shared deck, two with private decks, garden, porches, pool.
RESTRICTIONS	No smoking, no pets. Cleo is the resident Siamese cat.
MEMBER	Professional Association of Innkeepers International

SHINGLETOWN

This is the direct gateway into Lassen Volcanic National Park. Horse lovers take note, it's also the site of the Shingletown Wild Horse Sanctuary, a preserve where mustangs get a new lease on life. Shingletown is east of Redding on Highway 44.

WESTON HOUSE

6741 Red Rock Road, Shingletown, CA 96088　　　530-474-3738
Ivor & Angela Weston, Resident Owners

LOCATION	From Highway 44 east toward Mount Lassen National Park, travel 26 miles to the sign, turn right on Shingletown Ridge Road, drive 1.2 miles, and turn left on Red Rock Road.
OPEN	All year
DESCRIPTION	A 1979 two-story cedar shake country inn with Victorian and eclectic furnishings.
NO. OF ROOMS	Three rooms with private bathrooms and one room shares one bathroom. Angela suggests Helen's Room.
RATES	Please call for current rates and cancellation information.
CREDIT CARDS	MasterCard, Visa
BREAKFAST	Full breakfast is served in the dining room or on the deck.
AMENITIES	Refreshments upon arrival, use of the pool and outdoor Jacuzzi, gas grill available, TV/VCR in common room, wood-burning stoves in all rooms, massage available.
RESTRICTIONS	No smoking, no pets
MEMBER	Professional Association of Innkeepers International
KUDOS/COMMENTS	"A retreat in the foothills near Lassen Park; very pleasant owners and setting; a great massage is available." "Beautiful setting, lovely gardens, tastefully decorated rooms, delicious breakfast, and very gracious hosts."

Sierra City

In the Sierra Nevadas, this small mountain community sits alongside the North Yuba River and is surrounded by Tahoe National Forest. Sierra City offers easy access to some 40 lakes and more than 150 acres with groomed cross-country skiing trails.

High Country Inn Bed & Breakfast

100 Greene Road, Sierra City, CA 96125530-862-1530
Bob & Bette Latta, Innkeepers800-862-1530
EMAIL blatta@sccn.netFAX 530-862-1000

LOCATION	Off Highway 49 at Bassetts and Gold Lake Roads.
OPEN	All year
DESCRIPTION	A 1981 two-story ranch-style country inn decorated with wood and antiques on 2.5 acres along the north fork of the Yuba River.
NO. OF ROOMS	Two rooms with private bathrooms and two rooms with two shared bathrooms. Try the Sierra Buttes Suite.
RATES	Year-round rates are $90-125 for a single or double with a private bathroom, $80 for a single or double with a shared bathroom, and $125 for a suite. There is a two-night minimum stay during weekends and holidays, and cancellation requires 72 hours' notice.
CREDIT CARDS	American Express, Discover, MasterCard, Visa
BREAKFAST	Full gourmet breakfast includes fresh fruit and breads. Hot beverages are delivered to guestrooms in the morning.
AMENITIES	Fresh flowers; robes; trout pond stocked with trophy rainbows; trout feeding (they can be petted, too); wildlife can be observed from the inn.
RESTRICTIONS	No smoking, no pets, children over 10 are welcome.
MEMBER	California Association of Bed & Breakfast Inns

SMITH RIVER

Though the Smith River doesn't actually run through here (the town sits along the banks of Rowdy Creek), the river is nearby. Not surprisingly, the town is central to the Smith River National Recreation Area. Smith River's major events are in July: the Easter in July Lily Festival and the two-mile Smith River Gasquet Raft Race. Pelican State Beach is just up the road. North of Crescent City on Highway 101.

CASA RUBIO OCEANFRONT LODGING

17285 Crissey Road, Smith River, CA 95567   707-487-4313
Tony Rubio, Innkeeper   800-357-6199
Spanish and some French spoken
EMAIL casarubio@telis.org
WEBSITE members.aol.com/casarubio

LOCATION	On the beach, just 800 feet south of the Oregon–California border, five miles south of Brookings off Highway 101.
OPEN	All year
DESCRIPTION	A 1947 two-story contemporary beachhouse with contemporary furnishings. Very private, separate apartmentlike units surrounded by lush landscaping and exotic plants, with breathtaking ocean views.
NO. OF ROOMS	Four rooms with private bathrooms. Tony recommends the Suite or Cabin.
RATES	Year-round rates are $68-98 for a single or double and $88-98 for a suite. There is a minimum stay during holiday weekends and cancellation requires seven days' notice.
CREDIT CARDS	MasterCard, Visa
BREAKFAST	Continental breakfast is do-it-yourself in the guestrooms and includes croissants or bagels, juice, tea, and coffee. Lunch and dinner are also available.
AMENITIES	Complimentary dinner for two at Rubio's Restaurant in Brookings is included with a three-night stay (otherwise, 20 percent discount off all meals at Rubio's), fresh flowers, telephones, TV, fully equipped kitchens.
RESTRICTIONS	No smoking. Chica is the resident pooch and Cuca is the cat. "Both are very friendly and smart enough not to bother guests. Chica will join you on beach walks if desired."
REVIEWED	Pet Lovers Travel Guide

SODA SPRINGS

Off I-80 on the road to Lake Tahoe, this is a mecca for cross-country skiing, with over 200 miles of groomed trails.

ROYAL GORGE'S RAINBOW LODGE

9411 Hampshire Rocks Road, Soda Springs, CA 95728   530-426-3661
John Slouber, Resident Owner   800-500-3871
EMAIL info@royalgorge.com   FAX 530-426-7720
WEBSITE www.royalgorge.com

LOCATION	From I-80, take the Rainbow Road exit, turn left, and travel 0.5 mile to the lodge.
OPEN	All year
DESCRIPTION	A 1920s lodge of local granite and hand-hewn timber with mountain home decor, located in the Sierra Mountains by a bend in the Yuba River.
NO. OF ROOMS	Twelve rooms with private bathrooms and 19 rooms share four bathrooms.
RATES	November 15 through April, rates are $119 for a single or double with a private bath, $99 for a shared bath (sink only), $89 for a shared bath with a shower. Bridal and family suites are $139. May through November 14, rates are $109 for a single or double with a private bath, $79 for a shared bath (sink only), and $99 for a shared bath with a shower. $99. Bridal and family suites are $129. A minimum stay applies for winter and holiday weekends. In the winter, cancellation requires 21 days' notice for a full refund less a $10 fee; 24 hours' notice is required in the summer.
CREDIT CARDS	MasterCard, Visa
BREAKFAST	Full breakfast is served in the dining room and includes eggs, French toast, muesli, oatmeal, pancakes, melon with yogurt, juice, coffee, and tea. Lunch and dinner are also available.
AMENITIES	TV in bar, large fireplace in guest lounge, garden, deck, handicapped accessible. Facilities available for meetings, weddings, banquets, and parties.
RESTRICTIONS	No smoking, no pets

The Traverse Inn

PO Box 1012, Soda Springs, CA 95728　　　530-426-3010
Wes Ohlsen, Resident Owner

Sonoma

The birthplace of the state's wine industry has a fascinating history of foreign rule. Mexican General Mariano Vallejo's legacy is alive and well-preserved at Sonoma State Historic Park, which includes Sonoma Mission, a beautiful 8-acre plaza surrounded by adobe buildings. May and June are eventful, but the main attraction happens in August: the Sonoma County Wine Showcase and Auction. From San Francisco, drive about 35 miles north on Highway 121.

Adriana's Bed & Breakfast

19410 7th Street East, Sonoma, CA 95476　　　707-938-2939
EMAIL vhubbell@sonic.net　　　FAX 707-938-2290

Eller House Bed & Breakfast

56 Bradford Street, Sonoma, CA 95370　　　209-532-0420

Magliulo's Bed & Breakfast

691 Broadway, Sonoma, CA 95476　　　707-996-1031
WEBSITE www.sterba.com/sonoma/magliulo

Sonoma Chalet

18935 Fifth Street West, Sonoma, CA 95476 707-938-3129
Joe Leese, Resident Owner 800-938-3129
WEBSITE www.sonomabb.com

LOCATION	At the very north end of Fifth Street West, down the gravel road.
OPEN	All year except Christmas
DESCRIPTION	A 1940 two-story Swiss farmhouse and three country cottages on 3 acres.
NO. OF ROOMS	Five rooms with private bathrooms and two rooms with shared bathrooms.
RATES	Year-round rate for a single or double with a shared bathroom is $85. For a single or double with a private bathroom, the rates are $120-165 from April through October, and $120-145 from November through March. There is a two-night minimum stay during weekends and cancellation requires one weeks' notice.
CREDIT CARDS	American Express, MasterCard, Visa
BREAKFAST	Continental plus is served in the dining room or guestrooms and includes juice, fresh fruit, granola, cereals, hard-boiled eggs, coffee or tea, and pastries.
AMENITIES	Robes, hot tub, bicycles, sun deck, fireplace or wood-burning stove.
RESTRICTIONS	No smoking, no pets. Children are OK in cottages by prior arrangement. Resident pets include pygmy goats, geese, and Petapoo the golden retriever.
REVIEWED	*Frommer's California, Northern California Best Places, Wonderful Weekends from San Francisco, Inn Places, The Official Bed & Breakfast Guide*
MEMBER	Bed & Breakfast Inns of Sonoma Valley, California Association of Bed & Breakfast Inns, California Lodging Association

Starwae Inn

21490 Broadway, Sonoma, CA 95476 707-938-1374
Janice Crow & John Curry, Resident Owners 800-793-4792
WEBSITE www.sonomabb.com FAX 707-935-1159

LOCATION	On Highway 12, 2.2 miles south of downtown Sonoma.
OPEN	All year

DESCRIPTION	Two 1930 early California ranch-style stucco cottages on 3 acres across from a vineyard. Each cottage is divided into two rooms or suites and has a private patio and private entrance. Decor includes original art and pine and wicker furniture.
NO. OF ROOMS	Four rooms with private bathrooms.
RATES	April through October, rates for a single or double are $125-185, suites are $155-185, and the guesthouse is $295. November through March, rates are roughly 10 to 15 percent less. The minimum stay is two nights on weekends, three nights on holidays. Cancellation requires seven days' notice for one room and 14 days' notice for two rooms.
CREDIT CARDS	American Express, MasterCard, Visa
BREAKFAST	Continental plus, served in the guestrooms, includes juice, fresh scones, fruit, bagels, and coffee.
AMENITIES	Robes, kitchens, kitchenettes, air conditioning, TVs, telephones, beautiful gardens, sculpture, private patios and entrances.
RESTRICTIONS	No smoking, no pets, children OK by prior arrangement. Birds abound on the property, which is in a major migration flight path.
REVIEWED	*Sonoma Valley—The Secret Wine Country*
MEMBER	Sonoma Valley Bed & Breakfast Association

THISTLE DEW INN

171 West Spain Street, Sonoma, CA 95476
Larry & Norma Barnett, Resident Owners
German spoken
WEBSITE *www.thistledew.com*

707-938-2909
800-382-7895

LOCATION	Half a block west of the historic town plaza on West Spain Street.
OPEN	All year
DESCRIPTION	Two 1900 Victorian cottages furnished with period antiques.
NO. OF ROOMS	Six rooms with private bathrooms.
RATES	Year-round weekend rates are $125-210 for a single or double. Weekday rates are slightly cheaper and discounts apply from December through February. There is no minimum stay and cancellation requires two days' notice with a $10 fee.
CREDIT CARDS	American Express, MasterCard, Visa
BREAKFAST	Full breakfast, served in the dining room, includes an entrée cooked to order, fruit, breads, meats, and beverages.

AMENITIES	Evening hors d'oeuvres, garden hot tub, fireplaces, private decks, whirlpool tub, fresh flowers, two rooms are handicapped accessible.
RESTRICTIONS	No smoking, no pets, children over 12 are welcome.
REVIEWED	Fodor's California, Bed & Breakfast California, The Napa & Sonoma Book
MEMBER	California Association of Bed & Breakfast Inns

VICTORIAN GARDEN INN

316 East Napa Street, Sonoma, CA 95476   707-996-5339
Donna Lewis, Resident Owner   800-543-5339
Spanish spoken   FAX 707-996-1689
EMAIL vgardeninn@aol.com   WEBSITE www.victoriangardeninn.com

LOCATION	One-and-a-half blocks from the town square (plaza). Take the Highway 37 exit from Highway 101 north.
OPEN	All year
DESCRIPTION	An 1870s Victorian farmhouse and cottage with Victorian furnishings and wraparound porch.
NO. OF ROOMS	Three rooms with private bathrooms and two rooms share one bathroom.
RATES	Year-round rates are $129-175 for a single or double with a private bathroom and $95 for a single or double with a shared bathroom. April through November and holiday weekends, there is a minimum stay required when a Saturday is involved. Cancellation requires seven days' notice with a $10 fee.
CREDIT CARDS	American Express, Diners Club, JCB, MasterCard, Visa
BREAKFAST	Continental plus is served in the dining rooms or guestrooms, or outside in the garden, and includes fresh seasonal fruit, homemade pastries, granola, and beverages. Picnic baskets are also available.
AMENITIES	Fresh flowers and terry robes in every room, tea cart with beverages and cookies in the dining room, swimming pool in the back, air conditioning, hot tub.
RESTRICTIONS	No smoking, no pets, children are not encouraged. Rocky is the resident outdoor cat.
REVIEWED	*The Best Places to Kiss in Northern California; Northern California Wine Country Access; Country Inns of the Far West; America's Favorite Inns, B&Bs, & Small Hotels*
MEMBER	Professional Association of Innkeepers International, California Association of Bed & Breakfast Inns, Redwood Empire Association

SONORA

Once one of the richest and wildest of Mother Lodes, this pretty town now relies on lumbering and agriculture. Worth a visit are the Tuolumne County Museum, housed in the former jailhouse, and Bradford Street Park. Try a walking tour to view the many historic adobe and Victorian buildings. From Sonora, scenic Highway 108 leads into the Stanislaus National Forest. Sample the good old days during the Mother Lode Roundup Parade and Rodeo in May, and Wild West Days in September. Sonora is southeast of Sacramento via Highways 16 and 49, and east of Stockton.

BARRETTA GARDENS BED & BREAKFAST INN

700 South Barretta Street, Sonora, CA 95370   209-532-6039
Nancy & Detrich Brandt, Resident Owners   800-206-3333
Some Spanish understood
WEBSITE www.barrettagardens.com

LOCATION	One mile from downtown Sonora off Business Highway 108.
OPEN	All year
DESCRIPTION	A 1903 two-story Victorian with Victorian furnishings.
NO. OF ROOMS	Five rooms with private bathrooms. Try the Dragonfly.
RATES	Year-round rates are $90-105 for a single or double. There is a minimum stay on holidays and cancellation requires five days' notice.
CREDIT CARDS	American Express, MasterCard, Visa
BREAKFAST	Full breakfast is served in the dining room and includes eggs, quiche, crepes, pastries, fruit, and beverages.
AMENITIES	Fresh flowers, sunset view, gardens, facilities for small weddings, one room has a spa for two.
RESTRICTIONS	No pets. The two Labs, Shortcake and Jetta, are "smart, eccentric, humorous, and they eat grilled cheese sandwiches and Maine lobsters."
REVIEWED	Best Places in Northern California, The Best Places to Kiss in Northern California, The Best of the Gold Country, Bed & Breakfast California

HAMMONS HOUSE INN BED & BREAKFAST

22963 Robertson Ranch Road, Sonora, CA 95370 209-532-7921
Art & Linda Hammons, Resident Owners

LOCATION	Eighteen miles from Sonora and 5.5 miles from Twain Harte.
OPEN	All year
DESCRIPTION	A 1985 two-story ranch house and separate two-story bungalow with contemporary furnishings, on 6.5 acres.
NO. OF ROOMS	Two rooms with private bathrooms and one room shares one bathroom.
RATES	Year-round rates are $70-80 for a single or double with a private or shared bathroom. The bungalow is $110. There is no minimum stay and cancellation requires five days' notice and a $10 fee.
CREDIT CARDS	American Express, MasterCard, Visa
BREAKFAST	Full breakfast is served in the dining room or guestrooms, or on the deck, and includes fruit, meat entrée, home-baked breads, muffins, and cakes. Special and children's meals are available.
AMENITIES	The main house has a fireplace, swimming pool with deck, TV/VCR, and stereo. The bungalow has a kitchen, private deck, TV, stereo, and barbecue.
RESTRICTIONS	No smoking, no pets. Katy, who has been in the local paper, is an Australian shepherd, and the "Bigbird" guinea fowl goes by Stormer.
MEMBER	California Association of Bed & Breakfast Inns, Gold Country Inns of Tuolumne County, Tuolumne County Lodging Association
KUDOS/COMMENTS	"A fine country home on 6 acres in the Sierra foothills near Sonora."

LAVENDER HILL

683 South Barretta Street, Sonora, CA 95370 209-532-9024
Charlie & Jean Marinelli, Innkeepers 800-446-1333 (ext: 290)
Italian spoken
EMAIL lavender@sonnet.com
WEBSITE www.lavenderhill.com

LOCATION	On the east side of town on a hill overlooking downtown.
OPEN	All year

Lavender Hill, Sonora

DESCRIPTION	A 1900 two-story stick Victorian inn with a wraparound porch, year-round gardens, and an interior of Victorian mixed with country furnishings.
NO. OF ROOMS	Four rooms with private bathrooms. Try the Lavender Room.
RATES	Year-round rates are $65-95 for a single or double, $95 for a suite, and $340 for the entire inn. There is a minimum stay during holidays and cancellation requires five days' notice.
CREDIT CARDS	American Express, MasterCard, Visa
BREAKFAST	Three-course breakfast is served in the dining room and includes juice, coffee or tea, a fruit dish, sweet breads, and an entrée.
AMENITIES	Flowers in all rooms; robes for room with the bath down the hall; afternoon refreshments; porch swing; dinner and theater packages; massages; carriage rides; information on walking, biking, and spring flower trails; walking tour of historic Columbia State Park; baby grand piano for guests' use.
RESTRICTIONS	No smoking, no pets
REVIEWED	*Complete Guide to Bed & Breakfasts, Inns and Guesthouses; Recommended Country Inns—West Coast; America's Wonderful Little Hotels & Inns*
MEMBER	Gold Country Inns of Tuolumne County, California Association of Bed & Breakfast Inns
AWARDS	1997, Excellence in Service, Chamber of Commerce

MOUNTAIN VIEW BED & BREAKFAST

12980 Mountain View Road, Sonora, CA 95370   209-533-0628
Doris & Carl Disbrow, Resident Owners   FAX 209-533-1461
EMAIL mtvu@mlode.com   WEBSITE www.mtvu.com

LOCATION	Take Highway 108 east to the third Sonora exit. Go left on Mono Way (Business 108), right on Fir Drive, and left on Mountain View Road to the top of the hill.
OPEN	All year
DESCRIPTION	A 1981 two-story split-level contemporary inn surrounded by majestic blue oaks, with a view of mountains.
NO. OF ROOMS	Two rooms with private bathrooms and two rooms share one bathroom. Try the Floral Room.
RATES	Year-round rates are $70-80 for a single or double with a private bathroom and $60 for a single or double with a shared bathroom. There is a two-night minimum stay on holiday weekends and cancellation requires five days' notice.
CREDIT CARDS	Discover, MasterCard, Visa
BREAKFAST	A three-course country breakfast is served in the dining room and includes blue ribbon-winning breads and pastries. Individual dietary needs are accommodated.
AMENITIES	Swimming pool; theater packages; robes; special theme weekends, such as Chocolate Lovers Weekend; air conditioning; games and puzzles.
RESTRICTIONS	No smoking. Mickey-Do, the cat, lives outside and does not go inside the inn.
REVIEWED	*The Complete Guide to Bed & Breakfast Inns & Guesthouses*

RYAN HOUSE BED & BREAKFAST

153 South Shepherd Street, Sonora, CA 95370   209-533-3445
WEBSITE www.ryanhouse.com   800-831-4897

KUDOS/COMMENTS	"Professional, comfortable, and hospitable." "All the charm, grace, and perfect hospitality you expect from a B&B; as an innkeeper, I was impressed."

SERENITY, A BED & BREAKFAST INN

15305 Bear Cub Drive, Sonora, CA 95370 209-533-1441
Fred & Charlotte Hoover, Resident Owners 800-426-1441
WEBSITE www.serenity-inn.com

LOCATION	From downtown Sonora, take business Highway 108 east toward Pinecrest. Turn left onto Phoenix Lake Road, drive three miles to Bear Cub Drive, and turn right.
OPEN	All year
DESCRIPTION	A 1989 two-story Mother Lode colonial inn furnished with antiques and reproductions, with a wraparound veranda overlooking 6 forested acres.
NO. OF ROOMS	Four rooms have private bathrooms.
RATES	Year-round rates are $85-125 for a single or double. There is a minimum stay on holiday weekends and cancellation requires 72 hours' notice.
CREDIT CARDS	American Express, Discover, MasterCard, Visa
BREAKFAST	Full breakfast is served in the dining room and includes juice, fruit, an artfully presented entrée, and beverages. Dietary restrictions are accommodated with advance notice.
AMENITIES	Fireplaces, afternoon refreshments, mobile phone for guest use, library, flowers.
RESTRICTIONS	No smoking, no pets, maximum occupancy of two per room. There are two Siamese cats named Jupiter and Juno.
REVIEWED	*The Best of the Gold Country, Northern California Best Places, The Best Places to Kiss in Northern California, Country Inns & Back Roads—California, Bay Area Back Roads*
MEMBER	California Association of Bed & Breakfast Inns

WY'S ACRES

8773 Fraguero Road, Sonora, CA 95370 209-536-9004
WEBSITE www.wysguide.com

SOQUEL

This once-booming lumber town is the place to shop for antiques and things of oak. Or head down by the sea in Capitola for September's Begonia Festival or spend a day in New Brighton Beach State Park. Just south of Santa Cruz, off Highway 1.

BLUE SPRUCE INN

2815 South Main Street, Soquel, CA 95073 831-464-1137
Pat & Tom O'Brien, Resident Owners 800-559-1137
Spanish spoken FAX 831-475-0608
EMAIL *innkeeper@bluespruce.com* WEBSITE *www.bluespruce.com*

LOCATION	From Highway 17, exit onto Highway 1 south toward Monterey. Take the Bay Avenue/Porter Street exit, turn left, and drive 0.4 mile to the inn. Park in the rear.
OPEN	All year
DESCRIPTION	An 1875 two-story historic Victorian farmhouse and an 1893 carriage house with country furnishings, situated one mile from Capitola Beach.
NO. OF ROOMS	Five rooms with private bathrooms. Try the carriage house.

Blue Spruce Inn, Soquel

RATES	Year-round weekend rates are $95-150 for a single or double and $85-135 on weekdays. The entire B&B rents for the regular rates plus $100. There is a two-night minimum stay on weekends and cancellation requires seven days' notice.
CREDIT CARDS	American Express, Discover, MasterCard, Visa
BREAKFAST	Full gourmet breakfast is served in the dining room or guestrooms, or in the garden, and includes fresh orange juice, seasonal fruits, homemade muffins or coffeecake, an entrée, cold or hot cereals, and beverages. Lunch is available for business groups.
AMENITIES	Fresh flowers, robes, telephone, computer, gas fireplaces, spa tubs in rooms, original art.
RESTRICTIONS	No smoking, no pets, children over 12 are welcome. Samantha, the black Lab, doesn't go inside the inn. "Sam is happy to sit on the porch and enjoy little pats."
REVIEWED	*The Best Places to Kiss in Northern California; Country Inns and Other Weekend Pleasures—California; America's Wonderful Little Hotels & Inns; Northern California Handbook; Hidden Coast of California; Bed, Breakfast & Bike—Northern California; Fodor's California; Best Places to Stay in California*
MEMBER	Professional Association of Innkeepers International, California Association of Bed & Breakfast Inns
KUDOS/COMMENTS	"Warm hospitality; charming, cozy rooms; most comfortable beds and atmosphere."

SOUTH LAKE TAHOE

Three premier attractions separate sassy South Lake Tahoe from its sportier northern counterpart: glitzy casinos with celebrity entertainers, several sandy beaches, and the massive Heavenly Ski Resort, the only American ski area that straddles two states. If 24-hour gambling parties or schussing down the slopes of Heavenly is your idea of paradise, then you're in for a treat. As soon as you roll into town, stop at the South Lake Tahoe Chamber of Commerce, where you'll find an entire room filled with free maps, brochures, and guidebooks to the South Lake region.

THE CHRISTIANIA INN

3819 Saddle Road, South Lake Tahoe, CA 96150   530-544-7337
Jerry & Maggie Mershon, Innkeepers   FAX 530-544-5342
Spanish spoken
EMAIL thechris@sierra.net
WEBSITE www.christianiainn.com

The Christiania Inn, South Lake Tahoe

LOCATION	Across from Heavenly Valley ski resort. Take Ski Run Boulevard all the way to the top, turn left, and go two blocks.
OPEN	All year except mid-April through mid-May
DESCRIPTION	A 1965 three-story European chalet and restaurant furnished with country antiques.
NO. OF ROOMS	Six rooms with private bathrooms.
RATES	Thanksgiving to Easter, rates are $75-85 for a single or double and $155-175 for a suite. Off season rates are $50-60 for a single or double and $85-125 for a suite. There is a two-night minimum stay on weekends during the summer and winter seasons, and a 10-day cancellation notice is required.
CREDIT CARDS	MasterCard, Visa
BREAKFAST	Continental breakfast, served in the guestrooms, includes fresh orange juice, fruit platter, fresh-baked muffins, and beverages. Other meals are available in the restaurant.
AMENITIES	TV in rooms, brandy, two suites have saunas in the room, fireplaces and wet bars in four suites.
RESTRICTIONS	No smoking, no pets
REVIEWED	*The Best Places to Kiss in Northern California*
MEMBER	California Association of Bed & Breakfast Inns

Tamarack Creek Bed & Breakfast

7260 Sierra Pines Road, South Lake Tahoe, CA 96150 530-659-0325
WEBSITE www.net101.com/BBCA/tamarack

St. Helena

Where else can you find a small farming town that sells $1,600 owl-skin Japanese lanterns? St. Helena has come a long way since its days as a rural, Seventh Day Adventist village. On Main Street, with its Victorian Old West feel, farming-supply stores now sit stiffly next to chichi women's-clothing boutiques and upscale purveyors of home furnishings. Just off the main drag you can find more earthy pleasures at such shops as the Napa Valley Olive Oil Manufacturing Company, an authentic Italian deli and general store. Take your treats to Lyman Park on Main Street or to a more bucolic spot, Bale Grist Mill State Historic Park, which still has a 36-foot-tall wooden waterwheel that grinds grain into meal and flour. Nearby is St. Helena's popular tree-lined upscale outlet mall, where you'll find discounted designer wares.

Ambrose Bierce House

1515 Main Street, St. Helena, CA 94574 707-963-3003
John & Lisa Wild-Runnells, Innkeepers FAX 707-963-9367
EMAIL shdyoaks@napanet.net

LOCATION	From Napa, head north on Highway 29 for approximately 15 miles. Pine Street is the next street after the stoplight in St. Helena. The inn is the second house on the left after crossing Pine Street. Park in the rear.
OPEN	All year
DESCRIPTION	An 1872 two-story Victorian inn built by author Ambrose Bierce and decorated with antiques. Listed on the National and State Historic Registers.
NO. OF ROOMS	Three rooms with private bathrooms. Try the Ambrose Bierce Suite.
RATES	March through November and weekends and holidays, rates are $159-195 for a single or double and $195 for a suite for two ($29 for each additional person). December through February, rates are $129-175 for a single or double. There is a minimum stay during most weekends and cancellation requires 10 days' notice.
CREDIT CARDS	MasterCard, Visa

BREAKFAST	Gourmet champagne breakfast is served in the dining room and includes eggs Benedict, Belgian waffles, home-baked breads, fresh fruits, a special house-blend coffee, premium teas, juice, and champagne.
AMENITIES	Fresh flowers in rooms, complete collection of restaurant menus from the area, classical music in the parlor, central air conditioning, wine and cheese served each evening, innkeepers recommend restaurants and out-of-the-way wineries, port in rooms, TV in suite.
RESTRICTIONS	No smoking, no pets, children are not encouraged. Roger is the resident black Lab and Emily is the calico. The pets are not permitted in any common guest areas.
REVIEWED	*Northern California Best Places, The Insider's Guide to California's Wine Country*
KUDOS/COMMENTS	"I recommend it. Very nice innkeepers, very good breakfast."

ASPLUND COUNTRY INN

726 Rossi Road, St. Helena, CA 94574   707-963-4614

BARRO STATION BED & BREAKFAST

1112 Lodi Lane, St. Helena, CA 94574   707-963-5169
Carey Sculatti, Resident Owner

LOCATION	Two miles north of St. Helena on Highway 29, then right on Lodi Lane for 0.5 mile.
OPEN	All year
DESCRIPTION	A two-story farmhouse with southwestern and antique furnishings, located on a 7-acre vineyard.
NO. OF ROOMS	Three rooms with private bathrooms.
RATES	Year-round rates are $125-165 for a single or double. There is a two-night minimum stay on weekends and cancellation requires seven days' notice.
CREDIT CARDS	American Express, Diners Club, Discover, MasterCard, Visa
BREAKFAST	Continental breakfast is served.
AMENITIES	Private decks, fruit, view of mountains, 7 acres of vineyards.
RESTRICTIONS	Smoking outside only, no pets

ST. HELENA

Bartels Ranch & Country Inn

1200 Conn Valley Road, St. Helena, CA 94574 707-963-4001
Jami Bartels, Resident Owner 800-225-5288
Spanish spoken FAX 707-963-5100
WEBSITE innformation.com/ca/bartels

LOCATION	Drive three miles east of St. Helena on Pope Street to Silverado Trail, which becomes Howell Mountain Road. Continue for 0.25 mile and stay right at the fork.
OPEN	All year
DESCRIPTION	Built in 1979, this is a sprawling stone and redwood ranch-style country inn decorated with antiques and eclectic furnishings, situated on 100 acres.
NO. OF ROOMS	Four rooms with private bathrooms.
RATES	Year-round rates are $195-425 for a double. Ask about winter discounts. There is a two-night minimum stay on weekends, three nights on holidays and during harvest season. Ask about a cancellation policy.
CREDIT CARDS	American Express, Discover, MasterCard, Visa
BREAKFAST	Full breakfast is served in the dining room or guestrooms, or around the pool, and includes quiche or frittata, fresh fruit, English muffins, croissants, granola, yogurt compote, and beverages. Other meals are available upon request.
AMENITIES	Swimming pool, robes, flowers, candles, candy, telephones, TV/VCR (for movies only), wine and hors d'oeuvres, bicycles, darts, billiards, backgammon, table tennis, microwave, refrigerators and picnic tables, sun deck by lagoon, fishing in the lake, two rooms are wheelchair accessible.
RESTRICTIONS	No smoking, no pets, well-mannered children are OK by special arrangement. There are a variety of resident animals including two horses, Sugar and Irish (one a world champion); Sheba the German shepherd; two cats, Fluffy and Tuxedo; and Bobby the white dove.
REVIEWED	*Best Places to Stay in California*, *Bed & Breakfast California*, *Away for the Weekend*, *Bed & Breakfast in California*, *Taste of the Wine Country*, *Frommer's San Francisco*
MEMBER	Professional Association of Innkeepers International, California Association of Bed & Breakfast Inns, California Lodging and Industry Association
RATED	ABBA 3 Crowns

BYLUND HOUSE BED & BREAKFAST

2000 Howell Mountain Road, St. Helena, CA 94574   707-963-9073

CHESTELSON HOUSE

1417 Kearney Street, St. Helena, CA 94574   707-963-2238
Jackie Sweet, Resident Owner

KUDOS/COMMENTS   "Jackie Sweet is the best gourmet cook and serves a full breakfast with great style."

CINNAMON BEAR BED & BREAKFAST

1407 Kearney Street, St. Helena, CA 94574   707-963-4653
Cathye Raneri, Resident Owner   888-963-4600
EMAIL cinnamonbear@worldnet.att.net   FAX 707-963-0251

LOCATION	Eighteen miles north of Napa. From Highway 29 in St. Helena, turn left onto Adams at the second stoplight and go two blocks to Kearney.
OPEN	All year
DESCRIPTION	A 1904 three-story Craftsman with 1920s antiques and a wraparound porch. The inn is on the State Historic Register.
NO. OF ROOMS	Three rooms with private bathrooms. Cathye recommends the Vanilla Room.
RATES	May to October, rates are $135-190 for a single or double. December to February, rates are $90-150 for a single or double. There is a two-night minimum stay over Saturday, three nights during holidays. Cancellation requires seven days' notice with a $10 fee.
CREDIT CARDS	American Express, MasterCard, Visa
BREAKFAST	Full breakfast is served in the dining room or on the porch. The innkeeper is a professional chef. Her breakfasts include baked egg frittatas, scones, fresh fruit, homemade chicken apple sausage, almond-cinnamon pannetone French toast, fresh blueberry pancakes, and fresh orange juice.

AMENITIES	Afternoon refreshments (cheese board, hors d'oeuvres, iced tea, mineral water, soft drinks); port, sherry, and fresh-baked sweets; antique iron beds with handmade quilts; central heat and air conditioning; small collection of antique teddy bears.
RESTRICTIONS	No smoking, no pets, children over 10 are welcome.
REVIEWED	*America's Wonderful Little Hotels & Inns; Fodor's California; Northern California Wine Country Access; Wine Spectator's Wine Country Guide to California; The Napa Valley Guide*
MEMBER	California Association of Bed & Breakfast Inns

DEER RUN INN

3995 Spring Mountain Road, St. Helena, CA 94574   707-963-3794
Tom & Carol Wilson, Innkeepers   800-843-3408
WEBSITE *www.virtualcities.com*   FAX 707-963-9026

LOCATION	Take Highway 29 through St. Helena to the third traffic signal, turn left on Madrona Avenue, and go three blocks to Spring Mountain Road. Turn right and go 4.5 miles to the inn.
OPEN	All year
DESCRIPTION	A 1929 one-story cedar-shingled clapboard home with a carriage house, studio bungalow, and cottage with traditional antique furnishings. Located in the forest above the valley vineyards.
NO. OF ROOMS	Four rooms with private bathrooms.
RATES	Year-round rates are $140-175. There is a minimum stay during weekends and cancellation requires one week's notice and a $20 fee. Holiday and multiple-room cancellations require one month's notice.
CREDIT CARDS	American Express, MasterCard, Visa
BREAKFAST	Full breakfast is served in the dining room or brought to the cottage and includes fresh berries, cantaloupe, homemade breads and muffins, granola, frittatas, zucchini quiche, fruit juice, coffee, and tea.
AMENITIES	All rooms with TVs, brandy, coffee and tea service, robes, hair dryers, small refrigerators, shampoo/conditioner, air conditioning, fireplaces, down comforters, feather beds, king- and queen-size beds, fine linens, mints.
RESTRICTIONS	No smoking, no pets, no children under 12 months. The resident chocolate Lab is Cody and the three cats who "found" the innkeepers are Teddy, Annie, and Cricket.
REVIEWED	*California B&Bs, Best Places to Stay in California*
KUDOS/COMMENTS	"Clean, friendly, private retreat."

Elsie's Conn Valley Inn

726 Rossi Road, St. Helena, CA 94574   707-963-4614

Erika's Hillside Bed & Breakfast

285 Fawn Park, St. Helena, CA 94574   707-963-2887
Erika Cunningham, Resident Owner

Glass Mountain Inn

3100 Silverado Trail, St. Helena, CA 94574   707-963-3512
Jerry & Diane Payton, Resident Owners
Spanish spoken
WEBSITE *www.glassmountain.com*

LOCATION	One mile north of St. Helena on Silverado Trail.
OPEN	All year
DESCRIPTION	A 1978 two-story Victorian with towers, turrets, stained glass, and period furnishings.
NO. OF ROOMS	All rooms have private bathrooms.
RATES	Please call or check the website for current rates and cancellation information.
CREDIT CARDS	MasterCard, Visa
BREAKFAST	Full breakfast is served in the dining room.
AMENITIES	TV, phone, air conditioning, champagne, truffles, hot tub, fireplaces, decks, balconies, views, Roman soaking tubs.
RESTRICTIONS	No smoking, children over 10 are welcome.

Harvest Inn

One Main Street, St. Helena, CA 94574   707-963-9463
WEBSITE *www.harvestinn.com*   800-950-8466

HILLTOP HOUSE BED & BREAKFAST

9550 St. Helena Road, St. Helena, CA 94574 707-963-8743
Annette Gevarter, Resident Owner FAX 707-571-0263 (call first)
WEBSITE *www.innaccess.com/hti./*

LOCATION	At the second traffic light on Highway 29 in St. Helena, turn left on Madrona Avenue. Go three blocks to Spring Mountain Road, turn right and go 5.7 miles to Napa County Line. The inn is the first driveway on the left past the county line.
OPEN	All year
DESCRIPTION	A 1980 ranch-style inn decorated with a mixture of antiques and traditional furnishings and located on a ridge between Napa and Sonoma.
NO. OF ROOMS	Four rooms with private bathrooms.
RATES	Year-round rates for a single or double are $135-195. The suite is $195. There is a minimum stay on the weekends and cancellation requires one week's notice.
CREDIT CARDS	American Express, MasterCard, Visa
BREAKFAST	Full breakfast, served in the dining room or on the deck, includes homemade breads and muffins, fresh fruit, yogurt, granola, eggs, juice, and beverages.
AMENITIES	Hot tub with a view on the deck, afternoon refreshments, fresh flowers, ice bucket and glasses, spectacular views in all directions, turndown service, after-dinner sherry, hiking trails.
RESTRICTIONS	No smoking, no pets, children over six are welcome. The resident pets are two dogs, Rachel and Max, and a cat, Maude.
REVIEWED	*The Official Bed & Breakfast Guide*, *The Non-Smokers Guide to Bed & Breakfasts*, *Bed & Breakfast USA*, *The Complete Guide to Bed & Breakfast Inns & Guesthouses*
MEMBER	National Bed & Breakfast Association

HOTEL ST. HELENA

1309 Main Street, St. Helena, CA 94574 707-963-4388

INK HOUSE BED & BREAKFAST

1575 St. Helena Highway, St. Helena, CA 94574   707-963-3890
Diane DeFilipi, Innkeeper   FAX 707-968-0739
EMAIL inkhouse@aol.com   WEBSITE www.napavalley.com/inkhouse/

LOCATION	One-and-a-half miles from the town of St. Helena, on the corner of Whitehall Lane and the St. Helena Highway.
OPEN	All year except Christmas eve and Christmas day
DESCRIPTION	An 1884 Italianate Victorian inn with antique Victorian furnishings, family heirlooms, and original artwork. Listed on the National and State Historic Registers.
NO. OF ROOMS	Five rooms with private bathrooms and two rooms with one shared bathroom. Diane recommends the French Room or the Torino Room.
RATES	Rates vary by season, but run from $130-200 for a single or double with a private bathroom and $79-99 for a single or double with a shared bathroom. There is no minimum stay and cancellation requires seven days' notice.
CREDIT CARDS	MasterCard, Visa
BREAKFAST	Full breakfast is served in the dining room or parlor and includes fresh-baked scones, muffins, and breads; fruit dishes (baked pears with cream or fruit with warm mango butter sauce); and hot entrées (frittatas, stratas, or tortas).

Ink House Bed & Breakfast, St. Helena

AMENITIES	Robes for rooms with shared bathroom, air conditioning, wine and full appetizers daily, brandy and port, bicycles, antique pool table, two acres of Victorian gardens, glass observatory with 360-degree views, fresh flowers, grand piano, antique pump organ.
RESTRICTIONS	No smoking, no pets, children are not encouraged.
REVIEWED	Northern California Best Places; The Best Places to Kiss in Northern California; Frommer's; Fodor's; Napa Valley Guide; Damron Accommodations; Country Inns and Backroads: California; Best of the Wine Country; Official Guide to American Historic Inns
MEMBER	Independent Innkeepers Association, California Association of Bed & Breakfast Inns, International Luxury Accomodations
KUDOS/COMMENTS	"Lovely inn, beautifully done, very nice innkeepers, very good breakfast."

LA FLEUR BED & BREAKFAST INN

1475 Inglewood Avenue, St. Helena, CA 94574   707-963-0233
K.. Murphy, Resident Owner
Some Spanish spoken

LOCATION	Two miles north of Rutherford, 1.5 miles south of St. Helena, and 0.5 mile west of Highway 29, between the Beacon gas station and the Villa Helena Winery.
OPEN	All year except Thanksgiving, Christmas, and maybe January
DESCRIPTION	An 1882 two-story Queen Anne Victorian with country-style furnishings.
NO. OF ROOMS	Seven rooms with private bathrooms.
RATES	Year-round weekend rates are $166 for a double. There is a two-night minimum stay on weekends and cancellation requires seven days' notice and a 10 percent charge.
CREDIT CARDS	No
BREAKFAST	Full breakfast is served in the dining room or solarium, or on the back deck. The menu changes daily.
AMENITIES	Private tours of the Villa Helena Winery, rose garden, guest refrigerator.
RESTRICTIONS	No smoking, no pets
REVIEWED	The Best Places to Kiss in San Francisco and the Bay Area, Getaways for City Weary People, Northern California Wine Country Access

Milat Bed & Breakfast

1091 St. Helena Highway South, St. Helena, CA 94574   707-963-2612
WEBSITE *www.milat.com*

Oliver House Bed & Breakfast

2970 Silverado Trail, St. Helena, CA 94574   707-963-4089

Prager Winery Bed & Breakfast

1281 Lewelling Lane, St. Helena, CA 94574   707-963-3720
WEBSITE *www.pragerport.com*

Rose Garden Inn

1277 South St. Helena Highway, St. Helena, CA 94574   707-963-4417

RustRidge Ranch Bed & Breakfast

2910 Lower Chiles Valley Road, St. Helena, CA 94574   707-965-9353
Susan Meyer & Jim Fresquez, Innkeepers   800-788-0263
Spanish, German, and French spoken   FAX 707-965-9263
EMAIL *rustridg@napanet.net*

LOCATION	Nine miles east of the Silverado Trail at Rutherford. Take Highway 128 east around Lake Hennessey. At the fork in the road, veer to the left, and continue for 3.5 miles to Lower Chiles Valley Road. The B&B is 1.5 miles from the turn.
OPEN	All year
DESCRIPTION	A 1939 Southwestern ranch-style inn with Southwest ranch decor, on 442 acres with sweeping views of vineyards, pastures, hillsides, and ancient oak trees.

RustRidge Ranch Bed & Breakfast, St. Helena

NO. OF ROOMS	Five rooms with private bathrooms. In summer, try the Poolside Room; in winter, the Rustridge Room.
RATES	Year-round rates are $115-200 for a single or double and $250 for a suite. There is a two-night minimum stay and cancellation requires 72 hours' notice.
CREDIT CARDS	American Express, Discover, MasterCard, Visa
BREAKFAST	Full breakfast is served in the dining room and includes traditional hot breakfast items, fresh fruit salad, fresh orange juice, and plenty of coffee or tea. Special meals are available for groups by prior arrangement.
AMENITIES	Tennis, water sports, sauna, innkeepers can arrange for in-house massage with advance notice, decks and a fireplace in the living room, lots of hiking trails, wine and hors d'oeuvres in the evening.
RESTRICTIONS	No smoking, no pets. Bo and Buster are the resident yellow Labs and official tour guides on hikes. There are also approximately 20 cats and 10 Thoroughbred horses on the property. All animals are friendly, especially the dogs.
REVIEWED	*Northern California Wine Country Access; Bay Area Backroads; The Best of the Wine Country*
MEMBER	Bed & Breakfast Inns of the Napa Valley

Shady Oaks Country Inn

399 Zinfandel Lane, St. Helena, CA 94574   707-963-1190
John & Lisa Wild-Runnells, Innkeepers   FAX 707-963-9367
EMAIL shdyoaks@napanet.net   WEBSITE www.napanet.net/~shdyoaks

LOCATION	Traveling north on Highway 29, turn right on Zinfandel Lane and go 0.6 mile. The inn is on the right.
OPEN	All year except closed December 24 and 25
DESCRIPTION	A restored 1880s winery and 1920s Craftsman farmhouse on 2 acres decorated with unpretentious elegance.
NO. OF ROOMS	Five rooms with private bathrooms. Lisa recommends the Winery Retreat Room.
RATES	April through November and all weekends, rates are $159-190 for a single or double. December through March (except weekends), rates are $125-190. There is a minimum stay on most weekends (occasional exceptions) and cancellation requires 10 days' notice and a $10 per room fee.
CREDIT CARDS	MasterCard, Visa
BREAKFAST	Full breakfast is served in the dining room, in the garden, or in bed, and includes champagne, eggs Benedict, Belgian waffles, home-baked breads, fresh fruit, tea, juice, and inn-blend coffee.
AMENITIES	Wine and cheese served each evening, air conditioning, croquet, horseshoes, soft drinks, bottled water, beautiful patio with Roman pillars and wisteria, help with winery itineraries (owners are home winemakers).
RESTRICTIONS	No smoking, no pets, children are not encouraged.
REVIEWED	*Access California Wine Country; Napa Valley Guide; The Complete Guide to Bed & Breakfasts, Inns, and Guesthouses; Insider's Guide; B&Bs of Northern California*
KUDOS/COMMENTS	"Quaint; outstanding innkeepers and food; nice location." (1999)

Spanish Villa Inn

474 Glass Mountain Road, St. Helena, CA 94574   707-963-7483
Roy Bissemer, Resident Owner   FAX 707-967-9401
Spanish, Italian, and Portuguese spoken

LOCATION	Half a mile off the Silverado Trail.
OPEN	All year

DESCRIPTION	A 1981 two-story Mediterranean villa with Spanish interior.
NO. OF ROOMS	Three rooms with private bathrooms.
RATES	Seasonal rates are $145-185 for a single or double. There is a minimum stay on weekends and cancellation requires seven days' notice with a $15 cancellation fee.
CREDIT CARDS	Yes
BREAKFAST	Full breakfast is served in the dining room.
AMENITIES	King-size beds, Tiffany lamps, and a rose in each room.
RESTRICTIONS	No smoking, no pets, children are not encouraged.

Sunny Acres Bed & Breakfast

397 Main Street, St. Helena, CA 94574   707-963-2826
Edward & Susanne Salvestrin, Innkeepers
Italian spoken

LOCATION	One mile south of town on Highway 29 (Main Street), next to St. Helena High School.
OPEN	All year except Christmas
DESCRIPTION	An 1879 two-story Victorian host home, totally restored in 1991 and decorated with Victorian furnishings and historical photos and artifacts.
NO. OF ROOMS	Three rooms with private bathrooms.
RATES	May through October, rates are $150 for a single or double. November through April, rates are $10 less. There is no minimum stay and cancellation requires three days' notice.
CREDIT CARDS	MasterCard, Visa
BREAKFAST	A complete country breakfast is served in the dining room at 9 a.m.; continental breakfast is available in guestrooms anytime.
AMENITIES	Twenty-six acres of vineyards. Wine made on the property is for sale at the small winery.
RESTRICTIONS	No smoking, no pets, no children.
MEMBER	Bed & Breakfast Inns of the Napa Valley

TAYLOR'S CREEKSIDE INN

945 Main Street, St. Helena, CA 94574   707-963-7244
Virginia Toogood, Resident Owner   FAX 707-963-3012

LOCATION	In the heart of St. Helena. Turn left before crossing the bridge into downtown.
OPEN	All year
DESCRIPTION	A 1942 ranch-style country inn with country French decor.
NO. OF ROOMS	Three rooms with one-and-a-half shared bathrooms.
RATES	Year-round rates are $85 to $95 for a single or double. Two days' notice is required for cancellation.
CREDIT CARDS	MasterCard, Visa
BREAKFAST	Breakfast is served in the dining room or sunroom and includes fruit, homemade breads, muffins, croissants, coffeecakes, coffee, tea, and juice. Special meals are also available.
AMENITIES	Flowers in rooms; fireplace; acres of trees, lawns, and gardens.
RESTRICTIONS	No smoking, no pets, children are welcome when all three rooms are booked. Hooper is the resident black Lab.

VINEYARD COUNTRY INN

201 Main Street, St. Helena, CA 94574   707-963-1000

WHITE RANCH BED & BREAKFAST

707 White Lane, St. Helena, CA 94574   707-963-4635

WINE COUNTRY INN

1152 Lodi Lane, St. Helena, CA 94574   707-963-7077
WEBSITE www.winecountryinn.com

KUDOS/COMMENTS	"Excellent." "Our favorite for decor, service, food, and location." (1999)

Zinfandel Inn

800 Zinfandel Lane, St. Helena, CA 94574 707-963-3512
WEBSITE www.zinfandelinn.com

Stinson Beach

Natural wonders surround this little seaside gem in the Golden Gate National Recreation Area, just south of Point Reyes National Seashore. Check out Audubon Canyon Ranch, a sanctuary for great blue herons and great egrets.

Casa del Mar

37 Belvedere Avenue, Stinson Beach, CA 94970 415-868-2124
Rick Klein, Resident Owner 800-552-2124
EMAIL inn@stinsonbeach.com FAX 415-868-2305

LOCATION	From San Francisco, take Highway 101 north to the Mill Valley/Stinson Beach exit. Follow Highway 1 along the coast for 14 miles to Stinson Beach. As you drive into town, the first building on the right is the firehouse. Turn right onto Belvedere Avenue; Casa del Mar is located 100 yards up the street on the left.
OPEN	All year
DESCRIPTION	A 1989 three-story Mediterranean villa decorated with original art, with views of terraced gardens, mountains, and the ocean.
NO. OF ROOMS	Six rooms with private bathrooms. Rick gets raves about the Penthouse.
RATES	Year-round rates for a single or double are $150-250 and the entire villa rents for $1,200. There is a two-night minimum stay on weekends and cancellation requires seven days' notice with a $10 per night charge.
CREDIT CARDS	American Express, MasterCard, Visa
BREAKFAST	Full breakfast is served in the dining room and includes fresh-squeezed juice, yogurt, granola, fresh fruit, huevos rancheros with fresh salsa, blueberry/poppyseed coffeecake, apple or black bean pancakes, and fresh-ground coffee.
AMENITIES	Original art collection, fresh flowers, gardens, evening hors d'oeuvres, homemade cookies, phone on request.
RESTRICTIONS	No smoking, no pets, children are welcome.

Casa del Mar, Stinson Beach

REVIEWED The Best Places to Kiss in Northern California; Karen Brown's California Country Inns & Itineraries; Northern California Best Places; Berlitz Traveler's Guide—San Francisco and Northern California; Fodor's

MEMBER Professional Association of Innkeepers International, California Lodging Industry Association, Inns of Point Reyes

REDWOODS HAUS

1 Belvedere Avenue, Stinson Beach, CA 94970   415-868-1034

STIRLING CITY

STIRLING CITY HOTEL

16975 Skyway, Stirling City, CA 95978   530-873-0858

STOCKTON

OLD VICTORIAN INN

207 W Acacia Street, Stockton, CA 95203　　　　　　209-462-1613

SUTTER CREEK

Once a lumber mill and supply center during the Gold Rush, it is now one of the most charming and authentic of the Gold Rush-era towns. Browsing for antiques is a fun pastime, as is Poppy Days in May. But plan to be here in June for the Italian Benevolent Society's annual picnic. About 42 miles southeast of Sacramento via Highways 16 and 124.

CLEMENTINES BED & BREAKFAST

200 Hanford, Sutter Creek, CA 95685　　　　　　209-267-9384

THE FOXES IN SUTTER CREEK

77 Main Street, Sutter Creek, CA 95685　　　　　　209-267-5882
Pete & Min Fox, Innkeepers　　　　　　　　　　　　800-987-3344
EMAIL foxes@cdepot.net　　　　　　　　　　FAX 209-267-0712
WEBSITE www.foxesinn.com

LOCATION	The inn is 45 miles east of Sacramento on Highway 16 and 45 miles east of Stockton on Highway 88.
OPEN	All year except closed December 24 and 25
DESCRIPTION	An 1857 two-story Mother Lode Greek revival with gardens and trees, comfortable European antique furnishings, and a wraparound porch.
NO. OF ROOMS	Seven rooms with private bathrooms. Pick the Victorian Suite.
RATES	Year-round rates are $125-185 for a single or double. There is a two-night minimum stay on weekends and holidays, and cancellation requires seven days' notice and a $10 fee.
CREDIT CARDS	Discover, MasterCard, Visa

BREAKFAST	Full breakfast is made to order and served on silver in guestrooms or in the gardens. Dietary needs can be accommodated.
AMENITIES	Early coffee and morning newspaper delivered to your door, wood-burning fireplaces in five rooms, TV/VCR in four rooms, music in all rooms, air conditioning, robes, covered guest parking, complimentary soft drinks, garden gazebo, common areas.
RESTRICTIONS	No smoking. Two-person maximum occupancy per room.
REVIEWED	Best Places to Stay in California; The Best Places to Kiss in Northern California; Bed & Breakfast California; Recommended Country Inns—West Coast; America's Wonderful Little Hotels & Inns; Karen Brown's California Country Inns & Itineraries; Northern California Best Places; The Best of the Gold Country; Historic Inns of California's Gold Country; Bed & Breakfast American Style; Weekends for Two in Northern California: 50 Romantic Getaways; Fodor's; Northern California Discovery Guide; The National Trust Guide to Historic Bed & Breakfasts, Inns, and Small Hotels; Frommer's
MEMBER	Professional Association of Innkeepers International, Bed & Breakfast Inns of Amador County, California Association of Bed & Breakfast Inns, California Hotel and Motel Association
RATED	AAA 3 Diamonds, Mobil 3 Stars
KUDOS/COMMENTS	"Great inn, terrific innkeepers." "Very nice!"

GREY GABLES BED & BREAKFAST

161 Hanford Street, Sutter Creek, CA 95685 209-267-1039
Roger & Sue Garlick, Innkeepers 800-473-9422
EMAIL reservations@greygables.com FAX 209-267-0998
WEBSITE www.greygables.com

LOCATION	Two blocks north of downtown Sutter Creek on the west side of Highway 49.
OPEN	All year
DESCRIPTION	A restored 1897 three-story Victorian inn with Victorian decor and English country gardens with fountains and rose arbors.
NO. OF ROOMS	Eight rooms with private bathrooms. Try the Byron Room.
RATES	Year-round rates are $100-150 for a single or double. There is a two-night minimum stay during weekends and holidays and cancellation requires seven days' notice. Friday-only reservations require prepayment with no cancellation allowed.
CREDIT CARDS	American Express, Discover, MasterCard, Visa

BREAKFAST	Full breakfast is served on fine English bone china in the dining room or guestrooms. Breakfast consists of a fruit starter, followed by a hot entrée such as chicken-mushroom crepes or southwestern casserole, plus tea and/or coffee, juices, and homemade breads. Early tea and coffee are available.
AMENITIES	Each room is heated and air conditioned and has a gas log fireplace; the Shelly Room is wheelchair accessible; afternoon teas with cake or scones (in true English tradition); wine and hors d'oeuvres in the evening feature Amador County wines; English country gardens.
RESTRICTIONS	No smoking, no pets, children over 12 are welcome.
REVIEWED	Karen Brown's California: Charming Inns & Itineraries; The Best Places to Kiss in Northern California; Romantic California & the Pacific Northwest
MEMBER	Amador Bed & Breakfast Association, California Association of Bed & Breakfast Inns
RATED	AAA 3 Diamonds, Best Places to Kiss 3 Lips
KUDOS/COMMENTS	"Rebuilt by an English couple." "Excellent. Great decor. Charming English innkeepers." (1999)

THE HANFORD HOUSE BED & BREAKFAST INN

61 Hanford Street, Highway 49, Sutter Creek, CA 95685   209-267-0747
Bob & Karen Tierno, Innkeepers   800-871-5839
Spanish spoken   FAX 209-267-1825
EMAIL bobkat@hanfordhouse.com   WEBSITE www.hanfordhouse.com

LOCATION	Steps from the center of town. From the north, Highway 49 turns into Main Street.
OPEN	All year
DESCRIPTION	A 1984 two-story historic gold country inn—a classic, ivy-covered red-brick inn built over a 1920s Craftsman cottage. Listed on the National Historic Register.
NO. OF ROOMS	Ten rooms with private bathrooms. Try the Gold Country Escape.
RATES	Year-round rates are $89-149 for a single or double, $125-149 for a suite, $115-149 for the guesthouse, and $1,995 for the entire inn. There is a two-night minimum stay when a Saturday night is included and cancellation requires seven days' notice with a $10 per night charge.
CREDIT CARDS	Discover, MasterCard, Visa

BREAKFAST	Full gourmet breakfast is served in the dining room, on the rooftop deck, on the patio, or in the suites. Breakfast includes both a cold buffet and hot entrées; fresh breads, homemade Hanford House granola, smoothies, and yogurt available at each sitting.
AMENITIES	Robes; wine and hors d'oeuvres; CD players in most rooms; "raid the pantry" privileges; conference center; central air conditioning; five rooms with fireplaces, one with Jacuzzi tub; handicapped accessible; rose petals on pillows by request; champagne and fruit/cheese plates for sale; massage specialist on call.
RESTRICTIONS	No smoking, children over six are welcome. "Well-behaved children, please."
MEMBER	California Association of Bed & Breakfast Inns, California Lodging Industry Association, Amador County Bed & Breakfast Association, Professional Association of Innkeepers International
RATED	Mobil 2 Stars

PICTUREROCK INN

55 Eureka Street, Sutter Creek, CA 95685   209-267-5500

KUDOS/COMMENTS	"A comfortable B&B, tastefully decorated; excellent breakfast; warm and friendly innkeepers." (1999)

SUTTER CREEK INN

75 Main Street, Sutter Creek, CA 95685   209-267-5606
Jean Osborn, Resident Manager   FAX 209-267-9287

OPEN	All year
DESCRIPTION	An 1859 Greek revival inn surrounded by a half-acre of lawn, trees, a grape arbor, secret gardens, and patios.
NO. OF ROOMS	Eighteen rooms with private bathrooms
RATES	Year-round weekend rates are $95-175 for a single or double and weekday rates are $65-155. Call about the minimum-stay and cancellation policies.
CREDIT CARDS	MasterCard, Visa
BREAKFAST	Full breakfast is served in the dining room; the menu changes daily.

AMENITIES	Air conditioning and electric blankets in all rooms, game tables in the living room, refreshments in the kitchen every afternoon, 10 rooms with fireplaces, two rooms with hot tubs, massages, handwriting analysis, group facilities.
RESTRICTIONS	No smoking, no pets
REVIEWED	*Elegant Small Hotels and Inns, Very Special Places, America's Wonderful Little Hotels & Inns, Country Inns of the Far West*
MEMBER	California Association of Bed & Breakfast Inns
KUDOS/COMMENTS	"Comfortable, unique inn in beautiful Sutter Creek, a great central location." (1999)

TRINIDAD

This tiny coastal village has one of the most splendid harbors on the West Coast, and trolling for salmon is a full-time pursuit. Don't miss the town's massive crab feed in spring. Check out the Memorial Lighthouse and the aquarium, or Patrick's Point State Park and Agate Beach. Trinidad is just north of Eureka on Highway 101.

THE LOST WHALE BED & BREAKFAST INN

3452 Patrick's Point Drive, Trinidad, CA 95570 707-677-3425
Lee Miller & Susanne Lakin, Innkeepers 800-677-7859
EMAIL *lmiller@lostwhaleinn.com* FAX 707-677-0284

LOCATION	From Highway 101 north, exit at Trinidad and take an immediate right onto Patrick's Point Drive. The inn is four miles north on the left.
OPEN	All year
DESCRIPTION	A 1989 two-story Cape Cod-style country inn on 4 coastal acres with its own private beach. The interior is natural wood and lots of windows.
NO. OF ROOMS	Eight rooms with private bathrooms.
RATES	May through October and holidays, rates are $140-170 for a single or double and $230 for the farmhouse. November through April, rates are $110-140 for a single or double and $180 for the farmhouse. There is a two-night minimum stay during weekends and from June 15 through September 15. Cancellation requires seven days' notice.
CREDIT CARDS	American Express, Discover, MasterCard, Visa

BREAKFAST	Huge gourmet breakfast is served in the dining room. Breakfast changes daily and may include frittatas, casseroles, fruit cobblers and tarts, and other creative foods.
AMENITIES	Ocean view from all rooms; afternoon tea with wine and sherry cake; complimentary sodas; hot tub overlooking the ocean; two-mile private beach with hundreds of sea lions; chocolates by the bed; flowers; meeting, wedding, and reception facilities; playground with playhouse; close to Redwood National Park.
RESTRICTIONS	No smoking, no pets, all children welcome. There is one outdoor cat. Lee and Susanne raise pygmy goats at a farm down the street.
REVIEWED	*Bed & Breakfast Guide: California; America's Wonderful Little Hotels & Inns; Driving the Pacific Coast: California; Karen Brown's California Country Inns & Itineraries; Best Places to Stay in California; Fodor's; Frommer's*
MEMBER	Northern Redwoods Bed & Breakfast Association
RATED	AAA 3 Diamonds, Mobil 4 Stars
AWARDS	One of the Ten Most Romantic Inns, *American Historic Inns*
KUDOS/COMMENTS	"Clean, very well run, four star B&B"

TRINIDAD BAY BED & BREAKFAST

560 Edwards Street, Trinidad, CA 95570   707-677-0840
Paul & Carol Kirk, Resident Owners

LOCATION	From Highway 101, take the Trinidad exit, go west and follow Main Street toward the beach. The inn is on the corner across from the Memorial Lighthouse.
OPEN	All year except for December and January
DESCRIPTION	A 1950 two-story Cape Cod inn with country and antique furnishings.
NO. OF ROOMS	Four rooms with private bathrooms. Try the Mauve Fireplace Suite.
RATES	April through October, rates are $125 for a single or double, $155 for a suite, and $560 for the entire B&B. November, February, and March (excluding holidays), rates are $99 for a single or double, $119 for a suite, and $436 for the entire B&B. There is a minimum stay during holidays and weekends, and cancellation requires seven days' notice with a $15 charge.
CREDIT CARDS	MasterCard, Visa

BREAKFAST	Full breakfast includes local cheese, home-baked bread and muffins, homemade flavored butters, fresh fruit medley with yogurt, baked apples, coffee, and juice.
AMENITIES	All rooms overlook the ocean, self-serve snack and beverage area, fireplaces.
RESTRICTIONS	No smoking, no pets, children must be old enough to occupy their own room.
REVIEWED	Bed & Breakfast Guide: California, Karen Brown's California Country Inns & Itineraries, Bay Area Backroads
MEMBER	Northern Redwoods Bed & Breakfast Association

TURTLE ROCKS OCEANFRONT INN

3392 Patrick's Point Drive, Trinidad, CA 95570   707-677-3707
Roger & Francine Glidden, Innkeepers
EMAIL trocks@northcoast.com   WEBSITE www.turtlerocksinn.com

LOCATION	From Highway 101, exit Patrick's Point Drive and go west/southwest 1.5 miles down on the seaward side of the street.
OPEN	All year
DESCRIPTION	A 1995 two-story traditional gabled inn decorated with contemporary furniture and antiques, situated on 3 oceanfront acres.
NO. OF ROOMS	Six rooms with private bathrooms. Roger's favorite is the Patrick's Point Suite.
RATES	May through October, rates are $140-180 for a single or double. November through December and March 16 through April 30, rates are $130-170. January 1 through March 15, rates are $110-155. There is a two-night minimum stay on weekends and a three-night minimum on major holidays. Cancellation requires seven days' notice and a $15 per room fee.
CREDIT CARDS	Discover, MasterCard, Visa
BREAKFAST	Full breakfast is served in the dining room and includes two hot dishes (quiche, stratta, or casserole, plus a hot potato dish), yeast rolls, coffeecake, fresh fruit salad, yogurt, jams, granola, and fresh orange juice. Guests may take breakfast to their rooms on trays.
AMENITIES	Light, airy rooms; private glass-paneled decks; oversized tubs and showers; California king-size beds; love seats and overstuffed chairs in rooms; ocean views from rooms; soundproof walls; private phones; cable TV; afternoon desserts (homemade chocolate chip cookies with pecans, lemon meringue pie, and rum cake); antique refrigerator with sparkling juices, soft drinks, and ice; views of nearby sea lion colony.

RESTRICTIONS	No smoking, no pets, children over eight are welcome.
REVIEWED	America's Favorite Inns, B&Bs, & Small Hotels; Lonely Planet California and Nevada
MEMBER	Professional Association of Innkeepers International
RATED	AAA 3 Diamonds

TRUCKEE

Once Wild West wooly and wicked, the town still retains the flavor, along with upscale boutiques and down-home diners. This is the main gateway to north Lake Tahoe resorts and Donner Memorial State Park at Donner Lake. Head northeast of Sacramento on I-80.

BOCKS 10064 HOUSE

10064 SE River Street, Truckee, CA 96161   530-582-1923

DONNER COUNTRY INN BED & BREAKFAST

10070 Gregory Place, Truckee, CA 96161   530-587-5574

RICHARDSON HOUSE BED & BREAKFAST INN

10154 High Street, Truckee, CA 96161   530-587-5388
Jeannine Karnofsky, Resident Manager   888-229-0365
                                                    FAX 530-587-0927

LOCATION	One mile from I-80, one block from historic downtown Truckee, and 30 minutes from the Reno Airport.
OPEN	All year
DESCRIPTION	A restored 1886 two-story Victorian inn with Victorian decor and modern amenities.
NO. OF ROOMS	Six rooms with private bathrooms and two rooms share one bathroom. Try the Writer's Room.

RATES	Year-round rates are $75-150 for a single or double with a private or shared bathroom and $150 for a suite. There is a two-night minimum stay during holidays and peak times and cancellation requires five days' notice.
CREDIT CARDS	American Express, Discover, MasterCard, Visa
BREAKFAST	Full breakfast is served in the dining room and includes juice, fresh fruit, an entrée, breads, scones, muffins, Truckee roasted coffee, tea, and hot chocolate. Lunch, dinner, and special meals are available upon request.
AMENITIES	Complimentary refreshment center, transportation to and from Amtrack station, morning newspaper, air conditioning, feather beds, down comforters, fine linens.
RESTRICTIONS	No smoking, no pets, children over 10 are welcome.
REVIEWED	*Northern California Best Places, The Official Guide to American Historic Inns*
MEMBER	California Association of Bed & Breakfast Inns, Professional Association of Innkeepers International

TRUCKEE HOTEL

10007 Bridge Street, Truckee, CA 96161   530-587-4444
EMAIL *truckeeh@sierra.net*   WEBSITE *www.truckeetahoe.com/truckeehotel*

TUOLUMNE

This pretty mountain town stands out among Gold Country gems. In September, the annual Indian Acorn Festival is held at the Tuolumne Rancheria, one of the last remaining Miwok reservations. Southeast of Sonora off Highway 108.

OAK HILL RANCH BED & BREAKFAST

18550 Connally Lane, Tuolumne, CA 95379   209-928-4717
Sanford & Jane Grover, Resident Owners
Smatterings of Spanish and Japanese spoken

LOCATION	Take Road 17E off Highway 108 to Tuolumne. Turn right on Carter Street and go five blocks to Elm. Turn left and travel one block to Apple Colony Road. Turn right and travel five blocks to Connally Lane (private road) to the B&B.

OPEN	All year
DESCRIPTION	A 1980 two-story country Victorian and cottage built with genuine (collected) Victorian building materials on 56 wooded acres at an elevation of 3,000 feet.
NO. OF ROOMS	Two rooms with private bathrooms and two rooms share one bathroom.
RATES	Year-round rates are $80-85 for a single or double with a private bathroom and $75-80 for a single or double with a shared bath. Suites are $165 and the guesthouse is $120. A two-night minimum stay is required on national holidays. Cancellation requires seven days' notice with a $10 fee.
CREDIT CARDS	No
BREAKFAST	Full breakfast, served in the dining room, includes hot meats, fruit, home-baked breads, fresh fruit in season, iced juices, and entrées of crepes Normandie, eggs fantasia, Belgian waffles, crustless Swiss quiche, or French toast, plus hot beverages. Picnic lunches are available on request.
AMENITIES	Player piano sing-alongs after breakfast, meeting facilities available for up to 25 persons, two gazebos in the lawn and flower garden, refreshments on arrival, handicapped accessible.
RESTRICTIONS	No smoking, no pets. Children over 13 are welcome. One resident cat, Mitzi, "is never allowed inside the buildings."
REVIEWED	*Bed & Breakfast Guide: California; Recommended Country Inns—West Coast; Country Inns of America—California; Karen Brown's California Country Inns & Itineraries; Bed & Breakfast California; Northern California Best Places*
MEMBER	Gold Country Inns of Tuolumne County

TWAIN HARTE

On Highway 108 in the Stanislaus National Forest near Columbia State Historic Park, this small community celebrates Twain Harte Days and the Wild West Film Fest in September. The Jumping Frog Jubilee gets hopping in May. Skiing is less than 20 miles up the road at low-key Dodge River Ski Area.

COUNTRY INN AT SUGAR PINE

19958 Middle Camp Road, Twain Harte, CA 95383
Nancy Mulkey, Innkeeper
EMAIL *nancy @goldrush.com*
WEBSITE *www.mlode.com/~thcc/countryinn/*

209-586-4615
800-292-2093

LOCATION	On Highway 108, 2.4 miles above the second Twain Harte exit. Turn sharply left onto Middle Camp Road immediately after the blue and white "Welcome to Sugar Pine" billboard. The inn is the second house on the right.
OPEN	All year
DESCRIPTION	A 1947 three-story Mother Lode inn with knotty-pine paneling and country decor—a country home originally built as a hotel that sits on the edge of a ridge, with front and back porches that offer tremendous views.
NO. OF ROOMS	Four rooms with private bathrooms and one room with one shared bathroom. In winter, try the Cedar Room; in summer, the Tree Top Room.
RATES	Year-round rates are $65-100 for a single or double with a private bathroom, $65-85 for a single or double with a shared bathroom, and $395 for the entire inn. There is a two-night minimum stay during holidays and cancellation requires ten days' notice with a $25 charge.
CREDIT CARDS	MasterCard, Visa
BREAKFAST	Full country breakfast is served in the dining room and includes an egg dish, meat, fresh fruit, juice, choice of breads, and beverages.
AMENITIES	Robes, bottled water, and afternoon snacks.
RESTRICTIONS	No smoking, children are welcome. Scardy Claire is the resident cat. She will probably be invisible to guests as she spends most of her time under the bed.
MEMBER	Gold Country Bed & Breakfast Inns of Tuolumne County, Tuolumne County Lodging Association

McCaffrey House Bed & Breakfast

23251 Highway 108, Twain Harte, CA 95383   209-586-0757
EMAIL innkeeper@mccaffreyhouse.com   888-586-0757
WEBSITE www.mccaffreyhouse.com   FAX 209-586-3689

LOCATION	Eleven miles east of Sonora on Highway 108. Exit 0.5 mile beyond East Twain Harte Road.
OPEN	All year
DESCRIPTION	A 1995 three-story country inn with Irish country and pine decor, located in a grove of giant oaks and pines.
NO. OF ROOMS	Seven rooms with private bathrooms.
RATES	Year-round rates are $95-130 for a single or double. There is a minimum stay during weekends and holidays, and cancellation requires five days' notice.

McCaffrey House Bed & Breakfast, Twain Harte

CREDIT CARDS	American Express, MasterCard, Visa
BREAKFAST	Full breakfast is served in the dining room or on the decks and includes fresh-ground coffee, juice, fruit, an egg dish, potatoes, meat, muffins, and something sweet. Lunch and dinner are also available for groups.
AMENITIES	Fireplaces, TV/VCR, video library, telephone, data port, flowers, robes, tubs, showers, hair dryers, down pillows and comforters, outdoor spa, wine (or cider) and cheese in the afternoon, air conditioning and central heating in all rooms.
RESTRICTIONS	No smoking, no pets, children over six are welcome. Boysen, Logan, and Jeff are the resident dogs.
REVIEWED	*Northern California Best Places, Karen Brown's California Country Inns & Itineraries*
MEMBER	California Association of Bed & Breakfast Inns, Professional Association of Innkeepers International, Gold Country Bed & Breakfast Association
RATED	AAA 3 Diamonds
AWARDS	1996, Best New Construction, Tuolumne County Chamber of Commerce

UKIAH

Located in the upper reaches of California Wine Country, Ukiah is still what Napa, Sonoma, and Healdsburg used to be—a sleepy little agricultural town surrounded by vineyards and apple and pear orchards. Peopled by an odd mix of farmers, loggers, and back-to-the-landers, Ukiah is a down-to-earth little burg with few traces of Wine Country gentrification. That doesn't mean there isn't any wine, however. Take a soak at the clothing-optional Orr Hot Springs or in North America's only warm and naturally carbonated mineral baths at Vichy Springs Resort. Hikers will want to stretch their legs at Montgomery Woods State Reserve, 1,142 acres of coastal redwoods. In town, the main attraction is the Grace Hudson Museum and Sun House, featuring Hudson's paintings of Pomo Indians and a collection of beautiful Pomo baskets.

SANFORD HOUSE BED & BREAKFAST

306 South Pine Street, Ukiah, CA 95482   707-462-1653
Dorsey & Bob Manogue, Resident Owners   FAX 707-462-8987
EMAIL dorsey@sanfordhouse.com   WEBSITE www.sanfordhouse.com

LOCATION	Just five minutes from Highway 101. Take the Perkins Street exit and head west (toward central Ukiah) 0.75 mile on Perkins Street. Turn left on South Pine Street. The B&B is at the corner of South Pine and Stephanson.
OPEN	All year
DESCRIPTION	A 1904 two-story Queen Anne Victorian inn furnished with Victorian antiques.
NO. OF ROOMS	Five rooms with private bathrooms.
RATES	Year-round rates are $74-100 for a single or double. There is no minimum stay and cancellation requires at least seven days' notice.
CREDIT CARDS	American Express, MasterCard, Visa
BREAKFAST	Gourmet breakfast is made with fresh ingredients from the local farmers market.
AMENITIES	Flowers, wine and refreshments, koi pond, "ever-blooming" garden, front porch with wicker furnishings, air conditioning, close to Lake Mendocino.
RESTRICTIONS	No smoking, no pets, children over 12 are welcome. There are three resident dogs: Beauregard, a rare Dogue de Bordeaux; Spike, an English bulldog; and Bubba, a Boston terrier.
REVIEWED	Northern California Best Places

VICHY HOT SPRINGS RESORT BED & BREAKFAST

2605 Vichy Springs Road, Ukiah, CA 95482   707-462-9515
Gilbert & Marjorie Ashoff, Resident Owners   FAX 707-462-9516
EMAIL vichy@pacific.net   WEBSITE www.vichysprings.com

LOCATION	From Highway 101, take the Vichy Springs Road exit and travel three miles east to the resort.
OPEN	All year
DESCRIPTION	Several California Craftsman buildings from the mid-1800s decorated with chintz (waverley patterns) and hardwood floors, located on 700 acres two hours from San Francisco. Listed on the State Historic Register.
NO. OF ROOMS	Twenty-two rooms with private bathrooms. Choose one of the four cottages or five creekside rooms.
RATES	Year-round rates are $99-175 for a single or double. Cottages are $225. There is a two-night minimum stay on summer weekends.
CREDIT CARDS	American Express, Diners Club, Discover, MasterCard, Visa
BREAKFAST	Full breakfast, served in the dining room, includes coffee, orange juice, fresh fruit, sweet rolls, hard-boiled eggs, bagels and cream cheese. Lunch and dinner are also available and special meals can be catered.
AMENITIES	Flowers and phones in rooms, waterfall, rates include use of naturally warm (90 degrees) and Vichy baths, hot pool, Olympic-size mineral pool.
RESTRICTIONS	No smoking indoors, no pets. The inn is home to 10 cows.
REVIEWED	The National Trust Guide to Historic B&Bs, Inns and Small Hotels
MEMBER	American Historic Inns
RATED	AAA 3 Diamonds, Mobil 3 Stars

VOLCANO

Set in a deep, crater-like valley with a population hovering around 100, Volcano is almost a ghost town—but alive with history. The Volcano Theater Company performs year-round. Chow'se Indian Grinding Rock State Historic Park should not be missed. In spring, Daffodil Hill is a feast of blooms. Southeast of Sacramento off Highway 88.

THE ST. GEORGE HOTEL

16104 Main Street, Volcano, CA 95689   209-296-4458
Mark & Tracey Berkner, Innkepers   FAX 209-296-4457
EMAIL stgeorge@volcano.net   WEBSITE www.stgeorgehotel.com

LOCATION	Twelve miles east of Jackson (Highways 49 and 88) off Route 88. In Pine Grove, turn left onto Pine Grove–Volcano Road and follow for three miles to the town of Volcano.
OPEN	All year
DESCRIPTION	An 1867 three-story Gold Rush hotel with original furnishings and decorated with antiques and quilts. The hotel is situated on 1.5 acres and listed on the National and State Historic Registers.
NO. OF ROOMS	Six rooms with private bathrooms and 14 rooms share five bathrooms. Try the Jimtown Room.

The St. George Hotel, Volcano

RATES	Year-round rates are $50-80 for a single or double with a private bathroom and $40-80 for a shared bathroom. There is no minimum stay and cancellation requires 48 hours' notice.
CREDIT CARDS	MasterCard, Visa
BREAKFAST	Continental breakfast is served buffet style in the common area and includes fresh seasonal fruits, home-baked goods, fresh-ground coffee, assorted teas, and juice. An on-site full-service restaurant offers breakfast and lunch on the weekends, dinner Thursday through Sunday; the menu features local seasonal products.
AMENITIES	Full bar decorated with historic pictures and memorabilia; parlor with grand fireplace and games; conference center; facilities for weddings, anniversaries, birthdays, and family reunions; some rooms open onto the wraparound balcony.
RESTRICTIONS	No smoking, no pets, children under 12 are welcome in the annex only. Denali and Knick are the resident Malamutes. "The dogs are in charge of holding the floor down in the bar. They most likely will greet you or just roll over for the obligatory pet. Knick likes to take our guests for a tour of the creek road."
MEMBER	Professional Association of Innkeepers International
RATED	Sacramento Bee 3 Stars

WALNUT CREEK

From this large suburban city northeast of Oakland, Mount Diablo State Park is easily accessible. In town, children will enjoy the live animals at Lindsay Museum.

DIABLO MOUNTAIN INN

2079 Mt. Diablo Boulevard, Walnut Creek, CA 94598   925-937-5050

THE SECRET GARDEN MANSION

1056 Hacienda Drive, Walnut Creek, CA 94598   925-945-3600
Sharyn & Mike McCoy, Resident Owners   800-477-7898
WEBSITE www.secretgardenmansion.com   FAX 925-945-3608

LOCATION	Take Highway 24 from San Francisco to the Ignacio Valley Road exit. Head north to the seventh signal, turn right onto Homestead,

	go three blocks, and turn left on Hacienda Drive. Look for the white iron gates at the end.
OPEN	All year except closed two weeks at Christmas
DESCRIPTION	An 1860 two-story Victorian country estate surrounded by 3 acres of gardens.
NO. OF ROOMS	Seven rooms with private bathrooms.
RATES	Year-round rates for a single or double are $150-215 and $250-345 for a suite. Cancellation requires 72 hours' notice and a $10 fee. Inquire about special corporate rates.
CREDIT CARDS	American Express, Discover, MasterCard, Visa
BREAKFAST	Full breakfast is served in the dining room or guestrooms, or on the terrace, and includes heart-shaped waffles, quiches, baked eggs, fruit compotes, and beverages.
AMENITIES	Wildflowers and fresh fruit from the garden, hot cider in winter, old-fashioned lemonade in summer, TV/VCR in the library, wood-burning fireplaces, private phones, Egyptian cotton towels and robes, down pillows and comforters, AM/FM/cassette players in rooms, meeting facilities, handicapped accessible.
RESTRICTIONS	No smoking, no pets, children over 10 are welcome.
REVIEWED	*The Best Places to Kiss in Northern California*
MEMBER	American Bed & Breakfast Association, California Association of Bed & Breakfast Inns
RATED	ABBA 3 Crowns
KUDOS/COMMENTS	"Quiet elegance in an urban setting."

WESTPORT

The little coastal lumber mill town north of Fort Bragg is at the end of a long and beautiful northbound stretch of state parks and beaches. The Westport-Union Landing State Beach here is particularly nice.

BLUE VICTORIAN INN

38911 Main Street North Highway 1 707-964-6310
Westport, CA 95488 800-400-6310

DeHaven Valley Farm Country Inn

39247 North Highway 1, Westport, CA 95488
Christa Stapp, Innkeeper
Some Spanish spoken

707-961-1660
FAX 707-961-1677

LOCATION	On Highway 1, 1.7 miles north of Westport Village.
OPEN	All year
DESCRIPTION	An 1875 two-story Victorian farmhouse with high ceilings, light colors, antiques, and early American furnishings; situated on 20 coastal acres of meadows and farmland.
NO. OF ROOMS	Six rooms with private bathrooms and two rooms with one shared bathroom. Try the Eagle's Nest.
RATES	Year-round rates are $95-135 for a single or double with a private bathroom, $85-90 for a single or double with a shared bathroom, $125-140 for a suite, $135 for a cottage, and $920 for the entire inn. There is a minimum stay in August and during holiday weekends, and cancellation requires 72 hours' notice.
CREDIT CARDS	MasterCard, Visa
BREAKFAST	Full breakfast, served in the dining room, includes juice, fresh fruit, ham, bacon, or sausage, and an entrée such as apple pancakes with cranberries, waffles with fresh berries, or frittata with blueberry muffins. Dinner and special meals can be accommodated with prior notice.

DeHaven Valley Farm Country Inn, Westport

AMENITIES	Flowers, fireplaces, cookies, sherry, hot tub on the hill, large living room that can be used for meetings, hiking trails on property, picnic area with tables and benches, large patio, phones, tidepools nearby, and blackberry picking.
RESTRICTIONS	No smoking, no pets. The resident pets and farm animals include "a sheep, Starbuck, who thinks he's a horse;" two goats, Al and Al2; three horses; two donkeys; six cats; and one dog, Keeper.
REVIEWED	*Northern Califonia Best Places, Weekend Adventures for City Weary People, Complete Guide to American Bed & Breakfast, Feather Beds and Flapjacks, Recommended Country Inns—West Coast*
MEMBER	Professional Association of Innkeepers International, California Association of Bed & Breakfast Inns
RATED	AAA 2 Diamonds

HOWARD CREEK RANCH

40501 North Highway 1, Westport, CA 95488   707-964-6725
Charles & Sally Grigg, Resident Owners   FAX 707-964-6725
German, Spanish, Dutch, and Italian spoken
WEBSITE www.howardcreekranch.com

LOCATION	Three miles north of Westport on Highway 1.
OPEN	All year
DESCRIPTION	An 1871 two-story Victorian farmhouse furnished with period antiques and bordered by 40 acres of ocean beaches. Listed on the County Historic Register.
NO. OF ROOMS	Nine rooms with private bathrooms and two rooms with a shared bathroom.
RATES	Year-round rates are $75-145 for a single or double with a private or shared bathroom. There is a two-night minimum stay on some weekends and holidays, and one-week notice is required to cancel.
CREDIT CARDS	American Express, MasterCard, Visa
BREAKFAST	Full breakfast, served in the dining room, includes strawberry-banana hot cakes; omelets with garden tomatoes, scallions, and cheese; baked apples with granola and French whipped cream; sausage; fresh fruit; and beverages.
AMENITIES	Hot tub and sauna on the hill, massage, flower gardens, horse and wagon rides, farm animals, private decks and balconies, skylights, fireplaces/wood-burning stoves, piano and guitar, great books.

RESTRICTIONS	Smoking outside only, pets and children are OK by prior arrangement. Resident farm animals include cows, Percheron horses, dogs, and cats.
REVIEWED	*Best Places to Stay in California, Northern California Best Places, Fodor's Travel Guide—California, Bed & Breakfast North America, Feather Beds and Flapjacks*
MEMBER	Professional Association of Innkeepers International, California Association of Bed & Breakfast Inns, Mendocino Coast Innkeepers Association

PELICAN LODGE & INN

36921 North Highway 1, Westport, CA 95488   707-964-5588

WHITETHORN

SHELTER COVE BED & BREAKFAST

148 Dolphin Drive, Whitethorn, CA 95589   707-986-7161
Don Sack, Manager
WEBSITE *www.sheltercove.com*

WINDSOR

Here in the heart of Sonoma County, the grapes reign, just south of Healdsburg on Highway 101.

COUNTRY MEADOW INN

11360 Old Redwood Highway, Windsor, CA 95492   707-431-1276
Susan Hardesty, Resident Owner   800-238-1728
WEBSITE *www.countrymeadowinn.com*   FAX 707-431-2776

LOCATION	Traveling north on Highway 101, take the Healdsburg Avenue exit and turn left on Old Redwood Highway. Continue south for two miles. The inn is just after the Rodney Strong and Piper Sonoma Wineries.

OPEN	All year except closed Christmas Day
DESCRIPTION	An 1890 two-story Queen Anne Victorian with country and antique furnishings, situated on 6 acres of gardens.
NO. OF ROOMS	Five rooms with private bathrooms.
RATES	Year-round rates are $100-195 for a double. There is a two-night minimum stay on the weekends and a seven-day cancellation policy with a $10 fee.
CREDIT CARDS	American Express, MasterCard, Visa
BREAKFAST	Full breakfast is served in the dining room and includes a fruit dish (fresh and baked), a farm-fresh egg dish or pancakes, fresh-baked muffins, bread, coffee, and tea.
AMENITIES	Swiming pool, tennis court, fresh flowers in rooms, rooms with whirlpool tub, fireplaces, one room handicapped accessible, afternoon refreshments.
RESTRICTIONS	No smoking, no pets. Simon and Sheila are the resident cocker spaniels.
REVIEWED	*Weekends for Two in Northern California: 50 Romantic Getaways*

YOSEMITE NATIONAL PARK

This seven-square-mile international playground hosts some of nature's most incredible creations, including 4,500-foot-high El Capitan and Yosemite Falls, the highest waterfall in North America. From Merced, take Highway 140 east.

YOSEMITE PEREGRINE BED & BREAKFAST

7509 Henness Circle, Yosemite National Park, CA 95389   209-372-8517

YOSEMITE WEST HIGH SIERRA BED & BREAKFAST

7460 Henness Ridge Road   209-372-4808
Yosemite National Park, CA 95389
WEBSITE *www.sierranet.net/web/sierra*

YOUNTVILLE

The first vineyard in the Napa Valley was planted here in 1830, thanks to George Yount. Fine wineries have since proliferated to include the famous $42 million Domaine Chandon facility. The tiny town has gone upscale—with shopping centers around the Vintage 1870 complex housed in an old winery. Hot air balloons are the primary "way to go" here. Have a picnic in lovely City Park. Yountville is just north of Napa via Highway 29 from the Bay Area.

BORDEAUX HOUSE

6600 Washington Street, Yountville, CA 94599 707-944-2855
Jean Lunney, Innkeeper 800-677-6370
WEBSITE www.bordeauxhouse.com FAX 707-944-2855

LOCATION	From San Francisco, take Highway 101 north to Highway 37 east and its intersection with Highway 121. Turn left onto Highway 121 to Napa. At Highway 29, turn left and go north to Yountville. From Sacramento, take Highway 80 south to Highway 37 in Vallejo. Go west about two miles to Highway 29, turn right, and drive north to Yountville.
OPEN	All year
DESCRIPTION	A 1980 two-story contemporary red brick country inn with contemporary decor and French and English influences.
NO. OF ROOMS	Seven rooms with private bathrooms. Jean says the Chablis Room is her best.
RATES	April 1 through November 15, rates are $125-155 for a single or double. November 16 through March 31, rates are $95-125 for a single or double. High-season rates apply from December 26 through December 31. There is a two-night minimum stay on weekends and cancellation requires one weeks' notice.
CREDIT CARDS	MasterCard, Visa
BREAKFAST	Full buffet style breakfast is served in the reception room and includes an egg dish, cereal, fruit platter, hard-boiled eggs, yogurt, juice, coffee, tea, muffins, and breads.
AMENITIES	Air conditioning, flowers in rooms, private patio or deck, afternoon beverages in reception room, wood-burning fireplaces in guestrooms and reception room.
RESTRICTIONS	No smoking, no pets, no children
REVIEWED	Bed & Breakfasts and Country Inns, Non-Smokers Guide to B&Bs

Burgundy House

6711 Washington Street, Yountville, CA 94599 707-944-0889
Deanna Roque, Resident Owner

LOCATION	Take the Yountville exit off Highway 29 directly to Washington Street.
OPEN	All year
DESCRIPTION	An 1893 two-story country French inn constructed from river rock and field stone. Listed on both the National and State Historic Registers.
NO. OF ROOMS	Six rooms with private bathrooms.
RATES	April through November, rates are $125-165 for a single or double. December through March, rates are $100-140 for a single or double. There is a two-night minimum stay on weekends and cancellation requires seven days' notice with a $15 charge.
CREDIT CARDS	MasterCard, Visa
BREAKFAST	Full breakfast is served in the "distillery" or garden and includes juice, fruit platter, cereals, pastries, a hot casserole, coffee, and tea.
AMENITIES	Fresh flowers, decanter of local white wine in guestrooms.
RESTRICTIONS	No smoking, no pets, children over 12 are welcome.

Maison Fleurie

6529 Yount Street, Yountville, CA 94599 707-944-2056
Virginia Marzan, Resident Manager FAX 707-944-9342
WEBSITE www.foursisters.com

LOCATION	Take the Yountville exit from Highway 29. Turn right at the end of the ramp, then left onto Washington. When the road forks, stay right on Yount. The inn is on the left.
OPEN	All year
DESCRIPTION	Three 1880s French country-style brick buildings on landscaped grounds.
NO. OF ROOMS	Thirteen rooms with private bathrooms.
RATES	April through November, rates are $115-140 for a double and $190-245 for a deluxe room. December through March, rates are $110-125 for a double and $175-215 for a deluxe room. Rates are somewhat reduced on the weekdays during off season. There is no minimum stay and cancellation requires two days' notice.

CREDIT CARDS	American Express, MasterCard, Visa
BREAKFAST	Full breakfast is served either in the dining room or in guestrooms and includes home-baked bread and rolls, a hot dish, fresh fruit, cereals, and beverages.
AMENITIES	Morning paper, bicycles, afternoon tea, concierge, turndown service, phones, outdoor spa and swimming pool, beach towels, terry robes.
RESTRICTIONS	No smoking, no pets
KUDOS/COMMENTS	"Nice setting, very romantic."

OLEANDER HOUSE

7433 St. Helena Highway, Yountville, CA 94599   707-944-8315
John & Louise Packard, Resident Owners
WEBSITE www.oleander.com

VINTAGE INN—NAPA VALLEY

6541 Washington Street, Yountville, CA 94599   707-944-1112
WEBSITE www.vintageinn.com

YUBA CITY

Two-thirds of the nation's prunes are grown and processed here. The Prune Festival in September pays tribute to their yumminess. Check out the Punjab Bazaar for a glimpse of India. Most significant is the town's access to the Sutter Buttes, the world's smallest mountain range. North of Sacramento about 50 miles via Highway 99 along the Feather River.

HARKEY HOUSE BED & BREAKFAST

212 C Street, Yuba City, CA 95991   530-674-1942
WEBSITE www.gonative.com/inns/0015.html#directions

INDEX

5th Street Inn 171
Abe's Ocean View Redwoods
   Wilderness Chalet 152
Abigail Hotel 274
Abigail's Bed & Breakfast 267
Abigail's Elegant Victorian Mansion
   Bed & Breakfast 77
Above the Clouds Inn 104
Abrams House Inn 54
Adelaide Inn 274
Adriana's Bed & Breakfast 322
Agate Cove Inn 178
Aggie Inn 65
Alamo Square Inn 275
Albion House Bed & Breakfast 275
Albion River Inn 6
Alexander Inn 275
Amador Harvest Inn 248
Amber House Bed & Breakfast Inn ... 268
Ambrose Bierce House 334
American River Inn 101
Amsterdam Hotel, The 275
Anderson Creek Inn 28
Andora Inn 275
Andrews Hotel, The 276
Apple Blossom Inn Bed & Breakfast 1
Apple Lane Inn 13
Applewood 118
Arbor Guest House 203
Arbor House Inn 160
Archbishop's Mansion 276
Ark, The 135
Art Center Bed & Breakfast 277
Asplund Country Inn 335
Avalon House 89
Babbling Brook Bed & Breakfast 309
Bancroft Club Hotel 21
Barretta Gardens Bed & Breakfast Inn .326
Barro Station Bed & Breakfast 335
Bartels Ranch & Country Inn 336
Bass Lake Bed & Breakfast 17
Bayshore Cottage 136
Bayview Hotel Bed & Breakfast
   Inn, The 13
Bear Valley Inn 232
Beau Sky Hotel 21
Beazley House 204
Bed & Breakfast Inn, The 277
Bedside Manor 231
Bell Cottage 79

Belle de Jour Inn 125
Berkshire Inn 112
Bidwell House, The 48
Big Canyon Inn 168
Black Stallion Inn 277
Blackthorne Inn 136
Blair House Inn 179
Blanchard House, The 164
Blue Heron Inn Restaurant
   Bed & Breakfast 27
Blue Nile Inn 57
Blue Spruce Inn 331
Blue Victorian Inn 366
Blue Violet Mansion 205
Bock's Bed & Breakfast 278
Bocks 10064 House 357
Bodega Estero Bed & Breakfast 26
Bodega Harbor Inn 26
Bonita Studio Bed & Breakfast 22
Boonville Hotel, The 28
Bordeaux House 371
Boulder Creek Bed & Breakfast 171
Bradley House 88
Bradleys Alderbrook Manor 76
Brannan Cottage Inn 30
Brentwood Oaks 29
Brewery Gulch Inn 180
Briar Rose Bed & Breakfast Inn 302
Burgundy House 372
Bylund House Bed & Breakfast 337
Café Waterfront Bed & Breakfast 79
Cain House, The 29
Calderwood Inn 126
Calistoga Bear Flag Inn 31
Calistoga Country Lodge 32
Calistoga Wayside Inn 32
Camellia Inn 127
Campbell Ranch Inn 102
Candlelight Inn, The 206
Captain Walsh House 19
Captain's Cove Inn 180
Carol's Cow Hollow Inn 279
Carriage House Bed & Breakfast
   (Lake Arrowhead) 153
Carriage House Bed & Breakfast
   (Point Reyes Station) 251
Carter Cottage 79
Carter House 79
Casa Arguello Bed & Breakfast 280
Casa del Mar 348

375

Casa Madrona Hotel 316
Casa Rubio Oceanfront Lodging 320
Casita Blanca 280
Cats' Cradle Bed & Breakfast 15
Cavanagh Inn 239
Cazanoma Lodge 47
Cedar Gables Inn 207
Chalfant House, The 24
Chaney House .154
Chateau des Fleurs 17
Chateau du Sureau 229
Chateau Tivoli .281
Chateau Victorian, a Bed & Breakfast
  Inn 309
Chestelson House 337
Chez Duchene .281
Chibchas 47
Chichester-McKee House 242
China Creek 230
Christiania Inn, The 332
Christmas Tree Inn 189
Christopher's Inn 32
Church Street Bed & Breakfast 281
Churchill Manor Bed & Breakfast 208
Cinnamon Bear Bed & Breakfast 337
Cinnamon Teal Bed & Breakfast 49
Clarinett Cafe Bed & Breakfast 22
Claudia's Garden 90
Clearwater House 46
Clementines Bed & Breakfast 350
Cliff Crest Bed & Breakfast Inn 310
Coast Guard House 251
Coloma Country Inn, The 56
Columbia City Hotel 58
Combellack Blair House 243
Cooper House Bed & Breakfast 11
Cornelius Daly Inn 80
Cornell Hotel 282
Cottage Inn at Lake Tahoe 155
Country Garden Inn 209
Country Inn at Sugar Pine 359
Country Inn Bed & Breakfast 91
Country Meadow Inn 369
Country Rose Inn Bed & Breakfast 304
Court Street Inn 145
Courtyard Bed & Breakfast 272
Coxhead House Bed & Breakfast 305
Creekside Inn & Resort 119
Crickett Cottage 252
Crossroads Inn 210
Crystal Springs Inn 8
Cypress Inn on Miramar Beach 121
Dancing Coyote Beach 137

Darling House, a Bed & Breakfast Inn
  by the Sea, The 311
Davis Bed & Breakfast Inn 65
Deer Creek Inn 220
Deer Run Inn .338
DeHaven Valley Farm Country Inn 367
Diablo Mountain Inn 365
Doc's Country Inn 60
Dockside Boat & Bed 232
Dockside Boat & Bed 282
Dolores Park Inn 282
Donner Country Inn Bed & Breakfast . .357
Dorrington Hotel & Restaurant, The 66
Dorrington Inn .67
Dorris House B&B 9
Downey House B&B 221
Dream Inn Bed and Breakfast 198
Dreamwalkers Old Town
  Bed & Breakfast Inn 81
Druid House Bed & Breakfast 242
Dubord's Restful Nest 172
Dunbar House, 1880 201
Dunsmuir Inn 71
East Brother Light Station 265
Edward II Bed & Breakfast 283
Elam Biggs Bed & Breakfast 109
Elk Cove Inn 72
Eller House Bed & Breakfast 322
Elm House, The 210
Elms Bed & Breakfast, The 32
Elmwood House 22
Elsie's Conn Valley Inn 339
Emigrant Gap Inn 76
Emma Nevada House 221
Emma's Bed & Breakfast 167
Erika's Hillside Bed & Breakfast 339
Esplanade Bed & Breakfast, The 49
Eurospa & Inn 33
Evergreen 247
Fairview Manor .18
Fairwinds Farm Cottage 137
Falcon's Nest 33
Fallon Hotel 58
Fanny's 33
Farmhouse Inn & Restaurant, The 88
Faulkner House, The 260
Feather Bed, The 258
Felton Crest Hanna's Guest House 83
Fensalden Inn 7
Fernbrook Inn 61
Ferrando's Hideaway and Cottages 252
Finch Haven 172
Fitzpatrick Winery & Lodge 244

Flume's End .... .222
Foothill House Bed & Breakfast .... .34
Forbestown Bed & Breakfast
    Inn, The .... .161
Forest Manor .... .12
Foxes in Sutter Creek, The .... .350
Frampton House .... .128
French Gulch Hotel .... .99
Gables Inn Sausalito .... .317
Gables Inn, The .... .313
Garratt Mansion 3
Gate House Inn .... .146
George Alexander House, The .... .128
Gerstle Park Inn .... .306
Gingerbread Cottages Bed & Breakfast .227
Gingerbread Mansion Inn .... .84
Glass Beach Bed & Breakfast Inn ...... .92
Glass Mountain Inn .... .339
Glendeven .... .164
Glenelly Inn .... .105
Gold Country .... .153
Golden Gate Hotel .... .283
Golden Lotus .... .167
Golden Ore B&B Inn .... .110
Goose & Turrets Bed & Breakfast .... .191
Gramma's .... .23
Grandmere's Inn .... .223
Grandmother's House Bed & Breakfast . .85
Granny's Garden .... .172
Grape Leaf Inn .... .129
Gravenstein Inn .... .317
Green Apple Inn .... .98
Greenwood Pier Inn .... .73
Grey Gables Bed & Breakfast .... .351
Grey Whale Inn .... .92
Griffin House at Greenwood Cove ..... .74
Groveland Hotel, an Historic
    Country Inn, The .... .112
Hallman Bed & Breakfast .... .195
Hammons House Inn Bed & Breakfast .327
Hanford House B&B Inn, The .... .352
Harbor House .... .75
Harbor House .... .122
Harkey House Bed & Breakfast ...... .373
Harlan House .... .59
Hartley House Bed & Breakfast Inn ...269
Harvest Inn .... .339
Haskins Valley Inn .... .178
Haydon Street Inn .... .130
Headlands Inn, The .... .181
Healdsburg Inn on the Plaza .... .130
Heirloom, The .... .144
Helm's St Charles Inn .... .109

Hennessey House .... .210
Hensley House, The .... .303
Herb'n Inn, The .... .284
Heritage House .... .164
High Country Inn Bed & Breakfast ... .319
Highland Dell Inn .... .192
Highland House .... .173
Hill Point Bed & Breakfast .... .284
Hillcrest Bed & Breakfast .... .35
Hillegass House .... .23
Hilltop House Bed & Breakfast ...... .340
Hillview Country Inn .... .211
Holbrooke, The .... .110
Holly Tree Inn .... .253
Hollyhock Farm Bed & Breakfast .... .101
Homestead, The 1
Honor Mansion .... .131
Hope-Merrill House & Hope-Bosworth
    House .... .103
Hospitality Inn .... .68
Hotel California .... .237
Hotel Charlotte .... .113
Hotel David .... .285
Hotel Inverness .... .138
Hotel Jeffery .... .60
Hotel Mac Hotel .... .266
Hotel St. Helena .... .340
Hound's Tooth Inn .... .230
House of a Thousand Flowers ..... .48, 193
Howard Creek Ranch .... .368
Huckleberry Springs Country Inn
    and Spa .... .194
Hummingbird Hill Bed & Breakfast ...312
Imperial Hotel .... .10
Indian Creek Bed & Breakfast ...... .249
Ink House Bed and Breakfast .... .341
Inn 1890 .... .285
Inn at Depot Hill .... .45
Inn at Duncans Mills, The .... .69
Inn at Getchell Cove .... .114
Inn at Manresa Beach .... .14
Inn at Parkside .... .270
Inn at Pasatiempo .... .312
Inn at Shallow Creek Farm .... .234
Inn at Sugar Pine Ranch .... .113
Inn on Castro .... .285
Inn on Randolph .... .212
Inn San Francisco .... .286
Isis Oasis .... .104
Jack London Lodge .... .106
Jackson Court .... .286
Jarvis Mansion Bed & Breakfast ..... .261
Jasmine Cottage .... .254

377

Jean's Riverside Bed & Breakfast 235
Jefferson House 261
Jenner Inn 150
Jeter Victorian Inn 262
John Dougherty House 181
Johnson's Country Inn 50
Joshua Grindle Inn 182
Jughandle Beach Country
    Bed & Breakfast 93
Karen's Yosemite Bed & Breakfast 86
Kendall House, The 224
Klamath Inn 151
Knob Hill 254
Kristalberg Bed & Breakfast 108
Krusi Mansion Bed & Breakfast 4
L'Abri Bed & Breakfast 51
La Belle Epoque 213
La Chaumiere, a Country Inn 36
La Fleur Bed & Breakfast Inn 342
La Residence Country Inn 214
Lady Anne Victorian Inn 15
Lake Oroville Bed & Breakfast 236
Lake Shasta's True Bed & Breakfast 159
Lakehouse Bed & Breakfast 17
Larkmead Country Inn 36
Laurel Ridge Cottage Inn 139
Lavender Hill 327
Little Hotel Carter, The 79
Lodge at Manuel Mill 16
Lodge at Noyo River, The 94
Lord Bradley's Inn 98
Lost Inn, The 241
Lost Whale Bed & Breakfast Inn, The ..354
MacCallum House Inn 183
Madison Street Inn 307
Madrona Manor 131
Magliulo's Bed & Breakfast 322
Maison Fleurie 372
Mangels House 14
Mansions Hotel, The 287
Marina Inn 287
Mariposa Hotel & Inn 173
Mariposa Meadows Ranch 174
Marsh Cottage Bed & Breakfast 139
Marsh House 225
Matlick House, The 25
Mayfield House 155
McCaffrey House Bed & Breakfast 360
McClelland-Priest B&B 215
McCloud River Inn 177
Meadow Creek Ranch B&B Inn 174
Meadowlark Country House 37
Melitta Station Inn 314
Mendocino Farmhouse 184

Mendocino Village Inn 185
Milat Bed & Breakfast 343
Mill Rose Inn 123
Mill Valley Bed & Breakfast 189
Mill Valley Inn 190
Mine House Inn 11
Mokelumne River Lodge 191
Monarch Cove Inn 46
Monte Cristo Bed & Breakfast 288
Moon River Inn 271
Morning Rose Boat & Breakfast 5
Mount Shasta Ranch Bed & Breakfast ..199
Mountain Home Inn 190
Mountain Home Ranch 37
Mountain Seasons Inn 30
Mountain View Bed & Breakfast 329
Mountainside Bed & Breakfast 100
Murphy's Inn 110
Music Express Inn 52
Myers Country Inn 203
Napa Inn, The 215
National Hotel, The 148
New Davenport Bed & Breakfast Inn ...64
No Name Victorian Bed & Breakfast ...288
Nob Hill Lambourne, The 289
Noe's Nest 289
Norfolk Woods Inn 155
North Coast Country Inn 114
O'Brien Mountain Inn 229
Oak Hill Ranch Bed & Breakfast 358
Oak Knoll Inn 216
Obrero Hotel 290
Old Flower Farm Bed & Breakfast 167
Old Lewiston Inn 163
Old Milano Hotel, The 115
Old Monterey Inn 195
Old Saw Mill Lodge 238
Old Stewart House Inn 94
Old Thyme Inn 123
Old Victorian Inn 350
Old World Inn 217
Oleander House 373
Olema Inn 233
Oliver House Bed & Breakfast 343
On Mayacamas 218
On The Bluffs 271
One Fifty-Five Pine 27
Pacific Victorian Bed & Breakfast 124
Painted Lady Bed & Breakfast, The 20
Palisades Paradise B&B 262
Palm Hotel Bed & Breakfast, The 149
Palm House, The 306
Panama Hotel 307
Parker House 290

378

Parsonage B&B, The 225
Patterson House 140
Peacock Inn 111
Pebble Beach Bed & Breakfast 61
Pelennor Bed & Breakfast, The 175
Pelican Inn, The 201
Pelican Lodge & Inn 369
Pensione International 291
Pescadero Creek Inn B&B 239
Petite Auberge 292
Philo Pottery Inn 242
Picturerock Inn 353
Piety Hill Inn 225
Pillar Point Inn Bed & Breakfast 257
Pine Rose Inn 231
Pink Mansion, The 38
Pinoli Ranch Country Inn 242
Pleasure Point Inn 312
Plum Tree Inn 248
Plymouth House Inn 250
Point Arena Bed & Breakfast 251
Point Reyes Seashore Lodge 233
Poppy Hill 175
Power's Mansion Inn 16
Prager Winery Bed & Breakfast 343
Pudding Creek Inn 95
Pullman House Bed & Breakfast 257
Purple Orchid Inn Resort & Spa 166
Pygmalion House 315
Quail Mountain 39
Queen Anne Hotel 292
Rachel's Inn 166
Raford House, The 132
Rainbow Tarns Bed & Breakfast at
   Crowley Lake 62
Rambling Rose Bed & Breakfast 189
Rancho Caymus 266
Rancho San Gregorio 300
Red Castle Inn, Historic Lodgings 226
Red Victorian Bed, Breakfast, and
   Peace Center 293
Redbud Inn, The 202
Redding's Bed & Breakfast 263
Redwoods Haus 349
Reed Manor 186
Rendezvous Inn & Restaurant 96
Rhode's End Bed & Breakfast 152
Richardson House Bed & Breakfast
   Inn 357
Ridenhour Ranch House Inn 119
Ridgetop Inn & Cottages 234
River Ranch Lodge 156
River Rock 245
Riverview House 96

Riverwalk Inn B&B 72
Robin's Nest, The 273
Rockwood Gardens 176
Rockwood Lodge 157
Rose Garden Inn 343
Rosemary Cottage 140
Roundstone Farm Bed & Breakfast 234
Royal Gorge's Rainbow Lodge 321
Royal Hotel 150
RustRidge Ranch Bed & Breakfast 343
Ryan House Bed & Breakfast 329
Saint Orres 116
San Benito House 124
Sandpiper House Inn 75
Sandy Cove Inn 141
Sanford House Bed & Breakfast 362
Santa Nella House 120
Savoyard Bed & Breakfast 271
Scarlett's Country Inn 39
Scott Courtyard 41
Scotty's Bed & Breakfast 87
Sea Gull Inn 186
Sea Rock Bed & Breakfast Inn 186
Seafoam Lodge, The 166
Seal Cove Inn 196
Seasons Bed & Breakfast, The 245
Secret Garden Mansion, The 365
Serenity, a Bed & Breakfast Inn 330
Shadowridge Ranch & Lodge 246
Shady Oaks Country Inn 345
Shafsky House Bed & Breakfast
   Inn, The 246
Shangri La Bed & Breakfast 176
Shannon-Kavanaugh House 294
Shaw House Bed & Breakfast Inn 85
Sheehan Hotel 294
Shelter Cove Bed & Breakfast 369
Sherlock Homes Bed & Breakfast 61
Shiloh Bed & Breakfast 176
Shore House at Lake Tahoe, The 157
Sierra House Bed & Breakfast 176
Sierra Shangri-La 69
Silver Lady Bed & Breakfast 257
Silver Rose Inn 42
Silver Spur Bed & Breakfast 2
Snow Goose Inn 169
Sonoma Chalet 323
Sorensen's Resort 133
Southport Landing 167
Spanish Villa Inn 345
Spencer House 295
St. George Hotel, The 364
Stahlecker House Bed & Breakfast,
   Country Inn, and Gardens 218

Stanford Alpine Chalet, The 158
Stanford Inn by the Sea—
  Big River Lodge 187
Stanyan Park Hotel B&B 296
Starwae Inn 323
Stirling City Hotel 349
Stoney Brook Inn 178
Sunny Acres Bed & Breakfast 346
Sunset Edwardian 297
Superintendent's House, The 70
Sutter Creek Inn 353
Swan-Levine House 111
Tahoma Meadows Bed & Breakfast 159
Tall Timbers Chalets 219
Tamarack Creek Bed & Breakfast 334
Tanglewood House 107
Taylor's Creekside Inn 347
Ten Inverness Way 142
Terri's Homestay 255
Thatcher Inn and Restaurant, an 1890
  Bed & Breakfast 134
Thirty-Nine Cypress and Redwing
  Cottage 255
Thistle Dew Inn...................324
Thomas' White House Inn 27
Thompson House, The 161
Thorn Mansion Inn 274
Tiffany House Bed & Breakfast Inn 264
Todd Farmhouse Country
  Bed & Breakfast 96
Toll House Restaurant & Inn 29
Trailside Inn Bed & Breakfast 43
Traverse Inn, The 322
Tree House, The 143
Trinidad Bay Bed & Breakfast 355
Trubody Ranch Bed & Breakfast 219
Truckee Hotel 358
Tudor Rose Bed & Breakfast 232
Turtle Rocks Oceanfront Inn 356
Twenty Mile House 61
Twenty-Four Henry.................297
U. S. Hotel Bed & Breakfast 227
Union Hotel 20
Union Street Inn, The 297
University Inn Bed & Breakfast 65
Vichy Hot Springs Resort
  Bed & Breakfast 363
Victorian Farmhouse Bed & Breakfast ..166
Victorian Garden Inn 325
Victorian Gardens 170
Victorian Inn on the Park 298
Victorian on Lytton, The 237
Villa Messina 133
Villa Monti Bed & Breakfast 177
Vine Hill Inn B&B 317

Vineyard Country Inn 347
Vineyard View 191
Vintage Inn—Napa Valley 373
Vintage Towers Bed & Breakfast 55
Vintners Inn 315
Vizcaya 272
Wagon Creek Inn 199
Ward's Big Foot Ranch 200
Washington Inn, The 232
Washington Square Inn 299
Washington Street Lodging 43
Weaver's Inn, A 82
Webster House 5
Wedgewood Inn, The 147
Weston House 318
Whale Watch Inn 117
White Horse Inn, The 170
White Ranch Bed & Breakfast 347
White Sulphur Springs Ranch B&B 53
White Swan Inn 300
Whitegate Inn Bed & Breakfast 188
Wild Goose Victorian Bed & Breakfast,
  The 97
Willows Bed & Breakfast Inn 300
Windmist Cottage 66
Windsong Cottage 256
Wine & Roses Country Inn 167
Wine Country Inn 347
Wine Way Inn 43
Wisteria Garden Bed & Breakfast 44
Wooden Bridge B&B, The 162
Wool Loft, The 8
Wy's Acres 330
Ye Olde Shelford House 55
Yosemite Peregrine Bed & Breakfast ...370
Yosemite West High Sierra
  Bed & Breakfast 370
Yosemite's Carriage House 87
Zaballa House Bed & Breakfast, The ...124
Zinfandel House 44
Zinfandel Inn 348